Dual Language Education

BILINGUAL EDUCATION AND BILINGUALISM
Series Editors: **Professor Nancy H. Hornberger**, University of Pennsylvania, Philadelphia, USA and **Professor Colin Baker**, University of Wales, Bangor, Wales, Great Britain

Other Books in the Series
At War With Diversity: US Language Policy in an Age of Anxiety
James Crawford
Bilingual Education and Social Change
Rebecca Freeman
Building Bridges: Multilingual Resources for Children
Multilingual Resources for Children Project
Child-Rearing in Ethnic Minorities
J.S. Dosanjh and Paul A.S. Ghuman
Curriculum Related Assessment, Cummins and Bilingual Children
Tony Cline and Norah Frederickson (eds)
English in Europe: The Acquisition of a Third Language
Jasone Cenoz and Ulrike Jessner (eds)
Foundations of Bilingual Education and Bilingualism
Colin Baker
Language Minority Students in the Mainstream Classroom
Angela L. Carrasquillo and Vivian Rodriguez
Languages in America: A Pluralist View
Susan J. Dicker
Learning English at School: Identity, Social Relations and Classroom Practice
Kelleen Toohey
Language, Power and Pedagogy: Bilingual Children in the Crossfire
Jim Cummins
Language Revitalization Processes and Prospects
Kendall A. King
Multicultural Children in the Early Years
P. Woods, M. Boyle and N. Hubbard
Multicultural Child Care
P. Vedder, E. Bouwer and T. Pels
Reflections on Multiliterate Lives
Diane Belcher and Ulla Connor (eds)
The Sociopolitics of English Language Teaching
Joan Kelly Hall and William G. Eggington (eds)
Studies in Japanese Bilingualism
Mary Goebel Noguchi and Sandra Fotos (eds)
Teaching and Learning in Multicultural Schools
Elizabeth Coelho
Working with Bilingual Children
M.K. Verma, K.P. Corrigan and S. Firth (eds)
Young Bilingual Children in Nursery School
Linda Thompson

Please contact us for the latest book information:
Multilingual Matters, Frankfurt Lodge, Clevedon Hall,
Victoria Road, Clevedon, BS21 7HH, England
http://www.multilingual-matters.com

BILINGUAL EDUCATION AND BILINGUALISM 28
Series Editors: Nancy Hornberger and Colin Baker

Dual Language Education

Kathryn J. Lindholm-Leary

MULTILINGUAL MATTERS LTD
Clevedon • Buffalo • Toronto • Sydney

Library of Congress Cataloging in Publication Data

Lindholm-Leary, Kathryn J.
Dual Language Education/Kathryn J. Lindholm-Leary
Bilingual Education and Bilingualism: 28
Includes bibliographical references and index.
1. Education, bilingual. I. Title. II. Series.
LC3731.L568 2001
370.117'5–dc21   00-068234

British Library Cataloguing in Publication Data

A catalogue entry for this book is available from the British Library.

ISBN 1-85359-532-2 (hbk)
ISBN 1-85359-531-4 (pbk)

Multilingual Matters Ltd

UK: Frankfurt Lodge, Clevedon Hall, Victoria Road, Clevedon BS21 7HH.
USA: UTP, 2250 Military Road, Tonawanda, NY 14150, USA.
Canada: UTP, 5201 Dufferin Street, North York, Ontario M3H 5T8, Canada.
Australia: Footprint Books, Unit 4/92a Mona Vale Road, Mona Vale, NSW2103, Australia.

Typeset by WordWorks Ltd.
Printed and bound in Great Britain by Cambrian Printers Ltd.

Contents

Part 4: Conclusions and Implications for Language Education Programs

Acknowledgments

This project has been a labor of love – and much labor! I owe a debt of gratitude to a number of individuals who helped to make this book possible. First, many thanks to all the schools and the tireless administrators and teachers who provided the data and helped me to understand the dual language education model up close. In particular, I thank my colleague Rosa Molina with whom I had many hours of discussion that made me think in different ways about implementation and about parent education issues. Considerable gratitude is extended to my other colleagues who provided input into this manuscript or my understanding of issues discussed here – Donna Christian, Judy Lambert, David Dolson, Jim Cummins, Fred Genesee, Jim Crawford, Linda Luporini-Hakmi, and many more.

I also want to sincerely thank Colin Baker who spent numerous hours reading the manuscript and offering suggestions for improvement. His input has clearly made this a higher quality book.

This project was supported in part by a Sabbatical Leave from San Jose State University and by the National Center for Research in Education, Diversity and Excellence at the University of California, Santa Cruz.

Finally, I am very grateful to my family. To my son, Diego Padilla who inspired me to complete this project, my stepdaughter, Jessie Leary, and Terry Rowley, who provided cheers along the way. To all my other family as well, who listened to me talk about my book – many thanks. And to Dave, my husband, who lent support and expertise in his role as JOAT (Jack-Of-All-Trades), from repairing printer and computer hardware problems to introducing me to software that wouldn't freeze my computer, from making photocopies to making coffee, and much more. Thanks to you all.

Introduction

Across the globe, three major forces have created a surge of interest in various language education models. One concern is that, as the world communities develop business and political relationships, there is a greater need for individuals to develop multilingual competence. Immersion programs have thrived internationally as educators and politicians recognize the need to implement programs that promote higher levels of communicative proficiency than those offered by traditional foreign language models do. A second factor is that worldwide waves of immigration have forced many countries to address the educational needs of language minority students. In some instances, these students are children of guest workers who will return to their country of origin, while in other cases the immigrant students will stay in their host country. While these different outcomes may provoke the development of different educational models, there is still the need to meet the needs of these linguistically, if not culturally, diverse students. Still another force has led to increased interest in language education programs, which is the revitalization of languages in countries where the minority language has been suppressed or is in process of language loss (e.g. indigenous languages in many countries, Basque in Spain, Maori in New Zealand, Quechua in Peru). These factors have provided the impetus to challenge traditional language education models to assure that our models meet the increasingly diverse needs of the various student populations.

Dual language education (DLE) is a program that has the potential to eradicate the negative status of bilingualism in the US. The appeal of dual language education is that it combines maintenance bilingual education and immersion education models in an integrated classroom composed of both language majority and language minority students with the goal of full bilingualism and biliteracy.

While there has been a number of publications on the pedagogy and outcomes associated with bilingual education, immersion education, or other foreign language programs, there is little such information, especially empirically-based, available regarding dual language education (Lindholm, 1997, 1999b; Lindholm & Molina, 1998, 2000). Most publications on immersion and foreign language programs address the language majority student, and those on bilingual education focus on the language minority student. This book merges these two populations and programs to describe the implementation and outcomes of the dual language education model in the US and to discuss the implications for other student populations as well.

The research described here is based on my own data collection efforts, which in 1986 began to document the dual language education program. My research includes data from more than 20 schools at different stages of implementation, and comprises the major types of dual language education programs. Data collection efforts encompass considerable longitudinal and cross-sectional data, with students from diverse cultural, socioeconomic, and language backgrounds. Student outcomes, such as oral language proficiency, literacy, academic achievement, and attitudes, are available in addition to teacher and parent attitudes as well as classroom interactions. Where possible, data from dual language education programs are compared to outcomes in other forms of bilingual education or English-only programs. While considerable data are presented here, they do not begin to match the scope of data available for immersion education in Canada. However, data are offered here in the hopes that others will gather and publish further information about dual language education, and that the findings will have implications beyond the dual language education model in the US.

Overview of the Book

This book is organized into four parts. The first part sets the theoretical and conceptual stage for language education programs, and defines and describes dual language education. Part 2 provides contextual information, with data on school sites, teacher perceptions and attitudes, teacher talk in the classroom, and parental attitudes. Student outcomes are the focus of Part 3, which describes the language minority and language majority students' progress in oral language proficiency, academic achievement, and attitudes development. Finally, Part 4 summarizes and integrates the data to understand dual language education sites and students, as well as the implications of the findings for other language education designs and implementation in a variety of global contexts.

After working with dual language education programs for the past 15 years, I have an increasingly strong conviction that language education programs need a clear theoretical and conceptual framework in order to be successful. This is particularly true for bilingual education in the US, and is becoming true of dual language education programs as well. While recognizing the need to develop a program that meets particular needs at a school site, I have seen so much experimentation with the dual language education model without any consideration of the consequences on the students of such 'playing around.' Some of these programs that call themselves dual language are really not dual language programs at all.

Without a clearly defined pedagogy, bilingual education in the US has become a catch-all phrase for any form of instruction in which some first language (L1) activity is used in the classroom. The variety of programs that call themselves bilingual seems limitless, including programs in which the primary language is used for 1% of the day as well as those in which it is used for the entire instructional day. Bilingual education is also used to refer both to classrooms in which teaching is carried out by a certified bilingual teacher in that language and also to classrooms in which a volunteer with no professional training provides the student(s) with instruction or translation. Other times, bilingual education refers to classrooms that comprise students who speak a language other than English, whether there is any native language instruction or not. This problem of using the term bilingual education so loosely does not result from any of lack of understanding of bilingual education among bilingual educators, but rather is because definitions have not been carefully used in implementation. Thus, there is no operational definition that is stringently used to clarify whether or not a classroom is following a bilingual education model. Also, bilingual education has become caught in a web of political confusion regarding immigration reform, educational reform, and which populations deserve dwindling financial resources. Because of the political context in which language education functions, both in the US and other countries, it is important to discuss the context of and framework for language education programs.

Part 1

This section provides a conceptual grounding for effective language education models in general, and dual language education programs in particular. In Chapter 1 there is a description of demographic characteristics that affect language education in the US. Focus is on the changing demographics in the US, which reflect considerable cultural diversity and a significant language minority population, particularly among the school-aged population. To understand language education in the US also requires an understanding of the political context, which gives lip service to multilingualism and multiculturalism while promoting monocul-turalism and monolingualism through ethnic and linguistic prejudice and discrimination. Chapter 1 then goes on to provide information regarding the language education programs for language minority and language majority students in the US. The dual language education model is defined and described, with a brief history of its development and a discussion of the variability in model implementation across the US.

Chapter 2 examines the major theoretical and conceptual framework underlying language education models. The bodies of literature that are discussed for their relevance to language education include: effective schools, social context of language education, language development, and the relationship between language and thought. From these concepts, Chapter 3 discusses the specific design and implementation features that are critical to the success of language education programs in general. and dual language education in particular.

Part 2

The dual language education school communities are described in Part 2 to provide a context for understanding the school, classroom, teacher, and parent issues in the dual language education model. Chapter 4 describes the school sites that were involved in my data collection efforts, including the ethnic density and socioeconomic features of the school, and the ethnicity, language background and socioeconomic characteristics of the program participants. In this chapter, we see the variability in dual language education program types and populations. Also included is a description of bilingual education sites that are used for comparison purposes in subsequent chapters.

To examine teacher background factors and attitudes in dual language education programs, Chapter 5 presents a variety of data on teacher attitudes, efficacy and satisfaction. These data include background information on the teachers' education, training, proficiency in the two languages of the program, and ethnicity, along with these teachers' perceptions of their teaching efficacy, their satisfaction with the model, their perceptions of support, program planning, and whether the program is meeting the needs of its population. Findings demonstrate the complexity of teacher background; program type; administrative, peer and parent support; as well as program planning issues that are associated with teachers who report feeling efficacious as teachers and satisfied with the model implementation at their site.

Two studies in Chapter 6 examine teacher talk and patterns of teacher initiation–student response–teacher response in the classrooms. The results are consistent with previous classroom discourse, bilingual education and immersion research in demonstrating the lack of opportunity for students to engage in meaningful and extended discourse with the teacher.

Chapter 7 deals with a topic that is typically absent from education and language education studies. Parent attitudes and reasons for enrolling their child in a dual language education program are examined, comparing attitudes and reasons for enrolling children according to program type, parent ethnicity, and parents' language background. This chapter provides a rich description of the types of parents who participate in DLE programs.

Part 3

This section presents the evaluation outcomes of 4,900 students in dual language education programs, including longitudinal data collected over a period of 4–8 years. These outcomes are examined according to program type, school demographic characteristics, and student background characteristics. In addition, comparisons are made, wherever possible, with traditional bilingual education programs and English monolingual classrooms, wherever possible. Chapter 8 provides a description of the student participants from which data in subsequent chapters are drawn. In Chapter 9, the oral language proficiency and level of bilingual attainment are discussed. Oral language proficiency in the two languages is explored through teacher ratings of students' language proficiency and oral proficiency tests. From there, we move into Chapter 10 with an examination of reading and language achievement and Chapter 11, which includes and compares data from traditional standardized tests of reading achievement and reading rubrics developed as part of a language arts portfolio. A further look at content mastery is the topic of Chapter 12, which includes the level of achievement in mathematics, science, and social studies as indicated by traditional standardized tests of achievement. Students' attitudes and motivation are the topics of discussion in Chapter 13, which examines student attitudes toward the program, as well as student perceptions of their language and academic competence, motivation for challenge, integrative and instrumental motivation, cross-cultural attitudes, self esteem, and their beliefs about the benefits of bilingualism.

Part 4

Part 4 provides the opportunity to bring together data on teacher attitudes and student outcomes, and to examine implications of the data for language education pedagogy and student participants. Chapter 14 summarizes the findings and highlights key research results. This chapter clearly shows that the DLE model can produce its intended results – high levels of bilingualism, biliteracy, and achievement at or above grade level. Chapter 15 presents implications for language educational programs, including several issues that have been consistently important to dual language education and which may influence language education programs in general. These include: design and implementation issues, teacher training, parent recruitment and education, student population characteristics, evaluation and assessment issues, and transition to secondary school concerns.

Part 1

Social and Theoretical Contexts of Dual Language Education

Chapter 1

Language Education Programs and Politics

Language education is an increasingly vibrant issue in the United States, as it is in many other countries that have complex demographically- and politically-motivated language education programs. To provide a broader background for understanding language education programs, it is helpful to present the demographic and sociopolitical contexts that influence the implementation of these programs. Following a discussion of the demographic and political issues, this chapter will briefly present the existing language education models for language minority students as well as for language majority students. The final section will define the dual language education model.

Demographic and Political Issues Affecting Language Education in the US

Demographic issues affecting language education

The United States, along with many other countries, has experienced considerable immigration over many decades and particularly in the past 20 years. According to the last two decanal census reports and the most recent update (US Census, 1980, 1990, 1996), there have been significant population shifts, as shown in Table 1.1[1]. While the general US population grew at a rate of 17% (from 227 million to 275 million) from 1980 to 2000, the rate of growth varied tremendously across the different ethnic/racial groups in the US. The Hispanic population increased by 83% and represented 11.7% of the US population in 2000. One other group that expanded substantially was the Asian American population (at 3.8% in 2000), with a growth rate of 153%. More modest increases were witnessed among African Americans, who in 2000 represented 12.2% of the population. Thus, in 2000, the minority population encompassed 28.4%, or more than one quarter, of the US population. The remaining 71.6% of the population included European Americans, who decreased 9% in 2000, from 79.8% of the population in 1980. As one can see from Table 1.1, the non-European-American population is growing at a much faster rate, in part due to

Table 1.1 US population by race and Spanish origin: Percent distribution and rate of growth: 1980–2000

Ethnic Group	Distribution		Rate of Growth
	1980	**2000**	
Total	*227 million*	*276 million*	22%
Hispanic	6.4%	11.9%	86%
Asian American	1.5%	3.8%	153%
African American	11.7%	12.2%	4%
Native American	0.6%	0.7%	17%
European American	79.8%	71.3%	-10.7%

Source: US Census Bureau (2000).

continuing immigration. By 1999, 26.4 million foreign-born people resided in the US, representing 9.7% of the total US population (Brittingham, 1999; US Department of Justice, 1999).

This demographic shift has been widely discussed in the US, particularly in states where immigrants are most likely to settle (i.e. California, New York, Florida, Texas, and Illinois). The State of California is a prime example where the demographic shift has lead to political changes that have and will continue to impact language education programs. California has six of the top 20 cities that receive the most legal immigrants, accounting for about 100,000 new immigrants annually (Allen & Turner, 1988; US Department of Justice, 1999). Added to the legal immigrant figure are the estimated two million immigrants who have arrived illegally from many different countries (Allen & Turner, 1988; US Department of Justice, 2000).

The educational significance of this demographic shift is that many of these immigrants are children, or are adults who gave birth to children, who enter the school system speaking little or no English. In the US, an estimated 9.9 million of 45 million school-aged children, live in households in which languages other than English are spoken (US Census Bureau, 1996), a statistic which represents a 35% increase since 1980 (Waggoner, 1995). While Spanish continues to be the language of two thirds, or six million children, who speak a language other than English at home, speakers of languages that are Asian in origin have doubled from 1980 to 1990

(Waggoner, 1995). Close to eight million language minority children attended public schools, and one million entered private schools.

While language minority students live in each of the 50 states, only a few states have a significant language minority population. California has the largest language minority population, with an estimated 2.2 million students in 1999 (www.cde.ca.gov/demographics/). Other states with a significant number of language minority students include: Texas (1.4 million), New York (972,000), and five states each with at least a quarter million language minority students (Florida, Illinois, New Jersey, Arizona and Pennsylvania). It is in California where almost half of children entering school come from homes where a language other than English is used. Because California has the largest language minority population, it will be used to exemplify sociopolitical issues affecting language education as well as types of language education programs.

Political concerns affecting language education

At a national level is the appearance of a healthy respect for, and a desire to see in students, bilingual or multilingual language proficiencies and multicultural competencies. For example, in 1989, the National Governor's Conference and then-President Bush agreed on a national education agenda comprising six broad goals to be met by the year 2000. President Clinton largely adopted this Goals 2000 national education agenda. Though bilingual proficiency was not specified as one of the six goals, it was subsumed under Goal 3 (titled Student Achievement and Citizenship). Objectives (v) and (vi) under Goal 3 specified that:

(v)   The percentage of all students who are competent in more than one language will substantially increase; and

(vi) All students will be knowledgeable about the diverse cultural heritage of this Nation and about the world community. (Goals 2000: Educate America Act of 1994).

These goals have since been replaced by a new set of goals, none of which includes competence in a second language.

More recently, then US Secretary of Education Richard Riley (2000) was addressing the growth of Hispanic Americans, which he labeled a 'transformation of historic proportions', and the underachievement of this group. He noted:

This is why I am delighted to see and highlight the growth and promise of so many dual-language bilingual programs across the country. They are challenging young people with high standards, high expectations, and curriculum in two languages. They are the wave of the future ... Our nation needs to encourage more of these kinds of learning opportunities, in many different languages. That is why I am challenging our nation to increase the number of dual-language schools to at least 1,000 over the next five years, and with strong federal, state and local support we can have many more. (Riley, 2000)

At the state level, there was also some interest in increasing bilingual competence in the late 1980s and early 1990s. Nine states mandated elementary foreign language classes and a number of other states seemed likely to follow suit or, at least, to provide substantial incentives for schools that did so (Met, 1998). According to Rhodes (1992), 30 states have instituted new foreign language requirements at the elementary level. In addition, the National Association of Elementary School Principals passed a resolution supporting elementary foreign language education (Black, 1993). However, as Crawford (1999: 238) points out, neither states nor the US has ever really 'had a language policy, consciously planned and [for the US] national in scope.' This lack of a coherent language policy is further supported in August and Hakuta's (1997) report from the First National Research Council on Developing a Research Agenda on the Education of English Language Learners and Bilingual Students.

In direct opposition to this apparent interest in promoting the teaching and learning of other languages and cultures is the considerable attention and debate in recent years on the question of whether English should be designated the official language of the United States. Strongly organized movements, such as *US English* and *English First*, have made it their primary purpose to make English the *official* language of the United States, through an amendment to the US Constitution, through state legislation or through repeal of laws and regulations permitting public business to be conducted in a language other than English.

English only movement in the US

As of 2000, 20 states had enacted laws designating English as the official state language (http://ourworld.compuserve.com/homepages/JWCRAWFORD). One lone state, Hawaii, has not one but two official languages: English and Hawaiian. According to Crawford (1999: 70, emphasis added), Arizona's law 'imposed a blanket English Only policy: "This state and all political subdivisions of this state shall act in English *and no other language.*"' As various states (39 out of 50 to date) have considered constitutional amendments that would make English the official language, legal scholars have also examined the constitutional provisions that apply to language-rights issues in the classroom, workplace, courtroom, and social service agencies (Crawford, 1999; Piatt, 1990).

The major difference, however, between the concern for language then and today is that in earlier times language issues were confined to local or state arenas. Today, in contrast, the initiatives dedicated to establishing English as the official language are orchestrated at the national level by a powerful and heavily funded political organization. Further, this English Only movement has close connections to restrictionist, anti-immigration organizations, which suggests that the English Only movement has a wider, more far-reaching and more negative agenda than simply advocating an official English language policy. For example, until mid-1988, US English was a project of US Inc., a tax-exempt corporation that also supports the Federation for American Immigration Reform (FAIR), Americans for Border Control, Californians for Population Stabilization, and other immigration-restrictionist groups (Crawford, 1999).

Crawford (1999) suggests that *racist* attitudes appear to be behind English Only initiatives. The position that English Only may appeal to racist beliefs is also supported by Huddy and Sears (1990) who examined the attitudes of white Americans toward bilingual education. Similarly, in an analysis by MacKaye (1990) of letters to the editor of various California newspapers that appeared before and after the 1986 election which included Proposition 63 (the English Only Initiative), the signs of racism were clear in much of the public sentiment surrounding the initiative, as exemplified in Crawford's (1999) quotes from editorials in various newspapers around the US:

> We here in Southern California are overrun with all sorts of aliens – Asian, Spanish, Cuban, Middle East – and it is an insurmountable task if these million are not required to learn English. Many are illerate [sic] in their native language [Rolling Hills, California] …At the rate the Latinos (and non-whites) reproduce, [we] face a demographic imbalance if we do not change several of our dangerously outdated laws. Make English the official language everywhere in the USA. [Jersey City, New Jersey] …No other ethnic group has made the demands for bilingual education as have the Cubans. The more you give them, the more they demand. WHOSE AMERICA IS THIS? ONE FLAG. ONE LANGUAGE. [North Miami, Florida]. (Crawford 1999: 66)

Over the past decade there has also been a sharp increase in the number of *hate crimes* and other forms of anti-minority group sentiment (e.g. Sniffen, 1999). We have seen an increase in Ku Klux Klan demonstrations, neo-Nazi activities, and skin-head youth attempts to intimidate individuals because of differences in race, ethnicity, language, religion, or sexual orientation. In 1995 through 1998, almost 8000 hate crimes were reported annually (Summary of Hate Crime Statistics, 1998), and hate crimes against people far outnumbered crimes against property, accounting for 72% of the total hate crimes (*San Jose Mercury News*, 1996). So commonplace have these events become that in 1990 the US Congress passed, and then-President Bush signed into law, the Hate Crime Statistics Act, which requires local governments to keep track of bias crimes. Currently, the US legislature is considering the Hate Crimes Prevention Act of 1999. We have long known that the more favorably one's own group is perceived, the less attractive other groups are viewed, making *ethnocentrism* the psychological mechanism that promotes ingroup-outgroup cleavage and prejudice of all forms (Adorno *et al.*, 1950). The English Only movement and the arguments used by its supporters to justify their actions are very similar to those used at other times and in other places to force the domination of one group over another. As Cummins (2000) points out, the debate on the merits of bilingual education can only be understood by considering these types of power relations that are operating in the society-at-large.

Yet, more and more North Americans are cognizant of the need to be more sensitive to other cultural groups and the different languages they may speak. There are small movements, including *English Plus*, that clearly support the acquisition and use of English for all US citizens and residents. However, these groups also advocate enhancing second language training and proficiency for English speakers. In addition, groups such as English Plus also promote expansion of bilingual education programs for the growing number of immigrant and other linguistic minority children in US schools, for broadening the range of health and other social services available to individuals who speak languages other than English, and for increasing the number of Adult English-as-Second-Language (ESL) and literacy programs for adult immigrants (Padilla *et al.*, 1991).

Consistent with this movement are the results of a survey by Lambert and Taylor (1990, cited in Lambert *et al.*, 1993). Their study was conducted with Americans of Albanian, Arabic, Mexican, and Polish descent, as well as with African American, and working and middle class Anglo Americans (who were not identified by ethnicity) to examine their attitudes toward multiculturalism (i.e. maintaining language and culture while also demonstrating English language proficiency and acculturation) versus assimilation (i.e. giving up native language and culture to become American and speak English). Results showed that, overwhelmingly, all but the working class whites favored multiculturalism.

In several of the communities in which I work, the Dual Language Education (DLE) program is highly supported by both the language minority and language majority families who are participating. However, in one community, a lawsuit was filed charging the school with violating the new English Only law in California. While the lawsuit was dropped, it opened a chasm in the community around which the pro-US English Only and bilingual advocates vigorously fought. The outcome was actually a greater unity in the community for the DLE program. However, the community's attitudes toward multiculturalism cannot be underestimated with respect to the language education program's ultimate lifespan and success.

The realm most frequently targeted for opposition by English Only policies is the education of linguistic minority students. For example, in June, 1998, California voters passed an initiative (Proposition 227) that was labeled 'English for the Children' by its millionaire originator, Ron Unz, a software developer with absolutely no background in education. As Unz and his supporters could only have imagined, the name 'English for the Children' was the only support the bill needed for passage. Arguments about the effectiveness of bilingual education were moot in the face of such a title. As Krashen lamented in his description of the lay public's understanding of this measure:

It had been frustrating day. I had been scheduled to debate Ron Unz at Cal State LA, my first chance to debate him face to face. To my disappointment, Unz did not show up and he sent a substitute debater. Thanks to a very supportive, knowledgeable and sophisticated audience, the substitute was overwhelmed, but little was accomplished. Unz wasn't there and therefore the press wasn't there. On the way home ...was standing in line ...the woman behind me asked why I looked so depressed. I explained the situation briefly ..she asked what the debate was about, and I said that it was with Ron Unz and had to do with Proposition 227. Her response was immediate and animated: 'Oh yes, English for the children! I've heard of that. I'm voting for it. I'm for English.' I was stunned. I realized right then that my strategy of carefully presenting the research that contradicted the details of 227 had been all wrong. The woman had no idea what 227 was about: She was 'voting for English,' but she clearly had no idea that a major goal of bilingual education was English language development.' (Krashen, 2000: 20)

In reality, Proposition 227 was established to:

- Impose an English-only program for all limited-English-proficient (LEP) children – regardless of the wishes of parents, the recommendations of educators, or the decisions of local school boards.
- Mainstream 1.4 million LEP students after just one-year of English instruction – overtaxing teachers and holding back English-proficient students.
- Intimidate teachers and administrators, with threats of lawsuits and financial penalties, for using any language but English to assist a child.
- Restrict foreign-language instruction for all California students – including native English speakers.
- Restrict the California legislature by requiring a two-thirds vote to amend the English-only mandate – making it virtually impossible to modify or repeal.

This initiative has resulted in the replacement of many bilingual programs with English-only programs and the modification of other bilingual (including DLE) programs, if enough parents had requested a waiver to allow their child to be educated bilingually. Currently, thousands of teachers who have no training in working with language minority children or in English language development methodologies, have limited-English-proficient students in their classrooms (http://ourworld.compuserve.com/homepages/JWCRAWFORD).

To understand the significant impact of the English Only movement on the education of language minority students requires a slight demographic reminder. As indicated in the previous section, growth trends over the past twenty years have demonstrated that the number of language minority students has increased substantially. The great majority of these language minority students, about 75%, are Hispanic. In addition, it is probably true that, instead of providing bilingual education for these students, a disproportionate number of language minority students are tracked inappropriately into special education programs (Baca & Cervantes, 1998; Olneck, 1995).

Nationally, the academic performance of minority students is considerably below majority norms (e.g. August & Hakuta, 1997; Darling-Hammond, 1995; National Center for Education Statistics, 2000; Padilla & Lindholm, 1995; Portes & Rumbaut, 1990; Riley, 2000). Reading is critical to student achievement in all subjects, yet National Assessment of Educational Progress Reports (1990, 1998) for the period show that the achievement gap is greatest in reading. In addition, the highest drop-out rates are obtained in schools with large concentrations of Southeast Asian (48%) and Spanish speaking (46%) students, and large concentrations of language minority students in general (Sue & Padilla, 1986). While there are a number of risk factors implicated in school drop out for ethnic and language minority students, one of these risk factors includes limited English language proficiency at school entry. Fluency in English is also one critical factor in achievement. Although many students can acquire the basic communication skills in English necessary to carry on a normal everyday conversation with others, they often have difficulty mastering the academic language required of schooling tasks (see Chapter 3 for further information regarding communication skills and cognitive academic language skills).

English Only advocates and other opponents of bilingual education have vociferously disparaged the ineffectiveness of bilingual education for language minority children. This viewpoint received considerable support in 1985 when then-Secretary of Education, William Bennett, stated in a speech to the Association for a Better New York: 'After seventeen years of federal involvement, and after $1.7 billion of federal funding, we have no evidence that the children whom we sought to help have benefited.'

The central issue of the debate on bilingual education has been whether research supports the educational benefit of the program or whether federal monies could be better spent on other educational programs. As Crawford (1999) has pointed out, critics of bilingual education have had a decided edge in the controversy over its effectiveness. Where evidence is contradictory, the easiest position to defend and the hardest to disprove is that results are inconclusive. The US Education Department's request for proof that bilingual education is universally effective with every limited English proficient child from every background in every school is a standard that has been set for no other content area or program.

The strongest arguments against bilingual education came from two employees of the US Department of Education, Baker and de Kanter (1981, 1983) who reviewed the bilingual education evaluation literature and concluded that bilingual education was not effective in meeting the educational needs of language minority children. They went so far as to report that transitional bilingual programs were ineffective and harmful in some settings, instead endorsing a structured English immersion demonstration program, despite the lack of any evidence of its effectiveness in meeting the needs of language minority children. According to Crawford (1999: 112), 'During the 1980s it [the Baker and de Kanter report] was easily the most quoted federal pronouncement on the education of LEP children, and probably the most criticized as well.'

One critical reply to the Baker and de Kanter reports came from Willig (1985, 1987) who used meta-analysis procedures to re-analyze the Baker and de Kanter studies. In her analysis, Willig controlled for 183 variables that Baker and de Kanter had not taken into account and, most importantly, controlled for the design weaknesses in the studies. The results from the meta-analysis consistently yielded small-to-moderate differences supporting bilingual education. This pattern of findings was substantiated not only in English tests of reading, language skills, mathematics, and total academic achievement, but also in Spanish tests of listening comprehension, reading, writing, language, mathematics, social studies, and attitudes toward school and self. Methodological rigor also influenced the findings, such that higher quality study designs produced more positive effects favoring bilingually educated children over children in comparison groups.

Willig (1987), in a rebuttal to Baker (1987), elaborated upon her earlier study and argued even more convincingly for the soundness of her original conclusion. She also identified the numerous methodological flaws inherent in the Baker and de Kanter (1981, 1983) reviews of literature that contributed to their erroneous conclusions. While the policy questions that drove the Baker and de Kanter study are now quite moot, as Secada (1987) has so eloquently stated, the English Only movement has seriously eroded public and educator confidence in bilingual education as a promising educational program for language minority students.

In evaluation studies that compare bilingual education to structured English immersion and English-as-a-Second-Language (ESL) programs, these alternatives certainly fare far worse than bilingual education. One multi-million dollar study compared transitional bilingual education or early-exit (the most common bilingual education model, designed to transition students as quickly as possible to English mainstream), with late-exit (maintaining native language while developing English for several years), and structured English immersion approaches. This large-scale methodologically rigorous study showed that the immersion students scored lowest in almost every academic subject, while late-exit bilingual students scored highest, even when all groups were tested in English (Ramirez *et al.*, 1991). For a long time, the US Department of Education refused to officially release the results of this very expensive and well-designed study because it provided strong support for the effectiveness of *late-exit* bilingual education (Crawford, 1999).

Research has clearly shown that high quality bilingual education programs can promote higher levels of academic achievement and language proficiency in both languages, as well as more positive psychosocial outcomes (Holm & Holm, 1990). Similarly, the sink-or-swim structured English immersion approach, advocated by English Only, results in lower levels of academic achievement and English language proficiency, as well as a decrement in psychosocial competence (Hakuta & Gould, 1987). These views are consistent with the US General Accounting Office's (1987a, 1987b) own independent review of the findings of bilingual education research in light of the US Department of Education policy statements and many other studies (see August & Hakuta, 1997; Cummins, 2000).

At the core of the controversy regarding the effectiveness of bilingual education are some theoretical issues regarding the relationship between bilingualism and cognition (see Chapter 2 for a fuller description of this point). One controversial issue is whether there are positive or negative influences of bilingualism on cognitive ability. Considerable research on this point has demonstrated that balanced bilinguals (i.e. those who develop full competency in both languages) enjoy some cognitive advantages over monolinguals in areas such as cognitive flexibility, meta-linguistic knowledge, concept formation, and creativity (August & Hakuta, 1997; Bialystok, 1999; Bialystok & Hakuta, 1994). As Hakuta and Garcia (1989: 375) point out, 'Causal relationships have been difficult to establish, but in general, positive outcomes have been noted, particularly in situations where bilingualism is not a socially stigmatized trait but rather a symbol of membership in a social elite.' From this perspective, it is simple to understand why parents of a language majority child as well as language minority parents would want the *option* of enrolling their child in an enrichment bilingual program that promotes both languages. However, based on English Only goals, this type of language enrichment would not be possible in the public schools, because it would serve to strengthen proficiency in non-English languages. Interestingly, this contrasts sharply with recent concern for foreign language education and the need to prepare a language-competent society that is able to compete effectively with other nations in English and in the languages of our competitors.

Thus, psychological and educational research suggests that policies aimed at promoting English at the expense of other languages are misguided on at least three counts. First, there is considerable basic, applied, and evaluation research that shows that bilingual education can promote academic achievement, dual language proficiency, and psychosocial competence, whereas structured English immersion approaches may lead to lower levels of achievement, English proficiency, and psychosocial development. Second, there is no evidence that bilingualism causes any type of cognitive overload, causing children to become confused between the two languages. Third, bilingualism may lead to higher levels of intellectual development, a finding that should lend support for enrichment bilingual models rather than immersion English Only approaches, for both language minority and language majority students (August & Hakuta, 1997; Bialystok, 1999; Cummins, 2000; Tinajero & DeVillar, 2000).

In summary, the arguments against bilingual education by advocates of English Only (e.g. Imhoff, 1990) are inaccurate. Bilingual education, when properly implemented, can be a very effective pedagogical technique for assisting both in the smooth transition to English and in an orderly educational preparation of students from non-English-speaking homes. In fact, this may be the best way to achieve participatory democracy since the beneficiaries of bilingual education are both proficient in English and equipped educationally to contribute to society.

A final comment regarding the sociopolitical context is that support for bilingual education has always been paltry but, with the rise in the US English movement and escalating economic problems in educational settings, support for bilingual education is waning even further. Evaluation and research studies, even methodologically sound ones, are not awarded their due credibility (Crawford, 1999; Cummins, 2000; Krashen, 2000). Added to this enigma are the methodological challenges in conclusively demonstrating the superior effect of bilingual education over other educational approaches for language minority students. The net impact is that policy on language education for language minority and majority students is typically *not* guided by research and evaluation studies on the effectiveness of bilingual or immersion education programs, but rather by emotional appeals and myths based on misguided opinions.

Education of Language Minority Students

Almost without exception, language minority education in the US has been restricted to compensatory educational models based on a linguistic, academic, and socio-cultural deficit model. In Baker's (1996) and Skutnabb-Kangas' (1988) terminology, language education programs are largely submersion (devalue and attempt to eradicate the native language, as in immersion programs in English) or transitional (provide some L1 support, but move as quickly as possible into English). Both of these serve the societal and educational aim of assimilation, and result in English monolingualism.

This assimilationist aim is clearly seen in the manner in which educational services are decided for specific students. First, there is a determination of who requires language education services. All students from homes where a language other than English is spoken are potential language minority students. On the basis of their performance on English-language-proficiency tests, students are categorized as Limited English Proficient (LEP) or Fluent English Proficient (FEP). This terminology, which implies a deficit rather than the strength of a potential bilingual, sets the stage for further derogatory treatment, as seen in the reference to LEPs by educators, lawmakers or others as 'nonspeakers,' because the focus is on what the students lack rather than what they are able to do.

Only LEP students are offered placement in specialized language programs. Further, special services are typically offered only for the period of time that the so-called LEP students are considered deficient in English communication skills. Thus, all programs required by federal law for language minority students are transitional in nature. To reclassify as FEP and exit a student from specialized instruction, schools typically give the student some sort of oral language proficiency test that assesses the student's ability to communicate and understand English. Some schools go a step further and require that the student performs to a certain standard on an achievement test. However, when such achievement testing is carried out, the standard of attainment is typically quite low and certainly well below grade level.

Once students are reclassified as FEP, they are no longer protected by the educational laws that require bilingual or other specialized instructional services (Dolson, 1985). FEP students are rarely offered primary language, or L1 instruction by school districts. Certainly, they have no legal support in terms of linguistic human rights to petition the local school for mother tongue classes, although there are some school districts that provide ESL instruction for FEP students or that offer Spanish for Native Speaker classes at the high school level.

In 2000, 1.4 million language minority students enrolled in California's schools were categorized as LEP students (www.cde.ca.gov)[2]. While these students represented a wide variety of languages, the most common languages were:

- Spanish (81.9%)
- Vietnamese (2.9%)
- Hmong (2.0%)
- Cantonese (1.8%)
- Tagalog (1.3%)
- Kmer (Cambodian, 1.2%).

Table 1.2 depicts the manner in which these students were distributed among the various types of language education programs designed for language minority students. For further information about typologies of

Table 1.2 LEP Student enrollment in instructional programs: California summary

Number and Percent of LEP	Grades K–6	913,063 (69%)
	Grades 7–12 or ungraded	410,862 (31%)
	Total	*1,323,787*
	(1) English Language Development (ELD)	13.5%
	(2) ELD and Specially Designed Academic Instruction in English (SDAIE)	16.0%
	(3) ELD, SDAIE and Primary Language Support	19.7%
	(4) ELD and Academic Subjects Through the Primary Language	30.2%
	(5) Not in Program	20.6%

Source: California Department of Education (1996a).

language education programs, see Baker and his colleagues (Baker, 1996; Baker & Jones, 1998; Garcia & Baker, 1995) and Skuttnab-Kangas (1988).

Data in Table 1.2 were collected as part of the annual language census conducted by the California Department of Education (1996a). The survey used the following operational definitions for each of the program categories listed in rows 1 through 4 (Dolson & Lindholm, 1995):

(1) *English Language Development* (ELD): A specialized program of *English* language instruction appropriate for the student's identified level of language proficiency which is consistently implemented and is designed to promote second language acquisition of listening, speaking, reading, and writing. Instruction must be provided by a qualified bilingual teacher or by a teacher who is a language development specialist.

(2) *ELD and Specially Designed Academic Instruction in English (SDAIE)*: Each LEP student must receive a program of ELD and, at a minimum, two academic subjects required for grade promotion or graduation taught through specially designed academic instruction in *English*. SDAIE is an approach utilized to teach academic courses to LEP students in *English*. The instructional methodology must be designed for non-native speakers of English and must focus on increasing the

comprehensibility of the academic courses provided. Instruction must be provided by a qualified bilingual teacher or a teacher who is a language development specialist, or by any other teacher who has sufficient training to implement the SDAIE methodology.

(3) *ELD, SDAIE, and Primary Language Support*: Each LEP student must receive a program of ELD, SDAIE, and instructional support through the primary language in at least two academic subject areas. Primary language support may be provided by any teacher, or by any paraprofessional who has sufficient proficiency in the target language.

(4) *ELD and Academic Subjects Through the Primary Language*: In kindergarten through grade 6, *primary language* instruction is provided, at a minimum, in language arts (including reading and writing) and mathematics, science, or social science. In grades 7–12, primary language instruction is provided, at a minimum, in two academic subjects required for grade promotion or graduation. Lesson content and curriculum must be aligned with that provided to FEP and English-only students in the school district. Primary language instruction must be provided by qualified bilingual teachers.

It is interesting to note that 20.6% of the students are listed in Table 1.2 as 'Not in Program.' This refers to students who:

• Are not offered (contrary to law at that time) any specialized instruction.
• Have been withdrawn from a program by their parents.
• Are enrolled in a program that does not meet the operational definition of any of the programs indicated in rows 1 through 4.

Most of the students reported in row 5 receive some form of instructional assistance. However, such assistance rarely includes instruction in and through the *L1*, and almost never implies that the instruction is provided by a bilingual or other qualified teacher. None of the program options seeks to maintain the student's proficiency in his/her primary language. These potential bilinguals are forced into a monolingual mold because bilingualism is viewed as a liability rather than as a resource. Thus, close to 70% (rows 1–3 and 5) of these LEP students receive little, if any, L1 instruction and what L1 'support' they do receive may be provided by an untrained paraprofessional if the teacher is not proficient in the target language.

Language education for language minority students is further complicated by the lack of state and local support and by the lack of trained teachers. Public schools in California were required to abide by a mandatory bilingual education act from 1976 to 1987. In 1987, the governor and the state legislature were unable to reach an agreement on renewing the policy for language minority education in the state. Subsequently, programs for language minority students have been governed by a complex combination of state and federal laws, court cases, and local guidelines. All of this well-publicized legal uncertainty seems to have undermined efforts to obtain the human and material resources necessary to support bilingual programs. For instance, between 1987 and 1990, the number of bilingual teachers available for classroom assignments actually decreased slightly while the number of language minority students in the same period increased on average more than 10% annually (California State Department of Education, 1992). The demand for bilingual classroom teachers was estimated to be 22,365 for the 1.1 million LEP students in 1991 (California State Department of Education, 1991). The current supply of bilingual teachers is calculated at 13,543 for over 1.3 million LEP students. This results in a significant statewide shortage of teachers (Dolson & Lindholm, 1995). Currently, California State incentives to lower the teacher:student ratio to 1:20 in kindergarten through third grade have severely exacerbated this already-acute shortage of trained bilingual teachers.

Reviews of research on the scholastic underperformance of language minority students in the 1980s were reported by Dolson (1985), Cummins (1989), and Fishman (1989) among many others. More recent reports demonstrate that these negative trends continue in California and the US in general (August & Hakuta, 1997; National Center for Education Statistics, 2000; Riley, 2000; US Department of Education, 2001). Studies such as these, coupled with the California Department of Education language census reports on the quantity and quality of specialized language programs, provide an overall picture of the persistence of unfavorable educational conditions for language minority students in California and elsewhere.

Initially, many bilingual educators in the US mistakenly believed that transitional forms of bilingual education would be sufficient to provide language minority students with equal educational opportunities. What they did not realize at the time is that sociopolitical pressures would reduce the intervention to almost exclusive reliance on the *early-exit* version of this model, with its concomitant promotion of subtractive bilingualism (Hernandez-Chavez, 1984). These educators further underestimated the negative effects of minority status on bilingual program teachers and student participants (Cummins, 1989; Spener, 1988). The results of earlier investigations have been confirmed by the longitudinal study conducted by Ramirez and others (1991), which clearly indicates that the quick-fix versions of bilingual education are severely limited in their ability to address the scholastic needs of language minority students. This implication has stimulated interest among many educational practitioners and researchers who are concerned about the failure of current programs to adequately address the needs of language minority students.

These advocates of language minority students have worked to transform the compensatory nature of transitional programs into enrichment models of bilingual schooling (Cloud, Genesee & Hamayan, 2000; Dolson & Mayer, 1992; Genesee & Gándara, in press). Because enrichment models, or maintenance bilingual models, for language minority students have received such unfavorable media and popular attention as ineffective in promoting quick acquisition of English, they are rarely found in the US. Thus, educators have began to see the need for combining enrichment models that include language majority along with the language minority students as a way to allow enrichment language education for language minority students.

Education of Language Majority Students

As in most countries, the US provides two major types of foreign language instruction at the elementary school level. These major approaches include: FLES (Foreign Language in the Elementary School), and immersion. According to a national survey of public and private schools conducted by Rhodes and Oxford (1988), 59% of elementary-school foreign-language programs in the US can be categorized as either FLES or immersion.

The term FLES has a dual meaning. It is often utilized as an umbrella term to refer to elementary-school foreign-language education. However, the acronym also describes specific programs that usually last for two or more years and encompass a range of 5–15% of the weekly school curriculum (Lipton, 1985). In general, the objectives of FLES programs are:

- To develop a certain amount of listening and speaking skills (the amount varies from program to program).
- To acquire an understanding of and appreciation for other cultures.
- To reach a limited level of proficiency in reading and writing (in some programs).

When a FLES program emphasizes appreciation of culture rather than development of listening and speaking skills, the program is considered a FLEX (Foreign Language Experience) program.

The national Foreign Language in Elementary School (FLES) program, with its accompanying federal funds, generated a modest amount of

Table 1.3 Foreign language enrollments in California schools in Grades K–12

Language of Instruction	Total Course Enrollment			Totals
	Grades K–6	Grades 7–12	Advanced Placement (College Credit)	
Spanish	7,706	506,091	24,732	538,529
French	1,084	96,816	3,745	101,645
German	53	19,511	948	20,512
Japanese	23	6,451	n/a	6,474
Latin	56	4,626	315	4,997
Mandarin/Cantonese	73	3,859	0	3,932
Russian	0	1,328	0	1,328
Korean	0	874	0	874
Italian	29	623	0	652
Vietnamese	0	452	0	452
Portuguese	0	386	0	386
Other	2,756	15,580	0	18,336
Totals	*11,780*	*656,597*	*29,740*	*698,117*

Source: California Department of Education (1996a).

interest in kindergarten through grade 6 schools in the late 1960s. Most of these programs faded by the early 1970s, and activity in second language programs at these grade levels has remained paltry. Table 1.3 contains data that show that, in the 1995–96 school year, fewer than 11,780 elementary-level (grades K–6)[3] students were enrolled in such programs in California. The languages offered at the elementary level tend to parallel the traditional foreign language choices in the US (Spanish or French), but include a few other languages as well.

Including secondary students, fewer than 700,000 of California's 5.2 million public school students participated in some form of second language instruction. This represents only 11.5% of the state's total student enrollment. Only 29,740 students were enrolled in Advanced Placement courses, mostly in Spanish, which require higher levels of language proficiency. According to Dolson and Lindholm (1995), most English-speaking students in California tend to graduate from secondary schools with the following characteristics:

They are able to speak only one language, English, and even if they know something of another language, it is at a minimal, non-functional proficiency level. Further, since little or no attention is given to the development of their cross-cultural competencies, they are not well suited to participate in cooperative efforts to address global concerns of commerce, ecology, poverty or peace. (Dolson & Lindholm, 1995: 78)

Dissatisfaction with the dismal outcomes of traditional foreign language programs and the emergence of reports from Canada on the spectacular results of French immersion programs led some educators to speculate on the application of immersion education in the United States (California Department of Education, 1984).

Immersion is a method of foreign-language instruction in which the regular school curriculum is taught through the medium of a second language. Immersion education originated as a community experiment in the 1960s in Quebec, Canada (Lambert & Tucker, 1972). At the time, a group of parents was becoming increasingly concerned about deficiencies in the foreign-language pedagogy at local schools. In anticipation of a future in which a knowledge of French would be instrumental in their society, and with the help of Lambert and Tucker, two McGill University researchers, the parents founded an experimental French immersion program.

There are a number of alternative forms of the immersion approach. Two factors serve to differentiate among the existing variations of immersion:

- The amount of instruction provided in the second language (total or partial immersion).
- The grade level at which immersion commences (early, delayed or late immersion).

Not all of the different approaches will be described here as they are aptly described in a number of different sources (e.g. Baker, 1996; Baker & Jones, 1998; Cloud *et al.*, 2000; Genesee, 1987); rather, I will briefly define the major early immersion approaches.

In the *early total immersion* program, 90–100% of the students' instructional day is taught through the medium of the foreign language during grades K and 1. In grades 2 and 3, about 80% of the instructional day is devoted to teaching content through the foreign language. By the upper grades (typically grades 4–6), at least 50% of instruction continues to be offered in the second language (Snow, 1990).

Early partial immersion is a program in which less than 100% of curriculum instruction during the primary grades is provided in the second language. The amount of second-language instruction varies from program to program, but 50% first-language instruction and 50% second-language instruction is the most common formula from kindergarten through grade six (Snow, 1990).

The basic goals of immersion programs are usually the same (Lipton, 1985: v):

- Functional proficiency in the second language.
- The ability to communicate in the second language on topics appropriate to age level.
- Mastery of subject content material of the local school district curriculum (which is taught through the second language).
- Achievement in English language arts comparable to or surpassing the achievement of students in English Only programs.
- Cross cultural understanding.

Several *longitudinal* studies reflect the high degree of success that has characterized Canadian immersion programs (see Genesee, 1983; Johnson & Swain, 1997; Lambert & Tucker, 1972; Swain & Lapkin, 1981). For US educators, the first Canadian immersion model adapted to an 'American' context represented an encouraging solution to the lack of foreign language proficiency among US students. In 1971, Culver City, California became home to the first US immersion program. Culver City has since experienced positive results similar to those produced by the Canadian programs (see Cohen, 1974; Campbell, 1984; Genesee, 1985; Snow, Padilla & Campbell, 1988).

According to a survey of public schools by Fortune and Jorstad (1996), second-language immersion programs are on the increase in the United States, as parents and educators recognize the career advantages of having bilingual students. In this survey of schools offering immersion education, they located 79 schools, of which 43% provided instruction through Spanish and 35% in French. German, Japanese, and Hawaiian represented the remaining languages taught through immersion. About one third of these schools used a full early immersion model (at four hours of content instruction in the target language), and the remaining two thirds offered a partial immersion model. Most (87%) of these immersion schools were in predominantly English-speaking urban or suburban neighborhoods, with only a few programs situated in small towns or rural communities. These programs also are typically elite choice offerings that function much like private schools.

In general, immersion programs have been associated with solid advances in language skills as well as academic achievement in a variety of countries (e.g. Artigal, 1997; DeCourcy, 1997; Duff, 1997; Genesee, 1997). Genesee (1985: 559) confirms that 'the immersion approach is a feasible and effective way for English-speaking American students to attain high levels of second language proficiency without risk to their native language development or their academic achievement.' Snow (1986), reporting on twenty years of US and Canadian immersion research, concludes that the English language development and overall academic achievement of immersion students tends to equal or surpass that of their peers in mainstream class environments.

Genesee (1987) reviewed the evaluation results from three total immersion programs: the Culver City program in California; the Four Corners project in Maryland; and the Cincinnati immersion project. In terms of *first-language development*, Genesee reported that the immersion students did not experience any deficits in their English language development as a result of their participation in the immersion approach. During the first few years of immersion programs, there is usually a lag in English language arts performance due to the fact that English has not yet been introduced into the curriculum. However, upon the introduction of English language arts into the curriculum, the lag disappears (Snow, 1990).

In terms of the immersion students' *second-language development*, Genesee (1987: 130) reported that 'the American IM [immersion] students under evaluation attained functional proficiency in the target language.' Similarly, Snow (1990: 115) concluded that, in general, 'immersion students achieve a level of fluency rarely, if ever, attained in any other type of foreign language program; however, their speech and writing lack the grammatical accuracy and lexical variety of native speakers.' Yet research has demonstrated that the linguistic deficiencies of immersion students 'do not appear to impede their functional use of the language' (Genesee, 1985: 544, citing research from Genesee, 1983; Swain & Lapkin, 1981). Genesee (1987) reported that, with the occasional exception, early total immersion students achieve higher levels of second language proficiency than early partial immersion students do.

The positive results of immersion programs in Canada and other countries, and the handful of US experiments, although convincing, have not lead to large-scale implementation of this program model in California or other parts of the US (Fortune & Jorstad, 1996; Rhodes & Schreibstein, 1983). Apparently, both lack of interest in, and the scarcity of funds for elementary school foreign language education have, until recently, combined to limit the establishment of immersion programs to a few scattered attempts. In the past ten years, educators and especially English-speaking parents have expressed interest in preparing children for a more global future with necessary bilingual and multicultural proficiencies. This interest has lead to the resurgence of the practice of examining the advantages of immersion education in meeting these future needs. Further, because an immersion classroom does not provide students with the opportunity to talk and interact with children who are from the target culture and speak the target language, some parents have become interested in models that would integrate their English-speaking children with real target-language speakers to provide more opportunities for their children to acquire higher levels of proficiency in the target language. Dual language education provides this opportunity for English speakers to learn a second language through immersion, with the added advantage of using the language with, and learning about the culture from, target-language speakers.

Dual Language Education (DLE)

Program description and goals

Dual language education (DLE) programs have a variety of names in addition to dual language. These include: bilingual immersion, two-way bilingual immersion, two-way immersion, two-way bilingual, Spanish immersion (or whatever the target language is, combined with the word immersion), and developmental bilingual education (DBE – because of the name of the funding provided by the US Department of Education for this type of program). One reason some programs focus on the immersion aspect of the name is to affiliate it with enrichment or elitist programs. Another reason for focusing on the immersion aspect is to de-emphasize the 'bilingual' nature of the program because of the political connotations of bilingual education as a compensatory or lower quality education program.

Regardless of the name, DLE programs are similar in structure to immersion programs, but differ from the previously mentioned variations of immersion in terms of one very important factor: student composition. Unlike other forms of immersion, DLE includes native as well as non-native speakers of the target (non-English) language. In dual language programs, English-dominant and target-language-dominant students are purposefully integrated with the goals of developing bilingual skills, academic excellence, and positive cross-cultural and personal competency attitudes for both groups of students. While many immersion programs are elite and do not include language minority students, DLE programs serve a more diverse population.

Two major variants of the DLE model exist. Though they are usually referred to as the 90:10 and 50:50 models, they are parallel to the total immersion and partial immersion programs for language majority students. The principal factor distinguishing these two program variations is the distribution of languages for instruction. As Figures 1.1 and 1.2 show, the amount of time spent in each language varies across the grade levels in the 90:10, but not in the 50:50, design:

- In the *90:10 model* (see Figure 1.1), at kindergarten and first grade, 90% of the instructional day is devoted to content instruction in the target language and 10% to English. All content instruction occurs in the

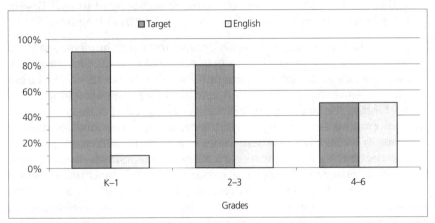

Figure 1.1 Distribution of languages, 90:10 model

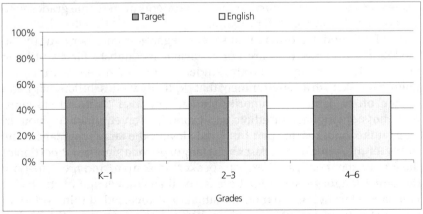

Figure 1.2 Distribution of languages, 50:50 model

target language, and English time is used to develop oral language proficiency. Reading instruction begins in the target language for both the target language-speaking and English-speaking students.

- At the second and third grade levels, students receive 80% of their day in the target language, and 20% in English. Students begin formal English reading in third grade, but they are exposed to English print and English literature as early as first grade.
- By fourth, fifth and sixth grades, the students' instructional time is balanced between English and the target language.
- In the *50:50 model* (see Figure 1.2), the students receive half of their instruction in English and the other half in the target language throughout all the elementary years. Students learn to read first in their primary language and then add on the target language.

Many school administrators must decide whether to implement a 90:10 or 50:50 model, or a proportion in between (80:20, 70:30). One simplistic answer is whether the school community wants more or less of the target language. However, the decision is actually more complex and involves understanding the language and educational background of the community, the expectations for language proficiency, trained personnel, and other community/school needs. These issues will be addressed in Chapter 15.

The content areas taught in each language depend on the available curriculum materials, supporting resource materials, and on particular needs at each school site. However, an attempt is made to assure that students are given opportunities to develop academic language in each of the major curricular areas. The instructional curriculum is based on state and local school district guidelines. Thus, the curriculum that the DLE students receive is equivalent to that for students at the same grades who are not enrolled in the DLE program.

The DLE model is different in several regards from other educational models for students who are not proficient in English. First and most importantly, language minority students are integrated with native English speakers in an environment that explicitly values the language and culture of the language minority student and that treats all students, regardless of language or ethnic background, in an equitable fashion. In DLE, at the kindergarten and first grade levels, the target language is the status (or more important classroom) language for a significant portion of the instructional day, and English speakers look up to and are helped by the target language speakers, because of their knowledge of the target language. During English time, the situation is reversed. It is important to note that both groups of speakers are highly valued, not only the English speakers, as is the norm in most classrooms. Second, the target language is never *replaced* by English, as it is in most transitional bilingual programs in the US. Rather, students are expected to learn to communicate and carry out complex academic learning in both languages. Third, teachers are trained to treat all students equitably and to have high academic expectations for all students. Further, teachers are expected to communicate this equity to students in the classroom so that all students value each other, regardless of their language, ethnic, religious, or social class background.

History of DLE programs

Dual language education programs emerged as a viable model as a result of four programs that began 20–30 years ago. During the mid-1960s, Dade County Public Schools in Miami, Florida, developed two 50:50 Spanish–English DLE programs. Shortly thereafter, in the 1970s, programs were formed in three other school districts (Washington, DC and Chicago, Illinois, developed a 50:50 model and San Diego, California, began a 90:10 model). Unfortunately, there were no *published* reports documenting these programs. However, the San Diego City Schools disseminated a comprehensive handbook in 1982 (ESEA Title VII Bilingual Demonstration Project, 1982), which was very influential in serving as the foundation for the development of other 90:10 DLE projects.

In the early 1980s, many schools had experienced tremendous increases in the number of students who entered school speaking little or no English. Thus, there was interest at the state and national levels in how to best teach language minority students. There was also renewed interest in successful methods of foreign-language instruction. Because of these coinciding agendas and the directive of the United States Department of Education's newly funded Center for Language Education And Research (CLEAR) to examine the DLE model, a consortium was formed of schools that were interested in beginning a DLE program in California, using the 90:10 model developed in San Diego (ESEA Title VII Demonstration Project, 1982). In 1988, I was commissioned to write a manuscript for the California Department of Education on DLE, based in part on the San Diego 90:10 model and Dolson's (1985) theoretical rationale for the DLE model. Because of changes in the political ideology of the administration, this manuscript was never published by the California Department of Education, but it was widely disseminated by the department's Bilingual Education Office and served the important purpose of a guiding principle for the 90:10 model.

Other states, such as New York, Massachusetts and Connecticut, were also becoming interested in the DLE model (e.g. Glenn, 1990; Glenn & LaLyre, 1991). Based on the success of the 50:50 models already in existence in Illinois, Florida and Washington, DC, other school districts began discussing whether and how to implement DLE programs in their schools.

Federal funding for DLE programs prior to 1990 was through the US Department of Education's Title VII program for Transitional Bilingual Education. Through this government-supported program, students had to be transitioned out of their native language and into English as quickly as possible. In the reauthorization of the Bilingual Education Act in 1994, new guidelines specified that up to 25% of instructional monies could be spent on alternative types of programs. At the same time, Mrs Rita Esquivel became director of the Office of Bilingual Education and Minority Languages Affairs (OBEMLA) in Washington, DC. Important for DLE programs, Mrs Esquivel had come from the Santa Monica-Malibu Unified School District in California, where a DLE program was ongoing. Because of the new reauthorization guidelines and Mrs Esquivel's support for DLE programs, there were finally funds for the DLE program model within the Title VII category of Developmental Bilingual Education (or DBE).

However, there was still very little research to document the effectiveness of DLE programs. Research such as Willig's (1985) meticulous analysis of the success of carefully designed and well-implemented bilingual programs was used to document the effectiveness of the maintenance bilingual component for language minority students. Similarly, Canadian and American research on immersion programs (e.g. Campbell, 1984; Genesee, 1987; Swain, 1984) was used to point out how effective the immersion model could be with English speakers. Anecdotal evidence from the existing DLE sites was also used. But, little hard evidence was published or readily accessible. I began to publish on the results of the 90:10 model, but these results were largely based on the first year or two of model implementation (Lindholm, 1992; Lindholm & Fairchild, 1990). There was also little available information on the 50:50 model (Baecher & Coletti, 1986), and no comparisons of the 90:10 and 50:50 models.

What research was available, though, showed that both language minority and language majority students were becoming bilingual and biliterate, achieving at or above grade level in at least their native language, and developing positive cross-cultural attitudes (Cazabon *et al.*, 1993; Christian *et al.*, 1997; Herbert, 1986; Lindholm, 1992, 1994; Lindholm & Fairchild, 1990).

Current state of DLE programs

From the five or so DLE programs in existence two decades ago, I was able to locate 30 DLE programs by 1987 (Lindholm, 1987). In an ongoing survey of DLE programs across the country, Christian and her colleagues (Christian & Mahrer, 1992, 1993; Christian & Montone, 1994; Christian &

Whitcher, 1995; McCargo & Christian, 1998; www.cal.org/db/2way) identified 124 schools with DLE programs in 1992. This increased to 156 school sites in 1993, 176 in 1994, 182 in 1995, 225 in 1998, and 261 in 1999.

These programs exist in 24 of the 50 states, with California having the most DLE school sites (83, or 32%) followed by New York (50, or 19%), Illinois and Texas (each at 22, or 8%), and Arizona and Massachusetts (each at 14, or 5%). Spanish is by far the most popular target language (240 programs, or 92%), followed by six Cantonese programs, four Korean, four French, two each of Navajo and Japanese, and one each of Arabic, Portuguese, and Russian. Almost all of these DLE programs were established at the elementary level, with very few programs established at the secondary level. As the demand for programs at the secondary level has grown, some middle school programs have begun to develop classes in the target language to enable students to continue their bilingual education experience. As of 1999, only 36 such programs were available.

Secondary DLE programs typically include a language arts class and one or two content courses that are offered in the target language. Some of these content courses are classes the student needs for graduation requirements, and others are electives. At some sites, the DLE program has enabled the schools to expand or develop a program for immigrant Spanish-speaking students who are new to the school. These classes, which integrate the DLE students with recently arrived immigrants, can serve to strengthen the need to use the target language and revitalize language development for the DLE students, particularly English speakers.

At most sites, the DLE program exists as one strand within the total school. That is, the school site offers regular English classrooms at each grade level in addition to one or more DLE classes at each grade level. In some of these schools, there are only two options – DLE and English only. At other school sites, there are three program options – DLE, English only, and transitional (early exit) bilingual education, or a structured English immersion. Only a few schools exist as magnet schools – schools that have only the DLE program at their site and are able to draw students from surrounding neighborhood schools.

Table 1.4 provides further information about the variability in DLE programs (www.cal.org/db/2way). As Table 1.4 shows, 50:50 ($n=90$) and 90:10 ($n=95$) programs were equally popular. In Table 1.4, we can also see the variation in DLE program designs. While the two most popular designs are the 90:10 and 50:50 models described previously, different school sites vary somewhat in whether they begin as 90:10 or as 80:20. The major reason for delivering an 80:20 as opposed to a 90:10 model lies in parental and administrative fear that there will not be enough English instruction. Fear

Table 1.4 Dual language education programs in the US: By language, model type, and language of initial reading instruction

Target Language	Number	Type of Model and Language of Initial Literacy			
		90:10 or 80:20 Literacy: T	90:10 or 80:20 Literacy: L1	50:50 Literacy: L1	50:50 Literacy: T & L1
Spanish	164	70	19	56	19
Mandarin/Cantonese	2	1		1	
Korean	4	4			
French	2				2
Navajo	2			2	
Japanese	1			1	
Arabic	2			2	
Portuguese	1	1			
Russian	1			1	
Totals	*179*	*72*	*23*	*63*	*21*

Source: Center for Applied Linguistics website: www.cal.org/db/2way.

Some program descriptions were too vague to determine which was the language of initial literacy. *Initial Literacy* indicates which language children learn to read in *first*. It is assumed that all children will eventually learn to read in both languages. *T Literacy*: all children learn to read in the target language first. *L1 Literacy*: all children learn to read first in their native language – target language speakers learn first in target language; English speakers in English. *T & L1 Literacy*: all children learn to read in both languages simultaneously. Not all programs could be classified.

also promotes the other major design variation – language of initial literacy. While most 90:10 models begin reading instruction in the target language (*n*=70), parents and administrators at some sites have worried that English-speaking students will fall behind in English reading. As a consequence, they use a 90:10 or 80:20 model with initial literacy in the student's L1 (*n*=19). Similarly, two major variations exist in the 50:50 model, with most sites (*n*=56) beginning reading in the students' L1, and other sites (n=19) beginning reading instruction in both languages. Currently, no research exists to determine which is the best approach. Such a comparison would be complicated by the cultural, social class, and linguistic diversity represented in the student populations at different school sites and in the different approaches used for literacy instruction (Christian *et al.*, 1997).

Summary and Conclusions

As these DLE and other language education programs become more popular, it is important that they are established according to the literature on effective language education programs. It is to this literature that we now turn, as we discuss the theoretical and conceptual foundations for language education programs.

This chapter has discussed the various language education programs in the US, and the demographic and political issues affecting these programs. Clearly, the demand for language education programs continues to increase with tremendous surges in immigration, and consequently the number of language minority students in US schools. In addition is the necessity for improving foreign-language proficiency on the part of English-speaking students.

Research has documented the effectiveness of the bilingual education model in promoting English proficiency and academic achievement on the part of language minority student participants. This research stands in contrast to the politically expedient message, voiced by the English Only movement stretching across the US, that bilingual education does not work.

Evaluation studies were also discussed to demonstrate the consistently positive findings of immersion education for language majority students.

Finally, the DLE model was presented as an educational program designed to simultaneously meet the language and academic needs of both language minority and language majority students.

Notes

1. The US Census categorizes the population into different ethnic/racial groups. The five groups include: (1) European Americans, also referred to as white, Caucasian, Anglo or white-non-Hispanic; (2) Hispanics, who are, or whose ancestors are, from any of the Spanish-speaking countries; (3) Asian Americans, whose ancestry traces from any of the Asian countries; (4) African Americans, who trace their ancestry to the African continent; and (5) Native Americans, whose ancestors belonged to one of the original Indian tribal groups in North America.

2. This information is provided for California because national data were not available, California has the largest population of language minority students, and California collects annual data on language minority students.

3. In some school districts, sixth graders are part of the elementary school whereas in other districts, sixth graders enter middle school, which comprises grades 6–7 or 6–8. Thus, some sixth graders may not be in an elementary program, but rather in a middle school program.

Chapter 2

Theoretical and Conceptual Foundations for Dual Language Education Programs

Introduction

Educational innovations must rely on sound educational theory and effective practices in order for program models to be successful in meeting their goals. The dual language education (DLE) model should be constructed on four theoretical and conceptual building blocks so that it can meet the language and academic needs of both language majority and language minority students. This chapter will examine the major theoretical and conceptual issues underlying language education models in general, but particularly the dual language education model. The major theoretical and conceptual issues include:

- Effective schools.
- Social context of language education.
- Language development.
- Relationship between language and thought.

While these issues will be examined with respect to the dual language education model, many concepts readily apply to other models of language education in many countries around the world. Each of these conceptual issues will be discussed separately.

Effective Schools

Over the past several years, an extensive literature has amassed on effective schools (see Levine & Lezotte, 1995 for an excellent review of the literature). Good and Weinstein's (1986) conclusion of the research is still as accurate today as it was over a decade ago:

> A general finding across all the studies that distinguish effective from ineffective schools is the belief on the part of teachers in effective schools that all children can learn and that the school is responsible for that learning .. *schools make a difference* [emphasis added]. Variation in

achievement among schools serving similar populations is often substantial and has significant implications for social policy. (Good & Weinstein, 1986: 1095–96)

Several salient characteristics of effective schools have been identified (Edmonds, 1983; Levine & Lezotte, 1995; Linney & Seidman, 1989; Lucas, Henze & Donato, 1990; Mortimore *et al.*, 1988; Purkey & Smith, 1983; Reynolds, 1985):

- An instructional focus and commitment to achievement that is shared by all.
- An orderly and safe environment conducive to teaching and learning.
- Whole school focus on positive performance, such as recognition for student citizenship, attendance, achievement, and leadership.
- A commitment to identifying and solving problems.
- A high level of faculty cohesion, collaboration and collegiality.
- Faculty input in decision making.
- The use of student achievement as the basis for program evaluation.
- In service training and other staff development, including intra-grade and cross-grade planning.
- Significant parental involvement, including the participation of parents in the classroom, in classroom activities, and in decision-making capacities.
- High expectations and requirements for all students.
- A mastery approach to learning skills, including an environment and faculty commitment with a focus on mastering academic content.

In addition, studies in immersion education have begun to highlight the need for specialized professional development (Day & Shapson, 1996; Lapkin *et al.*, 1990; Met & Lorenz, 1997).

Three other factors are also associated with effective schools (Levine & Lezotte, 1995). These will be described separately, because each requires more discussion than the characteristics listed previously. One factor is a clear understanding of the needs of culturally diverse students and of consolidating multicultural themes into instruction. This factor, while important in other schools, is vital in the dual language program model, with its emphasis on integrating language minority and majority students of different ethnic, language and social class backgrounds. Effective schools have faculty who share the commitment to 'breaking down institutional and community barriers to equality' (Stedman, 1987: 219). They demonstrate awareness of the diverse needs of language minority students, have been trained in multicultural understanding, and use multiethnic materials and curriculum (including the integration of students' cultural values into the classroom), and the target language is celebrated and encouraged. In addition, the shared belief that 'all children can learn' is a central operating principle that empowers language minority students (Garcia, 1988, 1991; Lucas *et al.*, 1990; Tikunoff, 1983).

Another factor associated with effective schools is outstanding leadership. According to Levine & Lezotte (1995: 528), several characteristics comprise particularly successful leadership:

- Assuming a major role in selecting and eliminating teachers.
- Description as 'mavericks who are willing to bend rules and challenge or even disregard pressure or directives from the central office or other external forces perceived as interfering with the effective operation of their schools' (p. 528).
- Frequent classroom visits and vigilance to all activities occurring in the school.
- A high output of energy and time on actions to improve the school.
- Pervasive support and concern for teachers.
- Acquiring necessary resources for teachers and school, including writing grant proposals to obtain additional funding.
- Exceptional instructional leadership.
- Instructional support staff, including resource teachers, to assist them.

The last characteristic of effective schools concerns appropriate instructional and organizational arrangements (Levine & Lezotte, 1995: 531). As with successful leadership, there are a number of components that comprise effective instruction and organization:

- While research on effective schools does not point to any particular grouping approach (i.e. homogeneous, heterogeneous) that is associated with higher student outcomes, 'one of the characteristics of an unusually effective school is the introduction and implementation of workable arrangements for helping low achievers'(p. 531).
- Pacing of instruction that is appropriate for students' level of performance, but is also accelerated for low achievers so that they can catch up to their grade level.
- The environment and instructional approaches facilitate and promote active and enriched learning in a context that includes a variety of interactions that engage with the teacher and with other students.
- Emphasis on higher-order learning and assessment materials that can measure this learning.

- Effective schools coordinate curriculum and instruction so that there is sharing of student information across grade levels, continued development of competencies and the instructional approaches to teach these competencies, and a coordination of support services.
- A wealth of appropriate instructional materials.
- Teachers adapt curriculum materials and instructional strategies for use in their classrooms.
- An emphasis on 'ensuring that students work meaningfully and diligently in mastering the content of instruction' (p. 535).

Lucas *et al.* (1990) would add that school counselors are available to language minority students. Many of these features are consistent with the results of other researchers who have examined the features of effective instruction for language minority students (Cloud *et al.*, 2000; Garcia, 1988, 1991; Lucas *et al.*, 1990; Tikunoff, 1983; Wong-Fillmore, 1985).

Research on bilingual and immersion education has also demonstrated that effective bilingual programs are integrated within the total school program, that strong support for the program is given from the school district administrators and local Board of Education, and that the principal is very supportive of and knowledgeable about the program (Cortés, 1986; Met & Lorenz, 1997; Troike, 1986).

One problem that frequently inhibits the operation of bilingual programs is that the school administration treats the program as peripheral to the central curriculum and organization of the school. The reason for this is a perceived temporariness about federally funded programs, which are expected to expire upon the cessation of government support. Troike (1986) also points out that school officials have applied for grants to supplement the regular school program, without any interest or commitment to the program for the linguistic minority students. Money, then, as opposed to concern for students, may motivate a school to institute such a program. In other cases, bilingual programs are viewed as a convenient way to help achieve school desegregation.

According to Troike (1986), successful bilingual programs are more likely to be housed centrally, and to be closely integrated structurally and functionally within the total school system. In addition, they receive strong support from the central administration and from building principals. In schools with successful programs, the administration does not regard bilingual education as remedial or as merely a temporary program, but rather makes a commitment to providing an equal education for linguistic minority students, even beyond any external funding, and ensures that the program is an integral part of the basic program in the school system. The administration also devotes attention and resources to promoting acceptance of the program among the community and other school staff by informing them of its methods and results. In addition, the administration supports acceptance of the bilingual program staff as part of the regular staff by insisting on comparable standards of certification and competence and by facilitating interaction among them. Finally, there is a serious effort to obtain high-quality materials in the non-English language for the students. Resources are allocated for the purchase and development of appropriate materials for linguistic minority students.

Implications for language education models

In sum, this literature base suggests that successful language education programs require: effective and supportive administrative leadership, a positive school climate that promotes achievement and positive performance for *all* students, well-trained teachers with high expectations for achievement of all students, faculty cohesion and program planning, and an appropriate well-paced and challenging instructional emphasis that comprises higher-order skills and assures that low achievers master academic skills. In addition, the program must experience actual integration within the total school. In addition, the program must be viewed as a long-term *enrichment* program, comparable to specialized math or technology programs, as opposed to a temporary compensatory program, as is typical of most bilingual programs. The program also requires an equitable share of resources. High quality educational materials in both languages and appropriate staff training are also essential for an enrichment program to develop high levels of student competence in *two* languages.

While many of these effective school issues are important in all educational programs, they are critical in dual language education programs (and bilingual programs) because of the compensatory label that most US bilingual programs possess, as well as the increased attention many programs receive because of the added goal of promoting the target language and academic competence among the English speakers. This added goal puts increased pressure on teachers and program directors to demonstrate as quickly as possible that the students are achieving academically at high levels. The pressure results from the political necessity to assure the community and school administrators that the program is truly an *enrichment* program of benefit to both groups of participants, that is, language minority and, particularly, language majority students.

Social Context of Language Education

The social context of education programs refers to the structure of the educational experience as it is shaped by attitudes and policies that are held regarding the education program and its participants. This social context can positively or negatively influence a program's outcomes (August & Hakuta, 1997; Cortés, 1986; Cummins, 2000; Genesee & Gándara, 1999; for excellent reviews of the literature, see Darling-Hammond, 1995; Knapp & Woolverton, 1995; Levine & Lezotte, 1995; Ogbu, 1995). Several bodies of research converge to indicate that students' educational experiences are influenced by their social class (Knapp & Woolverton, 1995), minority status (Darling-Hammond, 1995; Ogbu, 1995), and migrant status (Olneck, 1995). These factors are all important when we are talking about the populations in dual language education in the US, as well as in many countries with diverse populations such as Turks in Germany, Finnish in Sweden, Catalans and Basques in Spain, and Japanese in Australia.

Educational inequality

One way in which students have differential access to knowledge is through the structure of inequality in US education (Darling-Hammond, 1995).[1] 'From the time southern states made it illegal to teach an enslaved person to read, throughout the 19th century and into the 20th, African Americans faced *de facto* and *de jure* exclusion from public schools throughout the nation, as did Native Americans and, frequently, Mexican Americans' (Tyack, 1974: 110). Educational experiences for these minority students continue to be substantially unequal (Darling-Hammond, 1995; Ogbu, 1995), despite a number of lawsuits at the local, state, and national levels. For example, the percentage of minority students in predominantly minority schools [63% in 1986](Darling-Hammond, 1995) and the percentage of black and Hispanic [33% and 71%, respectively, in 1986] (Orfield *et al.*, 1989, cited in Schofield, 1991: 336) students in segregated schools has remained essentially the same over the past ten years. Furthermore, African American and Hispanic students are largely concentrated in central city public schools, with high enrollments (at least 50%) of minority students. As Percell (1993) points out, these students are also likely to go to school with others who share their common social class identity. The schools these students attend also vary considerably from suburban middle class schools:

> These schools are typically funded at levels substantially below those of neighboring suburban districts. The continuing segregation of neighborhoods and communities intersects with funding formulas

and school administration practices that create substantial differences in the educational resources made available in different communities ... Schools with high concentrations of 'minority' students receive fewer resources than other schools within these districts ...Together, these conditions produce ongoing inequalities in educational opportunity by race and ethnicity. (Darling-Hammond, 1995: 466)

Thus, many minority students attend schools with much poorer physical facilities, science laboratories, technological and library resources, and fewer and lower-quality books and instructional materials (Darling-Hammond, 1995; Knapp & Woolverton, 1995; Kozol, 1991). According to the US Census Bureau (1999), 24% of African American and Hispanic students have access to computers at home, while almost two thirds (62%) of white students use computers at home. The lack of resources would not be so perplexing if it were found across town in suburban schools as well. However, as many researchers have shown (e.g. Darling-Hammond, 1995; Knapp & Woolverton, 1995; Kozol, 1991), not only are the resources deficient in poorer schools with high concentrations of minority and poor students, but students are very aware of the large gap between what they have and what their richer peers have a few miles away:

You can understand things better when you go among the wealthy. You look around at their school, although it's impolite to do that, and you take a deep breath at the sight of all those beautiful surroundings. Then you come back home and see that these are things you do not have. You think of the difference. Not at first. It takes a while to settle in. (Kozol, 1991: 104, cited in Darling-Hammond, 1995).

In addition, the quality of instruction varies for minority and poor versus European American and middle class students. As Kaufman and Rosenbaum (1992) showed, minority and low-income students who were able to attend largely white and better-funded schools had access to more challenging courses, had additional academic help, graduated on time, and attended college. According to Darling-Hammond (1995):

Minority and low-income students in urban settings are most likely to find themselves in classrooms staffed by inadequately prepared, inexperienced, and ill-qualified teachers because funding inequalities, distributions of local power, and labor market conditions conspire to produce teacher shortages of which they bear the brunt ... All this means that districts with the greatest concentrations of poor children, minority children, and children of immigrants are also those in which incoming teachers are least likely to have learned about up-to-date teaching methods or about how children grow, learn, and develop – and what to do if they are having difficulties .. many children in central city schools are taught by a parade of short-term substitute teachers, inexperienced teachers without support, and underqualified teachers who know neither their subject matter nor effective teaching methods. (pp. 470–71)

Language education theorists and practitioners have also discussed the social context of language learning in terms of the additive/subtractive bilingualism dichotomy. Additive bilingualism is a form of enrichment in which 'children can add one or more foreign languages to their accumulating skills and profit immensely from the experience – cognitively, socially, educationally, and even economically' (Lambert, 1984: 19). Additive bilingualism is associated with high levels of proficiency in the two languages, adequate self-esteem, and positive cross-cultural attitudes (Lambert, 1984, 1987). As we saw in chapter one, these enrichment or additive programs are typically reserved for language majority students in the US.

In stark contrast, subtractive bilingualism refers to the situation in which children are 'forced to put aside or subtract out their ethnic languages for a more necessary, useful, and prestigious national language' (Lambert, 1984: 19). Subtractive bilingualism is associated with lower levels of second-language attainment, scholastic underachievement, and psychosocial disorders (Lambert, 1984). The reasoning behind these negative consequences is tied to the relationship between language and thought. When children are pressured to learn English as quickly as possible and to set aside their home language, they lose the critical linguistic foundation upon which their early conceptual development is based. These subtractive programs form the basis for the education of language minority students in the US.

As Linney and Seidman (1989) pointed out in their review of the literature on school and teacher effects on student outcomes, the quality of a child's school experience is important not only for academic and achievement outcomes, but also for fostering self-esteem, self confidence, and general psychological well-being. These positive outcomes are highly related to the attitudes held by administrators and other school staff, teachers, and peers, as suggested in the previous section on effective schools.

Administrative, staff and peer attitudes

There are many ways in which the attitudes of administrators and staff can influence the success of an educational program. At the administrative level, decisions reflecting resource allocation, space availability, placement of teachers and support staff, and professional development will all influence the extent to which a school will function optimally. Research on bilingual education programs in the US has clearly shown that favorable attitudes toward bilingualism and language minority students by the community, administration, and staff result in local language education policies that are more likely to produce high-quality programs and to facilitate language and academic achievement among program participants (Willig, 1985).

In contrast, when the community and administrative attitudes toward bilingualism and language minority students are negative, then it is unlikely that language education programs will be implemented unless there are laws requiring their implementation. If language education programs are developed only because they are required, they may receive fewer resources, untrained and inexperienced teachers, and the expectation for success may be minimal. This configuration of factors will tend to result in lower levels of academic achievement and language proficiency on the part of program participants (Willig, 1985).

Language minority children, while often subjected to subtractive bilingualism contexts, often experience different interactions with their teachers than do language majority students. Their teachers may also have different attitudes toward them. Research in non-bilingual classrooms shows that teachers tend to have lower expectations for success, praise less often but criticize more frequently, provide fewer opportunities for minority students to respond in class, and give them less time to respond (Brophy & Good, 1986; Olneck, 1995). Further, language minority children have additional barriers to overcome with accented English speech (Olneck, 1995). Language minority students are also more likely than language majority students to be placed in lower school tracks or assigned to special education classes (Olneck, 1995; Orum, 1986).

Research shows that expectations for European American students are higher than they are for ethnic-minority (except Chinese, Korean and Japanese) students, and higher for middle-class students than for lower-class students (Darling-Hammond, 1995; Knapp & Woolverton, 1995). When studies include comparisons of European American with minority students of both social classes, different results emerge. In research where teachers are given verbal or written *descriptions* of students, they do not base their assessments on minority status, only socioeconomic status. In contrast, when teachers are given *pictures* of students or have the opportunity to listen to them speak, then they base their assessments largely on minority group status. Social class and ethnic minority status thus appear to have different effects on teachers, where lower-class ethnic minority students have the lowest expectations and middle-class white students the highest expectations (Dusek, 1985).

Differential treatment by teachers leads to differential academic outcomes on the part of students (Banks & Banks, 1995; Brophy, 1986; Brophy & Good, 1986). Students who are labeled as bright or high achievers are praised more frequently, and given more opportunities and more time to respond to the teacher in class. Given extra praise and attention, these students are able to maintain their perceived high achievement status. In contrast, students who are labeled as low achievers are given fewer opportunities to respond, less time to answer when they are called upon, and receive more criticism and less praise.

Peer attitudes are also important to consider, as they can influence the social dynamics of the classroom so that the low-status peers are given fewer opportunities to:

> Participate meaningfully in group activities, while high-status peers tend to participate more, be listened to, and be allowed to take authority roles. Lack of low-status student participation in group activities not only reduces learning opportunities for these students, but reduces social opportunities as well by eliminating chances for them to demonstrate skills and abilities ...High-status peers are given the benefit of the doubt when not behaving as expected, while low-status student behavior tends to be negatively valued regardless of its actual content. (Knapp & Woolverton, 1995: 560)

Allowing only unplanned or incidental contact between majority and minority students may also reinforce negative expectations on the part of classmates. In his highly influential work on peer relations and school desegregation, Allport (1954) proposed four factors that are the core conditions for improving intergroup relations, and maximizing the achievement of minority and majority students. When minority and majority students have *equal status* in the classroom, *work interdependently* on tasks with common objectives, and have *opportunities to interact with each other as individuals*, student expectations and attitudes toward each other become more positive. Allport also pointed out that the effect of these contacts would be greatly enhanced if the contacts are *supported by teachers* and other authority figures.

Other researchers have provided evidence to support Allport's basic premises in demonstrating that instructional treatments which explicitly promote positive interdependence between minority and majority students result in positive outcomes in terms of an increased number of cross-racial friendships and greater self-esteem and academic achievement (Cazabon *et al.*, 1993; Lambert, 1984, 1987; Lindholm, 1994). It is particularly during the early school years that children are malleable in their cross-cultural attitudes. Children educated in immersion programs from early elementary school develop more positive cross-cultural attitudes than their non-immersion-program peers (Lambert, 1987).

Cooperative learning methods, which were developed based on Allport's four factors, use heterogeneous grouping and shared group leadership with activities that require the students to work interdependently, with clear individual and group accountability for the achievement of all group members (Cohen, 1994; Johnson & Johnson, 1989; Johnson *et al.*1986; Kagan, 1986; Qin, *et al.*, 1995; Slavin, 1995). Research demonstrates unequivocal support for the positive effects of cooperative learning on achievement, ethnic relations, and self esteem outcomes (Kagan, 1986; Stevens & Slavin, 1995; Slavin, 1995; see Qin *et al.*, 1995 for a meta-analytic review of the literature). When students work in ethnically mixed cooperative learning groups, they gain in cross-ethnic friendships.

Most research also shows positive effects of cooperative learning on achievement (Cohen & Lotan, 1995). Strong achievement gains have been found with minority and typically low-achieving students, with little or no effect for white (non-Hispanic) and higher-achieving students. However, the gains of minority and low-achieving students are not made at the expense of majority or high-achieving students, as these students also made gains at least as great as, if not greater than, in traditional classrooms. Thus, cooperative learning methods, which must be based on social equity in the group and classroom for these positive effects to occur (Cohen & Lotan, 1995), close the achievement gap between minority and majority students, and have positive effects on the self esteem and cross-cultural attitudes of both minority and majority children.

Implications for language education models

This review of literature on the social context of education yields important implications for promoting successful outcomes for communities that have some learners who do not possess the same social or linguistic status as others. While the literature and context have been largely US-based, it is well-known that in many other countries, immigrant, language minority or poor students do not function as effectively as they ought to, nor as successfully as their majority peers (Skutnabb-Kangas & Cummins, 1988; Lee, 1991; Ogbu, 1995). From this body of literature, it should be apparent that language learners should be provided a positive school context in which to develop bilingualism, biliteracy, and academic competence. Further, both language minority and majority students should have access to an additive bilingualism environment in which both languages and cultures are equally valued, and all students are treated equally. Finally, students should be integrated in a natural fashion to promote positive cross-cultural attitudes and psychosocial development, and higher levels of second-language development and academic achievement.

Language Development

Language development has been studied extensively for an understanding of how children acquire their first language, or first two languages for bilingual children, and how children and adults develop a second or even a third language.

Most language acquisition researchers agree that the capacity for native-like proficiency diminishes with age. Anecdotal evidence indicates that adults have considerable difficulty in learning a second language and, in fact, although they may be more effective language learners, often never achieve native-like pronunciation and sociolinguistic competence. Adults' greater propensity for language learning may result from more efficiently developed language-learning strategies (Genesee, 1987; Snow & Hoefnagle-Hohle, 1978) and/or positive transfer from a fully developed first-language system (Náñez et al., 1992). Further, long-term research shows that individuals who begin second-language learning early are more likely than those who begin later to achieve native-like levels of proficiency in their second language, particularly if given exposure to the language in extracurricular settings (Genesee, 1987).

Research in the process of language development has demonstrated that this process is systematic and rule-governed, and involves the learner's active cognitive attempts to formulate linguistic rules that underlie competence in the language. Considerable research has been conducted on language input in both first and second language acquisition to determine whether or how input influences language development (e.g. Gass & Madden, 1985). In first-language learning, input has been studied by examining the type of speech mothers, and occasionally fathers or other caretakers, use with children – usually dubbed 'motherese' in the literature. This literature has identified some distinct characteristics of speech addressed to young children, such as: slow rate of speech; simplified grammar, vocabulary and concepts; repetitious; oriented to the here and now; and containing few corrections, with the corrections that do occur being based on the truth value, or content, of the sentence rather than on the grammar (Lindholm, 1981). Second language researchers have also found similar input features in speech addressed to second language learners;

this special language is often termed 'foreigner talk' (e.g. Long, 1981). Research shows that, regardless of the input a child receives, the process of language development follows systematic patterns.

A final note on language input for child bilinguals concerns language mixing versus language separation. Most research on child bilingualism supports the notion that keeping two languages as distinct as possible is the better strategy for promoting high levels of bilingualism in children (e.g. Genesee, 1987; Hakuta, 1986; Padilla & Lindholm, 1984). Strategies in which the languages are distinguished by individuals (e.g. mother speaks Spanish, father speaks English), environment (e.g. German in the home, English in the day care), or time (e.g. Japanese in the morning, English in the afternoon) help children to distinguish the two languages and provide consistent rules for which language is to be used in particular settings or with particular individuals (Padilla & Lindholm, 1984).

Implications for language education models

Dual language education, like immersion education, is grounded in language acquisition research in several respects. First, it is based on the premise that considerable language learning can occur naturally during non-language arts classes, such as mathematics or social studies, and this is similar to first language acquisition in which children communicate with each other about issues that are not related to language (Genesee, 1984). Second, learners can progress according to their own rate and style, again in much the same way that first-language learners do (Genesee, 1987). Third, based on research regarding language learning and age, it has been argued that early immersion in a second language can facilitate a child's second language learning by taking advantage of his/her special neurolinguistic, psycholinguistic, and cognitive capacities to learn language (Genesee, 1984; Lambert, 1984). Fourth, language input to the students is adjusted to their conceptual and linguistic level, using many features of 'motherese' to facilitate language comprehension and acquisition on the part of the students. Fifth, concentrated exposure to language is important to promote language development. Finally, the two languages are kept distinct and never mixed during instruction in the early years of language acquisition.

Relationship Between Language and Thought

Many early studies that examined the cognitive functioning of bilinguals concluded that exposure of young children to two languages often had deleterious effects on their intellectual development, as measured by standard tests of intelligence (Baker, 1996; Hakuta, 1986). Careful examination of these early reports, however, led to questions concerning the validity of this conclusion. Almost without exception, the monolingual control groups in these studies who gave significantly higher performances on standardized intelligence tests were speakers of a socio-linguistically dominant language – dominant in the sense that it enjoyed greater prestige and greater communicative utility in the larger society from which the groups were selected. Moreover, in the majority of these studies, the bilinguals, regardless of their proficiency in the dominant language, suffered from socioeconomic and environmental factors specific to their lower status in the community. Because of these and other short-comings having to do with the tests themselves, many of these studies have been dismissed for their lack of valid scientific inquiry (Baker, 1996; Hakuta, 1986).

In a classic study by Peal and Lambert (1962), one of the better controlled studies comprising monolingual and bilingual adolescents on a series of intellectual tasks, the authors observed that proficiency in two languages gave French-English bilinguals an advantage. Intellectually, their experiences with two languages resulted in mental flexibility, superiority in concept formation, and a more diversified set of mental abilities. In contrast, the monolinguals appeared to Peal and Lambert to have more unitary cognitive structures, which restricted their verbal problem-solving ability. While the sample was limited to middle class and balanced bilingual children, a number of other studies have been conducted with a variety of bilingual children that substantiates Peal and Lambert's results, although not all research is totally supportive of this position (August & Hakuta, 1997; Baker, 1996; Bialystok, 1999; Cloud *et al.*, 2000; Hakuta, 1986; Homel *et al.*, 1987). The important point is that there is evidence to suggest that bilingual development may facilitate cognitive functioning. As Bialystok and Hakuta (1994) have noted:

> The result of this is that the mind of a bilingual speaker has a different structure than the mind of a monolingual. While it may involve a value judgment to describe it as richer, or more complex, it seems evident that the mind of a speaker who has in some way attached two sets of linguistic details to a conceptual representation, whether in a unified or discretely arranged system, has entertained possibilities and alternatives that the monolingual speaker has had no need to entertain. (p. 122)

The extent to which cognitive development may be influenced by language proficiency has been discussed by Cummins (1979, 1987) and Toukomaa and Skutnabb-Kangas (1977). They speculate that there may be threshold levels of linguistic proficiency a child must attain to avoid cognitive disadvantages and to allow the potentially beneficial aspects of becoming bilingual to influence cognitive growth. This hypothesis assumes that a child must attain a certain minimum or threshold level of proficiency in both languages to enable bilingualism to exert a significant long-term effect and positively influence cognitive growth. However, if bilingual children sustain only a very low level of proficiency in L2 or L1, the range of potential interaction with the environment through that language is likely to be limited and there will not be any positive effect on cognitive development.

Cummins and Toukomaa and Skutnabb-Kangas in fact, argue that there are two thresholds. Attainment of the lower threshold level of bilingual proficiency would be sufficient to guard against negative consequences of bilingualism. However, for long-term cognitive benefits to be manifested requires achieving the second threshold of a higher level of bilingual proficiency.

Thus, the differential effects of bilingualism on cognitive development that have been reported in the literature have been explained by understanding the child's level of bilingual proficiency. In research showing negative effects on cognition, the threshold hypothesis would explain the negative effects by proposing that the bilingual children's proficiency in one or both languages was low enough to impede the interaction that occurred through that language in the school environment. Thus, these children did not develop the school language to a sufficiently high level to benefit fully from their schooling. Conversely, children who attained the upper threshold of bilingual proficiency, or high levels of skills in both L1 and L2, demonstrated rapid academic and cognitive development. The threshold hypothesis predicts neither positive nor negative consequences on cognition of children who attain full native proficiency in their first language, but develop only intermediate levels of proficiency in the weaker language.

The type of language proficiency is also important to examine because it influences our understanding of cognitive and academic functioning across languages. Cummins (1987), among others, has conceptualized language proficiency along two continua, as shown in Figure 2.1. The first continuum represents the range of contextual support available for expressing or receiving meaning. At one extreme of this continuum is context-embedded language, and at the other is context-reduced communication. These two ends of the continuum are distinguished by the amount of shared and real-world knowledge regarding the communication. In context-embedded communication, knowledge is shared among the speakers, and the language is supported by a range of paralinguistic and situational cues. In context-reduced communication, knowledge may not be shared among the speakers, and thus there is a need for more precise and elaborated language and a dependence on the linguistic cues solely to interpret the communication. Examples of communicative behaviors going from left to right along the continuum might be talking with a friend, writing a letter to a close friend, reading (or writing) an article on theories of analogical reasoning. Context-embedded communication is more typical of everyday conversation, whereas many of the linguistic demands of the classroom reflect communication that is closer to the context-reduced end of the continuum.

This dichotomy in language skills has also been referred to as basic interpersonal communicative skills (BICS) versus cognitive/academic language proficiency (CALP) (Cummins, 1980, 1984). This distinction is important because it relates to the length of time required to become proficient in a second language. Collier (1989) and Cummins (1981) have proposed that students can acquire the BICS in about two years, whereas it takes about 5–7 years to develop CALP-type proficiencies.

The second continuum addresses the developmental components of communicative proficiency with respect to the level of active cognitive involvement in the task or activity. Cognitive involvement is defined as the amount of information that must be processed simultaneously or in close succession by the individual in order to carry out the activity (Cummins, 1987).

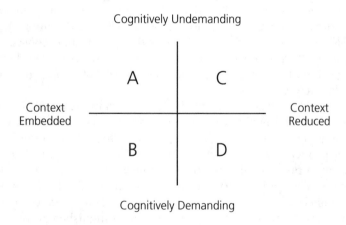

Figure 2.1 Two continua of language proficiency

Source: Cummins (1987).

The level of skill mastery underlies this continuum, where new skills are cognitively demanding, but move up to become cognitively undemanding as they are mastered and become processed automatically. For example, the acquisition of L1 sounds and syntax is cognitively demanding for a two-year old, but cognitively undemanding for a normal twelve-year old. Thus, whenever new linguistic skills must be used to communicate, active cognitive involvement occurs. As mastery occurs, specific linguistic skills travel from the bottom to the top of the vertical continuum. Cognitive involvement can be just as intense in context-embedded as in context-reduced activities.

Two important points can be made about this model (California State Department of Education, 1982). First, all human beings acquire the language proficiency, in at least one language, necessary to complete context-embedded, cognitively undemanding tasks (e.g. everyday conversation). Second, among monolinguals, the ability to complete cognitively demanding tasks in context-reduced situations (e.g. reading proficiency, math proficiency) differs significantly among individuals. The ability to complete context-reduced tasks is highly related to the amount of formal schooling. The capability to access information in any of these areas depends on how it is stored in memory.

There are two *major* views of how bilinguals store and retrieve language, although a number of different interpretations have been offered (e.g. Bialystok & Hakuta, 1994; Genesee, 1989). One view is that bilinguals develop the skills in each language independently, and store them separately in the brain. According to this model, termed Separate Underlying Proficiency, efforts to develop proficiency in one language do not facilitate development in another language and may, in fact, impede second language development because of limited storage space in the brain. The opposing view, labeled Common Underlying Proficiency, proposes that there is a common storage space and that the development of skills and knowledge in one language is not independent of the acquisition of information in a second language. Rather, developing knowledge and proficiency skills in one language facilitates learning in the second language (Cummins, 1987). Thus, acquiring the cognitively demanding tasks in context-reduced environments, typical of many school-related activities, in one language paves the way for the bilingual to perform similar tasks in the other language.

Considerable research supports the Common Underlying Proficiency viewpoint. Studies of academic skills in a bilingual's two languages typically show high relationships, with correlations in the 0.60–0.80 range (Cummins, 1979; Lindholm, 1990b; Lindholm & Aclan, 1991). Thus, a bilingual who performs well in math in one language is highly likely to perform well in math in a second language (Lindholm & Aclan, 1991; Lindholm & Fairchild, 1989), even after only one or two years of schooling in the second language, once the student has the language proficiency skills for demonstrating that knowledge (Lindholm, 1990b).

Content and literacy instruction in bilingual and immersion education programs have always assumed this interdependency across languages. According to the interdependency hypothesis, reading instruction in one language would result in literacy skills in the second language, in addition to a more advanced linguistic and conceptual proficiency. Furthermore, surface characteristics, such as oral fluency or the writing system (orthography), would develop separately, whereas cognitive/academic proficiency would be common across languages. Thus, while one would have to learn the particular sound/symbol relationships in reading in a second language, one would not have to learn strategies for how to make meaning from text. As a consequence, this common underlying proficiency enables the transfer of cognitive/academic, literacy-related skills across languages. Odlin (1989: 27) has defined transfer as 'the influence resulting from similarities and differences between the target language and any other language that has been previously (and perhaps imperfectly) acquired.'

Little empirical research has actually investigated whether and to what extent skills and knowledge transfer across languages. The positive correlations noted above clearly show relationships among content knowledge in two languages, and this is true in content areas as well as skills such as literacy (Cummins, 1991; Genesee, 1979; Lambert & Tucker, 1972; Ramirez, Yuen & Ramey, 1991; Verhoeven, 1994). While there are a number of criticisms of the common underlying proficiency hypothesis (see Verhoeven, 1994), there is clearly evidence that at least some skills and knowledge are mapped on to some type of representational system or systems that facilitate development across languages (Bialystok, 1999; Bialystok & Hakuta, 1994).

The questions of what literacy skills transfer across languages and what proficiencies are necessary for students developing literacy skills in a *second* language are important. Educators in the US have long assumed that oral language proficiency in English presupposed the ability of language minority students to develop literacy skills in English. To the chagrin of mainstream US educators, many language minority students have not transferred their English oral proficiency into English literacy proficiency skills. Consistent research has shown that oral proficiency in the L2 societal language of language minority students does not necessarily result in literacy proficiency in that language. What we have learned is that L2 literacy is better predicted by strong L2 oral proficiency *combined* with strong L1 literacy skills (Lindholm, 1994; Royer & Carlo, 1991; Verhoeven, 1994). However, it is not yet clear how the various literacy skills are represented in the brain, the extent to which particular skills transfer readily across the two or more languages of instruction, and what knowledge, language, or subject characteristics presuppose more ready transfer of literacy skills across languages (August & Hakuta, 1997; Bialystok & Hakuta, 1994; Odlin, 1989).

Implications for language education models

Three critical educational implications emerge for language education models from these theoretical and conceptual points. First, bilingual development may facilitate cognitive functioning if the dual language development is sustained over a long period of time so that the child attains a high level of proficiency in the two languages. Second, high levels of language proficiency require the development of both communicative and academic language skills in both languages. Third, some skills and knowledge learned in one language are accessible in another language as soon as the student possesses sufficient language proficiency to exhibit the knowledge.

Summary

In this chapter, the theoretical, conceptual, and empirical literatures have been reviewed to provide a rich and comprehensive conceptual foundation for language education models. Considerable research demonstrates the importance of several salient features for effective language education models, regardless of whether these models are for bilingual, heritage language, traditional foreign language, partial or full immersion, or dual language education programs.

Research on effective bilingual, immersion and non-language-education programs has provided consistent results that demonstrate the significance of outstanding leadership, including strong support for the educational program, faculty cohesion and support, and program planning and articulation. Further, in programs involving culturally diverse students, effective programs assure that all students' needs are met, that instruction integrates the cultures of the classroom and community, and that teachers are trained to treat students equitably.

While educators in various countries may subscribe to different philosophies of education, differ somewhat in their instructional methodologies, and have varying curricula, they nonetheless share the necessity of designing appropriate models to meet the language and academic needs of their students. Even in countries where language education programs are encouraged, and students share a middle class and majority status (e.g. European Schools model in several Western European countries; Canadian French immersion programs for English speakers; Basque and Catalan immersion programs in Spain) successful programs still require appropriate instructional designs based on sound theory and empirical evidence.

More critically, when we are dealing with diverse student populations or language minority students, many of the educational equity and effective school issues in language education programs require consideration – whether we are talking about the various racial/ethnic or linguistic minority students in the US, indigenous languages such as Quechua or Mayan in Central and South America, Aboriginal children in Australia, Sami children in Norway, guest worker children in European countries, Native Indian children in North America, or language minority groups in India.

In the next chapter, I will examine the design and implementation characteristics that emerge from these theoretical, conceptual and empirical literature bases, as well as from our experiential knowledge base in bilingual and immersion education.

Notes

1. Research in other countries clearly indicates that unequal educational opportunity exists in many countries other than the US (e.g. Lee, 1991; Ogbu, 1995).

Chapter 3

Critical Features of Successful Language Education Programs: Design and Implementation Issues

Several reviews have been conducted of research and evaluation studies concerning bilingual or heritage language and immersion education in many countries around the world (Artigal, 1995, 1997; August & Hakuta, 1997; Baetens Beardsmore, 1993, 1995; Baker, 1996; Baker & Jones, 1998; Buss & Lauren, 1995; Byram & Leman, 1990; Crawford, 1999; Cummins, 1979, 1983; Day & Shapson, 1996; De Courcy, 1997; Diaz, 1983; Dolson, 1985; Duff, 1997; Fisher & Guthrie, 1983; Fruhauf *et al.*, 1996; Garcia, 1988; García & Baker, 1995; Jaspaert & Kroon, 1991; Johnson & Swain, 1997; Lucas *et al.*, 1990; Moran & Hakuta, 1995; Skutnabb-Kangas, 1995; Skutnabb-Kangas & Cummins, 1988; Swain & Lapkin, 1982; Tikunoff *et al.*, 1980; Troike, 1986; Willig, 1985). An examination of these educational investigations points to certain pedagogical factors that tend to contribute to successful language education programs. The importance of these factors is evident from the frequency and consistency with which they are found in programs that promote positive outcomes. In addition, many of these critical features follow from the theoretical issues and empirical research discussed in Chapter 2. These factors form the core criteria for successful language education, particularly dual language education programs. This chapter will present these critical program and design features of the dual language education program.

Effective Leadership

In Chapter 2, we saw that successful schools typically have effective leaders. While there are a number of characteristics of particularly successful leaders, we can categorize these characteristics into two particularly salient features for dual language education and other language education models: (1) administrative and principal support; and (2) instructional leadership.

Administrative and principal support

Administrative support is important to schools in any community across the world (Johnson & Swain, 1997). For dual language and other language education programs, research has shown that administrative support includes strong support for the program by the school district and the local Board of Education. This support is demonstrated in the structural and functional integration of the program within the total school system. The program is not viewed as temporary, even if there is only temporary funding from an outside source (business or government). Resources are allocated to the program for staff training and for purchase and development of materials in each language.

Principal support is also critical for any successful education program. Within a particular school, a supportive principal assures that the language education program is integrated within the total school, that all teachers and staff understand the language education program, and that an appropriate and equitable amount of financial and instructional resources is allocated to the program (Cortés, 1986; Troike, 1986). In addition, the principal understands the language education model, truly supports its implementation at the school site, and understands the program well enough to explain it to others. Finally, the principal shows support and concern for the teachers. For a discussion on the importance of administrative and principal support in language education programs, see August and Hakuta (1997), Cloud *et al.* (2000) and Met and Lorenz (1997).

Instructional leadership

Instructional leadership for the language education program may or may not be provided by the principal. While the principal must be the main advocate for the program, s/he may be too busy with the needs of the whole school to provide the necessary instructional leadership for the language education program. Thus, this leadership may come from a vice principal, program coordinator or resource teacher. There are various titles for this support person, particularly from an international perspective, but the responsibilities are quite similar. This individual has extensive knowledge of the language education model being implemented at the site, second language development, bilingual and immersion education theory and research, instructional methodologies, effective classroom practices, and the belief that the selected language education model can work once it is implemented correctly.

At least three major tasks are required of this leader:

- program spokesperson;

- oversee model development, planning and coordination;
- staff training.

First, an effective leader serves the critical role of spokesperson for the program with the local school administration, local Board of Education, the parents, and the community. Second, an effective leader is in charge of development, planning and implementation of the model at the school site. This role necessitates a clear understanding of the theory underlying the model in order to make appropriate instructional decisions when implementation questions arise. In high quality programs, there is a high degree of faculty cohesion, collaboration, and collegiality (Cortés, 1986; Levine & Lezotte, 1995; Linney & Seidman, 1989; Troike, 1986). This means that, in schools with a dual language education (or immersion or bilingual) strand and an English-only 'mainstream' strand, teachers are integrated for school-wide planning and coordination. In addition, the non-dual-language education teachers are supportive of and knowledgeable about the dual language education program. Also, in the dual language education program at some school sites, teachers do not work together as a team, but rather plan and teach in isolation. In other school sites, teachers at the same grade level plan together and team for instruction.

The amount of planning within and across grade levels varies by school site, but a higher level of coordination across grades is almost always associated with more successful programs (Levine & Lezotte, 1995; Met & Lorenz, 1997). Once the instructional model is developed and implemented, it is important that the leader continues in the capacity of model development, with planning both within and across grade levels. An element in planning involves the ability to acquire the necessary financial and instructional resources for the program.

Third, effective leadership provides strong support for the teachers, oversees a program of staff training, and assures teacher involvement in program planning. This leader does not simply send teachers off to various unrelated in-service training courses, but tries to focus training on the topics most necessary for the program. In addition, the effective leader visits the classroom and provides feedback to teachers on the extent to which the instructional strategies are appropriately implemented in the classroom.

School Environment

The school environment is the atmosphere and ethos to which the student is exposed in the classroom and school. Chapter 2 pinpoints some characteristics that are particularly salient for the dual language education model, with its two distinct student populations. However, these characteristics are also important for other language education programs that include students who do not belong to the majority ethnic, language, or social group in their school.

A positive school environment

Research on effective schools, successful minority students and the social context of education (Darling-Hammond, 1995; Ford & Harris, 1996; Galindo & Escamilla, 1995; Gándara, 1995; Knapp & Woolverton, 1995; Levine & Lezotte, 1995; Olneck, 1995) has shown that successful schools have: (1) an orderly, safe, and warm environment that facilitates learning; (2) an instructional focus and commitment to achievement that is shared by all; (3) high expectations for all students; (4) students who feel pride in their school; and (5) students (including minority students) who participate in extra-curricular activities.

Additive bilingual environment

All students are given the opportunity to acquire a second language at no cost to their home language and culture (Cloud *et al.*, 2000; Cummins, 2000). This enrichment bilingualism results in high levels of proficiency in the two languages (Hernandez-Chavez, 1984; Skutnabb-Kangas, 1981), adequate self-esteem, and improved cross-cultural attitudes (Lindholm, 1994). Conversely, subtractive bilingual contexts in which the native language is replaced by a second language seem to have negative effects on the school performance of many minority language students. Native language loss is often associated with lower levels of second language attainment, scholastic underachievement, and psychosocial disorders (Lambert, 1984). Successful language development programs seem not only to prevent the negative consequences of subtractive bilingualism, but also to effectively promote the beneficial aspects of additive bilingualism.

Positive and reciprocal instructional climate

Promotion of positive interactions between teachers and students and between language minority and majority student peers is an important instructional objective (Levine & Lezotte, 1995). When teachers use positive social and instructional interactions in equal amounts with minority and majority students, both groups perform better academically (California State Department of Education, 1982; Kerman *et al.*, 1980). In addition, research suggests that a reciprocal interaction model of teaching is more beneficial to students than the traditional transmission model of teaching (Cummins, 1986, 2000). The basic premise of the transmission model is that the teacher's task is to impart knowledge or skills to students who do not yet have these abilities. In the reciprocal interaction approach, teachers participate in genuine dialogue with pupils and facilitate rather than control student learning. This model encourages the development of higher-level cognitive skills rather than just factual recall (Cummins, 1986), and is associated with more effective schools (Levine & Lezotte, 1995).

The achievement of language minority pupils is affected not only by the status perceptions of teachers, but also by the status perceptions of majority peers. Allowing only unplanned or incidental contact between majority and minority students may only reinforce negative expectations. Under the rubric of cooperative learning, a number of strategies have been developed that appear to optimize student interactions and shared work experiences (e.g. Cohen, 1994). Studies suggest that, when minority and majority students work interdependently on school tasks with common objectives, students' expectations and attitudes toward each other become more positive and their academic achievement improves (Cohen, 1994; Johnson & Johnson, 1990; Johnson *et al.*, 1986; Kagan, 1986; Qin *et al.*, 1995; Slavin, 1995). Also, language development is facilitated by extensive interactions among native and non-native speakers (Long & Porter, 1985).

It is important to point out that many years of research on cooperative learning show that, for cooperative learning to produce positive outcomes, the grouping must be based on particular operating principles. Many schools and teachers purport to use cooperating learning, but the grouping does not follow the necessary preconditions for successful cooperative learning. Perhaps this is why the literature on effective schools does not point to any specific grouping arrangement that is particularly effective (Levine & Lezotte, 1995). However, research on effective schools does show that, in successful schools, there is an emphasis on helping low achievers, not by slowing down instruction, but rather by accelerating instruction. Considerable empirical evidence and meta-analysis studies demonstrate the success of cooperative learning in promoting positive student outcomes. However, researchers also caution that successful grouping requires:

- that students work interdependently;
- clearly conceived individual and group accountability for all group members:
- social equity in the group and in the classroom (Cohen & Lotan, 1995; Johnson & Johnson, 1990; Johnson *et al.*, 1986; Kagan, 1986; Qin *et al.*, 1995; Slavin, 1995).

Cross-cultural components

Effective schools have staff who are committed to equality; who provide instruction in an equitable manner to students from different ethnic, social and language backgrounds; who have been trained in multicultural understanding and educational equity; and who use multiethnic materials (Levine & Lezotte, 1995; Lindholm & Molina, 2000). In these classrooms, every student is expected to participate in a variety of roles in the classroom or group, to serve in leadership roles, and students are socialized to treat each other with respect and equity. Thus, these teachers care about students with different learning needs, create an environment that includes books and instructional materials that represent ethnic and religious diversity, and take time to understand alternative points of view.

Teachers and Staff

Teachers in language education programs, as in mainstream classrooms, must possess the typical knowledge of content, curriculum, instructional strategies and classroom management skills. However, effective language education programs require additional teaching and staff characteristics (Cloud *et al.*, 2000; Day & Shapson, 1996; Johnson, 1997; Lapkin *et al.*, 1990; Met & Lorenz, 1997).

High quality instructional personnel

Teachers in language education programs have appropriate teaching certificates or credentials, have good content knowledge and classroom management skills, and training with respect to the language education model and appropriate instructional strategies (Cloud *et al.*, 2000; Met & Lorenz, 1997). Teachers in dual language education programs also need a native or native-like ability in either or both of the languages in which they are instructing. Native or native-like proficiency is critical. Research on language use in classrooms demonstrates two important points that severely influence dual language instruction. One point is that research in US classrooms shows that children do not receive cognitively stimulating instruction, as we saw in Chapter 2. To provide cognitively stimulating instruction, teachers need a high level of language proficiency. Second, how can teachers promote a high level of bilingual proficiency if they themselves do not possess high levels of proficiency as a part of their instructional interactions?

Teachers, although bilingual, may assume monolingual roles when interacting with students. In reality, because of the shortage of bilingual teachers, some English model (providing English instruction only) teachers are English monolinguals. It is important that these teachers be able to at least *understand* the child's mother tongue in the initial stages of language learning. If the teacher does not understand the native language, then s/he cannot respond appropriately in the second language to the children's utterances in their native language. In this case, comprehensible input, as well as linguistic equity in the classroom, may be severely impaired (Swain, 1985).

Many classrooms have an instructional assistant for part of the time, though the amount of time, and whether there is any assistance, varies by school site and even by grade level. In some classrooms, there is an instructional assistant all day and in other classrooms there may be a four- or six-hour a day assistant who is shared among two or three classrooms. To be maximally effective in the classroom, these instructional assistants require training.

Staff training

To be an effective teacher requires training. Researchers in immersion education have discussed the importance of specialized training in immersion pedagogy and curriculum, as well as materials and resources (Cloud *et al.*, 2000; Day & Shapson, 1996; Met & Lorenz, 1997). In the dual language education program, there must be pre-service and in-service training in:

- the dual language education model, including bilingual and immersion research and theory;
- second language development;
- instructional strategies in second language development;
- multicultural and educational equity training;
- cooperative learning.

Without this training, teachers will have difficulty implementing the model correctly in their classrooms. Chapter 15 includes more information on teacher training.

The educational equity component may be the most difficult to provide training in because teachers in the US (as in most countries) are socialized to believe that cute kids and middle class kids know more, that boys are better at math and girls are better at reading, that Asians work hard and Hispanics and African Americans are not as motivated. The stereotypes and expectations that guide our behaviors are the most difficult to retrain. Yet, it is important to train teachers about the dangers of stereotyping if there is to be educational equity observed in the classroom. Children as young as first grade are able to distinguish between the 'smart' and the 'dumb' kids in the classroom by noting how the teacher behaves with various children (Weinstein *et al.*, 1987).

Instructional Design and Features

The design and instructional features of the program are what most people think about when they are designing a language education program. There is considerable literature on bilingual and immersion instructional approaches, significant features and theory to guide us in model development, in addition to the theory and empirical research conducted in more mainstream classrooms.

Duration of instructional treatment

The instructional treatment is provided to the participating students for a period of *at least* four to six years. This is the average amount of time required to reach the second level of Cummins's threshold, or academic proficiency, but not to reach native-like proficiency, as confirmed by a number of evaluation studies on immersion and bilingual programs (Collier, 1989; Cummins, 1981; Swain, 1984; Troike, 1978). In its review of foreign language programs, the National Commission on Excellence in Education (1983) has concluded that achieving academic proficiency ordinarily demands from four to six years of study. Collier (1989) reported that achieving academic proficiency may necessitate six or seven years of study.

Exposure to optimal dual language input

Optimal *input* has four characteristics:

- It is adjusted to the comprehension level of the learner.
- It is interesting and relevant.
- There is sufficient quantity.
- It is challenging.

To accomplish this objective involves careful planning in the integration of language instruction and subject matter presentation. In the early stages of second language acquisition, input is made more comprehensible through the use of slower, more expanded, simplified, and repetitive speech oriented to the 'here and now' (Krashen, 1981; Long, 1980); highly contextualized language and gestures (Long, 1980; Saville-Troike, 1987); comprehension and confirmation checks (Long, 1980); and communication is structured so that it provides scaffolding for the negotiation of meaning by L2 students by constraining possible interpretations of sequence, role, and intent (Saville-Troike, 1987). Balanced with the need to make the second language more comprehensible is the necessity for providing stimulating language input (Kowal & Swain, 1997; Swain, 1987), particularly for the native speakers of each language.

There are two reasons why students need stimulating language input. First, it will facilitate continued development of language structures and skills. Second, when students are instructed in their first language, the content of their lessons becomes more comprehensible when they are then presented with similar content in the second language.

Language output: Promotion and opportunities

As noted earlier, immersion students, and foreign language students in general, have difficulty in producing native-like speech in the second language. Part of this difficulty stems from an absence of the opportunity to talk with fluent speakers in the language they are learning. According to classroom research, immersion students get few opportunities to produce extended discourse, where they are forced to make their language coherent, accurate, and sociolinguistically appropriate (Baker, S., 1996; Lindholm & Baker, 1997; Swain, 1985, 1987). This is true even in dual language programs in which teachers do not require students to use the language of instruction during group work. Thus, promoting highly proficient oral language skills necessitates providing both structured tasks and unstructured opportunities involving oral production skills in which students can engage. It also necessitates establishing and enforcing a strong language policy in the classroom that encourages students to use the instructional language and discourages students from speaking the non-instructional language.

Focus on academic curriculum

The instructional curriculum is based on state and local school district guidelines. Thus, the curriculum that the two-way bilingual immersion students receive is equivalent to that for students at the same grades not enrolled in the two-way bilingual immersion program. Schedules are carefully structured for teaching all required academic subjects using methods not only appropriate for specific grade levels, but also suitable for enabling both English-speaking and target language students to acquire language skills and vocabulary both in English and in the target language.

Integrated language arts instruction

Related to the previous two features is the need to provide language arts instruction in *both* the English and the non-English language and to design the instruction so that it is integrated with the academic curriculum. Considerable controversy exists about the importance of explicit second language instruction (e.g. Krashen, 1981; Long, 1983; Swain, 1987). Because many immersion programs were grounded in the natural approach, which eschews language arts instruction in the immersion language, two important but incorrect assumptions were made. The first assumption was that students would simply learn the language through the subject matter instruction, and the second was that students would achieve more native-like proficiency if they received the kind of language exposure that is similar to first language learning (see Swain, 1987).

As some immersion researchers have discovered (e.g. Harley, 1984, 1996; Swain, 1985; Swain & Lapkin, 1986), the fluency and grammar ability of most immersion students is not native like, and there is a need for formal instruction in the second language. However, formalized language instruction should not follow the route of traditional translation and memorization of grammar and phrases. It is important to utilize a language arts curriculum that specifies which linguistic structures should be mastered (e.g. conditional verb forms) and how these linguistic structures should be incorporated into the academic content (e.g. including preterit and imperfect forms of verbs in history subject matter and conditional, future, and subjunctive tenses of verbs in mathematics and science content).

Separation of languages for instruction

Monolingual lesson delivery (i.e. different periods of time devoted to instruction in and through each of the two languages respectively) seems to be superior to designs that rely on language mixing during a single lesson or time frame (Dulay & Burt, 1978; Legaretta, 1979, 1981; Swain, 1983). This is not to say that language mixing itself is harmful; clearly, the sociolinguistic skill of language mixing or code switching is important in bilingual communities. Rather, it appears that sustained periods of monolingual instruction in each language help to promote adequate language development. Because teachers need to refrain from language switching, they must have high levels of proficiency in the language for the content about which they are instructing. Teachers, instructional assistants and others who help in the classroom need to be told that they should not translate for children in the classroom. Some children in partial immersion programs have developed the strategy of looking confused when they have to respond in the second language. This is because some well-meaning adult who translates for the 'poor child' has reinforced the strategy. Initially, these children have no need to learn the second language, and fall behind their classmates.

Ratio of English to the target language

Immersion education was designed to promote high levels of second language proficiency while maintaining first language proficiency.

Although there are several program variations, many immersion programs utilize the target language for 100% of the instructional day, and English is not used at all for at least the initial stages of the program. Other partial immersion programs involve equal amounts of English and the target language. No research has yet determined the best ratio of English to the target instruction for both language minority and majority students. However, research on programs that utilize different amounts of instruction in the non-English language shows that students with greater exposure to the second language have higher levels of second language proficiency (Campbell *et al.*, 1985; Genesee, 1987), and that these students also maintain their English and perform at or above grade level in tests of English achievement (Campbell, 1984; Genesee, 1985). Furthermore, research in bilingual education shows that students with greater amounts of native language instruction achieve at higher levels than students with lesser amounts of native language instruction, at least in the early years of schooling (Ramirez, Ruen & Ramey, 1991; Willig, 1985).

From studies of bilingual students and immersion students, then, it appears that a minimum of 50% target language instruction is necessary to promote high levels of proficiency in the non-English language among language majority students, and to promote academic achievement among language minority students. Furthermore, although studies have not addressed the minimal level of English necessary, a minimum of 10% English instruction initially is important to promote English language development for the non-native speakers of English. Also, to develop a high level of academic English language skills among the language minority students, by the late elementary school years (grades 4–6), the amount of content instruction in English should be about 50%.

Meeting distinct needs during language arts instruction

There is considerable variation in how the English time is used in 90:10 dual language education programs. Unfortunately, not enough attention has been paid to English time in many school sites where English time has been used for assemblies, physical education, or other activities that do not provide a good basis for the development of cognitive academic language proficiency in English. It is important that teachers understand what language skills they need to cultivate at each grade level so that they develop the cognitive/academic English language skills necessary for literacy, particularly for language minority students who do not receive literacy training in the home. This is one example that requires the cross-grade coordination planning described previously in the section on Effective leadership.

Heterogeneous or homogeneous *grouping* also becomes a major consideration in dual language programs, with language minority and language majority students at very different levels of English language proficiency. The argument in favor of heterogeneous grouping is that it is consistent with the remainder of the day, wherein students receive all of their instruction in heterogeneous groups, including language arts in the target language. The counter-argument, in favor of homogeneous grouping by language background, is that each group's needs can be better met, particularly by providing second language learning activities and approaches for the target-language speakers (that is, those students who enter the program not speaking English). There is no research suggesting that one grouping strategy is more effective than another. However, successful 90:10 programs combine the two strategies. For portions of the week, target language speakers receive English as a Second Language (ESL) instruction and the English speakers work on further English language development. For other parts of the week, the students are kept together and given English oral input through content such as music, literature, or drama.

Literacy instruction in two languages

The major questions related to literacy instruction in dual language programs are:

- Should children be taught literacy in their native language first, and then have the second language added later?
- Can children be taught literacy simultaneously in two languages, or will they be confused?

These questions have not received much empirical attention, as we saw in Chapter 2. However, there is considerable evaluation research and experience to draw on in discussing this issue (see Cloud *et al.*, 2000, for a discussion of these issues).

Research demonstrates that the less socially prestigious and powerful language in a society is the one most subject to language loss. To promote the prestige of the target language and counteract the dominant status of the societal language, the target language must receive more focus in the early stages of an immersion program. Furthermore, for 90:10 dual language education programs in which students are receiving almost all of their instruction through the target language, it is important that literacy should begin in that language. This recommendation is based on two bodies of research. One is the bilingual education literature, which shows that students who receive considerable native language literacy instruction eventually score much higher on literacy tests in English – and in their native language – than do students who have been given literacy instruction largely or entirely in English (Ramirez *et al.*, 1991; Willig, 1985).

For language minority students, there is another important consideration. Some language minority students will do exceptionally well in English because their parents can provide the literacy-related experiences in the home that are needed to promote literacy. For language minority students without this literacy assistance, research suggests that they should receive literacy instruction in their native language first (Cloud *et al.*, 2000; Escamilla, 2000; Goldenberg, 2000).

Another large body of literature from Canada and the US that focuses on the language majority students shows that teaching literacy through the second language does not place language majority students at risk in their development of the two languages. Usually by third or fourth grade, they score at least as well as native English speakers in standardized tests of reading achievement (Baker, 1996; Genesee, 1987; Lambert *et al.*, 1993). These results even hold true for low-income and middle-income African American students in French immersion programs (Holobow *et al.*, 1991). Thus, the literature on bilingual and immersion education programs clearly supports early literacy instruction through the target language (Cloud *et al.*, 2000).

There is another very important reason for pushing literacy in the target language from the beginning. What we see in dual language education programs is that students will read for pleasure in the target language in first and second grade. However, once they are able to read in English, they read for pleasure largely in English. One reason is that English is the societal and prestigious language. The other reason is that there is considerably more literature to choose from in English, at least in the libraries and bookstores in these children's communities. The lack of available literature in the target language is more pronounced as the children move into the higher grades (grades 5–12). If children do not begin reading in the target language until second or third grade, after they have begun reading in English, they may never choose to read for pleasure in the target language, which will clearly impede any efforts to develop *high* levels of literacy in the target language.

Unfortunately, there are no comparative studies of dual language education programs that are 50:50 and teach literacy in both languages versus 90:10 programs that provide reading instruction in the target language for all students. The only study available (Christian *et al.*, 1997) described three different programs and their variant approaches to literacy instruction. However, because at one site there was no literacy assessment in Spanish, at another no literacy testing in English, and two schools did not provide test scores separately for language minority and language majority students, it is not clear whether particular approaches to literacy result in better outcomes than others for specific populations of students. Christian *et al.* (1997: 116) concluded that:

> These variations in program models reflect both differences in community needs as well as the distinctive populations served by the schools. At School 1: [50:50 model with simultaneous literacy instruction], the model has historically served a gifted population of English speakers and has screened out students who do not meet certain levels of language and conceptual development. As a result, their approach to literacy instruction in both languages is very appropriate in this context. Also, their high levels of achievement in English attest to a strong English language base and perhaps a more select student population. In contrast, at School 2: [80:20 model with L1 literacy instruction first for all students], there is a much larger population of free/reduced price lunch students (60%) of various ethnic groups (including a larger percentage of African American students). Their strategy for beginning literacy instruction in the primary language is suitable in this context. School 3: [90:10 model with initial literacy instruction in target language] students are a combination of largely middle class English speaking European-American and Latino students and Spanish speakers, most of whom are free/reduced price lunch participants and began with program with few, if any, skills in English. Thus, this context may be quite appropriate to support initial literacy instruction in Spanish. Understanding the population to be served is certainly an important prerequisite for a site in determining which model may be most effective at a particular school site.

Students

Last, but not least, is discussion of the features related to the students that will be served by the language education program.

Classroom composition

Little research has been conducted to determine the best classroom composition for bilingual education programs. To maintain an environment of educational and linguistic equity in the classroom and to promote interactions among native and non-native English speakers, the most desirable ratio is 50% English speakers to 50% target language speakers. To insure that there are enough language models of each language to promote interactions among the two groups of students, there should be no more than two speakers of one language to one speaker of the other language (a:b ratio).

In many school sites, segregated communities surrounding the school make it virtually impossible to include equal numbers of target-speaking and English-speaking students. Typically in the first or second year of model implementation, schools may have more difficulty recruiting a balanced population. After one or two years, though, most schools are able to balance their populations without too much difficulty. The populations represented in the dual language education model are heterogeneous by school site. Often the English-speaking and target language populations are not comparable in important ways that will be briefly described below.

Target language speakers

In programs in which the target languages include Korean, Chinese, or Portuguese, there is also diversity with respect to immigration status and socioeconomic status. However, language minority students in these language groups are more likely to be middle class and to come from homes with educated parents.

As a group, Spanish-speaking children can be characterized as largely immigrant and with parents who are working class, with typically 5–6 years of formal education (see Chapter 7). It is important to note that there is variation within this group, though. On the one hand, some Spanish-speaking students are US born or have parents who are highly educated and middle class. On the other hand, many Spanish-speaking students live in run-down inner cities or in rural areas in broken-down trailer homes without electricity or indoor plumbing. Some of these students' parents are very involved in their children's education and understand how to promote achievement in their children; yet other parents are not involved for various reasons or have no formal education to enable them to help their children with their schoolwork.

English speakers

The English-speaking population is also diverse in social class and parental education as well as in ethnic composition. In some schools, most of the English speakers are middle class and European American. In other schools, the majority of English speakers are African American students living in the poor and run-down sections of the city. In still other schools, the English-speaking population is diverse, including middle class and working class European Americans, African Americans, Hispanics, and Asian Americans.

Many educators have questioned whether African American students should participate in dual language education programs. While there is little research on the literacy and achievement of African American children in immersion programs, there is some research to indicate that these children are not negatively affected and may, in fact, realize positive outcomes in their achievement and attitudes (Holobow *et al.*, 1991; Lindholm, 1994).

Social class and language group confound

In many schools, a large social class and language group confound exists whereby the English speakers come from middle class and educated families and the target language speakers come from working class and undereducated (by US standards) families. These differences must be acknowledged to assure students equal educational opportunity in the classroom by both their teacher and their fellow students. These differences must also be recognized in the interpretations of the evaluation results.

Students with special learning needs

Consistent with immersion education (Genesee, 1987), students with special education needs or learning disabilities are typically accepted in the program (Cloud *et al.*, 2000). The only caveat is the scenario in which students have a serious speech delay in their native language; in these cases, the decision for admittance is carefully conducted on an individual basis. Further, students are typically not moved from the DLE program because of special education or learning disability needs.

Home/school collaboration

Another important feature of DLE is parental involvement and collaboration with the school. When parents are involved, they often develop a sense of efficacy that communicates itself to children, with positive academic consequences, especially in the case of language minority children (Cloud *et al.*, 2000; Met & Lorenz, 1997; Tizard *et al.*, 1982). In fact, most parents of minority students have high aspirations for their children, and want to be involved in promoting their academic success (Julian *et al.*, 1994; Lindholm & Cava, 1997; Stevenson *et al.*, 1990; Wong-Fillmore, 1985).

Dramatic changes occur in children's academic progress when parents interact with their children at home in certain ways. Activities such as reading and listening to children read are both feasible and practical, and contribute to improved scholastic achievement (Cloud *et al.*, 2000; Cummins, 1986; Bus *et al.*, 1995; Goldenberg, 2000). Effective programs tend to incorporate a variety of home/school collaboration activities. The general outcome on the part of students is an increased interest in schoolwork, and improved achievement and behavior. (There is more information on parental involvement in Chapter 7.)

Summary

In summary, based on the literature review presented in Chapter 2, a variety of programmatic, instructional, administrative, staff, and student characteristics are associated with more effective language education programs. These factors serve as a framework for effective language education programs, regardless of the type of program or its location. Not all features will be appropriate for all programs, particularly for language education programs that serve more homogeneous student populations. It is also important to point out that not all dual language programs have, or are even aware of, all these characteristics.

Part 2

Classroom, Administrative and Familial Contexts in Dual Language Education

Chapter 4

The Dual Language Education School Characteristics and Data Collection

This chapter describes the school characteristics from which the data in subsequent chapters are drawn, and a gives a brief explanation for the various data collection approaches used. These schools will be portrayed with respect to the school demographic and program factors that may influence program outcomes.

The schools are located in California, except for one in Alaska. One characteristic used to distinguish the communities was program type. There were two DLE models: the 90:10 and the 50:50 models, as described in Chapter 1. In addition, comparative data from four Transitional Bilingual Education (TBE) programs is presented in subsequent chapters and so the school sites housing the TBE model are also described. Another way in which the programs are delineated is with respect to the school demographic characteristics of ethnic density and socioeconomic status need (SES need). These two factors were shown in Chapter 2 to be important in influencing the quality of education, including teacher attitudes and the availability of educational resources and experienced teachers.

Demographic Characteristics of Schools and Programs

Schools were grouped into *HIGH* ethnic density (greater than 66% minority student representation in the *school*) and *LOW* ethnic density (fewer than 66% minority students). Then SES need (socioeconomic status need) defined as eligible, by government standards, for participating in the free lunch program at school)[1] was determined by calculating the percentage of English bilingual (EB, or students who began the program as monolingual English speaking) students who were eligible to participate in the free lunch programs at each school site. The reason that EB students were chosen is because at most sites a great majority of the SB (Spanish bilingual, or students who entered the program as Spanish speaking) students were participating in the free lunch program. Based upon this information, the fourteen 90:10 school sites were divided into two SES need

Table 4.1 Percentage of schools designated by SES need and ethnic density

SES need	Ethnic density	
	Low	High
Low	29%	7%
High	7%	57%

groups: *low SES need* (fewer than 20% of EB) and *high SES need* (more than 20% of EB) based on eligibility for the free lunch program. This distinction was made only for the 90:10 programs, as there were insufficient 50:50 programs to distinguish them on this basis.

Table 4.1 presents the percentage of 90:10 schools in the possible four quadrants of SES need by ethnic density. Four schools (29%) were *LOLO* (low in SES need and low in ethnic density), one school (7%) was *LOHI* (low in SES need, but high in ethnic density), another one (7%) was *HILO* (high in SES need, but low in ethnic density), and the remaining eight (57%) were *HIHI* (high in SES need and high in ethnic density). Because there was only one school in the HILO and LOHI categories, these two schools were reclassified into either LOLO or HIHI on the basis of SES need.

SES need might be more influential than ethnic density, because SES is highly affected by parental education and could thus influence the type of extra financial and educational resources the parents could provide the school and their children.

Table 4.2 provides the demographic characteristics of the 18 *school sites*, including the community type (urban, suburban, rural), student population in school, percentage of school population that is ethnic-minority, percentage of students classified as Limited English Proficient (LEP), and the percentage participating in the free lunch program. Table 4.3 presents ethnic and SES need data for the DLE and TBE *program participants*, which may vary from school-wide information for programs that operate as only one strand at a school site.

90:10 LOLO (90LO) school sites

Five school sites were designated as 90LO (90:10 LOLO). Table 4.2 shows that the three school sites classified as urban (located in large cities) and the one rural site (located in the country) were more similar to one another in the percentages of minority students (33–73%), LEP students (35–55%), students on the free lunch program (33–62%), and EB students on free

Table 4.2 Demographic characteristics of the school sites

Program type / School no.	Community type	Students in school	Minority %	Limited English %	Free lunch %
90:10 LOLO					
#1	Urban	390	73	54	62
#2	Urban	432	51	35	33
#3	Urban	715	62	43	58
#4	Suburban	658	19	12	12
#5	Rural	377	33	55	45
90:10 HIHI					
#6	Urban	707	91	47	87
#7	Urban	629	72	38	50
#8	Urban	362	74	48	55
#9	Urban	534	100	63	99
#10	Suburban	650	67	54	80
#11	Suburban	380	51	27	n/a
#12	Suburban	890	69	44	52
#13	Suburban	772	89	44	83
#14	Rural	598	67	49	77
50:50					
#15	Suburban	385	67	45	60
#16	Rural	584	38	25	35
TBE					
#10	Suburban	650	67	54	80
#14	Rural	598	67	49	85
#17	Suburban	514	87	46	85
#18	Suburban	632	98	58	100

Table 4.3 Demographic characteristics of student participants (percentages)

Program type / School no.	Euro Am.	Hispanic			African Am.	Asian Am. / Native Am.	Free lunch	
		EB	SB	Total			SB	EB
90:10 LOLO								
#1	27	2	64	66	5	1	80	15
#2	26	4	62	64	1	4	23	12
#3	32	19	47	66	3	0	76	9
#4	49	11	38	49	1	1	52	4
#5	38	8	54	62	0	0	85	18
90:10 HIHI								
#6	10	8	75	83	5	1	93	42
#7	10	19	63	82	7	2	95	22
#8	27	25	45	70	1	2	77	32
#9	1	5	64	69	30	0	96	96
#10	26	3	71	74	0	0	100	37
#11	13	10	73	83	2	1	87	30
#12	15	21	57	78	4	3	85	54
#13	7	24	62	86	5	2	70	35
#14	31	6	62	68	0	1	85	22
50:50								
#15	40	4	42	46	9	6	64	29
#16	39	9	52	61	0	0	89	16
TBE								
#10	0	0	100	100	0	0	100	n/a
#14	0	0	100	100	0	0	85	n/a
#17	0	0	100	100	0	0	100	n/a
#18	0	0	100	100	0	0	100	n/a

lunch (9–18%: see Table 4.3) than was the suburban site (located in a residential area outside a major city), which was much lower in these demographic characteristics. At each of the 90LO school sites, socioeconomic disparity was quite large, with 4–18% of English bilingual students on free lunch as compared with 52–85% of Spanish bilinguals (23% Portuguese bilinguals at School #2) on free lunch.

At four of the school sites, as Table 4.3 shows, two thirds of the program participants were Hispanic (see 'Total' column) and most of these were Spanish bilinguals ('Hispanic, SB' column)[2]. Relatively few African American, Asian American or Native American students were participants. Thus, these programs consisted largely of Hispanic Spanish bilinguals and European-American English bilinguals.

90:10 HIHI (90HI) school sites

As Table 4.2 depicts, nine school sites had populations consistent with a 90HI program. Of these sites, four were urban, four were suburban, and one was rural. Table 4.2 delineates the high ethnic density of these schools, with 67–100% of each school (except for school #11) comprising ethnic minority students. According to Table 4.3, while the percentage of Hispanic students in the *DLE program* was high (68–86%), in about one half of these programs (schools #7, 8, 12, 13), 20–25% of the Hispanics were English speakers, while in half of the programs (schools #6, 9, 10, 11, 14), about 3–10% were Hispanic English speakers. African Americans were included in very small percentages (0–7%) except at school #9 (30%). Few Asian American or Native American students (0–3%) were involved in these DLE programs. School #9 was distinct because all but one of the students there were ethnic minority and almost all of the SB and EB students (96% of each) were taking part in the free lunch program. Otherwise, Table 4.3 shows that between 22% and 54% of EB and 70–100% of SB students were participating in the free lunch program.

50:50 (5050) school sites

Two 50:50 programs were represented, one suburban and one rural. At these sites, the percentage of ethnic minority students varied at the school site (67% versus 38%: Table 4.2), but ethnic minority representation in program participants was similar (60–61%). Table 4.3 indicates that at school #16 all of the minority student participants were Hispanic, though 52% were Spanish bilingual and 9% were English bilingual. In contrast, school #15 program participants comprised 42% SB Hispanic students, 4% Hispanic EB students, 9% African American, and 6% Asian/Native American students. While there were twice as many EB student participants at school #15 compared to school #16 on free lunch (29% vs. 16%), school #16 had many more SB students on free lunch than school #15 (89% vs.64%).

Transitional Bilingual Education (TBE) school sites

Four Transitional Bilingual Education (TBE) programs were included, with two of the programs (#10 and #14) as strands along with the 90HI DLE programs already described. Three of the TBE programs were located in suburban areas, and one was in a rural community. As Table 4.2 shows, the percentage of ethnic minority students varied (from 67–98%), though all schools had a high percentage (80–100%) of students on free lunch. In these TBE programs, all participants were Hispanic SB, and all the students at three sites and most (85%) of the students at the fourth site were participating in the free lunch program.

Special needs students

While details of the extent of students with special education needs or learning disabilities are not available for each school, every program accepted such students. Further, students were not removed from the program because of special education or learning disability needs. Thus, none of the schools described here screened applicants for admission to the DLE or TBE program. The only exception to this policy of admitting all students was where students had a speech delay in their native language. In addition, a few EB children reacted negatively to the program. Most of these cases actually reflected home problems that caused the children to act out at school. Because the only difference between the DLE and regular classroom was Spanish, learning in Spanish became the culprit for these families. Some parents who removed their children from the DLE program, thinking that the problem resulted from the program itself, regretted the decision within a year when the child had the same problem in English instruction.

In sum, these 18 programs represent the diversity of students participating in DLE and TBE programs in US schools. Further, they comprise a complex array of student backgrounds with respect to ethnicity, language, and socioeconomic status.

Program Design Characteristics

Table 4.4 provides descriptive information about the program characteristics of the DLE programs, including a brief history of development, how languages are distinguished across the grade levels, how the languages are separated during instruction, the program configuration at the school site, and literacy instruction in the two languages.

History

As Table 4.4 indicates, the 90:10 LOLO (90LO) programs had different histories of implementation. School #1 was in jeopardy of closing because its enrollment was almost entirely ethnic minority. The district investigated various alternatives to attract European American students to the school site for desegregation purposes. After several months of discussion and research, the district, principal and teachers decided on a 90:10 DLE program. District personnel were also instrumental in the creation of schools #3 and #4. At school #4, the lone Hispanic bilingual administrator convinced the district and school to begin a DLE program. With no history of bilingual education in this district, it was difficult to garner the support. Despite three moves to different school sites, the program was able to grow and thrive. School #3 also had a strong advocate in the administration, which, along with a supportive principal and teachers, developed the program. Finally, school #2 has had a DLE program for Portuguese speakers that developed from a TBE program. It is small and has recently had difficulty attracting enough Portuguese speakers because the Portuguese community has slowly moved out of the area. The program in school #5 began through the consistent efforts of three bilingual teachers who convinced the community, principal and skeptical administration to implement the program. This program grew from one kindergarten class in its first year to three kindergarten classes, two first grade, and one second grade (for a total of six classes) in just two years. For each of these 90LO programs, community support has been consistently high.

Like the 90LO programs, the histories of the 90HI programs varied somewhat across the sites. At four school sites (#6, 9, 11, 12), the program was developed at the district level in the bilingual education office, and then placed into the schools, sometimes with little support from the principal or teachers. The major reason these programs were accepted by the school was because of the significant government funding that initially came with the program. Only one of these programs (school #6) currently has a strong DLE program and one program (school #11) no longer exists. Three 90HI programs were collaboratively developed by the principal and teachers, and two were cooperatively developed by the district and the teachers. These five collaboratively developed programs had a much easier start-up than the four programs developed solely at the district level.

Both 50:50 programs were developed at the district level. Importantly, in the development of these programs, there was input and support at the school site level.

Table 4.4 Program design characteristics of the DLE school sites

Prog. type / School no.	His- tory	Program configuration	Language distribution	How languages are separated	Literacy instruction
90:10 LOLO					
#1	T	Strand»Magnet	1b	Teacher/Time	SE (3)
#2	D/T	Strand/EO	2b	Teacher/Time	Port»E (3)
#3	D	Strand/EO	1c	Teacher/Time	S»E (4)
#4	D	Strand/EO	1a	Teacher/Time	S»E (3)
#5	T	Strand»Magnet	1c	Teacher/Time	S»E (3)
90:10 HIHI					
#6	D	Strand/EO	2a	Teacher/Time	S»E (4)
#7	D/T	Strand/EO	2b	Teacher/Time	S»E (4)
#8	P/T	Strand»Magnet	1a	Teacher/Time	S»E (3)
#9	D	Strand/EO	2a	Teacher/Time	S»E (4)
#10	P/T	Strand/TBE/EO	1a	Teacher/Time	S
#11	D	Strand/EO	1c	Teacher/Time	S
#12	D	Strand/EO	1c	Teacher/Time	S
#13	D/T	Strand/EO	1a	Teacher/Time	S»E (3)
#14	P/T	Strand/TBE/EO	1a	Teacher/Time	S
50:50					
#15	D	Strand/EO	3	Time	S + E
#16	D	Strand/EO	3	Alternate week	L1»L2

History: D=District/Admin., P=Principal, T=Teacher, D/T=District and Teacher(s).

Program configuration: Strand=program within a school; magnet=DLE program is the only one at the school site. Strand/EO=the other program at the site is a monolingual English Only program; Strand/TBE/EO=site that houses DLE, TBE and EO programs. Strand»Magnet=program began as a strand, but is currently a magnet.

Language distribution: See Table 4.5 for further information on language distribution.

How languages separated: Teacher/Time=Teacher for grades K–2 and by time of day for grades 3–6.

Literacy instruction: S»E (3) refers to a program that begins literacy instruction in Spanish and adds English at grade 3. S+E means that literacy instruction begins in both languages, L1»L2 indicates that literacy instruction begins in the primary language and later adds the second language. S=new program that has not yet begun reading in English.

Program configuration

There were three major program configurations at the DLE school sites. One configuration involved the development of the DLE program into a school-wide emphasis. At these three schools, which all started as a small program strand within a larger school structure, the program served as a magnet. A magnet school can attract students from other schools across the district.

Another configuration, which occurred in 11 schools, provided for the DLE program to co-exist with an English Only (EO) 'mainstream' program at the school site. In some cases, the DLE strand was larger than the EO strand and in other cases the DLE strand was smaller and comprised only one class at each of the grade levels. The last configuration involved three strands at the school site – one EO, one DLE and one TBE (transitional bilingual education). The two school sites with these three strands had to carefully distinguish the DLE and TBE programs and plan for staff development so that the teachers would understand how their programs were different.

The potential for staff problems had to be worked out at the sites in which the DLE program was a strand. Some TBE teachers felt threatened by the DLE model, and worried that Spanish bilingual students would not have enough exposure to English and consequently would not develop both languages. Other TBE teachers felt that the DLE program took the focus on bilingual instruction away from SB students and provided for bilingual instruction for EB students, leaving behind SB students in the process. Some EO teachers did not support the program, and worried about their job security if the DLE program grew and 'took over' the school. Finally, jealousies arose when DLE programs received funding for program development, and DLE teachers were provided with staff development and monies to purchase materials.

These problem situations require strong leadership skills of the principal to balance the needs of the teachers in the different strands, and to promote a school-wide focus. One principal (school #10) was very successful in this regard, and involved all strands in second language development. Thus, even students in the EO strand were learning Spanish. By having a school-wide emphasis and keeping teachers at all strands planning together, this principal was able to keep the staff unified.

Language distribution

As Table 4.4 indicates, the language distribution varied somewhat even within the 90:10 model. There were five variations (designated 1a, 1b, 1c,

2a, 2b in Table 4.4), as elaborated in Table 4.5. Model 1a is the standard 90:10 model, but in model 1b it was adapted at the third-grade level, with slightly less Spanish and more English. The adaptation of model 1a to model 1c provided for more Spanish at the fourth-grade level. Models 2a and 2b provided for less Spanish and more English at the lower grade levels. It should be noted that this variation in the 90:10 model was carefully planned to provide additional Spanish instruction at some sites.

In contrast, a couple of sites were surprised that their implementation was not consistent with model 1a, suggesting that they had not considered all of the instructional minutes in a day and the way these instructional minutes were allocated. For example, when a school site had only one music teacher who was a monolingual English speaker, music had to be taught in English. At some sites, this English time was built into the instructional minutes to be allocated to each language. At other sites, these minutes were subtracted from the total day, and the remainder was divided into Spanish and English time. This was not too great a problem when the English time amounted to only half an hour or so a week. But with music, physical education, library, computer and workshops presented in English, many instructional minutes were already used up in English. Some programs increased their English time to accommodate these time periods; other programs used this time for English, which did not leave sufficient time for the necessary English language arts, which is critical at the early grades to prepare students for reading in English. Thus, each program slightly adapted the 90:10 model to its own school-site needs. In some cases, these adaptations occurred because the model was new to the school site, the teachers were inexperienced, and the teachers and leadership made decisions without understanding what the consequences would be to the students at some later point.

As Table 4.5 shows, there was little difference across the 90:10 schools in the way the languages were separated for instruction. The major agreement was that the two languages must be separated at the early grade levels. At all school sites, the early grades distinguished Spanish and English time by teacher. *One teacher served as the Spanish model and one teacher as the English model.* In many cases, two DLE teachers teamed together. Usually, both teachers were at the same grade level or varied by just one grade level (e.g. grades K and 1). In addition, at some sites, a team comprised three teachers at the same grade level – one EO and two DLE teachers. Each teacher would leave his or her classroom and go to the classroom in which s/he was to be the model teacher. Thus, teacher A would go to classroom B, teacher B to classroom C, and teacher C to classroom A. In some of these cases, monolingual teachers had the DLE teacher provide Spanish instruction to their

English monolingual students. Other English-only teachers preferred that the DLE teacher provide content instruction in English. Some of the monolingual English teachers understood Spanish, and others did not. Further, some EO teachers supported the DLE model, and others did not. Thus, at one site, a monolingual EO teacher did not support the DLE program and required the first-grade SB students, many of whom still did not speak much English, to speak English. This is a violation of the DLE model in that there was not equity for the two groups of students – EB students could use English during Spanish time, but SB students could not speak Spanish during English time. Fortunately, this problem of a monolingual teacher with such an unfavorable attitude was rare. It is not possible to further distinguish school sites in their policy for language separation, because the policy varied by grade level at many sites.

At the upper grade level, some teachers continued to team-teach. When these teachers teamed, many used the opportunity to focus on their instructional strengths and cut their planning time. For example, at a couple of sites, one teacher would be responsible for the language arts/social studies/history instruction and the other teacher for the math/science curriculum. Students would go to one teacher for a designated portion of the day and receive Spanish language arts/social studies/history and to the other teacher for English math/science curriculum. In other classrooms, teachers did not team with another teacher and served as the language models for both languages. In these cases, *time of day* would serve as the indicator of when to switch languages. Thus, students would know that at time x, they would switch from one language to the other. Most teachers provided a very clear signal, announcing the language switch.

Table 4.5 Language distribution characteristics of the DLE school sites Spanish:English ratio

	1a	1b	1c	2a	2b
Kindergarten	90:10	90:10	90:10	90:10	80:20
First Grade	90:10	90:10	90:10	90:10	80:20
Second Grade	80:20	80:20	80:20	80:20	70:30
Third Grade	80:20	70:30	80:20	60:40	70:30
Fourth Grade	50:50	50:50	60:40	60:40	60:40
Fifth Grade	50:50	50:50	50:50	50:50	50:50
Sixth Grade	50:50	50:50	50:50	50:50	50:50

This typically coincided with a switch in curriculum. In addition, many teachers tried to have some natural break separate the languages, such as when students returned to the classroom from physical education, recess, library, computer room, etc. Students clearly understood the language separation and would adhere to the appropriate language of instruction.

In the 50:50 program, the two schools used two different approaches for language separation. At school #15, teachers divided each day in half, with Spanish in the morning and English in the afternoon, or vice versa. School #16, in contrast, alternated weeks, with one week in English and one week in Spanish. In both of these schools, there was less attention to the clear separation of languages. At each site, parent volunteers or instructional assistants might be working with a small group of students in English while the teacher worked with a group in Spanish. Thus, students could hear their L1 for at least some portion of the time they were supposed to be exposed to the L2.

During the early stages of implementation at school #15, it was noted that some teachers and instructional assistants or parents felt sorry for the EB students, who were still monolingual English speakers, and would translate for them. This is a common problem that 50:50 programs must overcome. Often the problem is not even noticed at the school site. A consequence of such translation is that the EB students realize that they do not have to develop much Spanish, because someone will translate for them. After discovering this problem, staff development can alleviate it, which is what occurred at school #15.

Literacy instruction

Literacy instruction in the 90:10 program largely followed the model, which specified that initial literacy instruction occurred through the target language (Spanish or Portuguese), and English reading instruction would begin in grade 3. While this overall structure was typically followed, how language arts and reading were actually taught varied considerably. At all sites, preliteracy activities in Spanish began in Kindergarten. However, the content of these preliteracy activities differed. The reason for the variation is that the beginning stages of the DLE program implementation (1987–1992) at most sites coincided with the new development of a strong whole-language movement in California. While the whole-language approach advocated learning literacy in a literature-rich environment, with authentic literature, many teachers and trainers interpreted 'whole language' to mean that traditional basal readers, phonics instruction, and worksheets were no longer appropriate. Thus, many teachers did not use phonics, and students were given little cognitive basis for learning how to read.

As a part of this whole-language approach, teachers were also trained to accept invented spelling and not correct spelling and grammar or have spelling lessons at the early grade levels. Only a few individual teachers and one school site (site #8) integrated whole language into their basal/phonics traditional approach to include a balance of skills. As California EO students educated in this whole-language approach advanced into the upper grade levels, some educators became alarmed at the lack of basic skills and cognitive understanding of reading in these students. This showed up in their reading comprehension strategies for higher level reading materials and also in their writing skills. California (California Department of Education, 1996b; California State Board of Education, 1998) now advocates a balance of the whole-language and phonics approaches. As a consequence, the outcomes of this whole-language movement and the DLE program are confounded; that is, in looking at reading achievement (see Chapter 10), it is difficult to distinguish to what extent the outcomes result from the DLE program and/or from the whole-language approach to reading instruction.

Another issue in literacy instruction involved the preparation for English literacy. Because the DLE program followed the immersion methodology for the EB students and the bilingual methodology for SB students, and because the DLE program advocated integrating students for instruction, teachers were not clear what to do during English time. During the early years of implementation at most sites, students received oral English at grades K–2 without any preparation for the academic language required for reading in English. Thus, for English speakers who possessed the Spanish literacy skills and had parents who read to them and discussed literacy in English, the addition of English literacy was almost automatic. At some sites, literacy instruction in English was delayed until fourth grade because many of their students, particularly Spanish bilingual students, were not ready for reading in English. However, these students were at a distinct disadvantage because they then needed to catch up with their English-only peers in English reading and writing in only two years before moving into middle school (grades 6–8).

Those schools that have moved English reading to fourth grade have struggled with two contrasting issues:

- Do we move our students into English reading while they are not yet strong in Spanish reading, which is inconsistent with the bilingual education framework that advocates establishing a strong literacy base in one language to promote literacy in the second language?

- Do we move into English earlier to keep the students up with their grade peers and what the DLE model specifies?

Another question has been whether Spanish bilingual and English students should be integrated or separated for English language arts so that each group's distinct language needs can be met more effectively. If students are homogeneously grouped by language, then the EB students do not serve as English-language models during English language arts instruction. In addition, students may wonder why they are not homogeneously grouped for Spanish, but are so grouped for English, which can lead to inherent linguistic inequity in the program. If students are heterogeneously grouped for instruction, then how can the two groups' distinct needs be met in such a short period of instructional time in English? Some teachers opted to separate the students for English language arts only, others kept them together, and still others balanced these approaches in order to provide some integrated instruction and some homogeneous instruction during the week. The approach that was used was not consistent at a particular school site, but tended to vary by teacher. Even at a specific grade level at one school site, two teachers could vary in their approach to English language arts/reading instruction.

Data Collection Approaches

Various approaches to data collection are included in the chapters that follow. Chapters 5, 7 and 13, describe how questionnaires were administered to teachers (Chapter 5), parents (Chapter 7) or students (Chapter 13) to examine their backgrounds and attitudes. These questionnaires appear in Appendix A. In Chapter 6, data collection included observational methods to assess teacher talk and teacher-student interactions. Chapter 9 relies on teacher rating rubrics (assessment frameworks) to assess language proficiency along with tests of language proficiency. In Chapters 10 and 12, norm-referenced achievement tests were used to collect the reading, mathematics, social studies and science achievement data. Chapter 11 used portfolios, consisting of teacher rating rubrics and parent and student questionnaires, to better understand students' reading and literacy.

A wide variety of data collection approaches is used in this book. However, most approaches are quantitative in nature, and rely on paper-and-pencil tests and surveys or questionnaires. Even the classroom observations are quantitative in nature, counting the frequency with which various categories of behavior occur. This quantitative approach is useful in describing the backgrounds, attitudes and various proficiencies of the teachers, parents and students.

What is missing is the richness of the ethnographic approach to understanding the students, teachers and classrooms. For example, there are no contextual descriptions of how children actually learn language in classrooms, how students initiate and respond to discussions with the teacher and their peers in each language, or the ethos of the classroom and school that support or inhibit expression of both cultures and languages. For example, in a dual language education classroom, McCollum (1993) used questionnaires to demonstrate students' positive attitudes toward bilingualism, but used ethnographic methods to demonstrate that students largely used English in the classroom. This was because the teacher constantly corrected the native Spanish-speaking students' speech, and made negative comments about the Spanish vernacular they used. This ethnographic approach has provided information that is considerably useful in understanding classroom and school contexts, particularly for minority and language minority students (e.g. Freeman, 1998; Gumperz *et al.*, 1999; Heath, 1983, 1995; Henze & Haliser, 1999; Hornberger & Micheau, 1993; Mehan *et al.*, 1995; Moll, 1992; Moll, Amanti & Gonzalez, 1992; Moll & Diaz, 1985; Salomone, 1992b). Hornberger and Corson (1997) and many other texts on research methods provide considerable depth in discussing the various approaches to data collection, as well as the strengths and weaknesses of these various approaches.

Discussion and Conclusions

The schools included here were representative of the schools in the US with respect to ethnic density, the percentage of students who were limited in English proficiency, and participation in the free lunch program. There were schools in wealthy suburban areas, schools in rural areas and poor inner city schools. What is missing is a larger percentage of African American and Native American children. Furthermore, no schools discussed here have an Asian language program or very many Asian American students. I did not work with the Asian language (Korean and Cantonese) programs that exist in California. However, Chapters 10 and 12 provide some achievement data for students in Korean DLE programs.

The majority of 90:10 school sites had high ethnic density (greater than 66% minority), and high SES need (more than 20% of EB participants on free lunch). Within these 90HI sites, there was further diversity, with some sites having 90–100% ethnic minority students and other sites 67–74%. Of these HIHI schools, half were located in urban and half in suburban areas, with one rural site. The other 90:10 programs were classified as low ethnic density and low SES need. These sites also varied, with two sites having 19–33% minority students, whereas others had over 50%. Overall, few English bilingual students participated in the free lunch program. While three programs were developed solely at the district level and put into the school, the remainder were developed with input from teachers and principals. Only three of the schools were a magnet program, with the remaining program strands at a school site.

These 90:10 programs, regardless of their ethnic density and SES need, followed a relatively similar program model. Language separation was considered an important design feature, and languages were separated by teacher in the early grades and by either teacher or time in the later grades. Language distribution varied across the 90:10 sites. However, most sites began with a distribution of 90:10 in the first two grades (Kindergarten and grade 1) and ended with 50:50 in grades 5 and 6. The differences in language distribution were strongest at third grade, when English reading instruction was added. Some programs used English for 20% of the day, others for 30%, and still others for 40% of the instructional day. This amounted to a difference of 30–60 minutes per day of less Spanish and more English in some schools.

Literacy instruction typically began in grade 3, but was delayed to grade 4 if the students were not ready for English reading. No school held off in English literacy instruction until fourth grade if students were ready sooner. While most of the sites that delayed English reading were 90HI, one 90LO site was included as well. The major reason students were not ready for literacy instruction in grade 3 was that the students, particularly language minority students, were not given sufficient cognitive academic language preparation in English to facilitate transfer to English reading. In large measure, these were new programs at the schools, and the teachers had little experience with the model and there was little program planning to meet the English language needs of the students. It was assumed that strong literacy skills in Spanish, combined with fluency in English, would produce the perfect union for literacy transfer to English. It did not. Another problem was that teachers were following the whole-language approach, which did not provide students with strong Spanish reading skills that they could transfer to English.[3]

The two 50:50 sites differed in that one was a HIHI suburban site, while the other was a LOLO rural site. While both programs operated as a strand within the school, their programs were implemented very differently. The HIHI site separated language by time and taught reading in both languages, while the LOLO site attempted Spanish and English instruction by week or unit, and began literacy instruction in the student's native language.

Finally, the TBE (transitional bilingual education) programs were all located at high ethnic density sites. Because there were no English bilingual students, SES need could not be designated in the same way as in the DLE programs. However, almost all students in TBE program were participating in the free lunch program. Two of these school sites were designated as HIHI for their DLE program, and the other two sites had almost all ethnic minority students, most of whom (85–100%) were on free lunch. Thus, one could argue that these were all HIHI sites.

It will be important to examine these variations across the different schools in ethnic density, SES need, and program implementation when we discuss, in subsequent chapters, teacher attitudes, language proficiency, and academic achievement outcomes.

Notes

1. In the US, parents may apply for their child to receive a free lunch at school if the household income falls below a designated level. All of these families are low income, and many are living in poverty.
2. It may not be obvious to the reader that Hispanic participants could be categorized as either Spanish speaking (SB) if they were classified as Limited English Proficient or as English speaking (EB). Many of the English speakers in various programs were Hispanic. These students entered the program as monolingual English speakers, or as bilingual speakers who were proficient in English.
3. While some whole-language promoters would argue that whole language does include phonics, this was not the way it was originally interpreted in the schools with which I worked.

Chapter 5

Teacher Background and Perceptions of Support, Program Planning, Instructional Practices and Efficacy

Introduction and Rationale

Research on teacher attitudes in language education programs is critical, given the consistent findings that teacher attitudes and expectations influence student achievement (Banks & Banks, 1995). There is little research on teacher satisfaction and perceptions in language education or in culturally and linguistically diverse classrooms. Various bodies of literature have examined teacher attitudes and expectations in different ways. These show that teacher attitudes are affected by teacher background, demographic characteristics of the school, program effectiveness, and perceptions of support by administration, other staff, and parents. To provide a conceptual framework for the various analyses discussed in this chapter, the literature is reviewed in somewhat more detail than in Chapter 1.

This chapter provides background information on DLE and TBE teachers from the schools examined in the last chapter, and discusses their perceptions of support, program planning, language attitudes and practices, and satisfaction. It also examines the teacher background and school demographic factors that may influence these teacher attitudes in ethnically and linguistically diverse schools implementing a DLE or TBE program.

School characteristics

Social class is an important school demographic characteristic. Learners who are identifiably from lower-class backgrounds tend to be perceived more negatively, while those from families located higher on the social-class hierarchy tend to be seen more positively (Knapp & Woolverton, 1995; Percell, 1993). Similarly, students with different languages, dialects, and cultural behaviors have been evaluated more harshly in the school context (Knapp & Woolverton, 1995). According to Baron et al. (1985), social class, race and ethnicity are major contributors to teacher beliefs about students. Further, researchers have shown that teachers' attitudes are influenced by a student's linguistic skills, with language minority students consistently rated lower in education, intelligence, socioeconomic status, and speaking ability (Johnson, 1994; Stern & Keislar, 1977). This research, and the social class findings presented in Chapter 1, suggest that the ethnic density and social class characteristics of the school's student population may affect teacher attitudes.

The type of language education program implemented at a school site is expected to affect teacher attitudes of support and instructional practices because different models (i.e. TBE, 90:10, 50:50) may be perceived and treated differently by school administrators, staff and parents. Because the DLE program includes an enrichment program, district-level administrators, principals, staff, and parents may perceive it differently than traditional TBE programs. In addition, the 90:10 model may differ from the 50:50 model with respect to perceptions of support and instructional practices (see Chapter 4 for a description of the 90:10 and 50:50 DLE models). While there is no research to substantiate these positions, the DLE program includes an immersion component for language majority students, and thus district, principal, staff and parents may appreciate it more than a traditional TBE program. Also, the 90:10 model may be viewed as distinct from the 50:50 model, because the 90:10 model has a much larger commitment to the minority language.

Teacher background characteristics

Research has shown that teacher background characteristics have an impact on teaching effectiveness in the classroom (Darling-Hammond, 1995). New teachers – those with fewer than three years of experience – are less effective as instructors than are more experienced teachers (Darling-Hammond, 1995; Veenman, 1984). Although these studies provide insight into the differences among teachers with differing years of experience, they do not specifically address teachers' attitudes and expectations according to their teaching experience. There is clearly an absence of research in this area, particularly in classrooms with culturally and linguistically diverse students. Teaching experience may be particularly important in language education programs with culturally and linguistically diverse students, as teachers have a greater range of student needs to meet. They must also provide instruction as any monolingual teacher would, but need to understand how to make the language and content accessible to the varying needs of their students. This experience usually requires considerable in-service and pre-service training, as well as classroom coaching.

A teacher's racial/ethnic background can also affect interactions in the classroom. For example, when teachers are unfamiliar with the ethnic and language backgrounds of students, miscommunications – both verbal and nonverbal – between teachers and students can occur (Brophy & Good, 1986). While teachers from European American backgrounds have been found to be more directive and authoritarian toward students of minority ethnic backgrounds and more democratic with students of European American background, similar ethnic background does not guarantee uncomplicated and productive relationships between teachers and their students (Foster, 1995). As Foster notes, teachers of similar background will sometimes judge students more harshly. Because European American teachers have learned the minority language and chosen to be bilingual teachers, they may not differ from Hispanic teachers. Because of the absence of literature in this area, the relationship between teacher attitudes and teacher ethnicity is unclear, especially in language education programs with culturally, socially and linguistically distinct student populations.

Program planning and support

As discussed in Chapter 2, research on effective schools (Levine & Lezotte, 1995) shows that:

- Teacher satisfaction and attitudes are influenced by the perceived support of principals, district administration, other staff and parents.
- Teacher attitudes can be affected by program characteristics, such as program planning and teamwork.

One characteristic of effective schools is outstanding leadership. School principals have been identified by a majority of studies as the most crucial leadership determinant of school effectiveness (Bullard & Taylor, 1993; Clancy, 1982; Glenn, 1981). Principals at unusually effective schools have high expectations for teachers while consistently offering support, particularly in the area of curriculum and instruction, where leadership is essential to maintain the improvement process (Mortimore *et al.*, 1988). Given the importance of leadership in effective schools, it is important to understand, in DLE and TBE programs, the teachers' perceived level of principal support and the extent to which principal support is associated with program development, teacher efficacy, and classroom practices.

Research on effective schools has also shown that support and leadership from district-level decision makers and school board representatives is vital, and can determine the ultimate success or failure of a school program (Bullard & Taylor, 1993). It is not clear whether district support will influence the attitudes and perceptions of teachers in language education programs. However, because the board of education and administrative leadership have the power to facilitate or impede the development of a language education program, the perception of language education teachers is probably more affected by district-level support than would be the case for monolingual teachers.

Although evidence regarding the role of parental involvement is mixed, research on effective schools generally has shown that strong home–school partnerships and parental involvement in the education process can have a positive influence on the school climate (see Chapter 7 for a review; Bermúdez & Márquez, 1996; Levine & Lezotte, 1995; Met, 1987; Moll, 1992; Moll *et al.*, 1992; Pecheone & Shoemaker, 1984; Stedman, 1987). If parents are involved, supportive of school endeavors and consistently communicate with teachers, positive results will follow (Hidalgo *et al.*, 1995; Levine & Lezotte, 1995; Levine & Stark, 1981; Mortimore *et al.*, 1988). In DLE programs, there are two distinct populations of parents with which to work, please, and garner support. It is not clear from research the extent to which perceptions of parent support may influence teachers' satisfaction, efficacy, and classroom practices.

Faculty cohesion and collegiality are other factors found to be important in effective schools (Purkey & Smith, 1983). Collegiality among school staff can strengthen communication, and help identify and solve problems (Rossmiller *et al.*, 1993). The extent to which a principal is effective in this capacity depends largely upon the successful establishment of positive communication patterns between the principal and staff, and among individual staff members (Rosenholtz, 1985). This staff support and unity is frequently absent from TBE and DLE programs where English monolingual staff feel threatened by the bilingual program or simply believe bilingual programs to be ineffective. Such attention can isolate TBE and DLE teachers. Thus, it is important to understand the level of staff support and unity in these programs in order to determine the influence of staff support on teacher satisfaction, teaching efficacy, and classroom practices.

Staff members in effective schools openly share ideas, expertise and observations on a regular basis (Clancy, 1982). This communication around program development enhances a staff's ability to coordinate curriculum and instruction that focus on specific objectives through careful planning and adoption of clear academic goals (Levine & Stark, 1981). Because several curricular subjects involve the continual development of academic skills and competencies across grade levels, it is crucial that the approaches used to teach these skills be utilized consistently by teachers at all grade levels (Venezky & Winfield, 1979). Further, such communication should include not only a shared commitment to educational equity (Stedman, 1987: 219), but also a plan for how to ensure that the commitment is exercised on campus. Since program planning is critical to program effectiveness, it is important to ascertain teachers' perception of the extent to which there is program planning, and whether it impacts on their ratings of satisfaction, teaching efficacy, and classroom practices.

This chapter will specifically examine:

- Teacher satisfaction, teaching efficacy, and language and classroom practices in the four language education models discussed in Chapter 4 (90HI, 90LO, 50:50, TBE).
- The language education model, school demography, teacher background, program, and perceived support factors that influence teacher satisfaction, efficacy and classroom practices.

Data Collection

All teachers in the study completed a questionnaire (presented in the Appendix) that consisted of two sections. Section A comprised questions that were divided into nine different categories of teacher attitudes, beliefs and behaviors The items for each category were rated on a five-point Likert scale ranging from 1 (strongly disagree) to 5 (strongly agree), with some items reverse-scored [see Table 5.1 for the categories and their items]. Most of the category items had high or acceptable *internal consistency*[1] as measured by *Cronbach's alpha*, given in parentheses:

- District/board support (0.80).
- Principal support (0.93).
- Staff support and unity (0.68).
- Parent support (0.79).
- Program planning (0.73).
- Multicultural equity concerns (0.73).
- Ability and competitive classroom structure (0.82).
- Positive classroom environment (0.85).
- Language instruction (0.68).
- Teaching efficacy (0.70).

The items for the scales were developed from the literature on teacher attitudes, and some items were adapted from Johnson (1974).

Section B of the questionnaire contained items that requested demographic information about the school site and teacher background (teaching experience, educational background, language proficiency, ethnicity) and training.

Table 5.1 Category items and reliabilities*

District/board support (0.80)
Board of Education helpful
Board of Education supportive
District committed to SB students
District has conflicting ideas about bilingual education*
District pushing for DLE exemplary program

Principal support (0.93)
Principal communicates high expectations for students
Principal expects high performance from teachers
Principal agrees with minority language use
Principal is assertive for improvement of instructional practices
Principal is assertive for meeting needs of students and school
Administration (on-site) is knowledgeable and good resource–for DLE model
Administration (on-site) supports program
Administration (on-site) shows interest in program

Staff support and unity (0.68)
Principal encourages communication among DLE and non-DLE teachers
Principal makes DLE teachers feel equal
Non-two way teachers well informed about program
Non-DLE teachers critical of program*

Parent support (0.79)
EB parents are supportive
SB parents are supportive
EB parents complain about program*
SB parents complain about program*

Program planning (0.73)
We have developed language objectives by grade level
We have discussed articulation across grade levels
Teachers work as team to plan
Teachers don't spend enough time as a group planning*

Multicultural equity concerns (0.73)
Expect more from EB than SB
SB community feels valued at school
Makes more sense to discuss ethnic themes at holidays*
Feel uncomfortable with EB parents*
Feel uncomfortable with SB parents*
Have effective program for EB students
Have effective program for SB students
Program better serves EB students*

Ability and competitive classroom structure (0.82)
Competition in school important preparation for life
Use competitive games
Competition enhances learning

(Table continues)

Table 5.1 *(Continued)*

Ability and competitive classroom structure (0.82) *(cont.)*

Contests increase motivation
Display work of high achievers
Use high achievers as models
Give privileges to academic achievers

Positive classroom environment (0.85)

Analyze mistakes in class
Encourage students to ask each other for help
Give students lots of choices
Students ask many content questions
Use cooperative games with mixed ability levels
Integrate multicultural themes throughout year
Tell students mistakes are essential to learning
Encourage students to monitor progress
Students capable of setting own goals
Important to teach social skills in class
Students always on task
Provide students time to think about answers
Provide group/pair activities
Provide activities for EB/SB to discuss
At-risk students get assignments even if difficult

Language instruction (0.68)

I accept all attempts at communication
I have developed specific language objectives I incorporate in content
All language in class is error free
I develop activities to address consistent language errors
I relate new information to previously learned information
During instruction, respond to questions in other language
I model writing through journals and other activities

Teaching efficacy (0.70)

I adjust my plans based on feedback from class
I organize lessons around themes
Enjoy teaching in program
I'm good at helping students improve
I make a difference in lives of students
Some students won't make progress no matter what I do*
Little I can do to assure all my students make progress*
Not trained to treat students equitably*
I don't understand all about DLE programs*
My Spanish isn't high enough level*
Math is my weak point*
Program has sufficient supply of non-English materials
Sufficient number of bilingual teaching paraprofessionals

Full scale (0.91)

---

* represents items that were recoded.

Teachers individually completed the questionnaire and, to assure confidentiality, returned their questionnaire in a sealed envelope to their school site, which forwarded the questionnaires in the sealed envelopes to the author.

Teacher Background Characteristics

A total of 126 teachers (117 females, 9 males), representing the four program types discussed in the previous chapter, participated in the study. The number and percentage of teachers in each type of program were as follows: 31% (n=39) in 90HI, 23% (n=29) in 90LO, 20% (n=25) in 50:50, and 26% (n=33) in TBE. While teachers varied with respect to ethnic background (45% Hispanic; 55% European American), teacher ethnicity differed among the program types. As Figure 5.1 shows, there were 57–59% of Hispanic teachers in 90HI and 50:50 programs, and 64–71% of European American teachers in 90LO and TBE programs. Almost all teachers (98%) taught in a Spanish/English program, while 2% instructed in a Portuguese/English program. Owing to the small sample of Portuguese teachers, further differences will not be discussed, and Spanish will be used to designate the language of the program and teachers so that it does not become too cumbersome to constantly write Spanish/Portuguese. However, it is important to remember that the sample includes a few teachers from a Portuguese program.

Close to two thirds (62%) of the teachers instructed primary-level students (grades K–2) while one third (38%) taught higher elementary-level students (grades 3–6). All of the teachers had a BA degree, one third had earned an MA, and one teacher had received a Ph.D.

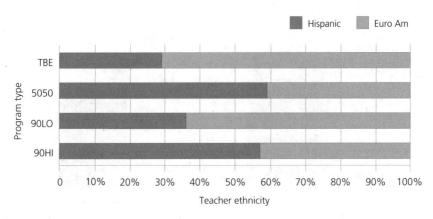

Figure 5.1 Teacher ethnicity by program type

Years of teaching experience with language minority students did not vary across the different program types. Overall, teachers had taught language minority students for an average of seven years. The percentage of new teachers, with one to three years of experience, did not differ by program type, with about one third new teachers at each program type.

Language proficiency

Self-reports of language proficiency indicated that most (72, or 92%) of the teachers were native speakers of English and the remainder (5, or 7%) claimed teaching proficiency. On a self-reported scale of language proficiency, from 1 (no practical proficiency), 2 (minimal communicative proficiency), 3 (basic communicative proficiency), 4 (professional proficiency), to 5 (full professional proficiency), teachers rated themselves between 4.9 and 5.0 in English, with no differences across program types (see Figure 5.2). In teachers' ratings of Spanish proficiency, there were differences across program types. In general, over half (42, or 54%) of the teachers were native speakers of Spanish and one third (26, or 33%) claimed teaching proficiency in Spanish (or Portuguese, for Portuguese-speaking teachers), with the remaining either reporting communicative proficiency (5, or 7%), or not responding to the question.

As Figure 5.2 indicates, 90:10 teachers rated themselves (on the scale of 1 to 5 described above) an average of 4.5, while 50:50 program teachers averaged 4.0 and TBE teachers averaged 3.9 – a difference that was statistically significant. Furthermore, Hispanic teachers (mean = 4.7) rated themselves higher in Spanish proficiency than did European American teachers (mean

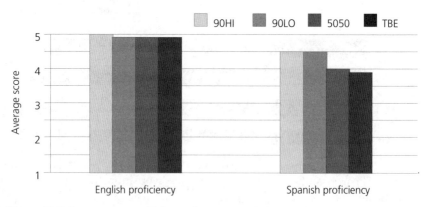

Figure 5.2 Language proficiency by program type

= 3.9). [Hereafter, unless otherwise stated, any differences discussed are statistically significant beyond the 0.05 level.]

Another way of determining Spanish proficiency was to look at teacher responses (from strongly disagree to strongly agree) to the item 'Sometimes I feel that my Spanish proficiency isn't at a high enough level to really provide students with different ways of expressing or understanding concepts or vocabulary items.' Agreement would suggest that teachers did not feel they were proficient enough in Spanish. About two thirds of DLE teachers, but one third of TBE teachers *disagreed* that their Spanish was not high enough – that is, they believed that their Spanish was of sufficiently high quality for instructional purposes. In contrast, 15–28% of DLE teachers, but a whopping 61% of TBE teachers *agreed* – they felt that their Spanish was not of high enough caliber for effectively teaching their students. Thus, consistent with the ratings of Spanish proficiency and the bilingual certification (which requires high levels of Spanish proficiency), teachers in DLE programs had higher levels of Spanish proficiency than TBE teachers had. This result is not surprising, since teachers in DLE programs cannot code switch, as TBE teachers can, when they do not know the correct word in Spanish. DLE teachers must keep the two languages separate. This is often not the case in TBE classrooms, where teachers often switch between the two languages.

Training

At most school sites, there was considerable ongoing staff training. In fact, at some sites, teachers were spending a considerable amount of time at a variety of in-service training sessions. Several items on the questionnaire related specifically to training. Many teachers came to the program with some training that helped them understand and teach in the program more effectively. As Figure 5.3 demonstrates, while 83–90% of 90:10 teachers held bilingual certificates, only 63% of 50:50 program teachers and 49% of TBE teachers had earned bilingual certification. About 40–48% of teachers from each program type held an ESL[2] certificate. The percentage of teachers in the different program types varied according to what certificate they possessed (e.g. neither bilingual nor ESL certificates, one of these certificates, or both certificates). As we can see in Figure 5.3, few teachers (10–13%) in 90:10 programs, but almost one third of teachers in 50:50 programs had not earned either certificate. Highly trained teachers with both certificates were more likely to be hired in the DLE programs (35–45%) than in the TBE (12%) program. While Hispanic teachers were more likely to have both certificates (41%) than European-American teachers (25%) were, the percentage of teachers with neither certificate was similar (15–16%).

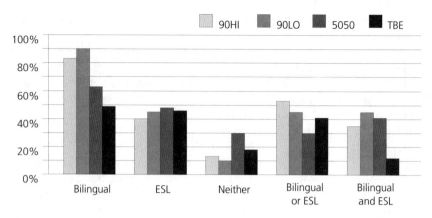

Figure 5.3 Certification by program type

However, teachers with both certificates (mean = 4.6) had higher levels of Spanish proficiency than teachers with only one certificate (mean = 4.1) or neither (mean = 3.7) of the certificates.

When teachers were asked if there was *not enough* training, the average score of 3.3 indicated that they tended to neither agree nor disagree that there was not enough training. DLE teachers, but not TBE teachers, agreed that there was *too much* training (mean = 3.7) and little follow-through on what training was provided (mean = 2.9). Most teachers agreed that there was not enough training in educational equity (mean = 3.8).

Of course, training is difficult in any new program when there are so many topics worthy of attention. However, one topic of prime importance in the DLE program is that teachers know and understand the model and its rationale; otherwise, how can they make informed instructional decisions? In asking teachers to rate the statement 'I understand all I should about the DLE model'(or the bilingual model, for TBE teachers), the average on this item was 3.9. The percentages of teachers who agreed and disagreed varied significantly across program types: while 5–12% of DLE teachers disagreed that they understood the model, 27% of TBE teachers responded in disagreement. Further, 75–83% of 90:10, but only 52% of 50:50 and 64% of TBE teachers agreed that they understood the model. Teachers' understanding of the model also varied depending on their level of certification. Teachers with both certificates (mean = 4.1) had higher levels of agreement that they understood the model than teachers with only one (mean = 3.9) or neither (mean = 3.1) of the certificates.

Perceptions of Support

The next topic was whether teachers in the various program types differ concerning their perceptions of support from the school district, principal, staff and parents.

School district support

As Figure 5.4 shows, local school district support varied, but not statistically significantly, across the program types, from a mean of 2.9 to 3.8. Results also showed that:

- The highest levels of support were experienced by 50:50 programs.
- The 90:10 and TBE program teachers felt neither support nor lack of support at the district level.
- While it may appear that 50:50 teachers felt more support, actually statistical analyses showed that the differences were really due to individual schools, rather than to the program type in which they were teaching.[3]
- Teachers with both (ESL and bilingual) credentials perceived more support than did teachers with neither or only one of these credentials.

The difference across schools rather than across program type is an important finding, as it suggests that district support varies by school and district needs, but not by the type of program a school may have in place. In addition, it implies that, while support may not always be positive for the DLE model, neither will it always be negative. Rather, support will reflect considerations at district and school level.

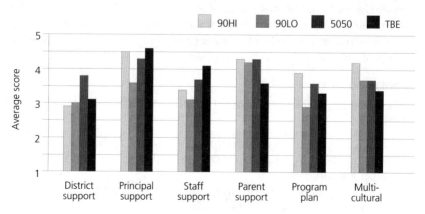

Figure 5.4 Teacher perceptions of support and planning

Support from school principals

Overall, teachers tended to agree that principals were interested in, knowledgeable about, and supportive of the program, had high expectations for students and teachers, agreed with the use of the minority language, and strove to improve instructional practices and meet student needs. Teachers did not vary in ratings of principal support by any teacher background variables. However, as Figure 5.4 illustrates, teachers differed in their ratings of principal support according to the program type in which they taught:

- 90LO program teachers perceived considerably less support than all other program types.
- Teachers at the different 90HI school sites gave very different ratings of principal support, but still high scores, from 3.8 to 4.9.

Staff support

Perceptions of staff support varied considerably depending on the program type and the school in which teachers instructed. As Figure 5.4 shows:

- TBE teachers (mean = 4.1) experienced significantly more staff support and unity at their schools than 90HI (mean = 3.4) and 90LO (mean = 3.1) teachers.
- 50:50 teachers (mean = 3.7) perceived significantly more support than 90LO teachers (mean = 3.1).

Most of the program type variation reflected differences in how effectively the principal unified the staff and treated teachers equitably. For the items 'Principal encourages communication among DLE and non-DLE teachers' and 'DLE and non-DLE teachers are treated equally', 90LO teachers scored only 3.5, while the other program types gave these items an average of 4.0 to 4.6.

Parent support

The last support category is parent support. As one can see from perusal of Figure 5.4:

- TBE teachers perceived less support (mean = 3.6) than DLE teachers (mean = 4.2–4.3), who generally agreed that the EB and SB parents supported the program.
- There were no statistically significant differences across the various schools, from a low of 3.3 to a high of 4.9.

One issue concerns the different perceptions of support experienced by TBE versus DLE teachers.

- TBE teachers perceived a lower level of support, but they actually only felt less support from EB parents.
- Hispanic teachers perceived significantly more support from SB parents (mean = 4.5) than European American teachers (mean = 4.1).

One important question was whether teachers perceived differences in the support, complaints, worry, and assisting child with schoolwork of EB versus SB parents. Results indicated that:

- SB parents were rated as more supportive than EB parents, though both groups were rated as supportive.
- EB parents were rated as worrying more about their children learning to read than SB parents.
- EB parents were rated as assisting their children more with homework than SB parents.

In general, these results suggest somewhat more support from SB parents and slightly elevated worry from EB parents, but only with respect to learning to read. Further, teachers felt that EB parents seemed more supportive and less concerned in DLE than in TBE programs.

Other findings showed that:

- Hispanic teachers gave higher scores to the SB parent support and SB and EB parents assisting their child with homework items than did European-American teachers.
- Teachers who had minimal or basic communication ability in Spanish rated SB parents as less supportive, more complaining and less assisting of children than teachers with either teaching proficiency in Spanish or full professional proficiency in Spanish.

In looking at the relationship among the various support categories:

- Principal support was strongly associated with staff support/unity for both DLE and TBE programs.
- For DLE programs, but not TBE programs, staff support/unity was also tied to district support and parent support.

These correlations demonstrate that important relationships exist among these various levels of support for DLE programs and that the relationships among the support variables differed for DLE and TBE programs.

Program Development

Program Planning

Ratings of program planning varied from 2.9 to 3.9, indicating agreement, but not strong agreement, that teachers planned together and discussed articulation across grade levels. As Figure 5.4 illustrates, teachers appeared to differ considerably across program types in their perception of program planning. However, the apparent variation across program types was actually due to considerable variation *across* different *school* sites.

Figure 5.5 shows teachers' average ratings for specific items related to program planning. Overall, teachers from 90HI programs were consistently more likely to be involved in program planning components: articulation across grade levels, establishing language objectives, to spend time planning as a group, and to plan as a team. Teachers were least likely to indicate that they plan together as a group, though they were likely to team with another teacher. If little time was spent planning as a group, it is not clear how much planning would have gone into articulation or into establishing language objectives.

Multicultural equity concerns

As Figure 5.4 shows, higher scores were given to multicultural equity concerns (mean = 3.4-4.2), indicating that:

- Teachers felt that there was an effective program for both SB and EB students.
- Teachers felt comfortable with both EB and SB parents.

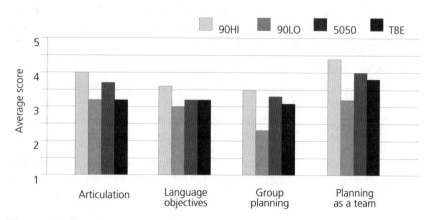

Figure 5.5 Teacher ratings of program planning

- SB parents were valued at school.
- Teachers did not expect more from EB than from SB students.

There were some very important differences that influenced how teachers rated multicultural equity concerns:

- Teachers with more years of experience perceived more attention to multicultural equity concerns.
- Teachers with both credentials (bilingual and ESL) gave higher ratings to multicultural equity concerns than did teachers with one (bilingual *or* ESL) or no extra credentials (neither bilingual nor ESL).
- Teachers at different schools gave very different ratings, regardless of program type.
- 90HI teachers rated their program higher in meeting multicultural equity concerns than did teachers from the other three program types.

For the multicultural equity concern items illustrated in Figure 5.6:

- There was no difference in teachers' ratings of their comfort level with Spanish bilingual (mean = 4.1) versus English bilingual (mean = 4.2) parents.
- Teachers did not vary significantly in their opinion that the program was effective for the two groups of students, with only slightly higher ratings for SB (mean = 4.0) than for EB (mean = 3.8) students.
- There was no significant difference, according to teacher background, program type, or school, in how comfortable teachers felt with EB or SB parents.
- In comparison to the scores given by the 90HI, 90LO and 50:50 teachers TBE teachers did not feel that the bilingual program was very effective for EB students (mean = 2.7 versus 4.6, 4.0 and 3.9).
- 90HI teachers were more confident than 90LO and TBE teachers (mean = 4.6 versus 3.8 and 3.5) that the program type they were teaching in was very effective for SB students.
- 90HI teachers were also more likely than 90LO, 50:50 and TBE teachers (mean = 4.0 versus 3.0 and 3.3) to believe that the program did *not* better serve EB than SB.
- Teachers agreed that they did *not* expect more from EB than from SB students (mean = 3.6–4.2).
- There was strong agreement (mean = 3.9–4.1) that SB families are valued at school, with some variation in this item across school sites.

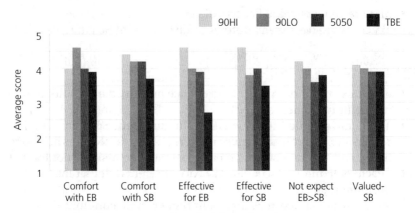

Figure 5.6 Teacher ratings of multicultural equity

In looking at the relationship among these variables:

- Program planning and multicultural equity concerns were highly correlated with each other, and teachers who felt multicultural equity concerns were being addressed tended to also believe that there was good program planning at their site.
- For DLE programs only, program planning and multicultural equity concerns were related to principal support.
- Multicultural equity concerns were positively associated with staff support/unity and parent support.

These relationships suggest that higher levels of principal support are associated with more program planning and more concerns for both groups of students and parents. In addition, parent support and staff support/unity are higher when there is respect and concern for meeting the needs of the culturally diverse population on campus.

Teacher Efficacy and Instructional Practices

The last set of scales relates to teacher efficacy and instructional practices. Ability items received a mean rating of 2.9 to 3.5 across the different program types, reflecting the teachers' overall belief that ability was not a salient component in the classroom, but competition and ability grouping were included to some extent.

Teaching efficacy

Teaching efficacy was rated medium to medium high (mean = 3.5–4.0), as Figure 5.7 demonstrates. While teachers in the various program types did not vary, there were many differences in teaching efficacy according to the school at which a teacher worked. In addition, yet not surprisingly, teachers with more teaching experience and both credentials (bilingual and ESL) rated themselves as having higher teaching efficacy.

The highest rated item was 'I enjoy teaching in the DLE/Bilingual program,' which teachers scored 4.2 (TBE), 4.4 (90LO and 50:50), and 4.8 (90HI). The lowest rated items pertained to sufficient Spanish materials (mean = 2.3–3.1), where teachers from different schools rated this item very differently, and 'There are enough bilingual paraprofessionals or teacher assistants to help me' (mean = 2.6–3.2). Most teachers felt that they would make a difference in their students' lives (mean = 4.2–4.5). In addition, DLE teachers expressed more confidence that they could help their students improve (mean = 4.0–4.2) than did TBE teachers (mean = 3.7).

Language instruction

As Figure 5.7 illustrates, most teachers ranged from agree to strongly agree that they used language instructional strategies. They accept all student attempts at communication; they respond to students' questions and answers, even if these are in the other language; they relate new vocabulary to previously learned material; and they model writing in the classroom. Furthermore, teachers tended to agree that they have developed specific language objectives as well as activities to address student errors. In looking at how teachers treated errors and whether they explained grammar, the results suggest that:

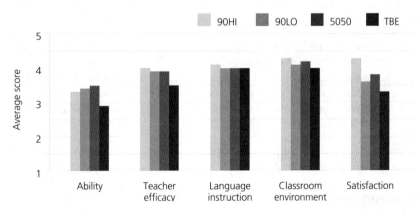

Figure 5.7 Teacher attitudes and satisfaction

- Teachers sometimes corrected grammatical errors and written errors.
- Teachers tended to correct pronunciation errors.
- Pronunciation errors were corrected more frequently than grammatical errors.
- Teachers tended to *disagree*, but not strongly disagree, that they *never* explain grammar.

In the item 'During content instruction, I use both languages to reinforce certain concepts,' a high score would indicate disagreement, and a low score agreement. Teachers in both types of 90:10 programs were more likely to *disagree* that they use both languages (mean = 4.6 for 90HI and mean = 4.2 for 90LO) than do TBE and 50:50 teachers (mean = 2.8). These results suggest that language mixing is not entirely absent in 90:10 programs, and may be fairly prevalent in 50:50 and TBE programs.

Classroom environment

Classroom environment was rated similarly across program types and schools (mean = 4.0–4.3). Teachers tended to rate the individual items between 4.0 and 4.5, indicating agreement to strong agreement with most items. The only items where there were important differences included:

- 'Students are usually on task', where TBE teachers rated lower than 90HI and 90LO teachers, and more teaching experience was associated with higher scores.
- Teachers with both credentials grouped students more frequently and provided more activities for SB and EB students to work together than did teachers with one or neither credential.

In examining relationships among these scales of efficacy and instructional practices, results showed that:

- Classroom environment and language instruction were highly correlated with each other in both DLE and TBE programs.
- Classroom environment and language instruction were associated with multicultural equity concerns in both DLE and TBE programs.
- Classroom environment was related to principal support in both DLE and TBE programs.

These correlations suggest that providing a more positive classroom environment is linked to using appropriate strategies for second language development, but also to school-wide concerns that student diversity needs were met, and to principal support.

Teaching efficacy was associated with almost all the other categories for both DLE and TBE programs, including:

- Principal support in DLE and TBE.
- Staff support in DLE and TBE.
- Parent support in DLE only.
- Program planning in DLE and in TBE.
- Multicultural equity concerns in DLE and TBE.
- Classroom environment in DLE and TBE.
- Language instruction in DLE and TBE.

Thus, teachers who rated themselves higher in teacher efficacy were teachers who perceived high levels of support from their principal, from non-DLE teachers at their site, and from parents. High efficacy was also influenced by the extent to which there was program planning at the site, and by whether student diversity needs were met. Finally, teachers with higher efficacy provided a more positive classroom environment and utilized second language development instructional strategies.

The ability scale was not correlated with any other scales in the DLE program, but was strongly associated in TBE programs with multicultural equity concerns, classroom environment, language instruction, and teaching efficacy.

Satisfaction with DLE or TBE Program

The satisfaction item invited teachers to select, on a scale from 1 (very dissatisfied) to 5 (very satisfied), how satisfied they were with 'the way the current bilingual or DLE program is operating.' Results showed that:

- Teachers' mean scores (see Figure 5.7) varied from 3.3 for TBE teachers to 3.6 for 90LO teachers, 3.8 for 50:50 teachers, and 4.3 for 90HI teachers, indicating a range from somewhat to very satisfied.
- While teacher satisfaction did not vary according to teacher background, or across school sites, teachers from 90HI programs were more satisfied than teachers from 90LO and TBE programs.
- Teachers rated enjoyment (mean = 4.5) much higher than satisfaction (mean = 3.8), indicating that teachers liked the model a lot, but not necessarily how it was implemented at their site.

There were a number of important relationships between satisfaction and the other categories for DLE, but not for TBE, programs. In DLE programs, satisfaction was related to:

- The support categories of principal support and parent support, but not to staff or district support.
- Program planning and multicultural equity concerns.
- None of the efficacy or classroom instructional strategies.

In TBE programs, satisfaction was associated only with parent support and program planning.

Summary and Conclusions

This chapter has provided information about backgrounds and attitudes of teachers in TBE and DLE programs. The results, which are summarized here, illustrate some important dynamics related to teachers' perceptions of support, program development, classroom instruction issues, and satisfaction, and to the way teacher attitudes may vary according to the teacher's background, to the school demographic characteristics, or to the type of program (90:10, 50:50, TBE) that is implemented.

With respect to teacher background, there are some important similarities and differences to keep in mind. First, years of teaching experience and educational background did not vary in the teachers from the four program types (90LO, 90HI, 50:50, TBE). However, there were considerable differences in other aspects of the teachers' backgrounds in the various program types. Hispanic teachers were more likely to be hired in 90HI and 50:50 programs than in 90LO and TBE programs, and Hispanic teachers were more likely to possess both the bilingual and ESL certificates and to be more proficient in Spanish. However, there were more teachers with both credentials in the 50:50 program than in the other programs. Thus, the TBE program stood out as the one with fewer teachers with bilingual or both certificates and with lower levels of Spanish proficiency. Because of the difference in training required for the certificates, it is not surprising that TBE teachers were least likely to understand the bilingual model that they were teaching in. Among DLE teachers, 90:10 teachers were more likely to agree that they understood the model than were 50:50 teachers.

Teachers perceived medium levels of support from the district and staff, and medium high levels of support from the principal and parents. In their ratings of support in any of the support categories (except district support), teachers did not differ according to their years of teaching experience, or type of credential. Teachers with both bilingual and ESL credentials felt higher levels of support than did teachers with neither or only one type of credential.

While teachers did not differ much according to their backgrounds in their opinions about the support they received in the program, there were important differences across the various programs and schools in terms of the support they felt. District support did not vary depending on the type of program, but teachers at different schools experienced quite distinct levels of support from the district. These results suggest that district administrations and boards of education are not more likely to support one model over another, at least from the perspective of teachers. Rather, support varies according to the particular concerns and needs of each district.

At the school-site level, teachers perceived medium staff support and unity. Teachers in 90LO programs felt much less support than TBE teachers and 50:50 teachers. Ratings of support were much higher for the principal, who was viewed as highly supportive – except in 90LO programs. It is interesting, but not surprising, that 90LO teachers experienced little support at their school site. At these school sites (see Chapter 4), there were typically fewer ethnic-minority students, a smaller percentage of students on free lunch, and fewer students who were rated as Limited English Proficient (LEP). However, there was a lot of variability at the different 90HI school sites in how much support they felt from their principal.

These district, principal and staff support items show an important and potentially negative impact on 90LO programs, which are distinct from 90HI and TBE programs because the population of students served in 90LO programs is not particularly diverse nor is it particularly needy. Thus, some of these schools have not had bilingual programs before, and staff perceive that they do not need bilingual programs, especially since, as noted in previous chapters, bilingual programs are typically not valued. Therefore, 90LO program teachers report that their principals are less supportive, knowledgeable and interested in the program, and do not see the need for the minority language. They do not work to integrate the program on the site, nor bring the staff together. Because the non-DLE teachers are not informed about the program nor encouraged to see it as an important strand within the school, they may feel disdain for the program. This is particularly the case if they believe that their jobs may be threatened at the school site as the program grows across the grade levels. If there is this perception at the school site, then it is no surprise that the 90LO teachers feel alienated from the staff and feel little support from the principal.

Parents were seen as very supportive of the program. While all DLE teachers felt support from both EB and SB parents, TBE teachers experienced the same levels of support from SB parents as DLE teachers did, but they experienced lower levels of support from EB parents. In general, while DLE teachers rated both groups of parents as supportive, they felt that SB parents were more supportive and less worried about their children learning to read in English than were EB parents. Hispanic teachers were also more optimistic about parent support than were European American teachers.

In program development issues, teachers were in general, but not strong, agreement that they have articulated the program across grade levels and have developed language objectives. It is not clear how this planning has occurred without the teachers spending time as a group to plan, which was rated as neither agree nor disagree. However, the extent to which planning occurred varied considerably by school site, though not by program type.

Program planning around multicultural equity concerns was very interesting. While program planning typically produces a program of high quality, at the core of the DLE and even the TBE program model is the necessity for assuring that the program meets the needs of the culturally and linguistically diverse population. Ratings of multicultural equity concerns differed widely depending on the background of the teacher, the program type, and the school site. With more teaching experience and more credential training, teachers were more likely to agree or strongly agree that the model at their site was equitable, effective for both groups of students, valued both SB and EB communities, and provided an integrated approach to multicultural education. Furthermore, 90HI teachers gave consistently higher ratings to meeting these needs than did the teachers from the other program types.

There was also considerable variation across different school sites in their rating of this set of questions. In general, most teachers expressed clear agreement that they felt comfortable with both SB and EB parents, that SB students were valued at their school, and that they did not generally expect more from EB than from SB students. However, SB students were not as valued at some school sites as at others, and 90HI program teachers were more likely then other teachers to believe that their program was effective for EB and for SB students, and that it did not have a preference for EB students over SB students.

These are important findings, because they indicate that some DLE programs are operating without the absolutely essential core foundation of educational equity. This conclusion is bolstered by the teachers' strong agreement that they have *not* received enough training in how to treat students equitably. It is also consistent with the agreement by many teachers that they do not fully understand the DLE model that they are implementing at their school.

These results provide the basis for three recommendations that will be discussed further in Chapter 15:

- Program development that focuses on curriculum and second-language development, as well as on the cultural and linguistic needs of the student population.
- Training on how to treat all students equitably.
- Training on the theory and foundations underlying the DLE or TBE model.

There were no differences in any of the classroom-related attitudes for teachers in different programs. In general, teachers believed in some *balanced* competitive activities and structures in their classroom, as well as homogeneous grouping to a limited extent. The classroom environment was rated positively by all teachers, with most teachers in general to strong agreement that they used cooperative activities, gave students sufficient time to answer questions, and activities that allowed them to work together in pairs or groups. Teachers also felt that it was important to teach social skills and to encourage students to help each other. 90HI teachers were more likely to integrate a multicultural perspective, to report that their students were on task and that their students ask a lot of content-related questions.

In language-related attitudes and practices, teachers tended to strongly agree that their students could ask and answer questions in the other language (i.e. the language the teacher was not currently using). In addition, teachers felt that they addressed language errors and had established language objectives. Neither agreement nor disagreement was the general view on correction of grammatical pronunciation and written errors, though teachers tended to *disagree* that they *never* explained grammar. While language mixing is in theory strongly discouraged in DLE programs, there was no difference in the use of language mixing for 50:50 and TBE teachers. In contrast, 90:10 teachers believed fairly strongly, though not consistently strongly, that they did not use two languages to reinforce concepts.

In examining how efficacious the teachers felt they were in the classroom, overall teachers believed that they could help students improve, that their Spanish was of high enough proficiency to help students understand, and that they used feedback from students to adjust their teaching. They tended to feel that there were not sufficient bilingual teaching assistants or Spanish materials, and this was particularly true of TBE teachers. Enjoyment in teaching in the program was very high across all program sites and all school sites.

There was not much difference in how teachers rated ability, classroom environment, language instruction, and teaching efficacy according to the type of program they taught in. In teaching efficacy, teachers rated their ability to be a successful teacher somewhat differently depending on the school at which they were teaching, but not according to the program type. The major factor that influenced how teachers felt about their teaching efficacy, classroom environment and language instruction was the credential they possessed. Teachers with both a bilingual and an ESL credential had more positive ratings of language instruction, classroom environment, and teaching efficacy. This result is important in developing a successful program, because it demonstrates the significance of teachers understanding:

- Bilingual theory.
- Second language development and theory.
- Strategies in establishing a positive classroom environment with appropriate language strategies.

Furthermore, this result is consistent with the effective schools literature in demonstrating the importance of training to promote more successful teachers, classrooms, and students (Levine & Lezotte, 1995; Met & Lorenz, 1997).

Teacher satisfaction was rated medium to medium high. Teachers in 90HI programs were more satisfied than 90LO and TBE teachers. Enjoyment in teaching in the DLE/TBE program was rated higher than was satisfaction with the way the program was currently operating at their site. Thus, while teachers enjoyed teaching in the program, they did not necessarily like the way the program was implemented at their site.

In summarizing the relationships among all of these different factors, the first point is that the relationships were not the same for the DLE and TBE programs, though there was some overlap. In the DLE program, teacher satisfaction related to the support of the principal and parents, whether or not there was program planning, and the degree to which multicultural equity concerns were addressed at the school site. These results are consistent with previous studies which demonstrate the importance of principal and parent support and program planning in teachers' perceptions of satisfaction (Levine & Lezotte, 1995). Classroom instructional factors, or those factors over which the teacher had control, were not related to satisfaction. Thus, feeling efficacious and having an effective classroom did not make a teacher more satisfied. Rather, teachers were more satisfied when they felt that the school had a good program, met the needs of both groups of students, had good leadership, parent support, and staff involvement in program planning.

It is no surprise that program planning was associated with higher levels of principal support, teacher efficacy and satisfaction. Further, the extent to which a school was meeting the culturally and linguistically diverse student needs was related to almost all the other factors: principal, staff and parent support, program planning, teaching efficacy, classroom environment, language instruction and satisfaction. As stated previously, this multicultural equity concern is a central component of the DLE program. The extent to which it is carefully executed is associated with a whole variety of other factors at the school-site level and the classroom level. For teachers who are drawn to this model because of its educational equity component, satisfaction and teaching efficacy were clearly a product of how well this central core was implemented.

Teaching efficacy was also strongly associated with almost all the other variables, except for satisfaction and district support (and parent support for TBE programs). Whether a teacher felt efficacious or not did not affect his/her satisfaction with the way the model was implemented at the school site. However, teaching efficacy was related, though only moderately, to principal, staff and parent support. Thus, a teacher's perception of being effective and having sufficient resources is clearly affected by whether s/he felt that the principal understood the program and student needs and assured that staff did not complain about the program. However, program development and effective classroom strategies also affected the extent to which a teacher felt effective. These results are not surprising, as previous research on teacher efficacy and the effective schools literature both demonstrate that effective teachers have supportive leadership and staff, that there is program planning, attention to multicultural student needs, and a positive classroom environment (Darling-Hammond, 1995; Levine & Lezotte, 1995; Levine & Stark, 1981; Mortimore *et al.*, 1988; Rosenholtz, 1985; Stedman, 1987).

Maintaining a positive classroom environment was associated with principal support, parent support and multicultural equity concerns. Because the teacher expectation literature shows that students are more likely to thrive in a positive classroom environment (e.g. Brophy & Good, 1974; Darling-Hammond, 1995; Levine & Lezotte, 1995), the importance of principal and parent support in contributing to a healthy environment cannot be stressed enough. Further, particularly in a culturally and linguistically diverse model, the attention to the equality of student status and to meeting all students' needs is a critical component of a positive classroom environment.

These results have important implications for parent recruitment and training, program planning, and staff development. These implications will be discussed in Chapter 15.

Notes

1. Reliability coefficients of 0.7 or above are usually considered respectable, regardless of the type of reliability calculated or the method of calculation used (Morris *et al.*, 1987: 118).
2. In California, teachers can receive certification for training in second language development (originally referred to as ESL and then later changed to LDS, or Language Development Specialist). More recently, teachers are required to have a CLAD certificate, which necessitates course work in second language development and cultural diversity. Similarly, bilingual certification (now termed B-CLAD) requires course work in second language development, cultural diversity, and demonstrated oral and written proficiency in a second language. To obtain ESL, LDS, CLAD or B-CLAD certificates requires passing a test administered by the California Department of Education.
3. Statistical note: a nested schools-within-program-type analysis of variance demonstrated that the variation in scores was not due to program type, but rather to the variation across different schools within the program type, $F_{12, 95} = 5.0$, $p < 0.001$. Within three program types (90HI, 50:50, TBE), there were highly statistically significant differences across the school sites in their perception of district support.

Chapter 6

Teacher Talk in Dual Language Education Classrooms

Introduction and Rationale

There is a growing body of literature on teacher talk and classroom discourse. Studies that have investigated the interactive relationship between teacher talk and student responses have concluded that teachers significantly influence classroom discourse (Dillon, 1985; Poole, 1992; Rowe, 1986). However, only a few studies have addressed teacher talk and teacher–student interactions in bilingual, immersion classrooms or DLE classrooms (Duff, 1995; Freeman, 1998; Genesee, 1987; Harley, Allen *et al.*, 1990; Hornberger & Micheau, 1993; Lapkin *et al.*, 1990; McCollum, 1994; Moll & Diaz, 1985; Wong-Fillmore, 1985; Ramirez *et al.*, 1991; Swain & Carroll, 1987; Swain & Lapkin, 1986; Tarone & Swain, 1995). This chapter presents the results of two studies in DLE classrooms (discussed in Chapter 4) that examined teacher talk and teacher–student interactions. First, a brief overview of the literature will provide a context for understanding analyses and results. Teacher instructional language will be examined for the language of teaching, instructional types, and complexity of sentences. These results will be compared, where possible, to the instructional language that the teachers in Chapter 5 said they used.

Research on Teacher Talk

Considerable previous research has focused exclusively on teacher talk, rather than on teacher–student interactions. Most teacher-talk research has been directed at the type of questions that teachers put to students. Beginning with Bloom's (1956) taxonomy, researchers categorized questions according to their cognitive complexity and social utility. Literature reviews of classroom discourse studies in traditional English mainstream classes as well as in transitional bilingual, maintenance bilingual, and immersion classrooms demonstrate that teachers tend to ask largely factual recall questions, which are considered very low in cognitive complexity (Hargie, 1978; Lapkin *et al.*, 1990; Lindsay, 1990; Ramirez *et al.*, 1991). Rarely are students required to think about or to apply the information they are learning in class during teacher–student interactions.

Given the overwhelming representation of factual recall questions used by teachers, it is not surprising that most student responses to teachers consist of short answers to factual-recall questions regardless of the type of classroom in which they are instructed – bilingual, immersion, or English monolingual (Johnson, 1974; Lapkin *et al.*, 1990; Ramirez *et al.*, 1991; Swain & Lapkin, 1986).

The low cognitive level of student responses in bilingual classrooms has been attributed to many factors, such as language ability (Moll & Diaz, 1985), cultural differences (Heath, 1983), or even the pace of teacher talk (Rowe, 1986). Most researchers believe that teacher talk, particularly the frequency of factual-recall questions, is one of the most significant factors in students' extensive use of more passive-recall-type responses.

A three-year analysis of effective bilingual education classrooms by Wong-Fillmore (1985) determined that certain characteristics of teacher talk lead to more efficient learning of English by both Chinese and Latino elementary school students. After analyzing hours of videotaped lessons, Wong-Fillmore reported that the teachers whose students demonstrated higher levels of English proficiency shared several common instructional practices. These include: a clear separation of languages during instruction (no language mixing); an emphasis on communication and comprehension; grammatically appropriate forms of language; repeated use of dialogue patterns and participation routines; repetitiveness; tailoring of questions according to a student's level of language proficiency; and a richness of language (simple, but highly diverse). Wong-Fillmore discovered that effective bilingual teachers tailor their verbal interactions according to the level of each student`s language proficiency, a practice also advocated by Ramirez *et al.* (1991).

Other studies of monolingual English classrooms show that teachers also adjust their verbal interactions with students according to the subject matter. For example, Florio (1978) determined that an arts and crafts period was characterized by more polite requests than other periods. Cazden (1979) suggested that science provides a richer, more natural environment for second language vocabulary acquisition than does math owing to the highly specific and technical words used in mathematics.

While immersion researchers (e.g. Harley, 1984, 1989; Lapkin *et al.*, 1990; Lyster, 1987, 1990, 1994; Swain & Carroll, 1987; Swain & Lapkin, 1986; Tarone & Swain, 1995) would all appear to agree that effective immersion teachers adjust their speech to accommodate the language proficiency level of their students, they would also suggest that the instructional language that teachers use with their students lacks systematic variety in verb forms and grammatical complexity. Thus, immersion students are not provided with a rich enough variety to produce native-like speech in their second language, and end up using what has been termed 'immersion speak.' This 'immersion speak' has been blamed on a number of factors, but there has been too little study of teacher talk or teacher–student interactions in immersion classrooms (Salomone, 1992a,b) to help us understand what kind of input students receive in immersion classrooms. A few studies have examined strategies used in the immersion classroom (Salomone, 1992a,b), but mostly for linguistic error correction (Chaudron, 1983; Lapkin *et al.*, 1990; Salomone, 1992a,b).

Many researchers have begun to recommend research that examines the totality of teacher–student interactive discourse, rather than simply focusing on particular aspects of teacher talk such as questioning styles (Lindsay, 1990). Mehan (1978, 1979) and Cazden (1988) studied the structure of classroom discourse and remarked that most lessons consist of a three-part dialogue termed I-R-E: teacher Initiation, student Response, and teacher Evaluation of student answer. These typical three-part dialogues are in fact what make classroom discourse unique from normal face-to-face interactions. Teacher initiations frame information and cue learning, student responses should then demonstrate acquisition and mastery of new material and, finally, teacher-evaluation remarks serve to guide the direction and pace of the lesson.

Few studies have examined the teacher–student interactions within the classroom. Even fewer studies exist that investigate student responses, and many of these have been concerned with qualitatively determining whether minority students demonstrate specific discourse styles that are culturally distinguishable within the classroom (i.e. Heath, 1983; Phillips, 1983). Researchers in bilingual (Ramirez *et al.*, 1991) and immersion (e.g. Swain & Lapkin, 1986; Lapkin *et al.*, 1990) classrooms have reported that the majority of student responses to teachers are anticipated short answers to teachers' factual-recall questions. Students rarely ask a question of the teacher or comment on the teacher's statement. These results are consistent across program types, languages, and grade levels.

Teacher remarks that follow student responses have also rarely been systematically studied. Nonetheless, the interactive nature of classroom dialogue (i.e. how teachers ask questions, how students respond, how teachers react to student responses) has begun to be questioned by researchers who seek better methods of instruction (see Moll & Diaz, 1985; Tharp & Gallimore, 1988). Researchers, like many educators, continue to believe that teachers and students mutually shape learning through their discourse patterns.

The purpose of the first study was to examine the teacher talk and student responses in 90:10 DLE classrooms to examine:

- the types of teacher utterances that characterize a 90:10 DLE classroom;
- the extent and types of student responses to teacher utterances;
- the characteristics of the teacher responses given to student responses;
- whether these teacher and student responses varied by subject matter or grade level.

The major purpose of the second study was to examine the complexity of teacher and student utterances in 90:10 DLE classrooms during Spanish language arts instruction.

Study 1

Eleven teachers were observed in their 90:10 DLE classrooms during regular instruction. Eight of these teachers taught at the primary level (grades K–2) and three taught at the elementary level (grades 3–5). All of the teachers were highly proficient in English and Spanish, had appropriate teaching certification and possessed bilingual-teaching authorization. The amount of teaching experience varied from 3–17 years of classroom experience, with most of the experience gained in a bilingual classroom.

The Teacher–Student Observation Coding Form was a time-sampling observation instrument that I developed with Jorge Cuevas to code various characteristics of the teacher-centered instruction and teacher–student interaction. The time sampling was in one-minute intervals, and the unit of analysis was the first teacher utterance that was produced in the minute time sample, as long as it was not a response to a student utterance. Included in the unit of analysis was any student response to the teacher's utterance, in addition to the teacher's response, if there was one, to that student response. The coding system, shown in Table 6.1, characterized the *teacher's primary utterance* in terms of:

- Target (to whom the utterance was directed).
- Language, the language of the utterance (English, Spanish, mixed).
- Instructional type, or the purpose of the utterance (see Table 6.1 for categories).

In addition, if a student responded to the teacher's utterance, the *Student response* was coded for the following information:

- Type of response;
- Language (English, Spanish, mixed).

Finally, if the teacher responded to the student's response, then the *Teacher response* was coded according to the *Response type*. Also examined was any correction that the teacher made in reference to a pronunciation or grammatical error in the student's response of the student. More detailed definitions of the categories are presented in Table 6.1.

In addition, other aspects of the instructional context were also indexed in the coding system. The two areas that will be discussed are: *classroom arrangement* (whole-class instruction vs. group instruction) and *student engagement* – the extent to which students were engaged in the instruction, categorized as *low* (few students were on-task), *medium* (most students were on-task, but several were not paying attention and were distracting to others), or *high* (most or all students were on-task).

Reliability was established separately for each variable in the coding system. Though there was only one rater, I coded a sample of 100 utterances to compare with the rater's codes in order to establish reliability in the coding system. Percentage of agreement was used as the criterion of reliability. The percentage of agreement was high across the coding system, with a high of 100% (e.g. Language, response type) to a low of only 92% (e.g. Instructional type).

One trained bilingual observed each teacher for his/her instruction in mathematics, social studies, science, and language arts. Observations were conducted over a four-month period in the spring semester. Because of program design restrictions in the languages used to teach the subject matter at each grade level, a much greater percentage of observations were made during instruction in Spanish than in English. For later clarification, a tape recorder was used to record the interactions.

Findings

Instructional context

The first sets of analyses provided information on the instructional context. Overall, close to two thirds (61%) of the teacher utterances were provided during instruction directed at the whole class, with the remaining utterances (39%) occurring during group instruction. There was no difference in the ratio of whole-class to group instruction for primary (grade K–2) versus elementary (grades 3–5) grade levels (62:38 vs. 60:40, respectively).

Table 6.1 Coding categories for teacher utterances

Teacher utterances					Student responses		Teacher response
Context	Target	Language	Content	Instructional type	Type	Language	Type
Language Arts Social Studies Math Science	Whole class Individual student	Spanish English Mixed	**Subject matter** **Language:** formal instruction of language **Other:** rules, conventions	**Information presentation:** presents factual and procedural information, including definitions, contrasts, classifications; object, person, and historical descriptions **Modeling:** provides model concept and student is expected to imitate it **Relating:** requires student to use high level mental processes, such as explanations, inferences, interpretations, generalizations, reasoning, etc. **Problem solving:** provides student with framework/algorithm for understanding concepts or rules. Goal is to make student think about problem and to discover appropriate solution **Expansion:** elaboration of previous utterance, rephrasing or expanding to clarify or extend meaning **Directive:** directs student to pay attention or to engage or refrain from engaging in activity **Movitational communication:** serves to keep students participating in the ongoing task **Factual display, referential, or clarification question:** Bloom taxonomy, categories 1–3 **Higher order display question:** Bloom taxonomy, categories 4–6 **Other**	**Correct response to the question** **Incorrect response to the question** **Clarification question** **Higher order display question**	Spanish English Mixed	**Neutral feedback:** acknowledge student response **Correction:** corrects or expands on student's utterance or models correct response **Positive evaluation:** contains positive evaluation of or reinforces student's response **Positive evaluation and expansion:** positive evaluation and corrects or expands on response **Negative evaluation:** contains or implies negative evaluation or criticism **Negative evaluation and expansion:** negative evaluation and corrects response or expands on response **Other**

Level of student engagement, however, did vary by grade level. While a low level of student engagement was not observed at either grade level, students were more likely to demonstrate high rather than medium levels of engagement at the elementary level (78% high) than at the primary level (43% high).[1]

The subject areas during which the teachers were observed were concentrated in language arts (39%) and mathematics (29%), but also included science (17%), and social studies (14%).

Language characteristics of the teachers and students

The next set of analyses focused on the percentage of Spanish used by the teachers and the students according to grade level. At the primary grade level (K–2), 98% of the teacher utterances were in Spanish, while at the elementary grade level (grades 3–5), 57% of the teacher utterances were in Spanish. This difference in language use reflected the program design characteristics in which the majority of content instruction at the K–2 grade levels was in Spanish, while the distribution of English and Spanish was more equivalent at the elementary grade levels (3–5). More important, though, teachers never shifted languages (i.e. spoke in Spanish during English time, or in English during Spanish time) during content instruction, and they never mixed the languages at all.

Language choice of the students within the context of the teacher's language choice was examined next. That is, in what language did students respond when the teachers were using each language? When the teachers used Spanish, 92% of the students' responses were in Spanish. Of the 8% English responses, there was no difference in the percentage of English responses produced by primary as opposed to elementary students. When the teachers used English, though, only 78% of the students' responses were in English, but again, there was no difference in the percentage of English utterances produced by primary and elementary students. Overall, there was considerable matching of student language choice to teacher language choice.[2] That is, students used Spanish during Spanish time when the teacher used Spanish, and conversely, they responded in English when the teacher spoke in English.

Instructional types used by the teachers

Figure 6.1 presents the percentage of different instructional types produced by the teachers. Not surprisingly, the most common type (25%) of teacher utterance recorded was factual questions (e.g. *¿Cómo se llama esto?* [What's the name of this?] *¿Quién puede leer esta palabra?* [Who can read this word?]) . The number of motivational remarks observed almost equaled that of factual questions and accounted for 22% of all teacher utterances (e.g. Yes, you've got it! I can't believe you guys know these so well!). Information was presented in 20% of the utterances (e.g. Sky ends in 'y'), while higher-order questions were asked about 14% of the time (Okay, let's extend this discussion a little. With such a cold climate, limited transportation, and the kinds of tools they had, think about this, how would they support the needs of their community during the cold dark winter?). Though directives represented 8% of the utterances (e.g. I want you to get into groups now. Jaime, *siéntate* [Jaime, sit down]), all other categories each accounted for less than 4% of the total.

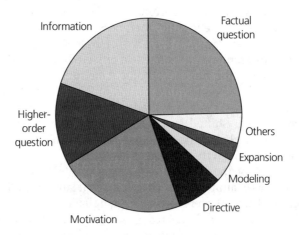

Figure 6.1 Instructional types

I was also interested in understanding whether these teacher instructional types varied according to grade level and subject matter. Teachers did not vary in their discourse directed at students according to grade level, but there was a relationship between subject matter and teacher talk type.[3] In Figure 6.2, instructional types are categorized by the different subject matters observed. When they were teaching *social studies*, teachers tended to use motivational remarks (32%), factual questions (23%), presentation of information (18%) and higher-order questions (13%). Social studies had by far the greatest percentage of expansion utterances (11%) and the smallest percentage of directives (3%). No modeling, relating or problem solving utterances were observed when social studies was taught.

During *language arts* instruction, there was a preponderance of factual questions (30%), motivational remarks (25%), information presentation

Table 6.2 Teacher utterances of each instructional type. Percentages categorized by subject matter

Instructional type	Total	Subject matter			
		Social studies	Language arts	Math	Science
Factual question	24.8	23	30	25	24
Higher order question	14.3	13	16	11	21
Motivational	22.0	32	25	19	20
Information presentation	19.7	18	23	22	15
Directive	7.7	3	4	15	9
Modeling	3.6	0	1	6	10
Expansion	2.8	11	1	2	1
Others	5.1	–	–	–	–

(23%), and higher order questions (16%). All the rest of the categories were rarely observed (< 2% each).

When *mathematics* was the subject of instruction, teacher utterances were also characterized by factual questions (25%), information presentation (22%), motivation (19%), higher-order questions (11%) and modeling (6%). Mathematics had by far the greatest percentage of directives (15%). The rest of the categories were rarely observed.

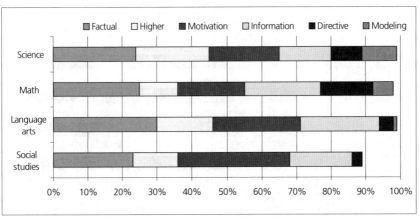

Figure 6.2 Instructional types categorized by subject matter

Table 6.3 Percentage of teacher utterances of each instructional type, categorized by grade level for mathematics and science

	Mathematics		Science	
	Primary	Elementary	Primary	Elementary
Factual question	23.7	25.9	26.7	22.0
Higher-order question	11.8	9.3	26.7	18.0
Motivational	27.6	5.6	6.7	28.0
Information presentation	13.2	35.2	23.3	10.0
Directive	13.2	18.5	13.3	6.0
Modeling	7.9	3.7	0.0	16.0
Expansion	2.6	1.9	3.3	0.0

When teaching *science*, teachers produced the highest percentage of higher-order questions (21%), the highest percentage of modeling (10%), and the lowest percentage of information presentation (15%). Like the other subject areas, science was also characterized by a large number of factual questions (24%) and motivational remarks (20%). Directives were also fairly frequently used (9%). The rest of the categories were rarely observed (< 1%).

The two subject areas of science and mathematics were examined further to determine whether teacher instructional types varied by grade

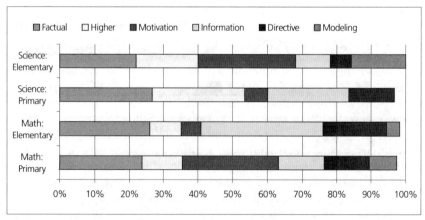

Figure 6.3 Instructional types used in science and math by grade level

level. Figure 6.3 presents the percentage of instructional types by grade level for science and mathematics. It shows that teachers used different instructional types for the primary and elementary grades when teaching mathematics[4] and science[5]. In teaching mathematics to elementary versus primary students, teachers tended to use considerably more information presentation, 35% (elementary) vs. 13% (primary), and much less motivation with elementary students as compared to primary students, 6% (elementary) vs. 28% (primary). However, these trends were reversed when teachers were instructing in science: primary students received more information presentation (23% vs. 10% for elementary) and elementary students received more motivation (28% vs. 7% for primary). Surprisingly, teachers used more higher-order questions with primary students than with elementary students (27% vs. 18%).

Student responses

Interesting findings emerged in terms of student-response characteristics. First, about 57% of the teachers' utterances received a response. Second, most (87%) of the students' responses to the teacher were correct, regardless of the teacher's utterance type. The few incorrect responses were more likely to be produced in response to factual and higher-order questions than to other teacher instructional types.

Of all the questions asked by teachers and responded to by students, 63% were lower-order factual-recall questions, while 37% were higher-order questions. The probability of a correct student response was not associated with the type of question. Students responded correctly 85% of the time when asked a lower-order question, and 83% of the time when asked higher-order questions.

The percentage of student responses answered correctly was also analyzed according to student language choice. It should be noted that 80% of all student answers, whether correct or incorrect, were produced in Spanish. When speaking Spanish, students made correct responses 80% of the time. Of the limited number of responses produced in English, students made correct responses 97% of the time.

Students tended to respond correctly across all subject areas, with more than 64% correct responses in each subject area. Students were more likely to produce an *incorrect* response during mathematics (25%) and science (15%) than during social studies or reading/language arts (< 5% each). Students were also more likely to ask a clarification question during social studies (23%) than during any other subject areas (< 7%). Higher-order questions were almost never produced by students during instruction time (1% during reading, 0% for the rest).

The teacher–student exchanges were examined to determine the most common teacher–student exchanges. About 88% of the teacher–student interactions could be characterized as:

- Teacher factual question – Student correct response (35%)[6]

  Teacher: How do you spell COW?
  Student: C-O-W.

  Teacher: What is the diameter of circle A?
  Student: Six.

- Teacher higher-order question – Student correct response (20%)

  Teacher: We know that these are all triangles, so what do you think is the definition of a triangle?
  Student: A figure that has 3 sides and 3 angles?

- Teacher motivation – Student correct response (12%)

  Teacher: Come on, I know you know the answer to this.
  Student: Is it 90?

- Teacher information – Student correct response (11%)

  Teacher: This is the diameter of the circle.
  Student: So, the diameter is 8.

- Teacher factual question – Student incorrect response (6%)

  Teacher: What is the capital of California?
  Student: San Francisco.

- Teacher higher-order question – Student incorrect response (4%)

These patterns did not vary by subject matter or grade level.

Teacher responses to student responses

One final set of analyses examined the types of response teachers gave to student responses. Overall, teachers responded to 85% of student responses. Teacher responses to student responses did not vary by grade level. However, teacher responses differed according to subject matter.[7] When teachers responded to students, they were more likely to give feedback, particularly during reading/language arts (54%) and science instruction (50%) than during social studies or mathematics instruction (35% each). Correction by teachers was more likely during mathematics (33%) than during any of the other subjects (all between 11–14%). By far the greatest percentage of simple positive evaluations occurred during reading/

language arts (27%, with all the rest < 19%), but social studies (21%) and science (17%) were characterized by more instances of positive evaluations plus expansion by the teacher. Teachers were more likely to use feedback when the student produced a correct response to a factual or a higher-order question (51% and 22% of all feedback responses, respectively). Thus, close to three fourths of all feedback responses from the teachers were produced in response to one of these two types of teacher–student exchanges. Much less frequent was teacher feedback when students responded correctly to teacher information or to teacher motivation utterances (7% and 8% of feedback responses, respectively).

Similarly, positive evaluation responses were most frequent when students produced correct responses to factual questions (38% of total positive evaluation responses), higher-order questions (33%), and motivational teacher utterances (14%). Teacher corrections were more frequently made when students produced an incorrect response to a factual question or to a higher-order question (29% and 17% of total corrections, respectively).

A second study was conducted to examine the complexity of teacher utterances during Spanish language arts instruction.

Study 2

Two DLE classrooms, one third-grade and one fourth-grade, were observed for the teachers' verb forms and utterance complexity. The classrooms were observed and taped for varying periods of time during the Spanish portion of the instructional day. Each observation and taping ranged in length from one and a half hours to three hours, and each teacher was observed four times by the same observer. Most observations occurred during language arts or integrated language arts/social studies.

Six 10-minute segments, accounting for 60 minutes, were transcribed from the four observations conducted with each teacher, giving a total of 120 minutes for the two teachers. Segments were chosen for the clarity of student and teacher speech, continuity of the teaching activity, and preponderance of discourse. A total of 918 utterances from the two teachers (43% from the third-grade teacher and 57% from the fourth-grade teacher) were used for analysis. Utterances were defined and coded according to:

- *target* (to whom the utterance was addressed);
- *language* (Spanish, English, mixed),
- *verb form* (present, preterit, imperfect, past subjective, conditional, imperative, multi-word, *'vamos a'* [we're going to],
- *utterance complexity* (1–2 words, short sentence or phrase, complex utterance with 1 or more clauses).

Findings

Consistent with Study 1, teachers spoke only in the target language, with 100% of their utterances in Spanish, and no mixed utterances.

Figure 6.4 presents the percentages reflecting the complexity of the utterances according to the utterance target (whole class or individual student). With respect to the complexity of the utterance, 38% were 1–2 word utterances, 43% were short sentences or phrases, and 19% were complex utterances with 1 or more clauses. The complexity of utterance varied according to the target. If the target was the whole class, then there were twice as many complex utterances, more short utterances, and almost half as many 1–2 word utterances as when the target was an individual student.[8]

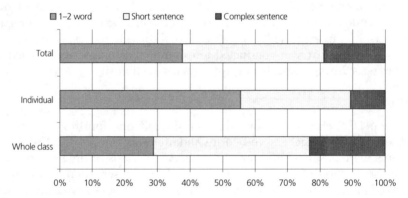

Figure 6.4 Sentence complexity by target

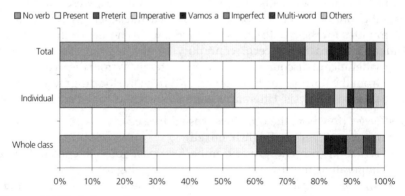

Figure 6.5 Verb forms by target

The verb form of the utterance was also examined. As Figure 6.5 shows, teachers used no verb in 34% of their utterances, present tense 31% of the time, preterit 11%, imperative 7%, *'vamos a'* [we are going to], which can imply future tense) 6%, and imperfect 5%. Other verb forms, such as past subjective, conditional, and multi-word forms were used infrequently (1–3% each). Thus, 65% of the utterances were in the present tense or contained no verb, and 82% were in the present tense, past tense (preterit, imperfect, or past subjunctive) or contained no verb.

Verb forms varied depending on whether the teacher was speaking to the whole class or to an individual student.[9] Present tense and imperative verbs were almost twice as likely to be used with the whole class (35% and 9%) than with an individual student (22% and 4%). Utterances with no verb were much more frequent with individual students (54%) compared with the whole class (26%).

The complexity of the utterance was associated with the verb form.[10]

Table 6.4 Teacher utterances of different complexity and verb forms. Percentages categorized by target

	Whole class	*Individual*	*Total*
Complexity* (*see Figure 6.4*)			
1–2 word	29	55	38
Short sentence	48	34	43
Complex sentence	23	11	19
Verb form* (*see Figure 6.5*)			
No verb	26	54	34
Present	35	22	31
Preterit	12	9	11
Imperative	9	4	7
Vamos + a (we're going to)	7	2	6
Imperfect	5	4	5
Multi-word	4	2	3
Past subjunctive	2	1	1
Conditional	1	2	1

*** $p < 0.001$

About one third (35%) of all the teachers' utterances consisted of 1–2 words and contained no verb. Most of these forms were used to motivate or acknowledge students' work or response ('Very good', 'That's right', 'Not quite'), to request students to do something ('Again' [repeat after me]), to determine whether students had questions ('Any questions?' 'Understand?'), or to follow up a previous utterance with a question ('Why?' 'How?' 'Where?' 'Any ideas?'). Thus, these forms were typically used to follow up on previous utterances, to give students more time to think, to call on students, or to praise or acknowledge students.

More complex utterances with at least one clause occurred most frequently in present-tense verb forms (45% of complex structures were produced with present-tense verbs), preterit forms (16% of complex structures), multi-word, imperative and *'vamos a'* [we are going to] forms (6–11% each of complex structures).

Conclusions and Implications

These studies examined the teacher talk and teacher–student interaction patterns at two 90HI DLE sites. One important observation was that the teachers did not mix the two languages at all, and students typically responded to the teacher in the language that the teacher used with them. This pattern ensued among both the primary and elementary students. Language matching also occurred more frequently in Spanish than in English. In the DLE model, language mixing was discouraged in order to maintain the separation of the two languages. These results are consistent with what the teachers reported in 90HI programs in the previous chapter; where we saw that 90HI teachers did not use the two languages to reinforce concepts. The findings are also encouraging in demonstrating that students were responsive to the language of the classroom and attempted to respond in the language appropriate to the task. Further, almost all responses were accurate in English, though students were able to respond correctly regardless of the language of instruction. In Chapter 5, we saw that teachers believed that they accepted all attempts at communication and responded to utterances in the other language. The results presented here are consistent with these teacher beliefs, as students did sometimes answer in the other language, and the teacher did reply to those utterances.

In looking at teacher responses to student responses, the findings showed that teachers rarely corrected students and they almost never corrected language characteristics, but rather focused on content. This was precisely what teachers stated in their ratings to questions of whether they correct grammar or pronunciation (see Chapter 5). Thus teacher reports of their language-related practices were consistent with the observations that little correction occurred with respect to student language errors. However, while teachers did not directly correct an utterance that was incorrectly formed, many classroom observations have shown that the DLE teachers often modeled the correct utterance without overtly saying it was wrong. This absence of direct correction is consistent both with advice given to immersion teachers (Krashen, 1981; Snow, 1990) and with other observations in immersion classrooms as diverse as English immersion in Hungary and French immersion in Canada (Duff, 1995; Lapkin *et al.*, 1990; Salomone, 1992a, b; Swain & Carroll, 1987).

Not surprisingly, this study has corroborated the frequently-reported result that teachers ask many more factual-recall questions than higher-order questions. Out of all the hours of instruction recorded, 64% of the questions asked were lower order and 36% were higher order. Based on research in structured English immersion, early-exit and late-exit bilingual programs (Ramirez *et al.*, 1991) and immersion programs (Lapkin *et al.*, 1990; Swain & Lapkin, 1986), findings have consistently shown that this type of learning environment is less than optimal for developing oral language skills or higher levels of academic and cognitive skills. Students rarely had opportunities to actually produce language with the teacher and, when they did, the language they produced was limited to short, simplistic, factual-recall responses. However, keep in mind that, within the DLE classrooms observed for this study, students spent a great deal of time working cooperatively in heterogeneous groups apart from the teacher, where discourse patterns may vary from those of teacher-centered lessons. Some immersion teachers believe that groups do not provide good opportunities for students to learn language because students make so many language errors (see Salomone, 1992a). The advantage of the DLE program is that when groups are formed there is always a native speaker of each language to serve as a good language model. Therefore, there should be more opportunities for students to produce longer and more complex utterances in their second language.

In regard to the student responses to teacher questions, it is imperative to note that students were no more likely to incorrectly answer a higher-order question than a lower-order one. Students responded with practically equal accuracy regardless of the cognitive difficulty of the question. A pedagogical implication of this finding is that teachers should not be reluctant to ask higher-order questions in the assumption that children would be more likely to respond incorrectly or to have more difficulty in answering higher-order than factual-recall questions. Further, teachers need training in how to ask higher-order, or more cognitively challenging, questions that require students to produce longer and more complex responses.

Results also showed that students produced a response to about half of the teacher utterances. Almost all of these student responses were the result of a teacher-directed question. Rarely did students ask teachers a clarification question and, even more infrequently, a higher-order question. These results are consistent with other studies suggesting that students are rather passive participants in the classroom (e.g. Ramirez *et al.*, 1991; Swain & Lapkin, 1986; Tikunoff *et al.*, 1980). Studies in bilingual (Ramirez *et al.*, 1991) and immersion (Tarone & Swain, 1995) classrooms and contexts (Liu, 1999) have shown that students rarely initiate a conversation with the teacher, and this lack of initiation increases with grade level. Students in *some* classrooms may also learn that their questions are not welcome when teachers tell students to stop asking so many questions. *Some* teachers also socialize children not to ask higher-order questions because they are afraid they will not know how to answer such questions.

Another observation verified by this study is that teachers adjusted their speech according to the subject area being taught. Cazden (1979) pointed out that science and mathematics provide different opportunities for learning. At the elementary school level, science was characterized by active participation where talk was necessary during data collection, laboratory investigation, and interpretation of the results, whereas mathematics was often a silent and solitary activity. Science, therefore, enabled more of an occasion for verbal interaction. Indeed, science lessons observed for this study produced higher levels of teacher modeling and higher-order questioning, whereas mathematics lessons yielded more directives and information presentation. Swain and her colleagues (Lapkin *et al.*, 1990; Swain & Carroll, 1987) have also pointed out that different subject areas provide distinct opportunities for a greater variety of verb forms and grammatical structures.

Study 2 results suggest that, in the two third- and fourth-grade classrooms with teachers who rated themselves as highly proficient in Spanish, there was some variety in verb forms and in complexity. Overall, while 37% were simplistic utterances (1–2 words with no verbs), 21% of the utterances were more complex (contained at least one clause). In some respects, these results are consistent with Swain and Lapkin (1986), who point out that a limited variety of verb forms is used in immersion classrooms, which restricts opportunities for students to learn how to use the language as native speakers. On the other hand, the results of study 1 indicate that the teacher utterances were similar in function to the teacher utterances in English-only classrooms. Thus, these teachers may be teaching content as they would in any classroom, and they have provided students with the basic academic and cognitive skills. However, as in most monolingual classrooms, the cognitive complexity could certainly be higher. In addition, the DLE teachers are following the advice of the acknowledged experts in the field (e.g. Krashen, 1981) not to teach grammar.

The results of this study concur with the results of other immersion studies that teachers need to learn how to integrate direct instruction of language structure into their classroom teaching so that students will hear a variety of verb forms and complex structures in their teachers' speech. Such advice is clearly consistent with immersion researchers and practitioners, particularly Day and Shapson (1996), Lyster (1987, 1990, 1994), and Swain (Lapkin *et al.*, 1990; Tarone & Swain, 1995), who advocate *integrating* the teaching of language structure with content in a meaningful context. Teachers must be trained in how to implement a 'linguistic syllabus' (Lyster, 1987), which consists of a systematic and graded presentation of grammar. Lyster (1987) also points out that the development of the linguistic syllabus would not be the responsibility of individual teachers, but rather would be the domain of the school board, or those who plan the immersion curriculum. Lyster (1990, 1994) and Day and Shapson (1996) have provided excellent frameworks for understanding analytic language teaching and for incorporating such teaching in an immersion classroom at the secondary level.

It is important that teachers and educators understand that these observations are not criticisms of their teaching. DLE teachers are already working hard to provide, to students with a diverse array of skill levels, the same curriculum and critical thinking skills that most monolingual teachers provide. In addition, they must balance the language needs of the two groups of students, providing challenging language input to L1 speakers and comprehensible input for L2 speakers, also recognizing that some L2 learners advance quickly and some slowly.

Thus, these teachers have a number of content- and language-related demands that go beyond traditional monolingual classroom teaching, bilingual teaching, or even immersion teaching where the students comprise slightly less heterogeneity than in DLE classrooms. Rather, these teachers need administrators, curriculum specialists, linguists and those trained in the pertinent bilingual, immersion or DLE model to develop the appropriate linguistic syllabus that is articulated across grade levels.

Notes

1. $\chi^2_2 (556) = 66.1, p < 0.001$.
2. $\chi^2_2 (244) = 103.2, p < 0.001$.
3. $\chi^2 (455) = 59.9, p < 0.001$.
4. $\chi^2 (130) = 17.0, p < 0.01$.
5. $\chi^2 (80) = 14.9, p < 0.01$.
6. Percentage refers to the percentage of total teacher–student exchanges that followed the described pattern.
7. $\chi^2 (244) = 41.7, p < 0.001$.
8. This relationship between target and complexity was highly significant, $\chi^2 (2) = 58.1, p < 0.0001$.
9. $\chi^2 (8) = 76.4, p < 0.0001$.
10. $\chi^2 (16) = 622.3, p < 0.0001$.

Parent Involvement, Attitudes and Satisfaction in Dual Language Education Programs

Introduction and Rationale

Considerable research has examined student performance or teacher attitudes in language education programs. However, relatively few studies have explored the parents of these children to determine their backgrounds, involvement, attitudes toward bilingualism, reasons for enrolling their child in a bilingual program, or satisfaction with the language education program in which their child is enrolled. Furthermore, because language minority and language majority students are not typically involved in a bilingual program that promotes bilingualism for both groups of students, no studies have examined whether these language minority and language majority parents who are participants in the same language education program differ in their involvement, attitudes, satisfaction and reasons for enrolling their child. The purpose of this chapter is to fill these gaps by discussing two studies that examine:

- Parents' second language and educational background.
- Parent involvement and attitudes toward involvement.
- Parent attitudes toward bilingualism and the language education program.
- Why parents enroll their child in a DLE program.
- Parent satisfaction with the DLE program.
- Whether parents' involvement, attitudes, and satisfaction differ according to the ethnicity, education, and language background of the parents, or according to the school demographic characteristics of the school.

Parental Involvement

Research has consistently demonstrated the importance of responsive and involved parents in the cognitive, language and socio-emotional development of children and adolescents (e.g. Maccoby & Martin, 1993).

Thus, it is not surprising that educational research also invariably shows that children benefit significantly when their parents are supportive of and involved in their education (Bermúdez & Márquez, 1996; Hidalgo, Siu *et al.*, 1995; Levine & Lezotte, 1995), and that schools should promote parents' involvement in education, and have high levels of home-school cooperation (Ascher & Flaxman, 1987; Chrispeels, 1992; Henderson, 1987; Levine & Lezotte, 1995). Research clearly shows that parents who take an active interest in their child's school activities and participate in school-related events facilitate:

- Academic achievement in their children (Bermúdez & Márquez, 1996; Hidalgo *et al.*, 1995; Levine & Lezotte, 1995; Mortimore *et al.*, 1988; Ramirez *et al.*, 1991; Slaughter-DeFoe, 1991; Snow *et al.*, 1991).
- Second-language proficiency in their children (Bermúdez & Padrón, 1990; Lindholm & Padilla, 1990; Padilla & Sung, 1995).
- More positive parent–child interactions (Henderson, 1989).
- Improved home–school relations (Bermúdez & Padrón, 1987; Bright, 1992; Herman & Yeh, 1980; Hidalgo *et al.*, 1995; Met, 1987).

In a comprehensive review of parental involvement in Puerto Rican American, Chinese American, African American and Irish American families, Hidalgo *et al.*, (1995) noted that:

> Studies are accumulating that show that family practices concerning children's education are more important for helping students succeed in school and in general than are family structure, economic status, or characteristics such as race, parent education, family size and age of child … The more schools do to involve families, the less parent behavior or student success can be explained by status variables. (p. 499)

While some research studies on school effectiveness have not found a relationship between parent involvement and effectiveness, many other studies comparing schools designated as more effective with those categorized as less effective have found that parental involvement is clearly linked to effectiveness (Levine & Lezotte, 1995).

Defining parental involvement

Reviews of literature point out that parental involvement is a complex variable to interpret and assess (Bermúdez & Márquez, 1996; Levine & Lezotte, 1995; Moran & Hakuta, 1995). In the school effectiveness literature, Levine and Lezotte (1995: 530) point out that: 'parent involvement has been a difficult variable to assess or identify as an effectiveness correlate, and that there are many forms and varieties of involvement, which make it difficult to define or measure.'

According to Levine & Lezotte (1995), some of the types of parental involvement that have been associated with effective schools include:

- Wielding pressure on public officials to procure resources.
- Participating in school meetings to make decisions regarding curriculum and school personnel.
- Participating in building-level governance and management decisions.
- Sitting in classrooms to monitor teacher performance.
- Assisting children in using library resources.

Parental involvement has also been discussed with respect to:

- Assisting teachers in and out of the classroom.
- Participating in planning and implementing school-related activities.
- Attending school-related events and activities.
- Attending workshops for parents (e.g. mathematics, literacy, technology, language instruction, childrearing).
- Helping children with homework or school-related projects.
- Encouraging and expecting children to do well in school.

Parent background issues influencing parental involvement

Clear differences in parental background distinguish various levels of parental involvement. One important factor is socioeconomic status (SES), or particularly the parents' level of formal education (Hidalgo *et al.*, 1995; Levine & Lezotte, 1995; Slaughter De-Foe, 1991). As Levine and Lezotte (1995: 530) note: 'involvement is so highly correlated with SES that controlling for SES in regression studies frequently eliminates its relationships with achievement.' Despite the correlation with SES, studies of low-income ethnic minority and language minority families show the beneficial effects of parent involvement on children's achievement (Bright, 1992; Cazden, 1992; Hidalgo *et al.*, 1995; Lucas *et al.*, 1990; Moran & Hakuta, 1995; Slaughter De-Foe, 1991; Snow *et al.*, 1991).

Considerable research demonstrates the importance of parent involvement on successful outcomes with language minority students (Bermúdez & Márquez, 1996; Cazden, 1992; Lucas *et al.*, 1990; Moll, 1992; Moran & Hakuta, 1995; Ramirez *et al.*, 1991; Snow *et al.*, 1991). Parents in late-exit bilingual programs tend to be more highly involved than parents in early-exit or ESL programs (Cazden, 1992; Ramirez *et al.*, 1991). According to Moran and Hakuta (1995: 456), 'exactly what kinds of parental involvement and what parental behaviors benefit minority-language students learning is another area for further study.'

Parents whose children are enrolled in immersion programs tend to have high levels of involvement (Cloud *et al.*, 2000). In fact, these parents have organized large parent organizations to support language immersion and language enrichment for their children. One such organization in the US is Advocates for Language Learning (ALL). This organization holds an annual conference, and has chapters in many communities where immersion or elementary-level foreign language programs exist.

These results are collectively important because they illustrate the importance of parental involvement in promoting children's academic achievement. This relationship holds regardless of factors such as:

- economic background;
- ethnicity;
- language background;
- family immigrant or native-born status.

While parental involvement may clearly benefit students, many parents experience barriers that prevent their active involvement. It is to this topic that we now turn.

Barriers to parental involvement

For minority families, barriers to parental involvement include: a sense of alienation, distrust, and for some parents, a perception that their low educational skills are not sufficient for them to assist in the classroom (Carrasquillo & Carrasquillo, 1979; Comer, 1986; Hidalgo *et al.*, 1995; Kozol, 1991; Ogbu, 1987; Petersen & Warnsby, 1992). Many language minority (e.g. Portuguese-, Spanish-, Yiddish-speaking) parents feel they lack appropriate English language skills to help their children or to assist in the classroom (e.g. Bermúdez & Márquez, 1996; Brisk, 1998; Dash Moore, 1981; Olneck, 1995). Further, many ethnic minority and low-income parents do not understand the school system, and do not recognize that parents' views are considered in decision-making at the school board, district and school level (Au, 1993). Also, many linguistically and culturally diverse parents have felt discriminated against by school personnel (García, 1990; Kozol, 1991). As Ortiz and Yates (1989: 187) have pointed out: 'School personnel commonly complain that parents of minority children do not care about their child and fail to take an interest in them ...are not involved, supportive, or helpful to the school or education professional.' These staff attitudes reflect the commonly-held societal perspective that low income, minority, and language minority parents do not care about the education of their children, despite research which demonstrates that such parents want their child to succeed in school, understand the importance of school, and support their children's school experience (Bermúdez & Márquez, 1996; Hidalgo *et al.*, 1995; Stevenson *et al.*, 1990).

Because there are distinct SES differences in the participation of parents in school monitoring and decision-making activities (Levine & Lezotte, 1995), and because of the barriers perceived by many low-SES language minority and ethnic minority parents, it is important to examine whether language minority parents feel as important as language majority parents do, and whether they participate in the education of their children.

Attitudes Toward Bilingualism and Language Education

Several studies have been conducted to assess parent or community attitudes toward bilingualism and bilingual education (Aguirre, 1984; Cazabon *et al.*, 1993; Edwards, 1977; Gribbons & Shin, 1996; Lambert, 1987; Lambert & Taylor, 1990; Ramirez *et al.*, 1991; Santos, 1985; Williams & Snipper, 1990; Torres, 1988; Youssef & Simpkins, 1985). A number of these studies conducted with language minority Mexican, Puerto Rican, and Arabic parents in various parts of the US have shown that these parents express positive attitudes toward bilingual education and believe that bilingualism is important.

Lambert and Taylor (Lambert, 1987; Lambert & Taylor, 1990: 540) conducted a community-based study on the attitudes of US working-class parents toward ethnic diversity and intergroup relations. The importance of this study of different ethnic groups (Polish, Arabic, Albanian, Mexican, Puerto Rican, European American, and African American) was in showing that:

- All but European working-class parents favored multiculturalism (groups should maintain cultural heritage as much as possible) over assimilation (ethnic, racial or cultural minorities should give up heritage culture and take on the American way of life) as the best strategy for America. Thus, these individuals clearly want the opportunities for themselves and their children to become bilingual and bicultural rather than lose their language and culture.
- Working-class African American and middle-class European American parents supported cultural heritage over assimilation as long as the language was not used in public settings outside the home and community.
- The working-class European Americans were the only group that rejected multiculturalism and expressed 'negative, racist attitudes toward other ethnic and racial groups' (p. 540).

- All parents, both ethnic minority and European American, saw advantages in bilingualism: 'The outcome was unanimous that being bilingual would mean not only better school performance for their children and a deeper sense of pride, but also more success in future careers in the world of work. Even the ethnocentric working-class White parents saw these advantages for their own children, although they did not believe ethnic minority children should become bilingual or bicultural' (p. 540).

Using the same data collection procedures with parents in a DLE program, Cazabon *et al.* (1993) compared parents in a DLE program with those in a non-DLE program. They found that:

- Parents of kindergartners through second graders enrolled in a DLE program, and English-speaking parents whose children were not in a DLE program, mostly agreed that requiring ethnic minority parents to relinquish their heritage cultural values and language 'would not necessarily disunify the nation' (1993: 9).
- Both DLE and non-DLE parents also agreed that 'heritage cultural abandonment would be a loss to the nation' (1993: 9).
- Both DLE and non-DLE parents were concerned that cultural maintenance could hamper communication and a common understanding.
- Both DLE and non-DLE parents were favorable to multicultural heritage maintenance in their agreement that 'a nation profits from a diversity of cultural and racial resources' (1993: 9).

These results are important because they provide information relating to the context of community attitudes surrounding language-education programs in the US, particularly those that support the maintenance of ethnic language and culture. These studies show that communities vary in their attitudes toward bilingualism and bilingual education, with middle-class and minority parents expressing more positive attitudes toward ethnic heritage cultural and language maintenance, and ethnic-heritage parents expressing the most positive attitudes toward keeping their language and culture.

Gardner (1985) considered the role of parents in the development of children's second language. While noting the lack of information available about the role of parents, he went on to suggest that parents can be classified as active or passive in facilitating their children's development of a second language. He concluded that parents who provide a warm and supportive environment that supports the development of an integrative motivational orientation (motivation to learn a second language in order to socially engage or integrate with people of another group) will lead to higher levels of second language development. However, Gardner's work is also important in demonstrating two major motivational orientations that inspire students to learn a second language: (1) *integrative*, as defined previously, and (2) *instrumental*, in which the learner sees some academic, intellectual or career gain in becoming proficient in the second language.

Only a few studies have examined parental attitudes toward the language education of their children (Choy, 1993; Kim, 1992; Padilla & Sung, 1995; Samimy & Tabuse, 1992; Yagi, 1991). Padilla and Sung (1995) assessed parental involvement and attitudes toward second language learning in their elementary and secondary-level students studying Chinese, Japanese or Korean. Their findings showed the importance of parental involvement in several different ways:

- Parents of elementary students (grades K–6) were more involved and had more positive attitudes toward foreign language learning than parents of secondary students (grades 9–12).
- Parents whose children were studying their ethnic heritage language had higher levels of involvement, regardless of the grade level.
- Parent involvement, especially by ethnic heritage parents, was associated with student interest in learning their ancestral language.

Reasons for enrolling child in a language education program

In examining why parents living in Wales placed their English-speaking child in a bilingual Welsh-dominant school, Bush (1983, cited in Torres, 1988) extended Gardner's (1985) concept of integrative and instrumental motivational orientation to learn a second language from the students to parents. Results suggested that most parents showed a high degree of integrative motivation in expressions of positive attitudes toward the Welsh language and Welsh speakers. Correspondingly, Torres (1988) found that Chicano parents communicated strong integrative motivation in placing their child in bilingual education classes, but also instrumental motivation in recognizing the value of bilingualism in their child's further education and career. Padilla and Sung (1995) discovered, as discussed in the previous section, that Chinese, Korean and Japanese parents displayed what might be called integrative motivational orientations in promoting their children's learning of their heritage language. Thus, regardless of the ethnic/language background of the parents, heritage language parents consistently demonstrate stronger integrative, and secondarily instrumental, orientations in promoting the development of the heritage language in their children.

The remainder of this chapter will describe two studies that examine four major questions:

- What are parents' levels of involvement and satisfaction with the DLE program?
- What are parents' attitudes toward bilingualism, the DLE program, and the multicultural atmosphere of the school?
- Do parents' involvement, attitudes, and satisfaction differ according to their ethnicity, language background, educational background, grade level of child enrolled, or type of school (90HI, 90LO)?
- Do Hispanic and European American parents differ in their motivational orientations (instrumental vs. integrative) for enrolling their child in the DLE program?

Data Collection

Questionnaire

All parents in the study completed a questionnaire (see Appendix) that consisted of two sections. The first section comprised questions regarding background information about the parents' ethnicity, language background, educational background, ability to communicate in Spanish/English, and experiences in studying Spanish/English. The second section contained items that asked parents about their involvement and attitudes toward the DLE program and bilingualism. These items were rated on a five-point Likert scale ranging from 1 (strongly disagree) to 5 (strongly agree). Because the first questionnaire focused on parental involvement and the second on reasons for enrolling the child, the questionnaires in Studies 1 and 2 varied somewhat.

Description of Parents

Study 1

A total of 201 parents, representing one 90HI elementary school, participated in the first study.[1] The 201 responses from a total of 272 parents who were sent questionnaires yielded a response rate of 84%.

Most of the parent respondents (146, or 83%) were mothers, while 17% were fathers. There was an important and significant difference in their level of education; slightly less than half of the mothers had a high school diploma or less education, compared with only one quarter of the fathers. Conversely, three quarters of the fathers had at least some college/vocational school; while about half of the mothers had such training.

In looking at the number of children that parents had enrolled in the DLE program:

- 60% had one child.
- 26% had two children.
- 9% had three children.
- 5% had four children.

The representation of the grade levels, including parents with children at different grade levels in the DLE program, was as follows:

- Parents with only kindergartners: 12%.
- Kindergartner and first/second (first or second) grader: 4%.
- Kindergartner and older child in grades 3–8: 9%.
- Only first/second graders: 28%.
- First/second grader and older child: 16%.
- Only third or fourth or fifth grader: 19%.
- Third/fourth/fifth grader and sixth/seventh/eighth grader: 6%.
- Only sixth/seventh/eighth grader: 6%.

Children's grade levels were collapsed and recategorized as

- *Kindergarten only* (parents were experiencing their first year of a DLE program).
- *Grades K–2* (parents with a first or second grader, and possibly a kindergartner as well, prior to English reading instruction).
- *Grades 3–5* only (after beginning English reading instruction, but prior to mastery of English reading).
- *Older* (parents with students in grades 6–8 who may also have students in earlier grade levels, i.e. full experience of elementary program and the skills it developed in students).

Ethnic and educational background of parents

Parents varied with respect to ethnic background (58% Hispanic, 27% European American, 15% other groups or unknown).[2] Parents were categorized into four ethnic/language groups based on their ethnicity and language background. Parents were classified as *EURO* if they were of European background and *Hispanic* if they identified as Hispanic. Then Hispanic parents were further distinguished according to their self-rated proficiency in English: as monolingual English speakers, monolingual Spanish speakers, or bilingual Spanish/English speakers:

- Euro American (EURO) parents: 32%.
- Hispanic-English speakers (Hisp-EB): 15%.

- Hispanic-Bilinguals (Hisp-Bil): 34%.
- Hispanic-Spanish speakers (Hisp-SP): 19%.

Parents varied considerably across these ethnic/language groups in terms of their educational background. Figure 7.1 presents the level of education for the parents in each group. As this figure shows, three quarters or more of the EURO (82%) and Hisp-Bil (74%) parents had a college education (on the graph, note that college education would include university/professional and community college), while half (58%) of Hisp-EB and none of the Hisp-SP parents had a college-level education. In looking more specifically at the level of education, we see that more than half of the Hisp-SP parents had an elementary-level education (59%), and another quarter (22%) had junior high/middle school education. Thus, 81% of these Hisp-SP parents had eight or fewer years of formal education. Only 0–2% of parents in the other groups had so little formal education. With respect to high school, 19–24% of Hisp-Bil and Hisp-SP, 16% of EURO and 42% of Hisp-EB had obtained this level of education. Community college (two-year college) and vocational training accounted for another 29–36% of EURO and Hisp-Bil, but half (54%) of Hisp-EB. The percentage of parents with a university or graduate degree was also quite different across the groups, representing only 4% of Hisp-EB, but 38% of Hisp-Bil, and 53% of EURO parents. Clearly, the EURO and Hisp-Bil parents had the most education, followed by Hisp-EB, and lastly by Hisp-SP parents.

In further understanding these groups, we see in Figure 7.2 that most of

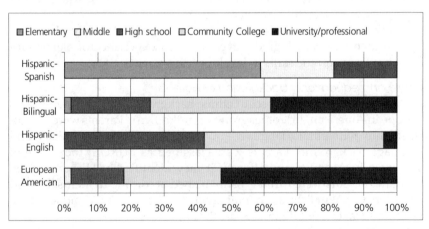

Figure 7.1 Education level of parents. Percentages by ethnic/language group

the EURO and all of the Hisp-EB parents were born in the US. In contrast, only one (3%) of the Hisp-SP parents was born in the US. Interestingly, in the Hisp-Bil group, overall half of the parents were born in the US. Among these Hisp-Bil parents, 80% of the high-school-level parents were born in the US while 60% of the college-level parents were born in the US. Thus, these Hisp-Bil parents were a third more likely to have received a higher level of education if they were born outside the US. As Figure 7.2 shows, most children (93%) were born in the US regardless of parental birthplace, though Hisp-SP parents were slightly less likely (77%) to have given birth to their child in the US than were other parents.

There were large differences across the ethnic/language groups in whether the parents had lived in or visited a Spanish-speaking country. As Figure 7.2 demonstrates, few (15–17%) EURO and Hisp-EB parents, but more than half (61%) the Hisp-Bil and almost all (97%) the Hisp-SP parents had lived in a Spanish-speaking country. With regard to visiting a Spanish-speaking country, at least two thirds of EURO, Hisp-Bil and Hisp-SP had done so, compared to half (54%) of the Hisp-EB parents

Language proficiency and language use in the home

Figure 7.3 presents further information about the language background of the parents. Most (76%) of the parents had studied a second language. While at least three-quarters of the EURO, Hisp-Bil and Hisp-SP had studied a second language, only half of the Hisp-EB parents had any instruction in a language other than English.

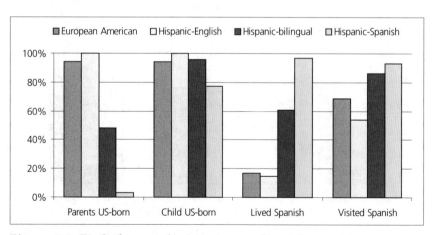

Figure 7.2 Birthplace and visitation to Spanish-speaking country. Percentages by Ethnic/language group

Proficiency levels in the second language (Spanish for English speaking and bilingual; English for Hisp-SP) varied across the groups. Parents rated their proficiency from 1 (no proficiency), to 2 (understand some) to 3 (speak some) to 4 (understand/speak well) to 5 (monolingual ability). As Figure 7.3 shows, few parents (0–13%) indicated that they had no proficiency in the second language. Not surprisingly, the Hisp-Bil group was the only group in which most or all of the parents rated themselves as understanding/speaking well or native-like in the second language. Also, 14% of EURO parents were included in this category of higher-level bilinguals. Figure 7.3 also shows that three-quarters to all of the parents in the EURO, Hisp-EB and Hisp-SP groups fit into these categories of understand or speak some. Thus, not surprisingly, the mean scores pertaining to proficiency in the second language were similar for the EURO (mean = 2.7), Hisp-EB (mean = 2.7), and Hisp-SP (mean = 2.4) groups, and significantly lower than for the Hisp-Bil (mean = 4.5) group.

Figure 7.4 presents further information about language use in the home, which varied tremendously across the groups. In EURO and Hisp-EB families, almost all the parents used English with their children and children used English with the parents and siblings. In Hisp-SP families, while almost all mothers used Spanish with their children, three quarters of the fathers spoke in both languages to the children, and children used both languages with the parents. However, in sibling interactions, Hisp-SP children were as likely to use Spanish (41%) as both languages (44%). Among Hisp-Bil families, half of the parents used English and a third spoke in

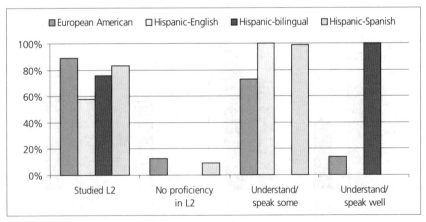

Figure 7.3 Language proficiency background. Percentages by ethnic/language group

Spanish. Two thirds of children responded back to parents and to siblings in English, while one quarter used both English and Spanish.

Most parents (86%) encouraged their children to use Spanish, though 10% more Hisp-Bil and Hisp-SP parents (90–93%) did so than EURO and Hisp-EB parents (81%). Fewer parents (68%) encouraged their child to use English. While two thirds of EURO and Hisp-Bil parents (61–66%) encouraged the use of English, three quarters of Hisp-SP and Hisp-EB (76–80%) parents encouraged English at home.

Study 2

A total of 69 kindergarten parents, representing three elementary school sites (two 90HI and one 90LO), participated in the study. Parents varied with respect to ethnic background (Hispanic, 41%; European American, 59%). Subjects were categorized into three ethnic/language groups, as in the previous study. However, because of the small sample size, only three groups were formed: 59% European American English speakers (EURO), 19% Hispanic English speakers or bilinguals (Hisp-EB), and 22% Hispanic Spanish speakers (Hisp-SP). In looking at the ethnicity of the spouse, 44% were Hispanic and 50% were EURO. In large measure, respondents had spouses with a similar ethnic background. Of those respondents who had a spouse from a different ethnic background, 11% of EUROs had a Hispanic spouse, 30% of Hisp-EB had a EURO spouse, and 8% of Hisp-SP had a EURO spouse.

Across these ethnic/language groups, parents differed significantly according to educational background. While 92% of EURO parents and

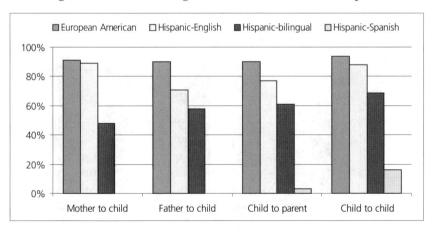

Figure 7.4 English use in home. Percentages by ethnic/language group

67% of Hisp-EB parents had at least some college education, all the Hisp-SP parents had high school education or less. Parents tended to have spouses with a similar education level: 85% of those with a high-school background and 81% of those with a college background had spouses with a similar level of education.

Combined samples: description of the parents

For some of the attitudinal items, parents from Study 1 were included with parents from Study 2, yielding the Combined sample with a total of 270 parents. In looking at the ethnic/language background, 39% were EURO, 15% Hisp-EB, 27% Hisp-Bil, and 19% Hisp-SP. Similar to what was observed in Study 1, 86% of EURO and 77% of Hisp-Bil parents had a college-level education; while only 50% of Hisp-EB and none of the Hisp-SP had a college background.

Findings

Administrative support and multicultural atmosphere of school

Parents responded to three questions that dealt with administrative support and the school's ability to promote diversity and balance the needs of the two groups of children – both English and Spanish speakers. Figures 7.5 and 7.6 present the average responses to these items, which varied from 1 (disagree strongly) to 5 (agree strongly), for ethnic/language groups (Figure 7.5) and for program type (Figure 7.6). As Figure 7.5 shows, parents

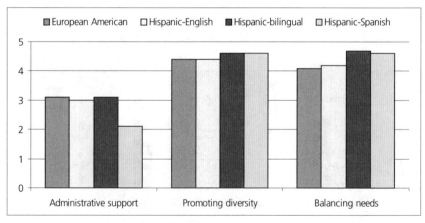

Figure 7.5 Attitudes toward socio-cultural diversity. Average response scores by ethnic/language group

scored low to neutral in terms of administrative support (mean = 2.1–3.1). Parents did not differ in their perceptions of administrative support according to their ethnic background. There were large differences in educational background and program type (see Figure 7.6), with college-level-parents and 90LO parents perceiving more administrative support than high-school educated and 90HI parents.

Parents gave high marks (mean = 4.4–4.6) to the staff's success in promoting diversity, and their responses did not differ according to their ethnic/language or educational background (see Figure 7.5). However, parents from the two program types (90HI vs. 90LO) answered this item differently (see Figure 7.6): parents in the 90HI programs gave schools significantly higher scores (mean = 4.5) in promoting diversity than did parents in the 90LO programs (mean = 4.1).

When parents were asked whether staff were successful in balancing the needs of both SB and EB students, their responses did not vary by educational background, but parents did answer differently depending on the program type (90HI vs. 90LO) and ethnic/language background (see Figures 7.5 and 7.6). Parents at 90HI sites gave higher ratings (mean = 4.4) to staff than parents at 90LO (mean = 3.8) schools. Interestingly, Hisp-SP and Hisp-Bil were most positive, with average scores of 4.6–4.7. Hisp-EB (mean = 4.2) and EURO (mean = 4.1) parents scored this item much lower, indicating their belief that the program was more focused on the needs of Spanish speakers than on English speakers, or on balancing the needs of both groups.

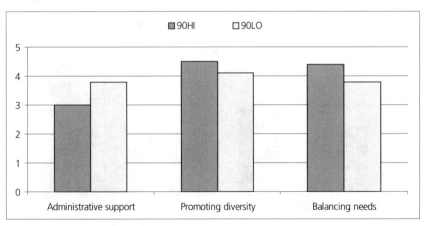

Figure 7.6 Attitudes toward socio-cultural diversity. Average response scores by program type

Parents in Study 2 responded to two questions about whether their child goes to homes of children from the other language group and whether those children come to their homes. As Figure 7.7 shows, there were large differences in parents' answers. Hispanic Spanish-speaking parents were significantly more likely to say that English-speaking children came to their house to play than were European American English speakers to indicate that Spanish-speaking children came to their home to play with their child. However, Hisp-EB parents were most likely to agree that their children go to the homes of Spanish speakers to play than were the largely monolingual parents (EURO and Hisp-SP).

Distance and transportation to school

Study 1 provided information about distance and transportation to the school site to determine whether these might be barriers to parental involvement. Distance to school varied by ethnic/language group. More Hisp-EB and EURO parents lived less than a mile away, while a third of EURO and Hisp-Bil lived at least five miles away. Thus, not surprisingly, transportation to school also differed by ethnic/language group. Three quarters of Hisp-SP, but only 13–28% of the other children, took the school bus to school. More than half to three quarters of EURO, Hisp-EB and Hisp-Bil traveled to school by car, compared with 25% of Hisp-SP. While one fifth of Hisp-EB children walked, only 6% of EURO and Hisp-Bil, and no Hisp-SP children walked to school. Interestingly, no child rode a bicycle to school.

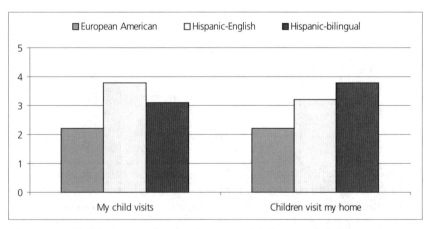

Figure 7.7 Child visits with other language background children. Average response scores by ethnic/language group

Parental involvement

Parents in Study 1 were asked a variety of questions about their involvement, the importance of involvement, and the types of support they received from the school. All parents strongly agreed that parental involvement was valued at the classroom (mean = 4.6) and school (mean = 4.7) levels. Parents neither agreed nor disagreed that involvement was valued at the district level. These perceptions did not vary according to the ethnic/language group, educational background of parents, children's grade level, or distance from school.

In rating the importance of parental involvement, again the parents provided strong agreement, regardless of the child's grade level and distance from school. However, importance differed for the ethnic/language groups, with Hisp-SP parents providing the strongest agreement (mean = 4.5). There was also a clear difference in education, with parents who had at least some college education more likely to value the importance of parental involvement than did parents who had a high school diploma or less. However, the lowest-educated group, Hisp-SP, had the highest level of agreement about the importance of parental involvement. In contrast, the Hisp-EB group with a high school diploma or less (mean = 3.8) had the lowest level of agreement about the importance of involvement.

To get some indication of their involvement at school, parents were also asked to check all the ways in which they give support to the school. The options and the percentage of parents, overall, who reported those options, were:

- none (6%);
- serve on committee (8%);
- helped in class at least once (36%);
- help in class often (19%);
- help outside class (23%);
- help with parent club (17%);
- help with or attend school activities or events (55%);
- other (11%).

The only ethnic/language differences in these categories were that EURO and Hisp-Bil parents were more likely to help outside class, to assist with the parent club and to help with or attend school activities/events. While a third of parents of each group reported that they attended the parent group meetings, only 12% of the Hisp-EB parents attended.

In looking at the support the parents felt they received from the school, the following categories and percentages were noted:

- none (14%);
- Spanish language class (13%);
- English language class (5%);
- workshops (24%);
- received information about program (59%);
- teacher/staff assisted me (39%);
- other (3%).

The only ethnic/language differences in these responses were that EURO and Hisp-EB parents were more likely to have taken Spanish classes and Hisp-SP parents to have taken the English classes. In addition, EURO parents reported that they received the most and Hisp-SP the least information from the school.

Attitudes toward bilingualism

Figures 7.8 and 7.9 show the attitudes of the group as a whole, as most attitudes did not vary according to the ethnic/language background of the parents in Study 2.

- Most parents also saw the value in their child studying Spanish (see Figure 7.8): to be comfortable with other Spanish speakers (mean = 4.6), to meet and converse with varied people (mean = 4.7), to under-

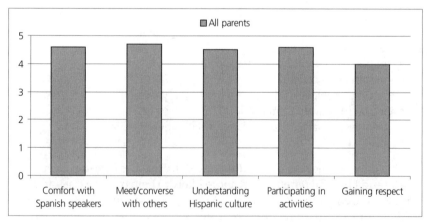

Figure 7.8 Attitudes toward bilingualism: Value for child studying Spanish. Average response scores

stand Hispanic culture (mean = 4.5), to participate in activities with people of other cultures (mean = 4.6), and that others will respect the child if s/he is bilingual (mean = 4.0).

- Parents also believed that studying Spanish was important for their children because (see Figure 7.9): they will need it for their career (mean = 4.1), it will make them more knowledgeable (mean = 4.8), and it will make them smarter (mean = 3.8).
- Parents' attitudes toward the program and toward bilingualism did not vary significantly according to their ethnic/language background, with the following exception: Hisp-EB parents (mean = 4.8) scored significantly higher than EURO (mean = 3.8) parents in the importance of Spanish for career advantages (see Figure 7.9).
- All parents in Study 1 highly valued the children's developing bilingual abilities: 92–100% of parents strongly agreed with this statement, and the remaining parents (except one Hisp-EB) agreed.

Reason for enrolling child in kindergarten DLE program

Parents in Study 2 selected reasons for enrolling their kindergartner in a DLE program. The possible reasons included: child will be able to communicate with others (categorized as integrative motivational orientation), child will have a stronger bilingual/bicultural identity (also classified as integrative), child will have academic/career advantages (categorized as instrumental), and it is a good neighborhood school (instrumental).

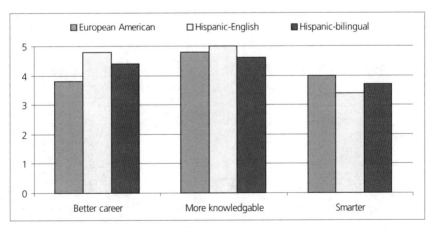

Figure 7.9 Attitudes towards bilingualism: Importance of studying Spanish. Average response scores by ethnic/language group

- In looking at the primary motivation for parents enrolling their kindergartner in a DLE program, the parents differed according to their ethnic/language background. Hispanic parents, whether English/Bilingual or Spanish speakers, were more likely to enroll their child so he/she would develop a bilingual/bicultural identity (73–90%) or language competence (0–9%). EURO parents were most likely to select academic/career advantages, though 22–27% also chose language competence and bilingual/bicultural identity. Thus, as Figure 7.10 shows, most Hispanic parents (82–90%) selected integrative motivation, whereas EURO parents were equally likely to choose integrative (49%) and instrumental (51%) reasons.

Parents in Study 1 were asked how they learned about the program. A third of parents found out through a friend or family member, 16–18% through the parent handbook distributed through the school, district, or by staff recruitment, and a quarter learned through other means. How they learned varied by ethnic/language group:

- Hisp-SP parents learned largely through staff recruitment and friends or family.
- In general, families and friends were important in recruiting EURO and Hisp-Bil, but especially Hisp-EB families.
- A parent handbook was more likely to attract EURO than other groups.

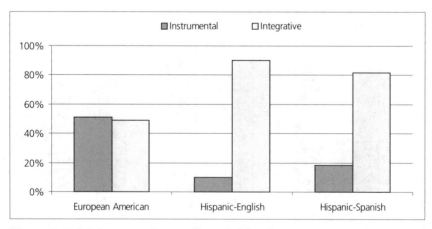

Figure 7.10 Main reason for enrolling child in DLE. Percentages by ethnic/language background

- Other types of strategy were used frequently to attract half of EURO families.

Satisfaction with program

Parents in both samples were satisfied (mean = 4.4–4.9) that their child was receiving access to the subject matter, though their satisfaction varied by ethnic/language group. While EURO parents were satisfied (mean = 4.4), their level of satisfaction was lower than that of Hispanic (mean = 4.6–4.9) parents.

In another analysis with the parents of Sample 1, this question was further examined to determine whether parent satisfaction differed according to their children's grade level. As Figure 7.11 indicates, there were large differences according to grade level. Parents of kindergartners were all completely satisfied (mean = 5.0), followed by parents who had older children in grades 6–8 (mean = 4.8). Parents of children in grades 3–5 were least satisfied, though their scores still clearly registered as 'agree' that they were satisfied (mean = 4.3).

Somewhat similar findings were obtained in examining whether parents were satisfied with their child's progress in reading English. Parents who had only a kindergartner, or who had children in upper grades (6–8), were most satisfied with their children's progress in English reading (mean = 4.8). The parents who had first and second graders were least satisfied (mean = 3.9), though still satisfied, and those with children in grades 3–5 were in between.

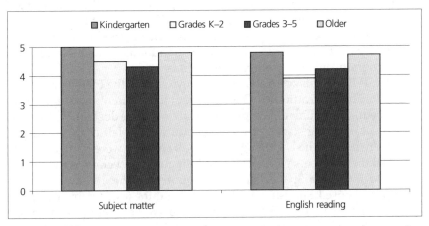

Figure 7.11 Satisfaction with the program. Average response scores by grade level of child

Finally, parents were asked whether they would recommend the program to other parents. From both samples, parents were highly consistent that they would recommend the program to other parents (mean = 4.8–4.9), regardless of their ethnic/language background, education level, their child's grade level, or the program type (90HI, 90LO).

Summary and Conclusions

This chapter has provided information about the backgrounds and attitudes of parents in DLE programs. The results summarized here illustrate perceptions that parents hold about their satisfaction, involvement, the support they receive, and parental attitudes according to their background and the school demographic characteristics (90HI vs. 90LO).

With respect to parent background, there are some important similarities and differences. First, parents differed in terms of ethnicity, language background, and education. Parents were categorized according to their ethnicity and language background as: European American English speaking (EURO), Hispanic-Bilingual (Hisp-Bil), Hispanic-English speaking (Hisp-EB), and Hispanic-Spanish speaking (Hisp-SP). These parents were quite distinct in some important ways:

- *EURO parents* had high levels of education, with more than half possessing a university/professional/graduate degree, and 82% having at least some college level education. Almost all parents (94%) were born in the US, though the majority had visited a Spanish-speaking country. Most parents had studied Spanish, though their proficiency was quite limited. Not surprisingly, the language of the home was almost exclusively English. EURO parents learned about the DLE program from the district/school handbook that described the program, and also from family/friends.

- *HISP-Bil parents* were similar in many ways to the EURO parents in education and attitudes. Over a third of these parents had high levels of education (university/professional/graduate degree), with a total of 74% having some college level education. Half of these parents were born in the US, though almost all children were born in the US. All these parents were proficient bilinguals, and close to two thirds had lived in a Spanish-speaking country. In these homes, half the parents used English with their child, a third used Spanish, and the remainder used both languages. Children were more likely to use English with their parents and siblings. These parents learned about the program from their family and friends.

- *Hisp-EB parents* were distinct from the Hisp-Bil parents in many ways. Only 4% of these parents had high levels of education, and only a half had some college-level education. While all parents and their children were born in the US, about half had visited a Spanish-speaking country. Only half (a lower percentage than the other parent groups) had ever studied Spanish, and all rated their proficiency as limited. While English was not used exclusively in these homes, most interactions between mothers, fathers and children occurred in English. These parents were much more likely than EURO or Hisp-Bil parents to agree that they encourage their child to use English. They learned about the program through family/friends.

- *Hisp-SP parents* had the lowest levels of education, with more than half possessing only an elementary-level education and the remainder split between 7–9 and 10–12 years of education. Almost all parents were born outside the US, whereas three quarters of their offspring were born in the US. Most parents (83%) had studied English, though all rated their proficiency in English as low. In these homes, parents used mostly Spanish, but some English, with their children. Among children, most used Spanish or both languages with their parents, but children were split between the use of Spanish and both languages with siblings. Most parents learned about the program through staff recruitment and friends/family.

Parents perceived medium levels of support from the district. Parents with children at 90HI sites and with lower levels of education felt lower levels of district support than did parents at 90LO sites and parents with college-level education. This lower level of perceived district support is consistent with literature reporting that low-income parents and minority parents feel alienation, distrust and discrimination from school personnel (Comer, 1986; Garcia, 1990; Hidalgo *et al.*, 1995; Kozol, 1995; Ogbu, 1987).

High marks were given to staff for promoting diversity at the school site and for balancing the needs of both SB and EB students. While most parents believed that staff were successful in promoting diversity, parents with children at 90HI sites gave staff higher scores than did parents with children at 90LO sites. Parents from different ethnic/language backgrounds did not differ in their scores in this area.

Ethnic/language and school demographic differences did influence how parents felt about the success of staff in balancing the needs of SB and EB students. Parents at 90HI sites gave higher ratings to staff than did parents at 90LO schools. While the scores of Hisp-SP and Hisp-Bil parents were very positive, the ratings of Hisp-EB and EURO parents were also similar and much lower. Thus, these results would suggest that English-speaking parents and the most culturally assimilated parents (Hisp-EB) were less confident that the program is successful in meeting the needs of their English-speaking children.

In looking at parents' perceptions about involvement, all parents strongly agreed that parental involvement was valued at both the class-room and school levels. These beliefs did not differ according to the parents' ethnic/language group, educational background, or their children's grade level.

Parents also strongly agreed that parental involvement is important. Parents rated the importance of involvement differently according to their ethnic/language and education backgrounds. Parents who had at least some college education were more likely to agree that parental involvement was important than were parents who had a high-school diploma or less. The one exception to this finding was that the lowest educated group (Hisp-SP) was most likely to agree about the importance of parental involvement. Hisp-EB parents with a high school diploma or less were least likely to agree about the importance of involvement.

When parents were asked about the ways in which they are involved, the majority of parents said they helped with attending school events, one third helped in class at least once, and one fifth helped in class often. Only a few served on committees, and few did nothing. EURO and Hisp-Bil parents, who were the most highly educated parents, were more likely to assist outside of class, to help with the parent club and to assist with or attend school activities/events. About one third of parents in each group reported that they attended the parent group meetings, though only a handful of the Hisp-EB parents attended.

Parent attitudes were very favorable toward bilingualism, as one might expect. Most parents agreed that it was important that their child study Spanish: to be comfortable with other Spanish speakers, to meet and converse with varied people, to understand Hispanic culture, to participate in activities with people of other cultures, and because others will respect the child if s/he is bilingual. Most parents also perceived that studying Spanish would be an asset for their child for career and intellectual benefits. Parents of different ethnic/language backgrounds did not differ in their attitudes except that Hisp-EB parents were more likely to believe in the importance of Spanish for career advantages than were EURO parents.

The findings are also important in validating the different reasons why parents enrolled their child in the program according to their heritage background. European American parents identify with both instrumental and integrative reasons. However, for Hispanic parents, for whom the target (non-English) language is their heritage language, the primary purpose is integrative in nature. These results hold true regardless of whether the Hispanic parent is a Spanish monolingual or a bilingual/ English speaker. The findings from this study are also consistent with research in Wales and in the US showing that Welsh and Chicano parents communicated strong integrative motivation for putting their child in a heritage language bilingual program (Bush, 1983, cited in Torres, 1988).

Parents were very satisfied with the program, and would recommend it to other parents. Parents differed somewhat in their satisfaction that their child was receiving access to the subject matter, with EURO parents less satisfied than Hispanic parents were. Parent satisfaction also varied considerably by the children's grade level. While all parents were satisfied, parents of kindergartners were most satisfied, followed by parents who had older children in grades 6–8. Parents of children in grades 3–5 were least satisfied. Similarly, in looking at parents' satisfaction with their child's progress in English reading, there was also a clear difference according to the children's grade level. Parents of kindergartners or upper graders (6–8) were most satisfied, parents of first and second graders were least satisfied, and those with third through fifth graders were in between.

We might expect that parents who enroll their kindergartner are optimistic about the program, especially toward the end of the year when both groups of children are beginning to use the second language and demonstrate preliteracy skills in Spanish. By second grade, we typically see the lowest levels of satisfaction. Since children do not begin formal English reading until third grade, parents see their children reading in Spanish but not in English, and become concerned that their children will fall behind. This is a typical outcome observed in 90:10 programs among parents, particularly English-speaking parents. In fact, this phenomenon is typically referred to as the 'Second-Grade Panic.' When children begin English reading instruction in third grade and become competent readers in English by fifth grade, there is less concern. By grades 6–8, parents are not at all concerned; they know their children can do all their academic work in English.

These results have important implications for understanding parental backgrounds in DLE programs, for parent recruitment and training, and for promoting parent involvement. These implications will be discussed in Chapter 15.

Notes

1. Only one school was selected because this school asked for parent information. Later, other schools were studied, as seen in the later sections of this chapter.
2. The unknown and two African American and Asian American parents were eliminated from further analyses involving *ethnic/language* differences because there were so few of them, but these individuals were otherwise included in the analyses.

Part 3

Student Outcomes in Dual Language Education Programs

Chapter 8

Student Outcomes: Introduction and Data Collection

Introduction

Educators have long been interested in understanding student outcomes in various types of educational programs (e.g. Binet & Simon, 1916; Rice, 1893; Thorndike, 1913). This focus is no different in language education programs, where researchers have examined the outcomes of program participants (e.g. California Department of Education, 1984; Cummins & Swain, 1986; Day & Shapson, 1996; Genesee, 1987; Johnson & Swain, 1997; Lambert & Tucker, 1972; Ramirez *et al.*, 1991; Swain & Lapkin, 1982; Willig, 1985).

Literature on student outcomes suggests that these are affected by the school and classroom environment, including teacher expectations (Battistich *et al.*, 1995; Brophy, 1998; Levine & Lezotte, 1995; Maehr & Pintrich, 1997), parent expectations and involvement (Hidalgo *et al.*, 1995; Levine & Lezotte, 1995; Slaughter-DeFoe, 1991), ethnic background and language proficiency (Darling-Hammond, 1995; Padilla & Lindholm, 1995; Portes & Rumbaut, 1990; Willig, 1985), socioeconomic background (Darling-Hammond, 1995; Knapp & Woolverton, 1995; Schultz, 1993), and grade level/age of the student (Eccles *et al.*, 1984; Harley, 1986; Harter *et al.*, 1992; Singleton, 1989; Snow & Hoefnagel-Höhle, 1978).

The chapters in this third section will present research and evaluation findings relating to:

- Language proficiency, academic achievement, and attitudes of DLE students.
- Whether student or school background variables influence these outcomes.
- The influence of attitudinal variables on language proficiency and academic achievement outcomes.
- Relationships between bilingual language proficiency and academic achievement.

These outcome issues have been examined with a large sample of data. The rest of this chapter will provide a description of the data that were

Table 8.1 Student background characteristics: ethnicity and free lunch participation by program type

Background: ethnicity	90HI	90LO	50:50	TBE	EO	Totals
Hispanic Spanish	849 (58%)	489 (56%)	580 (49%)	860 (93%)	176 (44%)	2954 (61%)
Hispanic English	244 (17%)	74 (9%)	204 (17%)	15 (2%)	57 (14%)	594 (12%)
European American	277 (19%)	273 (31%)	389 (33%)	2 (0%)	150 (38%)	1091 (23%)
African American	77 (5%)	31 (4%)	2 (0%)	33 (4%)	10 (3%)	153 (3%)
Asian American	18 (1%)	6 (1%)	9 (1%)	16 (2%)	3 (1%)	52 (1%)
Native American	5 (0%)	1 (0%)	2 (0%)	0 (0%)	2 (1%)	10 (0%)
Totals	1470	874	1186	926	398	4854
Background: % Free lunch	67%	48%	48%	91%	60%	64%

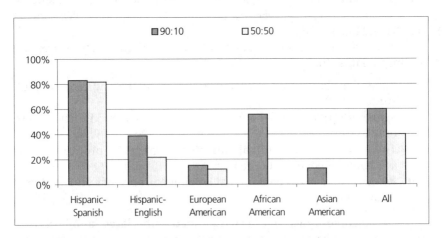

Figure 8.1 Free lunch participation by ethnicity and program type

collected in an attempt to understand language proficiency, academic achievement, and attitudes of students.

Data Collection

Oral language proficiency data are available for a total of 4854 students representing the five program types discussed in previous chapters: 90HI (n=1470); 90LO (n=874); 50:50 (n=1186); TBE (n=926); and EO (n=398). Table 8.1 presents background information related to ethnicity and SES for these students by program type. As the table shows, overall language proficiency data were available for: Hispanic Spanish speakers (Hisp-SB, 61% of the students), Hispanic English speakers (Hisp-EB, 12%), and Euro-Americans (EURO, 23%).[1] Few African American (3%), Asian American (1%) or Native American (<1%) participated. Across program types, ethnic distributions varied, with higher representations of Hisp-SB in 90:10 and TBE programs (56–93%), and lower representations in 50:50 and EO programs (44–49%). European Americans were more highly represented in 90LO, 50:50 and EO programs (31–38%) than in 90HI (19%) programs. Hisp-EB were more likely to participate in 90HI, 50:50 and EO (14–17%) than in 90LO (9%) or TBE (2%) programs.

The percentage of students who were receiving free lunch was 64% overall, but varied across program types. Close to 91% of TBE students were on free lunch, while 60–67% of EO and 90HI students, and 48% of 90LO and 50:50 students participated in the free lunch program.

Figure 8.1 illustrates the difference in free lunch participation across the various ethnic groups in 90:10 and 50:50 programs. The rates of free lunch participation across the various ethnic groups in 90:10 and 50:50 programs, respectively, were: 83% vs. 82% for Hisp-SB; 39% vs. 22% for Hisp-EB, 15% vs. 12% for EUROs, 56% for African Americans in 90HI, and 13% for Asian-Americans in 90HI.

Table 8.2 shows the number of students for whom there is oral language proficiency data by grade level and program type. This table indicates that there are data for a grand total of 8930 students. The reason for the discrepancy between the totals in Table 8.1 and Table 8.2 is that there are many students for whom there are multiple years of data. As Table 8.2 indicates, most data are available for the primary grade levels (K–2), and relatively little data for the upper grades (7–8). Further, more language proficiency scores are accessible for students in the 90:10 program, particularly the 90HI program, followed by the 50:50, then the TBE and EO programs.

Table 8.2 Student background characteristics: Grade level

Background: Grade level	90HI	90LO	50:50	TBE	EO	Totals
Kindergarten	800	451	409	210	46	1916
First	992	560	405	210	45	2212
Second	858	525	434	195	57	2069
Third	355	157	131	155	108	906
Fourth	211	80	74	120	161	646
Fifth	103	66	71	109	198	547
Sixth	55	61	65	84	112	377
Seventh	40	23	75	0	0	138
Eighth	35	23	61	0	0	119
Totals	3449	1946	1725	1083	727	8930

Table 8.3 Student background characteristics: Grade level

Background: Grade level	90HI Spanish English	90LO Spanish English	50:50 Spanish English	TBE Spanish English	EO Spanish English	Totals Spanish English
First	652 355	430 223	70 102	98 19		1250 699
Second	779 370	468 260	187 213	151 10		1585 853
Third	223 162	105 103	22 51	92 21	41 0	483 337
Fourth	117 80	64 64	12 34	67 13	26 0	286 191
Fifth	45 41	55 57	11 19	19 11	12 42	142 170
Sixth	22 23	28 31		10 11		60 65
Seventh	18 18	18 0				36 18
Eighth	19 0	15 0				34 0
Totals	2,924	1,921	721	522	121	6,209

Table 8.3 shows the number of students for whom there is academic language/reading achievement data by grade level and program type. The grand total for this table shows that there are data for 6,209 students. Primary grade levels (K–2) provided most of the data, while upper grade levels (7–8) yielded very little data. Further, more academic language-proficiency scores are accessible for students in the 90:10 program, particularly the 90HI program, followed by the 50:50, then the TBE and EO programs.

Longitudinal data were available for 149 students from four 90:10 schools who had participated since kindergarten or first grade, and had language proficiency and academic achievement scores for each year of grades 1–5. About two-thirds (69%) of the students were involved in 90HI and one third (31%) in 90LO programs. About half (56%) were mid-SES (non-free-lunch students) and the remainder (44%) were low-SES (free lunch). Ethnicity breakdown was as follows: 45% Hispanic Spanish speakers, 18% Hispanic English speakers, 28% European American English speakers, 8% African American English speakers, and 1% Asian American English speakers. Participants in the free lunch program varied considerably by ethnic group, as shown in Figure 8.2. Three-quarters of Hispanic Spanish speakers, half of African American, but only 15–17% of Hispanic English speakers and European Americans took part in the free lunch program.

In comparing the longitudinal sample with the cross-sectional sample, the smaller longitudinal sample seems to be a good representation of the larger cross-sectional sample in terms of student background characteristics.

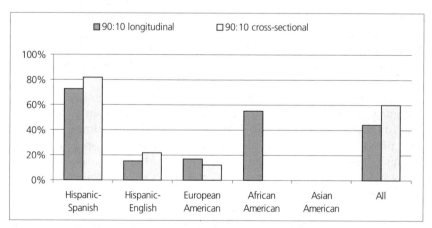

Figure 8.2 Free lunch participation of 90:10 students. Percentages by ethnicity and sampling method

The major differences between these samples related to SES and ethnicity. That is, the percentage of low SES students was 44% in the longitudinal sample compared to 60% (of 90:10 students) in the cross-sectional sample. In addition, the longitudinal sample had a smaller representation of Hispanic Spanish speakers, and a greater number of African American students.

Instruments

Analyses of oral language proficiency are based largely on teacher ratings of students' oral language proficiency in both languages. The measures used for the teacher ratings are the *Student Oral Language Observation Matrix* (SOLOM) developed by the California Department of Education and the *Stanford Foreign Language Oral Skills Evaluation Matrix* (FLOSEM), which was an upgraded version of the SOLOM developed by Amado Padilla and his colleagues at Stanford University. Because the FLOSEM was developed from the SOLOM, both rating scales assess oral language proficiency in five domains: (1) *comprehension*, (2) *fluency*, (3) *vocabulary*, (4) *pronunciation*, and (5) *grammar* [see Appendix for the FLOSEM and SOLOM]. Teachers do not administer a test, but reflect on the students' language abilities after extensive interaction with the student in a number of different situational contexts. The scores range from 1, representing almost no ability, to 5 (SOLOM) or 6 (FLOSEM), designating monolingual native-speaker ability for each domain. The FLOSEM is more precise in describing the language-proficiency requirements for each score, and it enables a finer distinction for higher levels of oral proficiency. Scores in each domain can be summed to provide a total language proficiency score, or kept distinct for subscale scores. These scales can be administered in any language. Teachers complete the SOLOM or FLOSEM, in both English and Spanish, at the end of the school year. A score of 19 or higher places a student in the Fluent (or Proficient) range, while a score lower than 19 designates Non-Fluent.

Other measures of proficiency available for a few students included the Language Assessment Scale (LAS) and the IDEA Proficiency Test (IPT). The *Language Assessment Scale* (LAS) is an individually administered test that provides an overall picture of oral linguistic skills in English and Spanish. It assesses the basic sounds of language (phonemic skills), vocabulary (referential skills), grammar (syntactic skills), and ability to use the language (pragmatic skills).

The *IDEA Proficiency Test* (IPT) places students in one of seven oral language-proficiency levels (from beginning to mastery) and assists in the classification of students according to relative levels of bilingualism.

The test can be individually administered in both English and Spanish, and measures four basic areas of oral language proficiency: vocabulary, comprehension, syntax, and verbal expression.

For both the LAS and the IPT, scores were converted by the school to three language proficiency levels: (1) Non-English Proficiency (NEP), Non-Spanish Proficiency (NSP); (2) Limited English Proficiency (LEP), Limited Spanish Proficiency (LSP); and (3) Fluent English Proficiency (FEP), Fluent Spanish Proficiency (FSP).

Data are available for both cross-sectional and longitudinal perspectives, though there is substantial cross-sectional data and sparse longitudinal data, as schools were funded for periods ranging from two to five years. In addition, some schools used the SOLOM and others used the FLOSEM, and yet other schools began with the SOLOM and then switched to the FLOSEM. Thus, longitudinal and cross-sectional analyses are complicated by these methodological limitations.

At the end of the oral language proficiency section, data are presented to suggest that the SOLOM, FLOSEM and other proficiency measures provide similar assessment outcome information. That is, where we could get a school to administer both the FLOSEM and SOLOM, the correspondence between ratings of Proficient vs. Non-Proficient in each language was very high in rating students in their L1 (96–100% agreement) and moderate to high in rating students' L2 (74–100%). In addition, there was a high level of correspondence between students classified by the IPT/LAS and the SOLOM/FLOSEM as Proficient vs. Non-Proficient in L1 (95–100%), but a moderate to high level of agreement in L2 (67–100%).

Schools administered different academic achievement tests over the time. Three different achievement tests were used: *Comprehensive Tests of Basic Skills*, Form U (CTBS-U), *Metropolitan Achievement Test* (MAT), and *CAS*[2] Each test is a norm-referenced achievement test that was developed to measure achievement in English in the basic skills normally found in US State and district curricula. The CAS^2, a short-lived test, was developed to align with the California curriculum frameworks in assessing basic skills. The subject areas typically assessed in all of these tests included reading, language arts, and mathematics. Content areas of science, social studies, spelling and other areas were not often assessed or reported and thus there is little data on these areas. Where it is available, it is discussed.

In Spanish, most schools used one of three common Spanish achievement tests: *La Prueba Riverside de Realización en Español* (La Prueba), *Aprenda: La Prueba de Logros en Español* (Aprenda), and *Spanish Assessment of Basic Education* (SABE). These norm-referenced achievement tests were designed for Spanish-speaking students, and assessed educational objectives such as reading, language and mathematics. The tests were developed by Spanish-speaking experts and normalized with a native Spanish speaking US student population.

Different achievement tests were used because school districts required the schools to use their mandated achievement tests. Thus, it was impossible to select one test and have that test be the standard for all schools. Accordingly, the normal curve equivalents (NCEs) were the scores used to assess performance across all tests. NCEs were used for all statistical analyses, so the tables in the chapters that follow include NCE scores.

Testing procedures

All students were group-administered the achievement tests each spring (April–May) by their teachers. Also, teachers completed the SOLOM or FLOSEM ratings in May each year in both English and Spanish.

Summary and Conclusions

This chapter has presented information about students for whom there is language proficiency, academic achievement, and attitudes data. There is a large sample of students for whom there is cross-sectional data and a smaller sample of students for whom there are several years of longitudinal data. This group of students represents largely Hispanic and European American students, and some African American students. Students vary with respect to socioeconomic background, though most Hispanic and African American students are lower income while most European Americans are middle income. Finally, for some of the data, there are students from different types of language education programs (DLE, TBE, English Only) and from different types of dual language education programs (90:10 and 50:50 programs). In subsequent chapters, where there is sufficient data, comparisons will be made across program types.

Notes

1. SB designates that the students were Spanish bilinguals; that is, they began as Spanish speakers, but became bilingual. Similarly, EB refers to English bilinguals; these students began the program as native English speakers, but became bilingual.

Chapter 9

Student Outcomes: Oral Language Proficiency

Introduction to Language Proficiency

A large body of research has amassed on the language proficiency of students in various types of language education programs. Results from this research are consistent in demonstrating that students can develop high levels of first and second language proficiency through various types of bilingual and immersion programs that include adequate exposure to both languages.

When we talk about language proficiency, we will distinguish between the two types of language proficiency discussed in Chapter 2: oral language proficiency or basic interpersonal communicative skills, and cognitive/academic language proficiency (Cummins, 1984). As mentioned in Chapter 2, students can become orally proficient in about two years, but require approximately five to seven years to develop full academic language proficiency (Collier, 1989; Cummins, 1981). Oral language proficiency will be examined in this chapter, and cognitive/academic language proficiency in the next chapter.

With respect to academic language skills, research shows unequivocally, that on various types of cognitive/academic tests of reading and language skills, students can score on a par with their peers who are not in immersion programs. For example, students studying in four languages in the European Schools model in Belgium were proficient enough in their first two languages to take the examinations in either language (Baetens Beardsmore, 1995). Similarly, Hungarian immersion students scored as well as native English speakers in a Cloze test in English (Duff, 1997); Catalan students performed as well in L2 (Spanish) as students not in immersion (Artigal, 1995, 1997); Basque immersion students outperformed controls in both languages in writing and reading achievement (Lasagabaster & Cenoz, 1995); and the narrative structures of Finnish immersion students in their L2 approached those of monolingual native speakers (Lauren, 1998). Jones (1995), reporting on Welsh immersion students, found that the children could retell a story, using a variety of linguistic resources, though they lacked some linguistic structures. Thus, these results are consistent in demonstrating that immersion students develop the appropriate academic language skills to perform on a par with their peers not in immersion programs, though they may possess too few of the sophisticated grammatical structures or lexical elements to perform as a monolingual in that language (Snow, 1990).

In looking at oral language proficiency, the concept of 'immersion speak' has been used to characterize language majority students' language output in immersion programs. It has been well documented that immersion students do not reach native-like proficiency in their output of the second language (Hamers & Blanc, 1989; Lyster, 1987; Pellerin & Hammerly, 1986; Spilka, 1976; Swain & Lapkin, 1982). However, immersion students outperform their non-immersion (students in foreign language programs) peers in listening and speaking in L2 (Campbell *et al.*, 1985; Genesee, 1987; Lasagabaster & Cenoz, 1995; Lindholm & Padilla, 1990).

Day and Shapson's (1996) conclusion relating to the linguistic development of French immersion students in Canada represents a good summary of the results found in a variety of immersion programs across the world:

> Overall, grade 7 immersion students performed well in French speaking. They were able to engage in fairly complex discussions requiring them to use French for a range of purposes, and they did so with ease and enjoyment. The immersion students were not comparable to a group of native French-speaking students in their pronunciation/intonation and oral grammar. However, except for fluency, they were comparable on the more communicative measures (e.g. quality of information, quality of description). (Day & Shapson, 1996: 11)

Other studies show that the lexicon expands rapidly in immersion students (for example, Björklund, 1995, in Sweden; Wode, 1998, in Germany). Jones (1995), reporting on Welsh immersion students, found that the grammatical and sociolinguistic aspects of the children's communicative competence were weaker than the discourse and strategic competence, a finding consistent with other research on immersion programs in Canada (Harley, 1986; Day & Shapson, 1996; Genesee, 1987).

Large-scale studies and reviews of evaluation studies of bilingual (including heritage language) programs in the US that have examined the academic language of language minority students demonstrate that high quality maintenance bilingual programs result in reading and language arts scores that approximate or exceed grade-level norms (August & Hakuta, 1997; Cloud *et al.*, 2000; Thomas & Collier, 1997; Genesee & Gándara, 1999 ; Padilla *et al.*, 1991; Ramirez *et al.*, 1991; Willig, 1985; for reviews of these issues, see also August & Hakuta, 1997; Baker, 1996; Baker & Jones, 1998; Crawford, 1999). Few studies have assessed the oral language proficiency of language minority students, though what research exists shows that these students can develop high levels of proficiency in both their native language and English (August & Hakuta, 1997; Padilla *et al.*, 1991; Ramirez *et al.*, 1991; Willig, 1985).

It is important to point out that the extent to which students become proficient in both languages is influenced by the type and quality of the program. Additive programs (maintenance bilingual/late exit) as compared to subtractive programs (transitional/early exit) programs and more intensive programs (immersion) versus less intensive programs (foreign language/FLES) promote higher levels of proficiency in both languages (see Chapter 2).

Another factor that is important to consider is the development of the L1 prior to program entry. As discussed in Chapter 2 and consistent with the notions of linguistic interdependence (Cummins, 1979; Skutnabb-Kangas, 1988; Skutnabb-Kangas & Toukomaa, 1976), researchers have consistently reported that language proficiency in one language influences proficiency in the second language (e.g. August & Hakuta, 1997). Some students enter school with low levels of proficiency in their L1 and others enter school with low levels of bilingual proficiency – in L1 *and* L2. While there is little research on the influence of bilingual programs on the language proficiency of these students, the few studies examining this issue have reported that maintenance bilingual programs can promote the L1 and L2 development in these students (Escamilla & Medina, 1993) and do so more adequately than transitional programs (Medina & Escamilla, 1992).

Some attitudinal factors have been found to influence language proficiency. Several researchers have pointed out that *integrative motivation* (as discussed in Chapter 7), or seeking out opportunities to use the language, promotes higher levels of language proficiency (Baetens Beardsmore, 1995; Gardner & Lambert, 1972; Lambert, 1987; Lindholm & Padilla, 1990). Others have pointed out that interaction with native speakers is required in order for students to develop a high level of language proficiency in L2 (Peirce, 1995), a finding clearly consistent with the language proficiency results found in immersion programs. For language minority students, willingness to use, and proficiency in, the L2 depends on factors such as: the reaction they receive from native speakers of that language (Zanger, 1987, reported in Brisk, 1998), the amount of native language used in the home (Hakuta & D'Andrea, 1992), and whether students believe they have to give up the home language (Dorian, 1982).

Information about students' development of oral language proficiency is limited to teacher ratings and language tests. Unfortunately, there is still little specific information about the language structures and sociolinguistic competencies of DLE students, unlike the considerable documentation of second language development provided by immersion researchers (e.g. Björklund, 1995; Day & Shapson, 1996; Jones, 1995; Lyster, 1987; Snow, 1990; Swain & Lapkin, 1982; Wode, 1998).

In this chapter, several research questions will be examined:

- What is the students' level of oral language proficiency (L1, L2 and bilingual proficiency) after participating in a DLE program?
- What student background (ethnicity, SES, level of L1), school demographic (high vs. low ethnic/SES density), and program type (90:10, 50:50, TBE, EO) influence L2 proficiency?
- Does L1 proficiency at program entry influence L1 and L2 proficiency after several years of participation?
- Does the students' motivation relate to their level of L2 proficiency?

Oral Language Proficiency in Native Language (L1)

Table 9.1 and Figures 9.1 and 9.2 present cross-sectional SOLOM data for oral language proficiency in the native language (L1) according to the language background (Spanish vs. English), school demographic and program type factors (90HI, 90LO, 50:50, TBE) and grade level of the students. As Figure 9.1 shows, both groups were rated close to the top of the scale (25). While the L1 scores of 90:10 English and Spanish speakers were similar, English speakers' ratings were significantly higher than those of Spanish speakers at grades 1, 2 and 4, but not at grades K, 3 and 5.

For English speakers rated in English, Table 9.1 shows that there were no program differences at any grade level between 90LO, 90HI, and 50:50 program students (where such analyses were possible). Almost every student was rated as proficient in the L1, or English.

In contrast, at every grade level, Spanish-speaking students' scores varied by program type (see Table 9.1 – Spanish speakers rated in Spanish – and Figure 9.2):

- Students in the 90HI program scored higher than students in the 90LO (in first grade) and 50:50 (kindergarten and second grades) programs.
- Students in the 90:10 (90HI and 90LO) programs outscored students in the TBE program at every grade level.
- Students in 50:50 programs were rated higher than students in TBE programs.

Table 9.1 Oral language proficiency in L1: Cross-sectional perspective. SOLOM scores (and percentage of students rated as proficient) by grade level and program type

English speakers rated in English

Grade level	90HI	90LO	50:50	Program differences
Kindergarten	24.2 (98%)	23.9 (95%)	23.9 (98%)	None
First	24.4 (97%)	24.5 (98%)	24.2 (99%)	None
Second	24.6 (99%)	24.7 (100%)	24.6 (100%)	None
Third	24.5 (97%)	24.5 (98%)		None
Fourth	24.7 (100%)	24.9 (98%)		None
Fifth	24.5 (100%)	24.7 (100%)		None
Sixth		23.9 (100%)		n/a

Spanish speakers rated in Spanish

Grade level	90HI	90LO	50:50	TBE	Program differences
Kindergarten	23.4 (92%)	23.0 (90%)	21.8 (83%)	10.9 (6%)	90HI>50:50 90HI,LO,50>TBE
First	24.3 (96%)	23.6 (95%)	24.0 (96%)	18.2 (54%)	90HI>90LO 90HI,LO,50>TBE
Second	24.2 (97%)	23.7 (96%)	22.5 (93%)	16.1 (46%)	90HI,LO>50,TBE 50:50>TBE
Third	24.6 (99%)	24.7 (100%)		19.1 (57%)	90HI,LO>TBE
Fourth	24.6 (100%)	23.9 (95%)		18.7 (69%)	90HI,LO>TBE
Fifth	23.8 (100%)	24.9 (100%)		21.0 (75%)	90HI,LO>TBE
Sixth		24.4 (100%)		20.3 (84%)	90LO>TBE

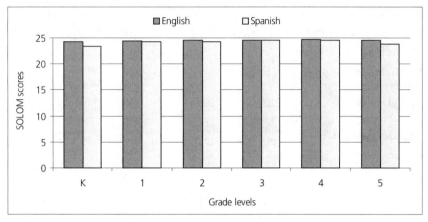

Figure 9.1 L1 SOLOM scores for English and Spanish speakers in 90HI programs

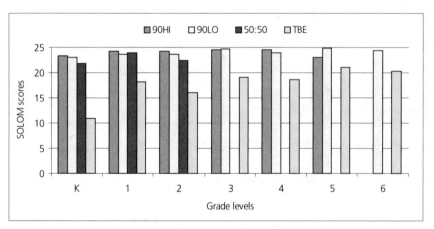

Figure 9.2 L1 SOLOM scores for Spanish speakers by program type and grade level

Longitudinal data for students in the 90:10 programs appears in Table 9.2. This longitudinal data represents students who participated in a 90:10 program from kindergarten or first grade through fifth grade and had language proficiency scores for each year from grades 1–5. The repeated measures of *analysis of variance* (ANOVA) for students' L1 SOLOM scores revealed a statistically significant effect for time and language background. Thus, both English and Spanish speakers made significant growth across

Table 9.2 Oral language proficiency in L1: Longitudinal perspective. Mean SOLOM scores by grade level for 90:10 students (standard deviations in parentheses)

Grade level	Spanish speakers	English speakers
First	23.8 (2.4)	24.4 (2.0)
Second	23.9 (2.1)	24.8 (1.4)
Third	24.3 (1.4)	24.7 (1.4)
Fourth	24.3 (1.4)	24.8 (1.2)
Fifth	24.3 (1.6)	24.5 (1.3)

the grade levels, though English speakers had significantly higher ratings of L1 proficiency than Spanish speakers across all grade levels.

FLOSEM data (see Table 9.3) were based on a different subset of students and thus, there were slight variations in the results from the SOLOM data. However, most trends were similar. Among English speakers, EO program students scored higher than TBE students in grades K–1. Otherwise, there were no differences by program type. Significant program type differences were evident for Spanish speakers. At all grade levels, the 90:10 students outscored the 50:50 students. Also, the TBE students were rated higher than the 50:50 students in grades K–3.

Analyses were also conducted to determine whether there were differences according to the children's gender and SES. Although girls scored slightly higher than boys did, this difference was not statistically significant. Similarly, overall there was no significant effect due to SES; students on free lunch scored as high as children who did not participate in the free-lunch program. However, for students who had SOLOM scores in grade 5, higher SES students (not on free lunch) had significantly higher scores than lower SES students (receiving free lunch).

Table 9.4 presents SOLOM data for English speakers[1] according to students' ethnic background, as many school administrators, teachers and parents question whether African American and Hispanic English speakers should be placed in DLE programs. As Table 9.4 shows, there were no program type differences for any of the English-speaking ethnic groups, except for kindergarten African American students, where students in the 90HI program outscored students in the 90LO program.

Table 9.3 Oral language proficiency in L1: FLOSEM scores (and percentage of students rated as proficient) by grade level and program type

English speakers rated in English

Grade level	90HI	50:50	TBE	EO	Program differences
Kinder-garten	28.3 (94%)	29.2 (97%)	14.9 (20%)	29.5 (96%)	EO>TBE
First	29.6 (100%)	29.9 (100%)	16.1 (31%)	29.7 (100%)	EO>TBE
Second	29.7 (100%)	29.3 (100%)	n/a	29.3 (100%)	None
Third	28.7 (100%)	29.6 (100%)	20.9 (63%)	29.3 (100%)	None
Fourth	29.9 (100%)	19.6 (100%)		29.3 (100%)	None
Fifth	n/a	29.6 (100%)		29.7 (100%)	None
Sixth	30.0 (100%)			29.8 (100%)	None

Spanish speakers rated in Spanish

Grade level	90HI	90LO	50:50	TBE	EO	Program differences
Kinder-garten	28.2 (91%)	28.0 (100%)	18.6 (51%)	26.8 (93%)		90HI,LO,TBE>50
First	29.1 (97%)	28.2 (100%)	24.0 (76%)	29.3 (98%)		90HI,LO,TBE>50
Second	29.2 (99%)	28.0 (100%)	22.5 (64%)	29.4 (100%)		90HI,LO,TBE>50
Third	28.2 (100%)		25.1 (85%)	29.2 (100%)	28.7 (96%)	90HI,TBE,EO>50
Fourth	29.6 (100%)		25.2 (81%)	29.4 (100%)	27.7 (97%)	90HI >50

Table 9.4 Oral language proficiency in L1 for English speakers by ethnicity. SOLOM scores (percentage rated as proficient) by grade and program type*

English speakers in English: African Americans

Grade level	90HI	90LO	Program differences
Kindergarten	24.0 (96%)	20.5 (82%)	90HI>90LO
First	24.4 (98%)		None
Second	24.9 (100%)		None
Third	25.0 (100%)		None
Fourth	25.0 (100%)		None
Fifth	24.4 (100%)		None

*At grade levels 1–5, there were no differences between the 90HI and 90LO programs, or the sample size for each program type was too small to ascertain differences.

English speakers in English: Hispanic Americans

Grade level	90HI	90LO	50:50	Program differences
Kindergarten	23.9 (96%)	22.7 (88%)	23.5 (100%)	None
First	23.9 (96%)	24.4 (96%)	23.5 (100%)	None
Second	24.2 (97%)	24.0 (97%)	23.9 (100%)	None
Third	24.2 (96%)	24.2 (100%)		None
Fourth	24.1 (100%)	24.4 (100%)		None
Fifth	24.8 (100%)	24.3 (100%)		None

English speakers in English: European Americans

Grade level	90HI	90LO	50:50	Program differences
Kindergarten	24.6 (99%)	24.3 (97%)	24.1 (98%)	None
First	24.7 (98%)	24.5 (98%)	24.4 (99%)	None
Second	24.5 (98%)	24.8 (100%)	24.8 (100%)	None
Third	24.3 (91%)	24.6 (98%)		None
Fourth	25.0 (100%)	24.7 (100%)		None
Fifth	24.8 (100%)	24.6 (100%)		None

Table 9.5 Percentage of students (all 90:10) rated non-proficient, limited proficient and proficient on other proficiency measure evaluations by grade level and language background

English speakers in English

Grade level	Non-proficient (NEP)	Limited prof. (LEP)	Proficient (FEP)
Kindergarten	0%	1%	99%
First	0%	1%	99%
Second	0%	0%	100%
Third	0%	0%	100%
Fourth	0%	0%	100%
Fifth	0%	0%	100%

Spanish speakers in Spanish

Grade level	Non-proficient (NSP)	Limited prof. (LSP)	Proficient (FSP)
Kinder	8%	9%	83%
First	2%	3%	96%
Second	0%	1%	99%
Third	0%	0%	100%
Fourth	0%	0%	100%
Fifth	0%	0%	100%

Table 9.5 presents the percentage of students rated as non-proficient (NEP, NSP), limited proficient (LEP, LSP), or proficient (FEP, FSP) by the other proficiency measures (IPT and LAS). As the table illustrates, almost all students scored high enough to be classified as proficient, whether they were native English or Spanish speakers. By third grade, all students scored as proficient.

Table 9.6 shows the correspondence in scores between the SOLOM and the FLOSEM in ratings of L1 proficiency. There was 'agreement' when both the SOLOM and FLOSEM gave the student a 'proficient' rating or a

Table 9.6 Correspondence between SOLOM and FLOSEM in L1 (all 90:10 students)

Grade level	Same rating for English speakers	Same rating for Spanish speakers
Kindergarten	100%	96%
First	97%	98%
Second	100%	100%

Table 9.7 Correspondence between SOLOM and other proficiency measures (all 90:10 students)

English speakers in English

Grade level	Same	SOLOM>Other	Other>SOLOM
Kindergarten	99%	1%	0%
First	99%	1%	0%
Second	100%	0%	0%
Third	96%	0%	4%
Fourth	100%	0%	0%
Fifth	100%	0%	0%

Spanish speakers in Spanish

Grade level	% Same	% SOLOM>Other	% Other>SOLOM
Kindergarten	83%	3%	14%
First	95%	3%	2%
Second	95%	1%	4%
Third	100%	0%	0%
Fourth	100%	0%	0%

'non-proficient' rating, while 'disagreement' meant that one scale rated the student as 'proficient' and the other scale provided a 'non-proficient' rating. Clearly, these measures were providing very similar information, as the percentage of agreement was 96–100% for all grade levels and both language backgrounds.

Correspondence between the SOLOM and other proficiency measures (IPT, LAS), which was determined in similar fashion as for the SOLOM and FLOSEM, appears in Table 9.7. A high level of congruity characterized the classification of students as proficient or non-proficient across these measures. Thus, 95–100% of English and Spanish speakers (except Spanish kindergartners, where the correspondence was only 83%) were categorized as proficient by both measures.

Table 9.8 Oral language proficiency in L2. SOLOM scores (and percentage of students rated as proficient) by grade level and program type

English speakers rated in Spanish

Grade level	90HI	90LO	50:50	Program differences
Kinderg.	14.4 (26%)	12.6 (12%)	9.3 (2%)	90HI>90LO,50 90LO>50
First	17.5 (38%)	16.8 (35%)	10.7 (2%)	90HI, 90LO>50
Second	19.0 (60%)	18.6 (56%)	12.3 (4%)	90HI, 90LO>50
Third	20.2 (80%)	20.2 (68%)		NS
Fourth	22.0 (89%)	19.8 (63%)		90HI>90LO
Fifth	24.0 (100%)	20.7 (75%)		90HI>90LO
Sixth		21.3 (93%)		

Spanish speakers rated in English

Grade level	90HI	90LO	50:50	TBE	Program differences
Kinderg.	14.1 (26%)	13.2 (21%)	14.6 (21%)	22.4 (94%)	TBE>90HI,LO,50
First	16.6 (41%)	15.6 (32%)	16.9 (36%)	24.7 (100%)	TBE>90HI,LO,50
Second	18.5 (55%)	17.7 (53%)	17.7 (42%)	22.0 (78%)	TBE>90HI,LO,50
Third	18.7 (65%)	19.4 (64%)		22.7 (92%)	TBE>90HI,LO
Fourth	21.4 (87%)	19.8 (66%)		22.7 (91%)	TBE>90LO
Fifth	24.1 (100%)	22.4 (94%)		23.3 (96%)	90HI>90LO
Sixth		21.3 (93%)		21.7 (79%)	TBE>90LO

Oral Language Proficiency in Second Language (L2)

Table 9.8 and Figures 9.3–9.5 present the oral language proficiency data in L2 by language background, grade level and program type. As Figure 9.3 shows, Spanish-speaking and English-speaking students in 90HI programs were very similar in their advancement toward L2 proficiency across the grade levels. Interestingly, there was more variation within English speakers and within Spanish speakers in different program types than between Spanish and English speakers in 90HI programs. However, two multivariate analyses of variance (grades 1–3 and grades 4–5) indicated that in grades 1–3 English speakers were rated higher than Spanish speakers, whereas in grades 4–5, there was no significant difference between these two language groups. Regardless of the program type, students' scores were higher at each increasing grade level.

English speakers in 90HI and 90LO programs developed high levels of proficiency. By fifth grade, 90HI students scored near the top of the SOLOM (24 out of 25) and all students were rated as proficient. As Table 9.8 and Figure 9.4 indicate, 90HI students outscored 90LO students at most grade levels. However, even at the third grade level where the scores were equivalent, 12% more 90HI students were rated proficient (80% total) compared to 90LO students (68%). By fifth grade, 25% more 90HI than 90LO students scored as proficient. At each of the primary grade levels, where there are data available, 90:10 students outscored 50:50 students. By second grade, 50:50 students scored only 12.3, and only 4% were rated as proficient in Spanish.

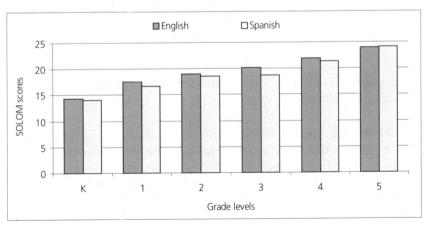

Figure 9.3 L2 SOLOM scores for English and Spanish speakers: 90HI programs

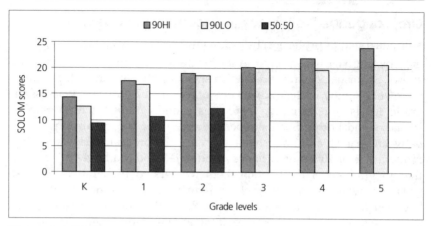

Figure 9.4 L2 (Spanish) SOLOM scores for English speakers by program type and grade level

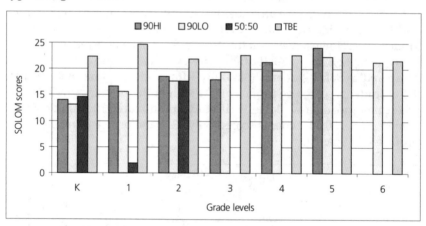

Figure 9.5 L2 (English) SOLOM scores for Spanish speakers by program type and grade level

Table 9.9 shows that FLOSEM results were fairly comparable to SOLOM results (Table 9.8) SOLOM results. That is, across the grade levels, for the most part, more English speakers in each program type were rated as proficient in Spanish. Also, at the upper-grade levels, most 90:10 English-speaking students were rated as proficient in Spanish.

Among Spanish speakers, SOLOM data (Table 9.8) show that, across grade levels, scores increased and more students were rated as proficient in English. By fifth and sixth grades, all students in the 90HI and almost all (93–94%)

Table 9.9 Oral language proficiency in L2. FLOSEM Scores (percentage of students rated as proficient) by grade level and program type

English speakers in Spanish

Grade level	90HI	90LO	50:50	EO	Program differences
Kinder.	12.5 (12%)	10.1 (0%)	10.7 (5%)	5.8 (4%)	90HI,50>EO
First	17.0 (23%)	16.7 (18%)	11.5 (8%)	5.4 (0%)	90HI,LO>50,TBE 50>EO
Second	21.1 (58%)	19.6 (50%)	13.2 (18%)		90HI,LO>50,TBE
Third	22.7 (88%)		15.9 (29%)	7.2 (7%)	90HI,LO>50,TBE 50>EO
Fourth	24.9 (100%)		17.1 (38%)	8.9 (13%)	90HI,LO>50,TBE 50>EO
Fifth	n/a				
Sixth	20.4 (70%)			9.7 (18%)	
Seventh	25.3 (100%)				

Spanish speakers in English

Grade level	90HI	90LO	50:50	TBE	EO	Program differences
Kinder.	10.6 (10%)	13.5 (36%)	22.9 (76%)	10.1 (7%)		50>90HI,LO,TBE
First	15.9 (32%)	17.8 (49%)	22.0 (58%)	15.7 (40%)		None
Second	19.3 (52%)		24.9 (86%)	18.6 (58%)		50>90HI,TBE
Third	22.3 (87%)		25.7 (92%)	18.4 (42%)	20.2 (60%)	50>TBE,EO 90HI>TBE
Fourth	21.9 (68%)		24.6 (84%)	17.4 (31%)	20.4 (53%)	50>TBE,EO
Fifth	n/a			21.8 (68%)	22.5 (73%)	None
Sixth	27.9 (100%)				25.3 (73%)	90HI>TBE

students in the 90LO programs were rated as proficient in English. While almost all (91–96%) TBE students in grades 3–5 scored as proficient, only 79% of sixth graders received high enough SOLOM scores to rate them as proficient. At all grade levels, TBE students were rated higher than 90:10 students and 50:50 students. What is interesting is that from kindergarten, almost every TBE student (94%) scored as proficient. Yet, these students were identified as limited English proficient because of their oral language scores. Further, while the scores of the students in the 90:10 and 50:50 programs increased across the grade levels, those of TBE students stayed fairly constant.

Another interesting comparison is between 90:10 and 50:50 Spanish-speaking students. At each grade level, from K to 2, more 90HI than 50:50 students were rated as proficient in English. Yet, 90HI students received only 10% of their instructional day in English in grades K–1 (20% in grades 2–3) compared to 50:50 students, who spent half of their instructional day in English.

Table 9.9 presents FLOSEM results that are slightly different from the SOLOM results we saw in Table 9.8. That is, students in the 50:50 program were rated significantly higher than students in 90:10 at kindergarten and second grade, though there were no significant differences at grades 1, 3 or 4. Students in the TBE program showed increasing English proficiency across grade levels, but their scores were not as high as 90HI students. Finally, EO program students, despite receiving instruction only in English, did not outscore students in any other program type. In fact, only 73% of sixth graders in the EO program, compared with 100% of 90HI sixth graders, scored as proficient in English.

Thus, these results clearly indicate that students in the 90:10 program made good progress toward developing proficiency in English. Despite receiving lower levels of instruction in English than their 50:50 and EO peers, they scored as high or higher than their peers at the upper grade levels.

Table 9.10 presents the L2 longitudinal data for English and Spanish speakers. The repeated measures analysis of variance (ANOVA) for oral language proficiency in L2 revealed a highly significant effect for time. As the table shows, these results indicate that students' scores increased significantly across the grade levels from first through fifth grade. An analysis of the contrasts from each grade level to the next produced significant contrasts, and thus significant growth: from grade 1 to grade 2, from grade 2 to grade 3, from grade 3 to grade 4, and from grade 4 to grade 5. Overall, there was a highly significant effect for language background, in which Spanish speakers outscored English speakers. These longitudinal results are consistent with the findings discussed according to the cross-sectional perspective.

Table 9.10 Oral language proficiency in L2: Longitudinal perspective. SOLOM scores by grade level for 90:10 students

Grade level	Spanish speakers	English speakers
First	17.8 (5.6)	15.0 (5.8)
Second	20.4 (4.0)	19.7 (3.3)
Third	21.8 (3.3)	19.7 (3.1)
Fourth	22.4 (2.8)	20.9 (3.1)
Fifth	22.9 (1.9)	21.4 (3.2)

Table 9.11 presents oral language proficiency in L2 (Spanish) for English speakers according to grade level, program type and ethnicity. As this set of tables shows, for all three ethnic groups, students made continued progress across the grade levels, with higher scores and more students rated as proficient. For each ethnic group, most or all of the students in the fifth grade were rated as proficient in Spanish. In the primary grade levels, Hispanic and EURO students in the 90:10 programs outscored students in the 50:50 programs. From the first grade level, there were no differences between proficiency ratings for the 90HI and 90LO participants.

Table 9.11 Oral language proficiency in L2 by ethnicity. SOLOM scores (percentage of students rated as proficient) according to grade level and program type

English speakers in Spanish: African Americans

Grade level	90:10	Program differences
Kindergarten	9.0 (5%)	None
First	14.2 (21%)	None
Second	17.9 (49%)	None
Third	19.3 (54%)	None
Fourth	21.0 (88%)	None
Fifth	22.3 (80%)	None

At grades K–5, there were no differences between the 90HI and 90LO programs, or the sample size for each program type was too small to ascertain any differences.

Table 9.11 *Continued*

English speakers in Spanish: Hispanic Americans

Grade level	90HI	90LO	50:50	Program differences
Kindergarten	16.8 (40%)	15.2 (28%)	9.9 (5%)	90HI>90LO,50
First	18.9 (59%)	18.4 (52%)	11.3 (6%)	90HI, 90LO>50
Second	19.4 (61%)	19.2 (67%)	12.9 (0%)	90HI, 90LO>50
Third	20.5 (78%)	21.3 (82%)		NS
Fourth	22.9 (100%)	21.3 (83%)		NS
Fifth	24.3 (100%)	22.6 (86%)		NS

English speakers in Spanish: Euro Americans

Grade level	90HI	90LO	50:50	Program differences
Kindergarten	14.3 (26%)	12.4 (11%)	9.1 (1%)	90HI>90LO 90HI,LO>50
First	17.3 (44%)	16.7 (32%)	10.6 (2%)	90HI, 90LO>50
Second	19.1 (55%)	18.7 (62%)	12.1 (6%)	90HI, 90LO>50
Third	19.7 (78%)	20.2 (71%)		NS
Fourth	21.5 (80%)	19.0 (48%)		NS
Fifth	23.1 (100%)	20.7 (82%)		NS

Thus, these data demonstrate that, as with L1 proficiency, students of the three major ethnic groups studied made excellent progress in developing proficiency in a second language. Students' progress in L2 development was also examined for gender and SES differences. These analyses showed that students' scores did not vary according to their gender or SES.

Table 9.12 shows the percentage of students rated as non-proficient (NEP/NSP), limited proficient (LEP/LSP), and fluent proficient (FEP/FSP) in their second language. These data demonstrate that, across the grade levels, fewer students were rated as NEP/NSP and LEP/LSP and correspondingly more students were rated as FEP/FSP. By third grade, at

Table 9.12 Percentage rated non-proficient, limited proficient and proficient in L2 on other proficiency measure evaluations by grade level and language background (all 90:10 students) ·

English speakers in Spanish

Grade level	Non-proficient (NEP/NSP)	Limited prof. (LEP/LSP)	Proficient (FEP/FSP)
Kindergarten	63%	24%	13%
First	38%	28%	34%
Second	10%	24%	66%
Third	0%	4%	96%
Fourth	0%	0%	100%
Fifth	0%	0%	100%

Spanish speakers in English

Grade level	Non-proficient	Limited proficient	Proficient
Kindergarten	46%	28%	26%
First	27%	18%	55%
Second	10%	14%	76%
Third	0%	5%	95%
Fourth	0%	6%	94%
Fifth	0%	0%	100%

least 94% of the students were rated as proficient and, by fifth grade, all English and Spanish speakers scored as proficient.

Table 9.13 presents the correspondence between the SOLOM and the FLOSEM ratings for 90:10 students in their development of the second language. As this table indicates, there was considerable similarity (86–100%) between SOLOM and FLOSEM categories (proficient vs. non-proficient) in grades K–1 for English and Spanish speakers. However, at grade 2, the level of agreement between the two measures was lower than at grades K–1, though it was still fairly high (74–77%) for both English and Spanish speakers.

Table 9.13 Correspondence between SOLOM and FLOSEM in L2 (all 90:10 students)

Grade level	Same rating English speakers	Same rating Spanish speakers
Kindergarten	100%	93%
First	86%	92%
Second	77%	74%

Table 9.14 Correspondence between SOLOM and other proficiency measures (all 90:10 students)

English speakers in Spanish

Grade level	Same	SOLOM>Other	Other>SOLOM
Kindergarten	67%	32%	1%
First	70%	6%	24%
Second	72%	11%	16%
Third	77%	0%	23%
Fourth	100%	0%	0%
Fifth	100%	0%	0%

Same means that both measures rated the students as proficient, or SOLOM rated as not-proficient and Other rated as limited or non-proficient.
SOLOM>Other means the SOLOM score gave students proficient rating while Other measure gave students non-proficient or limited proficient rating.
Other>SOLOM means the Other measure rated the student as proficient while the SOLOM classified the student as non-proficient.

Spanish speakers in English

Grade level	% Same	% SOLOM>Other	% Other>SOLOM
Kindergarten	74%	12%	14%
First	77%	6%	17%
Second	82%	2%	16%
Third	90%	0%	10%
Fourth	89%	6%	6%
Fifth	100%	0%	0%

Table 9.15 Correlations between L1 and L2 SOLOM scores for 90:10 (and 50:50) students

	English speakers	*Spanish speakers*
L1/grade 1 with L2/grade 1	-0.09* (0.25*)	-0.02 (0.03)
L1/grade 2 with L2/grade 2	-0.13** (0.06)	-0.03 (0.02)
L1/grade 3 with L2/grade 3	-0.304***	-0.06
L1/grade 4 with L2/grade 4	-0.23	-0.09
L1/grade 5 with L2/grade 5	-0.11	-0.08

Correlations for 50:50 students shown in parentheses. *$p<0.05$; **$p<0.01$; ***$p<0.001$

However, in looking at the correspondence between the SOLOM ratings and other proficiency measures (IPT, LAS) scores, there was moderate agreement (74–90%) at the kindergarten through third grade levels and high agreement (89–100%) for grades 4 and 5. When the ratings did not agree, from first grade on, the other measures produced higher scores than the SOLOM ratings (see % Other>SOLOM column in Table 9.14).

Relation Between Proficiency in L1 and L2

Correlations were run to examine the extent to which proficiency in L1 was related to proficiency in L2. These correlations were conducted separately for English speakers and Spanish speakers and separately for 90:10 and 50:50 programs, as there were differences in students' proficiency levels according to program type. As Table 9.15 shows, for the Spanish speakers, the correlations were very close to 0, signifying no relationship between proficiency in L1 and L2. Thus, scores in L1 were not associated with particular scores or score clusters in L2. Correlations for English speakers were not much higher, and most were negative. It is interesting that, even by fifth grade, the correlations were very small and more negative than positive.

Level of Bilingualism

Students were categorized according to their total SOLOM or FLOSEM scores in each language (Spanish and English) as High, Medium or Low proficient bilinguals. The scoring was as follows:

- *High*: students scored at the *top of the scale* (23–25 for SOLOM, 26–30 for FLOSEM) *in both languages*.
- *Medium* included one of the following:

  high in their L1 (23–25 for SOLOM, 26–30 for FLOSEM) and *moderate in L2* (SOLOM score of 19–22, FLOSEM score of 19–25)

  moderate in their L1 (SOLOM score between 19 and 22 or FLOSEM score between 19 and 25) and *high in their L2* (23–25 for SOLOM, 26–30 for FLOSEM)

- *Low* was defined as:

  Low or moderate in the L1 and the L2 (5–22 for SOLOM and 5–25 for FLOSEM)

  Low in the L1 (5–19 for SOLOM and FLOSEM) and *high in the L2* (23–25 for SOLOM, 26–30 for FLOSEM)

Table 9.16 Level of bilingualism by grade level and language background

English speakers

Grade level	90:10			50:50			Significant relationship
	Low	Med	High	Low	Med	High	
Third	4%	79%	17%	3%	90%	7%	None
Fourth	1%	72%	26%	0%	94%	6%	None
Fifth	2%	49%	49%	–	–	–	
Sixth	0%	79%	21%	–	–	–	

Spanish speakers

Grade level	90:10			50:50			Significant relationship
	Low	Med	High	Low	Med	High	
Third	4%	76%	20%	23%	50%	27%	***
Fourth	6%	64%	31%	20%	52%	28%	*
Fifth	2%	41%	57%	17%	44%	39%	*
Sixth	0%	41%	59%	22%	44%	33%	*

$* p < 0.05; *** p < 0.001$

Table 9.16 and Figures 9.6 and 9.7 present the percentage of students in the 90:10 program who were categorized by their SOLOM or FLOSEM scores as Low, Medium or High bilinguals. As the table and figure show, for English speakers between grades 3 and 6 in the 90:10 program, the percentage of Low bilinguals was rare (0–4%) and the percentage of High bilinguals varied between 17% and 49%. The great majority of 90:10 students were classified as Medium (49% in grade 5, 72–79% in grades 3, 4, and 6). In the 50:50 program, few students were categorized as Low (0–3%) or High (6–7%), and almost all

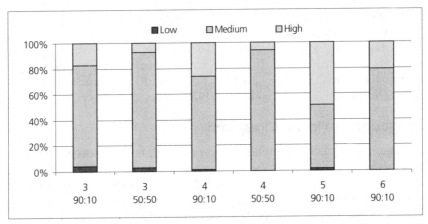

Figure 9.6 Level of bilingualism for English speakers by program type and grade level

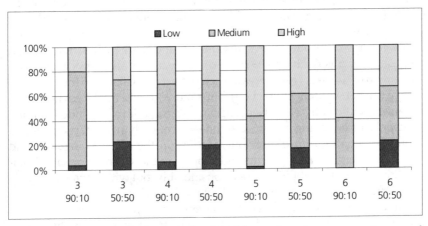

Figure 9.7 Level of bilingualism for Spanish speakers by program type and grade level

students (90–94%) as Medium. At the third and fourth grade levels, there was no statistically significant relation between program type (90:10, 50:50) and level of bilingualism (low, medium, high).

Results differed for the Spanish speakers in terms of variations across program types and percentage of students rated as High bilingual. At all grade levels, few (0–6%) 90:10, but one fifth (17–23%) of 50:50, students were categorized as Low bilingual. Fewer students at grades 5–6 (41–44%) than at grades 3–4 (50–76%) were categorized as Medium, and correspondingly more upper-grade than lower-grade students made the High bilingual rating. At all grade levels, there was a significant relationship between program type and bilingual level.

As these data show, for grade 5–6 students, half of 90:10 Spanish speakers and one third of 50:50 Spanish speakers were rated High bilinguals. Among English speakers, half of 90:10 fifth graders but only 20% of 90:10 sixth graders were High bilinguals.

Language Use in the Classroom

Language proficiency ratings are very useful, but they do not indicate whether students could use the languages in the classroom. Throughout the grade levels, as the proficiency measures showed, both Spanish and English speakers maintained their fluency and gained greater accuracy in using various grammatical, vocabulary, sociolinguistic, and semantic components. In the second language, as students became more proficient, all comprehended and most were able to fluently produce the L2 with appropriate pronunciation, grammar, and vocabulary. Furthermore, they demonstrated an understanding of a variety of sociolinguistic rules during communication exchanges. Students showed high levels of comprehension skills during classroom lectures, discussions and work in both Spanish and English. Students tended to respond correctly across all subject areas, with more than 64% correct responses in each subject (see Chapter 6 for a description of teacher–student interaction). Thus, students had mastered the second language sufficiently to fully participate at grade level in understanding teacher lectures, taking part in question–answer exchanges, participating in large and small group discussions, reading in the second language, and completing written assignments and projects in the second language. Their reading and writing abilities varied considerably, but within the same range of abilities one might see in a monolingual classroom.

Across grade levels and in both academic and non-academic classroom situations, the speaking of English between students was generally tolerated during Spanish time. At the upper grade levels, students were expected to speak Spanish during Spanish time, and teachers often requested students to use Spanish if they were using English. When students were distanced from linguistic authority and given the opportunity to choose a language, more often than not the students at the upper-grade levels spoke in English.

There was some language switching in student–student interactions. In the lower grades, students switched languages because they did not have the appropriate vocabulary or grammar. In the upper grades, though, both English-speaking and Spanish-speaking students spoke more completely in one language or another. Thus, often when they deviated from the language-use rule of 'Spanish during Spanish time', they were making a choice to change languages.

Overall, students were able to use both languages in the classroom to work at grade level. There was considerable matching of student language choice to teacher language choice. That is, students had sufficiently developed the vocabulary and grammar in both languages to use Spanish during Spanish time and English during the designated English time.

Summary and Conclusions

These oral language proficiency data clearly show that DLE students scored at or near the top of the SOLOM in their first language and almost all students were rated as proficient in their two languages, particularly by the upper grade levels. Students made statistically significant growth in both languages across grade levels. These data are consistent whether we examine them from a cross-sectional or longitudinal perspective, and regardless of the language measures that we used.

L1 proficiency

Both English and Spanish speakers were highly proficient in their native language, especially in the upper grades. English speakers did not vary in their English language development according to the type of program in which they were participating. Students receiving as little as 10% or 20% of their instruction in English scored as well as students spending half their instructional day in English, and both types of bilingual participants were rated as highly as monolingual English speakers in English Only programs. These findings were just as true for African American and Hispanic students as they were for EURO students, and the results held whether these students were low or mid SES.

For Spanish speakers, there were significant program differences associated with their Spanish proficiency. Students in 90:10 programs received higher ratings than did students in 50:50 and TBE programs. Thus, Spanish speakers clearly benefited from the additional instruction in Spanish to promote their Spanish language development.

With respect to program and school demographic factors, then, program type was influential for Spanish but not for English speakers. Ethnic density/SES need (90HI vs. 90LO) was not a significant factor in L1 proficiency. In terms of student background characteristics, English speakers received higher ratings than Spanish speakers. Overall, SES was not a significant factor, though it was important by the final year of elementary school (fifth grade), where mid-SES students were rated higher than low-SES students were. While girls generally scored higher than boys did, these differences were not significant at any grade level.

L2 proficiency

In summarizing L2 proficiency, Spanish speakers scored higher than English speakers did. There were important program type and school demographic differences in these students' proficiency ratings. For English speakers, 90:10 students outscored 50:50 students. Thus, receiving a much larger percentage (80–90% compared with 50%) of instruction in Spanish in the early grade levels produced a larger gain in Spanish proficiency. Thus, school demographic characteristics were important in promoting higher levels of proficiency for English speakers. Furthermore, English-speaking students from all ethnic groups made good gains in developing Spanish, even when a significant percentage was low-SES.

Among Spanish-speaking students, there were important program-related findings. While TBE students outscored DLE students, they began kindergarten with fairly high scores and made little growth across the years in English proficiency. In contrast, DLE students made significant gains across the grade levels, with sixth-grade DLE students outscoring TBE students in the percentage of students rated as proficient in English. Another important program effect was the absence of any significant difference between 90:10 and 50:50 participants. Despite receiving only 10–20% of their instructional day in English compared with 50% for 50:50 students, in their proficiency ratings 90:10 students scored similarly to 50:50 students. Thus, receiving less English in their curriculum did not negatively affect these students' English language proficiency relative to students receiving half of their instruction in English.

In examining the development of L2 proficiency, program and school demographic factors were important, but in different ways for English and Spanish speakers. English speakers benefited from the additional Spanish in their curriculum, as the 90:10 students were more proficient than the

50:50 students. In contrast, Spanish speakers developed just as high levels of English proficiency whether they participated in a 90:10 or a 50:50 program. However, at the upper-grade levels, English-speaking 90HI students were rated more proficient in Spanish than 90LO English-speaking students. Other student-background factors were not significant. Thus, students of all ethnicities and both genders and SES categories made excellent progress in developing proficiency in a second language.

English speakers in the 50:50 sample described here were rated lower on the SOLOM in Spanish than were English-speaking students in another 50:50 program (Key School) using the SOPR, a SOLOM-like measure (Christian *et al.*, 1997). At grades 1 and 2, the 50:50 students in this sample, compared with the Key sample, scored 10.7 vs. 14 (grade 1) and 12.3 vs. 16.4 (grade 2). Further, in the Key sample, 21% of the second-grade students were rated as proficient in Spanish compared to only 2–4% in my sample. However, using FLOSEM data (another SOLOM-type measure) at the second-grade level, 18% of students in my 50:50 sample were rated as proficient in Spanish compared to the 21% proficiency rate found with Key students.

In comparing the results for Spanish speakers, the findings were very comparable for first language proficiency. At grade 1, about 88% of Key students and 96% of students in my sample and at grade 2 100% of Key and 93% of students in my sample were rated as proficient in Spanish. Thus, there was fairly good consistency across the samples with different instruments for both groups of students.

The results for L1 and L2 proficiency are similar to results from immersion research, showing that English speakers develop high levels of proficiency in their *first language*, regardless of whether they participate in a partial (50:50 type) or full (90:10 type) immersion program (Genesee, 1987; Swain & Lapkin, 1982). Further, immersion students develop high levels of L2 proficiency in both partial and full immersion programs (Campbell *et al.*, 1985; Genesee, 1987), though their proficiency is higher in full immersion programs (Campbell *et al.*, 1985).

In addition, the findings for Spanish-speaking students are comparable to those reported in the literature on bilingual education. That is, previous studies have reported that good bilingual programs promote high levels of proficiency in the native language (August & Hakuta, 1997; Escamilla & Medina, 1993; Padilla *et al.*, 1991; Ramirez *et al.*, 1991; Willig, 1985). Further, the results presented here showed that additional instruction in Spanish was associated with both higher average scores in Spanish and more students rated as proficient in Spanish (comparing 90:10 students with 50:50 and TBE students), especially at the upper-grade levels. This result is consistent with previous research demonstrating that LEP students in late-exit programs (such as 90:10 program) acquire higher levels of proficiency in English than students in early-exit (TBE) programs (August & Hakuta, 1997; Escamilla & Medina, 1993; Medina & Escamilla, 1992; Padilla *et al.*, 1991; Ramirez *et al.*, 1991; Willig, 1985).

L1, L2 and Bilingual Proficiency

There was little significant relationship between L1 and L2 proficiency for English or Spanish speakers at any grade level. Thus, as a group, their L1 scores were not related to L2 scores. This lack of a positive and significant relation between L1 and L2 proficiency is probably due to the fact that the students were at different levels of bilingual proficiency: some students were very high in both languages, some were high in one language and moderate or low in the other. However, there were no students who were low in both languages at the upper-grade levels, though there were a few students who were moderate in one language and low in the other.

Among English speakers, most were medium bilinguals, with one fifth to one half of 90:10 students classified as high bilinguals. By fifth and sixth grades, over half of the Spanish-speaking 90:10 and 50:50 students were medium bilinguals. However, over 20% more 90:10 Spanish speakers (57–59%), compared to 50:50 Spanish-speaking students (33–39%), were high bilinguals.

What these results show is that both DLE models (90:10 and 50:50) promoted proficiency in two languages. Students in 90:10 programs developed higher levels of bilingual proficiency than did students in the 50:50 program. In developing proficiency in the English language, both English and Spanish speakers benefited equally from 90:10 and 50:50 programs. Thus, whether they spent 10–20% or 50% of their instructional day in English, students were equally proficient in English. In contrast, developing high levels of Spanish proficiency for both English and Spanish speakers was much more likely to occur in 90:10 than in 50:50 programs. Further, for English speakers, 90HI programs augmented Spanish proficiency even more than 90LO programs did.

Clearly, there is no evidence to suggest that participation in DLE programs retards the native language development of Spanish or English speakers. In contrast, almost all students, regardless of their student characteristics, were proficient in English and Spanish.

Notes

1. Data for Spanish speakers are not disaggregated by ethnicity, as all of the students were Hispanic and their scores were presented in Tables 9.1–9.3.

Chapter 10

Student Outcomes: Academic Language Proficiency – Reading and Language Achievement

Introduction to Academic Achievement

Considerable research shows that students in various types of high quality language education programs perform on various measures of academic achievement at least at grade level or at levels comparable to or exceeding those of their peers who are not enrolled in the language education program. These results hold true for partial and total immersion as well as for bilingual programs in the United States and many other countries – Australia, Brussels, Canada, Hong Kong, Hungary, South Africa, Spain (both Basque and Catalan programs) (e.g. Artigal, 1995; Baetens Beardsmore & Swain, 1985; Byram & Leman, 1990; Cummins & Swain, 1986; Day & Shapson, 1996; De Courcy, 1997; Dolson & Lindholm, 1995; Duff, 1997; Genesee, 1987; Johnson, 1997; Nuttall & Langhan, 1997; Ramirez *et al.*, 1991; Slaughter, 1997; Willig, 1985).

Academic achievement in bilinguals is also influenced by the level of bilingual proficiency, whereby higher levels of proficiency in the two languages is associated with higher levels of performance on academic achievement tests (e.g. Dawe, 1983; Fernandez & Nielsen, 1986; Lindholm, 1991; Lindholm & Aclan, 1991). In addition, a high level of bilingualism is related to factors that affect achievement performance, such as cognitive flexibility (Cummins, 1979; Peal & Lambert, 1962) and metalinguistic awareness (Ben-Zeev, 1977; Hakuta & Diaz, 1985; Ianco-Worrall, 1972).

According to a recent report by the Education Trust (1998), 'More than two decades of academic gains by minority students – particularly Hispanics and blacks – have largely disappeared in the 1990s.' As discussed in Chapter 1, the academic performance of minority students at a national level is considerably below that of non-minority students (e.g. Darling-Hammond, 1995; Padilla & Lindholm, 1995; Portes & Rumbaut, 1990). Though reading is critical to student achievement in all subjects, it is in reading where the achievement gap is greatest (National Assessment of Educational Progress Report, 1990). Although this achievement gap between non-minority and minority students has narrowed from 1971 to 1996, the scores of minorities increased during the 1980s, but have declined or flattened out in the 1990s (National Assessment of Educational Progress Report, 1998).

In addition, the highest secondary school drop-out rates are obtained in schools with large concentrations of Southeast Asian (48%) and Spanish-speaking (46%) students, and large concentrations of language minority students in general (Sue & Padilla, 1986). Thus, fluency in English is also a critical factor in achievement.

Research on both resilient students (those living in very adverse situations who appear to adjust quite well) and successful ones (those who come from high-risk environments, but achieve at high levels in school) has produced a set of factors that are related to the achievement and adjustment of successful African American students (Ford & Harris, 1996; Fordham & Ogbu, 1986; Kraft, 1991; Luster & McAdoo, 1994) and Hispanic students (Galindo & Escamilla, 1995; Gándara, 1995; Gándara et al., 1998; Okagaki et al., 1995). These factors include: (1) the students' achievement-related attitudes (e.g. self-efficacy, motivation); (2) family support; (3) positive and supportive peer group; and 4) supportive school environment.

This literature on achievement leads to some important questions to examine with the DLE students:

- How well do DLE students perform on achievement tests that assess reading and language?
- Does the level of bilingual proficiency relate to DLE students' academic achievement?
- Do student background (ethnicity, SES, gender, language background), and school demographic and program factors (90HI, 90LO, 50:50, TBE, EO) influence achievement performance?

Data are available from the reading and language sections of standardized achievement tests described in Chapter 8. Ratings of students' reading and writing proficiencies are presented in the next chapter (Chapter 11).

Academic Language Proficiency in the Native Language (L1)

Reading achievement in L1

Table 10.1 and Figures 10.1 through 10.3 present the reading achievement Normal Curve Equivalent (NCE)[1] scores for English and Spanish speakers in their first language (L1). As Table 10.1 shows, English speakers in 90HI programs performed below grade level in first and second grade, but average after that. Their scores were comparable with statewide aver-

Table 10.1 L1 reading achievement (NCE scores) by grade level and program type: Cross-sectional perspective

English speakers in English

Grade level	90HI	90LO	50:50	CA state average*	Program differences
First	40	58	59		90LO,50>90HI
Second	41	61	55	52	90LO,50>90HI
Third	49	59	74	51	50>90HI,90LO
Fourth	53	59	62	52	None
Fifth	50	61		51	None
Sixth	52	78		52	90LO>90HI

*Based on 1998 California-wide testing; scores provided by California Department of Education.

Spanish speakers in Spanish

Grade level	90HI	90LO	50:50	TBE	EO	CA avge	Program differences
Kinder.	56						
First	47	39	51	33			90HI,50>90LO,TBE
Second	50	43	41	39		52	90HI>90LO,50,TBE
Third	55	43	52	42	35	54	90HI>90LO,TBE,EO
Fourth	53	38	56	37	38	53	90HI>90LO,TBE,EO
Fifth	47	39	56	17	41	51	90HI,LO>TBE
Sixth	57	41				49	90HI>90LO
Seventh	78	44				50	90HI>90LO
Eighth	58	42				50	90HI>90LO

ages for English-speaking (non-LEP) students studying in English-only classrooms. Students in 90HI programs scored significantly lower than students in 90LO programs at the first, second and sixth grade levels. At all grade levels, students in the 90LO and 50:50 programs scored above

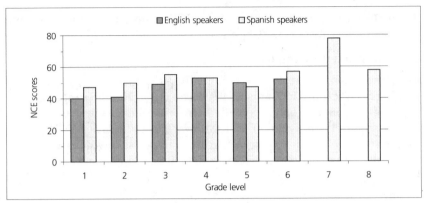

Figure 10.1 L1 reading for English and Spanish speakers in 90HI programs

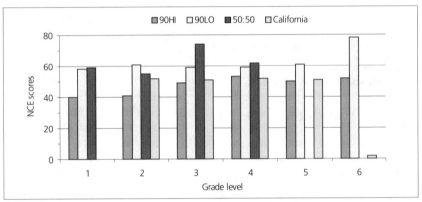

Figure 10.2 L1 reading scores for English speakers by program type

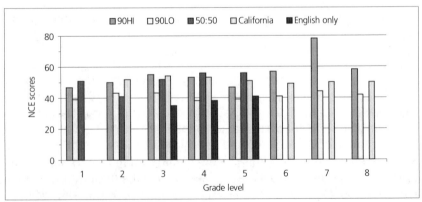

Figure 10.3 L1 reading scores for Spanish speakers by program type

average (55–61) to very high (74–78). What is interesting about the performance of the English speakers is the level of achievement related to the initiation and duration of formal English reading. At the first and second grade levels, students in 90:10 programs were reading in Spanish only. Thus, their scores represent their ability to transfer what they know about reading from Spanish to English. This places the 90:10 students at a performance disadvantage compared with their 50:50 peers and their EO peers in EO classrooms (state average). By the time 90HI students began reading in English (grade 3), their scores were comparable to statewide averages.

Results varied for Spanish speakers in their native language. Students in the 90HI and 50:50 programs scored average at most grade levels and comparable to statewide averages for Spanish-speaking students tested in Spanish. In contrast, peers in 90LO, TBE and EO programs scored below grade level and much lower than the statewide averages for LEP students. In the 90:10 programs, there was a slight dip in Spanish at the fourth and fifth grades as students focused more on reading skills in English.

Analyses of variance showed that there was a significant interaction between program type and language background; these results revealed that 90HI programs promoted *higher* reading performance for Spanish speakers, while 90LO programs were associated with higher reading scores for English speakers. We will re-examine this finding in light of results from L2 reading achievement.

Analyses were also conducted to determine whether SES and gender significantly affected students' scores in L1 reading achievement. There were significant gender differences in grades 3 and 4, with females outscoring males. At the other grade levels, there was no significant difference between boys and girls. While SES was highly significant as a main effect, there was also a statistically significant interaction between SES and language background. Thus, the gap in scores between students on free lunch versus students not on free lunch differed for Spanish and English speakers. For English speakers, there was a greater difference in scores between lower and middle SES students, whereas there was not much variation between the scores of Spanish-speaking free-lunch versus non-free-lunch participants. This interaction may reflect the rather small variation in SES among Spanish-speaking students and the few Spanish speakers who were not participating in the free lunch program.

Longitudinal data are presented in Tables 10.2 and 10.3 and Figure 10.4. Table 10.2 shows the NCEs for students' reading achievement for grades 1–8, for those students who participated in a 90:10 DLE program from kindergarten or first grade through at least fifth grade and had reading achievement scores for each year. As this table illustrates (and as a repeated

Table 10.2 L1 reading achievement by grade and language background: NCE scores, longitudinal perspective

Grade level	*Spanish speakers*	*English speakers*
First	52	44
Second	65	50
Third	55	55
Fourth	57	59
Fifth	52	57
Sixth	59	56
Seventh	65	57
Eighth	59	

measures analysis of variance demonstrated), students made statistically significant growth over time from grade 1 to grade 5. Furthermore, across the grade levels from first through fifth, English speakers outscored Spanish speakers. There were no main effects due to SES. However, there was a significant interaction between program and language background, wherein English speakers scored higher in 90LO programs, while Spanish speakers received higher NCEs in 90HI programs. These results are consistent with the cross-sectional results presented earlier.

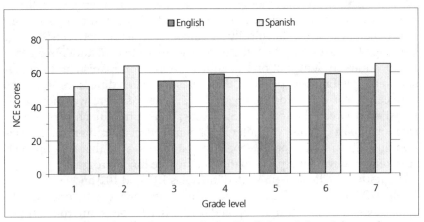

Figure 10.4 L1 reading achievement for English and Spanish speakers: NCE scores, longitudinal perspective

Table 10.3 L1 reading achievement for 5th graders by SES and program type: NCE scores, longitudinal perspective

Grade level	Spanish speakers	English speakers
90HI	58	54
Mid SES	56	55
Low SES	60	47
90LO	40	69
Mid SES	47	69
Low SES	39	–
Combined		
Mid SES	55	58
Low SES	51	47

Table 10.3 and Figure 10.5 present the longitudinal perspective for fifth graders who had participated since kindergarten or first grade, categorized by language background, program type (90HI vs. 90LO) and SES. Clearly, among Spanish speakers, low SES (free lunch) 90HI students scored higher (NCE=60) than the other Spanish-speaking groups. However, in the 90LO program, it was the non-free lunch students who outscored their free-lunch peers (NCE = 47 vs. 39). Among English speakers, mid-SES students also scored higher than their free-lunch peers in the 90HI program (55 vs. 47), though these students scored much lower than the mid-SES students in the 90LO program (69).

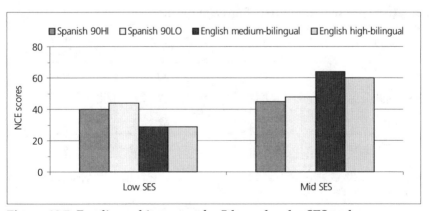

Figure 10.5 Reading achievement for 5th graders by SES and program type: Longitudinal perspective

Table 10.4 L1 English reading achievement in L1: NCE scores by ethnicity, grade level and program type

English speakers in English: African Americans and Asian Americans

Grade level	90:10 African Am	90:10 Asian Am
First	54	63
Second	49	52
Third	37	
Fourth		
Fifth	42	

English speakers in English: Hispanic Americans

Grade Level	90:10	50:50	Program differences
First	34	54	50>90:10
Second	35	47	50>90:10
Third	44	76	50>90:10
Fourth	50	66	50>90:10
Fifth	57		

English speakers in English: Euro Americans

Grade Level	90:10	50:50	Program differences
First	49	60	50>90:10
Second	53	57	
Third	60	62	
Fourth			
Fifth	60		
Sixth	69		
Seventh	61		

Table 10.4 presents the English reading achievement scores of English speakers by ethnicity. As this table shows, Hisp-EB students in the 50:50 program scored at or above average at all grade levels. These 50:50 participants also performed at a higher level than their 90:10 peers did. However, a year after they began English reading instruction, 90:10 students scored average to slightly above average (50–57). Among EURO first-grade students, 50:50 students who were reading in English outscored 90:10 students, who were only exposed to reading instruction in Spanish. At the other two grade levels, even though 50:50 students received more English reading instruction, their scores were not significantly higher than those of the 90:10 students.

African American students scored at grade level in first and second grade, but below grade level in grades 3 and 5. Interestingly, the African American students at the first and second grade levels scored similar to European American English-speaking (EURO) students and higher than Hispanic–English speaking (Hisp-EB) students. Finally, Asian American students scored the highest in first grade and comparable to EURO and African American students in second grade.

Language achievement in L1

Considerably fewer data were available for examining language achievement in either language because this assessment was not required for schools, and they were already spending a considerable amount of time testing the students. However, we will discuss what data exist.

In looking at the English speakers in Table 10.5, we see that students in the 90HI program scored below grade level during the first and second grades, when they were doing all of their academic work in Spanish. Their scores increased in third grade, when they began reading in English, and stayed in the average range after that. Students in 90LO and 50:50 programs all performed at grade level. Thus, despite having been instructed in Spanish, their performance compared favorably with EO students who were instructed only in English.

For Spanish speakers in the DLE program, performance was average up until fourth grade. As we saw with Spanish reading, the scores dipped in fourth and fifth grades. LEP students in EO and TBE programs scored well below average at all grade levels, and below statewide averages.

Academic Language Proficiency in the Second Language (L2)

Reading achievement in L2

Table 10.6 and Figures 10.6 through 10.8 present the scores for English

Table 10.5 L1 language achievement: NCE scores by grade level and program type

English speakers in English

Grade level	90HI	90LO	50:50	State average for English-only speakers	Program differences
First	36	50			90LO>90HI
Second	39	59	53	54	90LO>90HI
Third	44	50		52	None
Fourth	56	NA		52	
Fifth	49	49		53	None
Sixth	54			54	

Spanish speakers in Spanish

Grade level	90HI	50:50	TBE	EO	State average for LEPs	Program differences
First	55	59				None
Second	50	48	38		53	None
Third	50			32	53	90HI>EO
Fourth	34			31	51	None
Fifth	42			35	52	None

and Spanish speakers' reading achievement in their second language. Several points are interesting. First, English speakers scored in the average range in the 90HI program, average to below average in 90LO programs, and low in the 50:50 program. In fact, students in 90HI programs significantly outperformed their peers in 90LO programs at most grade levels.

For Spanish speakers, performance in English was low or below average in both 90:10 programs, below average to average in the 50:50 program, and low in the EO (English only) program. While students in the 90LO program outper-

Table 10.6 L2 reading achievement by grade level and program type: NCE scores, cross-sectional perspective

English speakers in Spanish

Grade level	*90HI*	*90LO*	*50:50*	*State avg. for LEPs*	*Program differences*
Kinder.	66				
First	53	45			90HI>90LO
Second	49	44	19	52	90HI,LO>50
Third	48	53		54	None
Fourth	49	39		53	90HI>90LO
Fifth	45	33		51	90HI>90LO
Sixth	50	47		49	None
Seventh	81			50	

Spanish speakers in English

Grade level	*90HI*	*90LO*	*50:50*	*EO*	*State avg. for LEPs*	*Program differences*
Kinder.	22					
First	30	35				90LO>90HI
Second	27	35	26		34	90LO>HI
Third	29	28	49		31	50>90HI,LO
Fourth	36	33	48		30	50>90LO,TBE
Fifth	22	39	34	29	29	90LO>90HI
Sixth	34	35	39		31	None
Seventh	43				27	

formed those in the 90HI program at first, second and fifth grades, there were no differences at the third, fourth and sixth grades. Students in the 50:50 program outscored students in the 90:10 program at the third and fourth grades, but not at the second, fifth or sixth grades. These findings suggest that both approaches yield equivalent performance in English reading achievement.

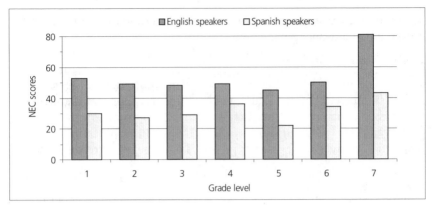

Figure 10.6 L2 reading for English and Spanish speakers in 90HI programs

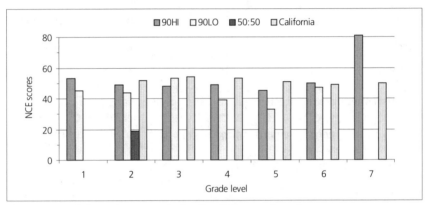

Figure 10.7 L2 reading scores for English speakers by program type

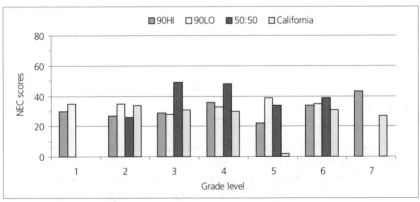

Figure 10.8 L2 reading scores for Spanish speakers by program type

A multivariate analysis of variance was conducted for grades 1–3[2] to determine whether language background, SES and program type significantly affected students' L2 reading achievement scores. From this analysis, language background was statistically significant, with English speakers outperforming Spanish speakers. In addition, mid-SES students scored significantly higher than low-SES students did. Another univariate analysis of variance was conducted at fifth grade to determine whether these variables were still significant. SES was still significant, as was an interaction between program type and language background. That is, consistent with the data previously presented, 90HI programs promoted higher L2 achievement for English speakers while 90LO programs increased the L2 achievement of Spanish speakers. Finally, analyses of gender suggested no differences between boys and girls.

Tables 10.7 and 10.8 (and Figures 10.9 and 10.10) provide the longitudinal L2 reading achievement data. As these tables show (and as demonstrated by a repeated measures analysis of variance for grades 1–5), the scores of students changed significantly over time. The scores of Spanish speakers increased significantly (from 29 to 41) across the grade levels, while the scores of English speakers stayed constant (59 to 54). Further, there was again a significant interaction between language background and program type: Spanish speakers scored higher in 90LO programs, while English speakers performed at higher levels in 90HI programs. This difference is clearly apparent in Table 10.8, where 90LO free-lunch Spanish speakers scored at grade level (NCE=47) in English reading achievement,

Table 10.7 L2 reading achievement by grade level and language background: NCE scores, longitudinal perspective

Grade level	Spanish speakers	English speakers
First	29	59
Second	31	60
Third	36	58
Fourth	38	51
Fifth	38	46
Sixth	37	53
Seventh	41	54
Eighth	41	

while even their mid-SES peers in 90HI programs scored 7 NCE points below them (NCE=40). Among English speakers, 90HI mid-SES students scored average (NCE=53), while their 90LO mid-SES peers scored *20 NCE points* lower.

Comparing the achievement of fifth graders in the two samples (longitudinal versus cross-sectional) yields slightly different findings. In the fifth grade, Spanish speakers in the longitudinal sample scored much higher (38) than their peers in the cross-sectional sample (22).

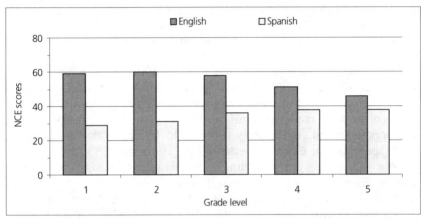

Figure 10.9 L2 reading achievement for English and Spanish speakers: NCE scores, longitudinal perspective

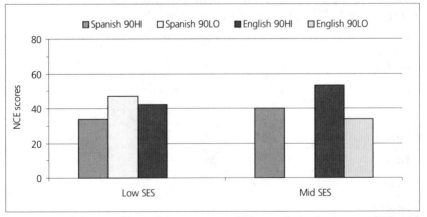

Figure 10.10 L2 reading achievement at fifth grade by language, SES and program type

Table 10.9 provides Spanish reading achievement scores according to ethnicity, grade level and program type. As this table indicates, Hispanic-English, EURO American and Asian American students scored about average at most grade levels (except for low-scoring EURO second graders in the 50:50 program, and high-scoring EURO American seventh graders in the 90:10 program). African American students scored low (NCE=24–30) at all grade levels (NCE=24–30).

Table 10.8 L2 reading achievement for 5th graders by SES and program type: NCE scores, longitudinal perspective

Grade level	Spanish speakers	English speakers
90HI	36	51
Mid SES	40	53
Low SES	34	42
90LO	47	34
Mid SES	—	34
Low SES	47	—
Combined		
Mid SES	40	47
Low SES	39	42

Table 10.9 L2 Spanish reading achievement (NCE scores) by ethnicity, grade level and program type

English speakers in Spanish: African Americans, Asian Americans and Hispanics

Grade level	90:10 African American	90:10 Asian American	90:10 Hispanic English
First	24	57	53
Second	26	52	50
Third	29		52
Fourth	26		46
Fifth	30		49

Table continues overleaf

Table 10.9 *(continued)*

English speakers in Spanish: European Americans

Grade level	90:10	50:50	Program differences
First	52		
Second	50	17	90:10>50:50
Third	53		
Fourth	48		
Fifth	50		
Sixth	51		
Seventh	73		
Eighth	52		

Table 10.10 L2 language achievement by grade level and program type

English speakers in Spanish

Grade level	90HI	90LO	Program differences
First	60	20	90HI>EO
Second	55		

Spanish speakers in English

Grade Level	90HI	90LO	Program differences
First	34	29	None
Second	28	30	None
Third	32		
Fourth	46	29	None
Fifth	27	40	90LO>90HI
Sixth	40		
Seventh	43		

Language achievement in L2

Table 10.10 indicates that English speakers in 90HI programs scored in the average range in Spanish at the primary levels. Spanish speakers performed in the low to slightly below average range in both 90HI and 90LO programs. The only significant different was the higher scores of 90LO students over 90HI students at the fifth-grade level. By sixth and seventh grades, Spanish-speaking students were scoring closer to average in their language achievement in English.

Relationships Between Oral Language Proficiency/Bilingual Proficiency and Academic Achievement for DLE Programs

Table 10.11 presents results from Pearson correlation analyses between oral language proficiency and reading achievement, and between reading achievement in the two languages, separately for English and Spanish speakers in 90:10 and 50:50 DLE programs. As this table shows, most of the correlations were statistically significant, though most were in the moderate range (0.2 to 0.3) rather than high (0.7 or 0.8). Patterns of correlations were similar for the Spanish and English speaking students. For both English and Spanish speakers, there was a low to moderate correlation (0.10 to 0.55) between L1 oral language proficiency (using the SOLOM) and L1 reading achievement. Correlations between oral language proficiency and reading achievement were higher (0.10 to 0.62) for L2, for both English and Spanish speakers. Also, there were low to high correlations between

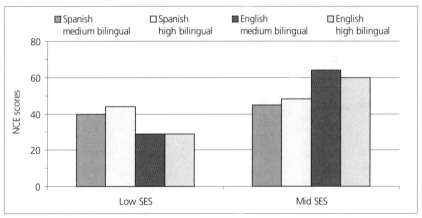

Figure 10.11 Relation between language background, SES, bilingual proficiency and L1 reading achievement at grade 5

Table 10.11 Correlations between oral proficiency and reading achievement by grade level, program type and language background

	Spanish speakers		English speakers	
	90:10	*50:50*	*90:10*	*50:50*
Grade 1				
L1 oral & L1 read	0.18**	0.34**	0.10	0.47**
L2 oral & L2 read	0.22**		0.33**	
L1 read & L2 read	0.29**		0.29**	
Grade 2				
L1 oral & L1 read	0.19**	0.55**	0.13*	0.45**
L2 oral & L2 read	0.23**	0.29	0.37**	0.28
L1 read & L2 read	0.31**		0.37**	
Grade 3				
L1 oral & L1 read	0.22*	0.51	0.13	
L2 oral & L2 read	0.39**		0.38**	
L1 read & L2 read	0.66**		0.61**	
Grade 4				
L1 oral & L1 read	0.30*		0.27*	
L2 oral & L2 read	0.62**		0.32*	
L1 read & L2 read	0.56**		0.63**	
Grade 5				
L1 oral & L1 read	0.22		0.43**	
L2 oral & L2 read	0.10		0.41**	
L1 read & L2 read	0.43**		0.55**	
Grade 6				
L1 read & L2 read	0.79**		0.81**	
Grade 7				
L1 read & L2 read	0.77**		0.48*	
Grade 8				
L1 read & L2 read	0.88**			

Statistical significances: * = $p<0.05$, ** = $p<0.01$, *** = $p<0.001$.

reading scores across the two languages (from 0.29 to 0.88). Once students began reading instruction in grade 3, the correlation (0.6) between English and Spanish reading increased dramatically (from 0.31 to 0.66). For the most part, the correlations between oral proficiency and reading achievement and between reading achievement in the two languages were stronger at increasing grade levels (except for grade 5 Spanish speakers).

Analyses of variance were conducted at grade 5 (the terminating grade level in elementary school) to determine the extent to which various program and student background factors, including level of bilingualism, affected reading achievement. The results of these analyses are illustrated in Figures 10.11 (L1 reading achievement) and 10.12 (L2 reading achievement). In examining L1 reading achievement in grade 5, language background, SES, and level of bilingualism were not statistically significant. However, L2 reading achievement at grade 5 was significantly affected by students' level of bilingualism, program type (90HI vs. 90LO), SES, and an interaction between program type and language background:

- *At grade 5, for English and Spanish speakers, higher reading achievement in L2 was associated with*: English speakers slightly outscored Spanish speakers, high bilinguals outperformed mid bilinguals, mid-SES students scored higher than low-SES, *Spanish speakers scored higher in 90LO than in 90HI programs*, while *English speakers scored higher in 90HI* than in 90LO programs.

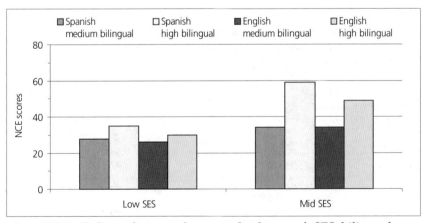

Figure 10.12 Relation between language background, SES, bilingual proficiency and L2 reading achievement at grade 5

Comparing Reading Achievement Results with Other Studies

Table 10.12 presents comparative data for students in my 90:10 sample (Lindholm 90:10) with data for students in other DLE programs that used similar models. With both English and Spanish speakers, the Inter-American Magnet School (IAMS) in Chicago, Illinois (Christian *et al.*, 1997) follows an 80:20 model (80% Spanish and 20% English at kindergarten and first grades, then reducing the amount of Spanish while increasing the amount of English over the grade levels, as in the 90:10 model). The 90:10 San Diego, California model is the model upon which the 90:10 DLE models in California were based. The Spanish and English speakers participated in the Spanish/English program from kindergarten until sixth grade. The Korean-speaking and English-speaking students in the Korean program were also involved in a DLE model similar to the Spanish DLE model except that Korean was initially used for 70% of the day and English for 30%, and students began reading in both languages.

Because IAMS did not disaggregate their data to enable comparisons between English and Spanish speakers, they are listed as combined, and are compared to my sample (Lindholm 90:10) with the English and Spanish speakers combined together. In comparing the Lindholm 90:10 and IAMS 80:20 students, the performance in Spanish was slightly higher for the IAMS students in grades 3–6, but the Lindholm 90:10 students scored slightly higher at grade 7. Overall, though, their scores were fairly similar.

Table 10.12 Reading achievement (NCE scores) in non-English language by grade level and program

Grade level	Lind. 90:10	IAMS 80:20	San Diego 90:10		Lindholm 90:10		Korean 90:10	
	Comb.	Comb.	Eng.	Span.	Eng.	Span.	Eng.	Korean
First	47				59	52		
Second	47		57	64	60	65	27	52
Third	52	60	53	58	58	55		
Fourth	47	58	66	62	51	57		
Fifth	41	56	55	59	46	52		
Sixth	48	56	62	60	53	59		
Seventh	61	55			54	65		

In looking at the other comparisons that allowed distinctions to be made between language groups, the San Diego Spanish speakers only slightly outperformed my sample at every grade level by a few NCE points. Thus, my sample and the San Diego sample scored slightly above grade level. Also, the Korean-speaking students scored at grade level in Korean. In comparing the performance of the English speakers, students in my sample scored higher than the San Diego students at grades 2–3, but the results were reversed for grades 4–6, where San Diego students outperformed my sample. All groups outperformed the English speakers assessed in Korean reading. Of course, the English speakers learning Korean had the much more complicated task of learning an entirely different and more complicated alphabet.

Tables 10.13 and 10.14 and Figures 10.13 and 10.14 compare different samples on English reading, using normal curve equivalent (NCE) scores from standardized achievement tests. Comparing the combined samples of English and Spanish speakers from Lindholm and IAMS, we can see that the two samples provided very similar scores in English reading achievement from grades 4–7, with students scoring around grade level.

Among English speakers, Table 10.13 and Figure 10.13 show that all samples scored at or above grade level from grade 3 (when students in the 90:10 program began reading in English), except for the Korean sample #2, which scored below grade level in grades 2–4. The San Diego and Lindholm samples had scores that were fairly comparable for grades 3–5.

Table 10.14 and Figure 10.14 show the reading achievement in English for language minority students (Spanish and Korean speakers) across a variety of samples. As Table 10.14 shows, the Korean-speaking students perform well above the Spanish-speaking students in their reading achievement in English, with scores that are average to above average. Given the difference between the educational backgrounds of Koreans and Hispanics in the US, this difference could be predicted on the basis of social class differences, if the Korean students at the schools are typical of the Korean sample in the US Census (US Census Bureau, 1996).

Comparing the Spanish-speaking samples, we see that there are increases across the grade levels, slowly but steadily inching toward average performance by sixth or seventh grade. Further, while there is little difference between the various samples at second and third grade, the gaps between groups begin to increase until there are larger differences in fifth grade. Compared to their California State peers, the San Diego and Lindholm samples, as well as the national Thomas and Collier samples, continued to increase, while the California group maintained the same low scores (see Figure 10.14). Thus, by seventh grade, the Lindholm and

Table 10.13 Reading achievement (NCE scores) in English language by grade level and program: Combined and English-speaking samples

Grade Level	*Lindholm* 90:10	*IAMS* 80:20	*San Diego* 90:10	*Lindholm* 90:10	*Korean* 70:30		
	Com-bined	Com-bined	English	English	#1 Eng.	#2 Eng.	#3 Eng.
First	39			44	53	57	77
Second	39		30	50	67	43	
Third	39		51	55	69	41	
Fourth	44	50	52	59	68	38	
Fifth	44	48	56	57			
Sixth	45	47	63	56			
Seventh	51	49		57			

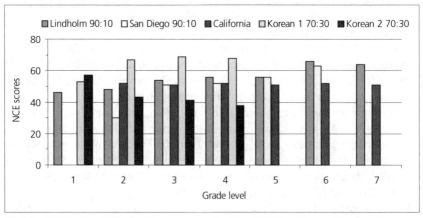

Figure 10.13 English reading scores for English speakers: Comparison samples

Table 10.14 Reading achievement (NCE scores) in English language by grade level and program: Combined and Spanish-speaking samples

Grade Level	*Lindholm* 90:10	*IAMS* 80:20	*Lindholm* 90:10 & 50:50	*Thomas & Collier* 90:10 & 50:50	*San Diego* 90:10	*Lindholm* 90:10	*Korean* 70:30		
	Com-bined	Com-bined	Span-ish	Span-ish	Span-ish	Span-ish	#1 Kor.	#2 Kor.	#3 Kor.
First	39		33	23		32	50	66	67
Second	39		30	28	35	31	46	60	73
Third	39		31	35	36	29	52	52	57
Fourth	44	50	37	42	36	34	61	49	
Fifth	44	48	33	45	40	33			
Sixth	45	47	35	50	43	37			
Seventh	51	49	43	52		41			

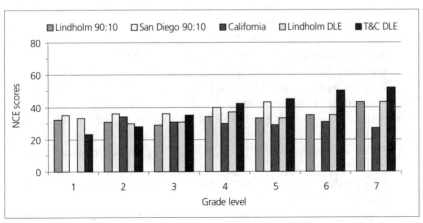

Figure 10.14 English reading scores for Spanish speakers: Comparison samples

Thomas and Collier samples were scoring close to grade level, but the California statewide group of limited English proficient (LEP) students was still hovering around NCEs of less than 30. Finally, the Lindholm combined 90:10 and 50:50 sample, which more closely approximated the Thomas and Collier sample composed of both 90:10 and 50:50 students, did not score quite as high as the Thomas and Collier sample. It is not clear how similar or different the student backgrounds and program types were between these two samples. But we can conclude that, regardless of any student background or program differences, students in both samples made slow but steady increases toward average performance in English reading by the seventh grade.

Summary and Conclusions

Reading and language achievement in L1

In examining the English and Spanish speakers' reading achievement in their native language (L1), the students made significant growth across the grade levels, and students scored on a par with their peers using California State norms for English and Spanish speakers. However, results varied somewhat depending on the language background, program type, and grade level of the students:

- By the time English-speaking DLE students began English reading instruction in grade 3, they scored average and at least as high as the California statewide norms for English speakers instructed only in English. Students in 90LO programs performed at levels similar to students in 50:50 programs. These results clearly show that the DLE English-speaking students were able to catch up to their peers in English-only instruction. For the most part, students in 90LO and 50:50 programs were performing about 10 NCE points higher than the state average for English-speaking students educated only in English. Further, at all but the third grade level, the 90LO and 50:50 students had similar scores.
- Spanish speakers in 90HI and 50:50 programs also scored average, and at least as high as their peers across the State of California. However, students in 90LO, TBE and English-only programs scored below grade level.
- Longitudinal and cross-sectional results were very similar for L1 reading achievement.
- Language achievement results paralleled the reading achievement results.

- In terms of student background characteristics, girls outscored boys in grades 3–4, but at no other grade levels. There was also a significant interaction between SES and language, wherein the gap between the performance of low-SES and mid-SES students was greater among English speakers than among Spanish speakers. This is probably because there was less real variation between Spanish speakers on free lunch compared with those not on free lunch, since most of the students not on free lunch were probably still in the low-SES range (see Chapter 7). This was less true among English speakers, where there was a greater range from high SES to low SES.
- African American students performed similarly to the other ethnic groups at grades 1 and 2, but scored lower and below grade level in grades 3 and 5, though the grade 5 score was only slightly below grade level. These results demonstrate that African American students can perform at or close to grade level in English while being instructed largely in Spanish. Since the great majority of these students were low-SES, these results are encouraging in demonstrating that African American students benefit from DLE programs.

Reading and language achievement in L2

In the second language, students also made good progress in academic reading and language proficiency. As with L1 achievement, results varied according to the language background of the students as well as the program type:

- Among the English speakers, students' scores in Spanish reading achievement differed depending on the program. In 90HI programs, English speakers performed average to high, and about comparable to statewide norms for Spanish speakers. In 90LO programs, though, their scores were average to below average and they did not reach the statewide norms for Spanish speakers.
- Spanish speakers also varied in their English reading achievement by program type, with 90LO students scoring higher than 90HI students in grades 1, 2 and 5. In both 90HI and 90LO programs, students scored below grade level, but only slightly below grade level by seventh grade. However, Spanish speakers in the 90LO program who were not receiving the free-lunch program (mid-SES) scored at grade level (NCE=47). Students in the 50:50 program outscored students in the 90:10 program in grades 3 and 4, but not in grades 5 and 6. At sixth grade, students in all DLE program types (50:50, 90LO, 90HI) scored comparably.

- Where language achievement data were available, the scores and results tended to mirror the reading achievement outcomes. This finding is not surprising, as there are high correlations between reading and language achievement in most studies. The relatively small sample size precluded more elaborate analyses.
- For both Spanish and English speakers, mid-SES students scored significantly higher than low-SES students did. Otherwise, there were no student background characteristics that differentiated the students.
- In the longitudinal sample, Spanish speakers' scores increased across the grade levels in English, while English speakers' scores decreased from grade 1 to 5 in Spanish.

In considering both L1 and L2 reading achievement, results showed the important influence of bilingual proficiency on students' reading achievement scores. While this finding was not robust for English speakers in English reading, it was certainly true for English speakers in Spanish reading and for Spanish speakers in English and Spanish reading. Thus, higher levels of bilingual proficiency were associated with higher levels of reading achievement. Further support for this interpretation is that, across the grade levels, as students became more proficient in both languages, the correlation between reading achievement in English and Spanish increased. These results are consistent with previous studies showing that higher levels of proficiency in two languages are associated with increased performance on academic achievement tests (e.g. Dawe, 1983; Fernandez & Nielsen, 1986; Lindholm, 1991; Lindholm & Aclan, 1991). Such an interpretation is also congruent with bilingual research demonstrating that higher levels of bilingual language proficiency lead to elevated academic and cognitive functioning (Cummins, 1979; Cummins, 1987; Toukomaa & Skutnabb-Kangas, 1977).

Comparisons of students in the samples reported here with those in other DLE programs yielded some differences, but more parallels. In reading achievement in Spanish, we found that the DLE students in the current sample received scores similar to those at another site across the country, though slightly lower than students at a comparable 90:10 site in California. Overall, though, the trends were analogous, with average to above-average performance across grade levels.

For limited English proficient (LEP) students' reading achievement in English, results across different samples produced similar trends of increasing performance, from very low NCE scores in the primary grades to about average performance by seventh grade. DLE former-LEP students also outscored their LEP peers across the state. Among English speakers, students scored average to above average by the time they received reading instruction in English. They also performed as well as or superior to their English monolingual peers in English-only instruction in tests of English reading and language achievement. Further, they could read and write in Spanish, which their English monolingual peers could not!

In sum, these results clearly show that both English and Spanish-speaking students benefited from instruction in DLE programs. These findings were true regardless of the students' background characteristics (ethnicity, socioeconomic class, gender, language background, and grade level), program type (90:10, 50:50), or school characteristics (90LO, 90HI).

Notes

1. Normal Curve Equivalent (NCE) scores provide information about how well students scored on a test, compared with other students in the norm group. NCEs range from 1 to 99, with 50 as average and 10 as the standard deviation. Normal curve equivalents are standardized scores, and thus enable comparisons between different achievement tests (Popham & Sirotnik, 1992).
2. Grades 1–3 were selected as the sample size dropped considerably after grade 3, and results were not as robust.

Chapter 11

Student Outcomes in Reading and Literacy: Standardized Achievement Tests vs. Alternative Assessment

Over the past several years, there has been growing discontent with traditional student assessment practices (e.g. AERA *et al.*, 1999; California Council on the Education of Teachers, 2001; Linn, 2000; National Research Council, 1999). As a consequence, many school districts and states (e.g. California, Connecticut, Michigan) as well as professional associations (e.g. California Mathematics Council) and publishing companies (e.g. Psychological Corporation) have developed various alternative assessment procedures. As Linn *et al.* (1991: 20) point out, though, while there is a need and an interest in developing alternative methods for assessment, we need to think about the 'complementary roles served by traditional and alternative assessments and ultimately to clarify the ways in which each contributes to true educational reform.' We also need to be concerned with whether these alternative measures are equitable for students from different ethnic groups (Darling-Hammond, 1995) and English language learners (California Council on the Education of Teachers, 2001; Lacelle-Peterson & Rivera, 1994).

The purpose of this chapter is to compare and contrast the results obtained from a traditional standardized achievement approach with those of an alternative assessment approach in evaluating the progress in reading of native English speakers and native Spanish speakers enrolled in a dual language education program. This chapter will examine three sets of questions:

- Using a traditional assessment approach, how well do native Spanish speakers and native English speakers perform on standardized tests of Spanish reading achievement?
- Using an alternative assessment approach, how well do native Spanish-speaking and native English-speaking students read in more naturalistic contexts in the classroom? How do students rate their own reading competence? How often do parents read to their children at home?

- Do the two approaches to assessment provide comparable or contradictory results regarding the reading accomplishments of Spanish
  speakers versus English speakers? Are there complementary roles
  that the two assessment approaches provide to our understanding of
  the reading achievement of English and Spanish speakers in DLE
  programs?

Data Collection

Data from four elementary schools implementing a Spanish/English
dual language education program were included in the study. The 395
students (grades 1–4) included in this study had been enrolled in a DLE
program since kindergarten or first grade. Information about the students'
ethnic background, SES, grade level, and language background appears in
Table 11.1. Socioeconomic status was measured by participation (designated as *low*) or non-participation (designated as *mid*) in the school's free/
reduced price lunch program. Language background is indicated as
Spanish or English, and refers to whether students entered the program as
native Spanish speakers or native English speakers. There were more
Hispanic (301) than African American (43) or Euro American (51) students.
It is important to note that not all of the African American and Hispanic
students were categorized as low in SES, nor were all of the Euro American
students classified as mid-SES. Thus, the data do not represent a total
confounding of ethnicity and social class, as typified by most quantitative
educational or developmental research involving ethnic groups (Graham,
1992; Padilla & Lindholm, 1995). In addition, while all the African American
and Euro American students were native speakers of English, close to 13% of
the Hispanic students were also native English speakers. Recognizing the
diversity of this sample is important in examining the appropriateness of the
alternative assessment procedures for all students in the classroom.

Instruments

Standardized academic achievement scores in reading were obtained for
grade 1–4 students in Spanish. Two of the schools used the *Spanish Assessment of Basic Education (SABE)* and two of the schools used the *Aprenda: La
Prueba de Logros en Español* (APRENDA)[1]. Both are norm-referenced achievement tests designed for Spanish-speaking students. They both have empiri-
cally verified reference group norms that relate performance to a representative US sample of students who are receiving their primary instruction in
Spanish. The SABE was developed to be comparable to, though not a transla-

Table 11.1 Number of students by ethnic background, SES, language background and grade level

Ethnicity and SES	Grades 1 & 2	Grades 3 & 4	Totals
African American: low-SES	29	7	36
African American: mid-SES	4	3	7
Hispanic: low-SES	217	32	249
Hispanic: mid-SES	30	22	52
Euro American: low-SES	15	0	15
Euro American: mid-SES	27	9	36
Spanish speakers	219	42	261
English speakers	103	31	134
Totals	322	73	395

tion of, the Comprehensive Test of Basic Skills (CTBS). For both tests, normal curve equivalent (NCE) scores were used for all analyses.

As part of a cooperative effort in developing a Language Arts Portfolio, the four schools, along with other schools in Southern California, worked together to create a portfolio packet and collect language-arts information using the same procedures. The Two-Way Bilingual Language Arts Portfolio was developed by teachers and project directors from Title VII-funded Developmental Bilingual Education programs in the Los Angeles Unified School District, Los Angeles County Office of Education (ABC Unified School District and Long Beach Unified School District), and Santa Monica-Malibu Unified School District. Parts of the portfolio were adapted from the current portfolios and/or work of Dr Barbara Flores, Elena Castro, Erminda Garcia, and ABC Unified School District.

The following portfolio data were collected for each student:

(1) *The Reading Rubric Assessment Scale*: teachers rate each student in the language(s) in which s/he is reading. Teachers select the appropriate descriptor, on a scale of 1 (low) to 6 (high), that characterizes the student's reading competence. There are separate forms for Grades 1-2 and Grades 3-6. For current purposes here, only ratings completed for students with regard to Spanish reading will be included.[2]
(2) *The Parent Questionnaire*: this requests parent input on literacy activi-

ties and materials in the home, including one question that will be used here: *How often do you read with your child'* For each question, the parent answered Rarely, Sometimes or Often. Parents had the choice of completing the questionnaire in English or Spanish.

(3)   *Student Reading Attitudes*: students responded to questions about their attitudes toward reading and their self-assessment of their reading competence. On the form for grades 1–2, students chose from a three-point scale of Never, Sometimes or Always to answer the question *Do you think you are a good reader?* For students in grades 3–6, the responses were along a five-point scale, from Always (4 or 5), to Sometimes (2 or 3) to Never (1). The item examined for this study was: *I am a good reader*.

Procedures

Most of the assessments were completed in the spring, except for the Parent Questionnaire, which was completed during parent–teacher conference time in the fall.

Results

Standardized achievement test performance

The first row of Table 11.2 presents the NCE scores for Spanish reading achievement by grade level, ethnicity, and SES. In the next three rows of Table 11.2 are the portfolio scores categorized by grade level, ethnicity, and SES. Table 11.3 also displays these NCE and portfolio scores, but classified according to language background (native English or Spanish speaker). As Table 11.2 shows, students' NCE scores ranged considerably, from 18 (very low) to 49 (or average). Students' scores were analyzed separately by grade level to assess differences according to language background and also by ethnicity and SES. At the first/second grade levels, both ethnicity ($F_{2,199} = 4.3$, $p < 0.05$) and SES ($F_{1,199} = 8.6$, $p < 0.01$) were significant, though the interaction was not. Scheffé comparisons for ethnicity indicated that no two groups were significantly different from one another. In a separate analysis of variance examining native English and Spanish speakers (see Table 11.3), there was no statistically significant difference between these two groups ($F_{1,212} = 0.90$, ns).

Among third/fourth graders, analyses of variance indicated that there were no significant differences associated with ethnicity ($F_{2,65} = 0.64$, ns), SES ($F_{1,65} = 0.08$, ns), or language background ($F_{1,75} = 0.04$, ns).

Table 11.2 Average scores for standardized achievement test (in NCEs) by grade level, ethnicity and SES

	African American		Hispanic		Euro American	
	low-SES	*mid-SES*	*low-SES*	*mid-SES*	*low-SES*	*mid-SES*
Spanish reading achievement						
Grades 1–2*++	21	18	34	49	26	39
Grades 3–4	34	38	40	41	—	43
Teacher: rubric[1]						
Grade 1-2**+[ab]	2.7	5.0	4.0	4.3	4.0	5.0
Grades 3–4	3.9	4.5	4.2	4.1	—	4.3
Student: comp[2]						
Grades 1–2	2.2	2.5	2.4	2.3	2.3	2.3
Grades 3–4	4.3	4.0	4.4	4.1	–	4.6
Parent: freq[3]						
Grades 1–2++	2.1	2.3	2.4	2.7	1.9	2.6
Grades 3–4+	2.3	1.3	1.9	2.7	—	2.4

[1] Scores ranged from 1 (low) to 6 (high).

[2] First/second graders' scores ranged from 1 (low) to 3 (high). Third/fourth graders' scores ranged from 1 (low) to 5 (high).

[3] Scores were 1 (Never), 2 (Sometimes), 3 (Often).

* Significant ethnic effect ($p < 0.05$).

** Significant ethnic effect ($p < 0.01$).

+ Significant SES effect ($p < 0.05$).

++ Significant SES effect ($p < 0.01$).

[a] African American students were rated significantly lower than Hispanic or Euro American students were.

[b] Analysis of covariance with Spanish reading achievement score as covariate lead to non-significant ethnic effect and significant SES effect ($p < 0.05$).

Portfolio assessment in reading: Teachers' assessment

Tables 11.2 and 11.3 also display the mean scores from the Reading Rubric Assessment scale according to the students' grade level and ethnicity, SES, and language background. As Table 11.2 indicates, Reading rubric scores ranged from 2.7 to 5.0 at the first/second grade levels and

Table 11.3 Average scores for standardized and portfolio instruments by language background and grade level

	Spanish speaking	*English speaking*
Spanish Reading Achievement		
Grades 1-2	35	35
Grades 3-4	40	40
Teacher: Reading Rubric[1]		
Grades 1-2	3.9	3.8
Grades 3-4	4.0	4.2
Student: Reading Competence[2]		
Grades 1-2	2.4	2.3
Grades 3-4	4.1	4.5
Parent: Frequency read in home[3]		
Grades 1-2	2.4	2.5
Grades 3-4*	2.0	2.5

[1] Scores ranged from 1 (low) to 6 (high).

[2] First/Second graders' scores ranged from 1 (low) to 3 (high). Third/Fourth graders' scores ranged from 1 (low) to 5 (high).

[3] Scores were 1 (never), 2 (sometimes), 3 (often).

* Significant language background effect ($p < 0.05$).

from 3.9 to 4.5 at the third/fourth grade levels. In the first/second grade group, there were statistically significant main effects for ethnicity ($F_{2,99} = 5.1, p < 0.01$) and SES ($F_{1,99} = 3.7, p < 0.05$), but no significant interaction ($F_{2,99} = 0.35$, ns). According to Scheffé comparisons, African American students scored significantly lower than Hispanic and Euro American students. In conducting an analysis of covariance controlling for Spanish achievement reading scores, reading rubric ratings no longer differed significantly on the basis of ethnicity ($F_{2,75} = 2.3$, ns), though they were still significantly different for SES ($F_{1,75} = 4.4, p < 0.05$). Looking at language background, results showed that there was no statistically significant difference in reading rubric scores between students who began the program as native English vs. Spanish speakers ($F_{1,109} = 0.10$, ns). At the third/fourth grade levels, no significant effects were found for ethnicity ($F_{2,60} = 0.10$, ns) or SES ($F_{1,60} = 0.99$, ns). Similarly, students' reading rubric scores did not vary as a function of language background ($F_{1,70} = 0.84$, ns).

Student Reading Attitude and Competence Assessments

Students' ratings of their reading competence are exhibited in Tables 11.2 and 11.3. As Table 11.2 indicates, neither first/second nor third/fourth graders rated their reading competence differently as a function of ethnicity [first/second: ($F_{2,232} = 0.14$, ns); third/fourth: ($F_{2,60} = 1.35$, ns)] or SES [(first/second: $F_{1,232} = 0.09$, ns); third/fourth: $F_{1,60} = 2.28$, ns)]. Similarly, Table 11.3 shows that students did not vary in their ratings of their reading competence by language background either [first/second: ($F_{1,245} = 2.14$, ns); third/fourth: ($F_{1,69} = 3.37$, ns)].

Parent information

Tables 11.2 and 11.3 show the parents' responses to the item asking about the frequency with which parents read to their children at home. As Table 11.2 indicates, for both grade level groups, mid-SES parents read to their children significantly more frequently than low-SES parents did [first/second: ($F_{1,194} = 12.6$, $p < 0.001$); third/fourth: ($F_{1,49} = 6.5$, $p < 0.05$)]. However, there was no ethnicity effect at either grade level [first/second: ($F_{2,194} = 2.7$, ns); third/fourth: ($F_{2,49} = 0.93$, ns)]. Examining language background at the first/second grade levels (see Table 11.3), Spanish-speaking and English-speaking parents did not vary in the frequency with which they read to their children ($F_{1,206} = 1.13$, ns). In contrast, third/fourth grade Spanish-speaking parents read significantly less often to their children than did English-speaking parents ($F_{1,57} = 5.7$, $p < 0.05$).

Integrating standardized and portfolio approaches

Two approaches were employed to examine the relationship between the reading performance of students using the standardized and alternative assessment approaches. Table 11.4 displays the correlations between the standardized test scores and the reading rubric (teacher rating), student reading rating, and parent reading frequency. Above the diagonal are presented the correlations for the first/second grade group and below the diagonal are the correlations for the third/fourth grade group. Table 11.4 indicates that, at the first/second grade level, standardized reading achievement scores were significantly related to all three other alternative assessments: teacher rating ($r = 0.83$, $p < 0.001$), student rating ($r = 0.32$, $p < 0.01$), and parent reading frequency ($r = 0.19$, $p < 0.05$). In the third/fourth grade group, the reading NCE scores were significantly correlated with the teacher rating ($r = 0.64$, $p < 0.001$), student rating ($r = 0.44$, $p < 0.01$), but not the parent reading frequency ($r = 0.007$, ns). Also in Table 11.4 was the rather high correlation between the teacher rating and the student rating at

Table 11.4 Correlations between standardized achievement for reading and alternative assessment measures for reading

	Standardized	*Teacher*	*Child*	*Parent*
Read–Standardized		0.83**	0.32**	0.19*
Read–Teacher	0.64**		0.40**	0.26*
Read–Child	0.44**	**0.47****		0.08
Read–Parent	0.27	0.15	0.48**	

Correlations above the diagonal are for first/second graders; those below diagonal are for third/fourth graders. * $p < 0.05$; ** $p < 0.01$

both the first/second grade level ($r = 0.40$, $p < 0.01$) and the third/fourth grade level ($r = 0.47$, $p < 0.01$). Interestingly, at the third/fourth grade level, but not the first/second grade level, the correlation between the student rating and the parent reading frequency was statistically significant [third/fourth: ($r = 0.48$, $p < 0.001$); first/second ($r = 0.08$, ns)].

Another way of examining the relationship between the standardized and alternative approaches is to look at the teacher reading rubric scores at each performance quartile on the Spanish reading achievement test. One might expect that students in the lowest quartile would receive the lowest teacher ratings and those in the highest quartile, the highest teacher ratings. Table 11.5 depicts the reading rubric ratings for first/second and third/fourth graders by quartiles on the Spanish reading achievement test. Table 11.5 demonstrates that, with each higher quartile, teachers gave students higher reading scores, students rated themselves as more competent in reading, and parents read to their children more frequently.

Discussion

While there has been a resounding cry for methods of assessment that are more reflective of the knowledge that students are learning rather than the discrete facts and basic skills characterizing most standardized tests, producing such alternative assessments has proved to be a difficult task (e.g. Baron, 1991; Linn, 2000). While many educators would argue that we should be entirely rid of standardized tests, Linn and his colleagues (Linn, 2000; Linn *et al.*, 1991) remind us that before we throw out the baby (traditional tests) with the bath water, we need to consider the complementary roles that traditional testing and alternative assessment can serve in our

Table 11.5 Alternative assessment scores by reading achievement:
Grades 1–2

Quartile	Reading rubric	Student rating	Parent reading frequency
Quartile 1: 1-25	3.0	2.2	2.3
Quartile 2: 26-50	4.6	2.4	2.4
Quartile 3: 51-75	5.2	2.6	2.6
Quartile 4: 76-99	5.5	2.6	2.6

Grades 3–4

Quartile	Reading rubric	Student rating	Parent reading frequency
Quartile 1: 1-25	3.7	4.0	2.0
Quartile 2: 26-50	4.1	4.3	2.1
Quartile 3: 51-75	4.7	4.7	2.9
Quartile 4: 76-99	5.0	5.0	3.0

understanding of student achievement. We also need to make sure that our alternative assessments are at least as valid as traditional tests, and that alternative assessment procedures are appropriate for our culturally and linguistically diverse student populations, without hindering or promoting the achievement of some groups over others (August & Hakuta, 1997; Darling-Hammond, 1995; Lacelle-Peterson & Rivera, 1994).

The objective here was to compare the results obtained from a traditional standardized achievement approach with an alternative assessment approach in evaluating native English-speaking and native Spanish-speaking students' progress in Spanish reading achievement. Two approaches will be used to accomplish this comparison. First, it is important to understand if there are differences in the way that each approach measures reading progress of culturally and linguistically diverse students. Second, a couple of examples will illustrate the difference in the knowledge gained from standardized versus alternative assessment approaches.

Before discussing the results, it is important to recognize that the schools reported here are all in the early stages of developing a dual language education program. Thus, the students' scores are lower than the average Spanish reading achievement scores at other sites that have implemented a DLE program for a few years. At other school sites implementing a DLE model, students demonstrated average to high NCE scores (Lindholm, 1994; see Chapter 10).

Results were presented according to the ethnicity, SES, and language backgrounds of students to determine whether these factors were systematically related to differences in how students were rated. In the DLE classroom, most teachers are trained to treat students equitably, to use cooperative learning to equalize student status in the classroom, and to give equal status to the two languages (Spanish and English) of the classroom (Lindholm, 1990a, b, c). However, because of the consistent literature demonstrating that teachers treat students in a manner that is compatible with their expectations of the students, and that teachers' expectations may be based on social class, ethnicity, language background, and perceived attractiveness (see Chapters 2 and 5), it was important to assess whether ratings varied as a function of cultural or linguistic diversity. At the third/fourth grade level, teachers' and students' scores were not significantly different on the basis of any of these background variables. In contrast, first/second grade ratings differed according to ethnicity and SES, but not on the basis of language background. However, when students' reading achievement scores were controlled for, there were no longer significant effects due to ethnicity or SES. These results are important because they attest to the equity of these assessment procedures for culturally and linguistically diverse students. That is, using these measures does not introduce additional bias if teachers who are sensitive to cultural and linguistic diversity implications in the classroom utilize them. Next we will compare and contrast the results obtained from the standardized versus alternative assessment procedures.

Example 1: First/second graders in the first quartile

The standardized achievement tests for students in the first quartile indicate that 75% of all students who took the test scored higher than this group of students did. As a group, they averaged an NCE score of 17, with average NCE scores across the ethnicity by SES groups ranging from 14 to 19. These low scores clearly indicate that the students have very low levels of word attack skills (sound/symbol relationships), vocabulary, and reading comprehension. The average teacher-rated reading rubric score for this group signifies that the students are not in the lowest two categories of 1 (pre-reader) or 2 (emergent reader), but that students are in category 3 (Developing Reader: 'Has increasing confidence in reading familiar and predictable material independently. Has growing ability to use a variety of strategies to gain meaning from the material. Understands the sound/symbol relationship'). Thus, this same group of students is rated by the teacher as understanding the sound/symbol relationship, as well as using different strategies to gain meaning from the literature material. Clearly, these two scales show some overlap in that these measures are highly correlated ($r = 0.83$, $p < 0.001$).

However, these two measures are also examining student reading somewhat differently. While the standardized test assesses more discrete skills, the reading rubric relies on the teachers' extensive interactions with and observations of the student in different reading contexts. This allows the teacher to determine whether the student not only understands discrete reading skills, but also is beginning to utilize various strategies to draw inferences from text and can read text, though this may be limited to familiar and predictable texts. The average student rating for whether they are a good reader is Sometimes, not Never, an encouraging sign, and a more realistic rating than an Always response. Thus, students' ratings indicate that they are fairly confident of their reading ability, consistent with the teacher rating that students show 'increasing confidence in reading familiar and predictable material independently.' Thus, this confidence in reading is clearly being developed in the classroom along with the ability to read predictable material, yet these important components associated with successful reading are absent from standardized achievement tests. In this first quartile group, parents are likely to indicate that they Sometimes, as opposed to Rarely or Often, read to their child. However, we need to also remember that some parents may not want to admit to the teacher that they rarely or never read to their child.

In summary, the standardized achievement score shows that these children are far behind other children in reading at their grade level. In fact, this score alone would indicate to a teacher, parent, or administrator that the child is not succeeding at reading. By way of contrast, the reading rubric indicates that the student is not at the bottom of the reading heap, but has developed some sound/symbol relationships and strategies to enable him/her to progress in reading. The student rating shows that the student feels capable of reading, rather than discouraged, perhaps because he/she can read independently, at least in predictable and familiar texts. Finally, the information on the parent reading frequency indicates that even the parents of the lowest readers do at least sometimes read to their children, whatever 'sometimes' means.

Example 2: Third/fourth graders at the second quartile

These students are achieving in the below-average to average range. As a group, their NCE score was 42, and the NCE scores ranged from 40 to 45 among the different ethnicity by SES groups. This group of students was performing a little below grade level in Spanish vocabulary and reading comprehension, according to the standardized test. Using the teacher-rated reading rubric, the students were rated 4.1, which is in the category of competent reader: 'A reader who feels comfortable with books. Is generally able to read silently and is developing confidence as a reader. Selects books independently, but still needs help with unfamiliar material. Uses some strategies to derive meaning.' At the third/fourth grade level, like the first/second grade level, the correlation between the teacher rating and the standardized test's NCE score was positive and highly significant ($r = 0.64, p < 0.001$). Also, like the first/second grade, there was some variation in what these different scores tell us. While both scores indicate that the students are around average, the standardized score is slightly below average, while the reading rubric score reflects a 'competent reader', not a below-average reader, though not a strong reader either. The standardized score reflects reading skills such as vocabulary and comprehension of reading passages, while the reading rubric alludes more to developing an interest and confidence in books, and the ability to read independently. In addition, the reading rubric category indicates that the students use some strategies to derive meaning from text. Thus, the scores from these two different assessment approaches tell us somewhat different information: one tells us about reading skills, and the other about reading confidence and independence. As with the first/second grade group, teachers' ratings of students' confidence is expressed in students' positive rating of their reading ability. Students' self-rated competence averaged 4.3, indicating that students almost always agree with the statement that they are good readers. Finally, parents in this group scored 2.1, demonstrating that the parents read to their children Sometimes, but not Often, though not Rarely either.

In both examples, the standardized and alternative assessment scores are consistent with each other, and this is supported by the correlations, which were significant. However, neither approach alone provides sufficient information to understand students' reading progress. Standardized tests focus exclusively on reading *skills*, which the reading rubric and other assessments largely ignore, except for reference to the sound/symbol relationship at the first/second grade level. To diagnose reading skill deficiencies, one clearly could not use the reading rubric, though the standardized test might provide some relevant information. However, to further understand those reading skill deficiencies, the standardized test would not distinguish whether the student is able to read predictable passages, or no passages at all. In addition, the standardized test does not provide any information about a student's confidence in reading. The reading rubric could be used in both situations to assist in determining approaches that would remedy reading problems. The student and parent information is not necessary, but is very helpful , as it indicates how confident students feel about their own reading ability and also whether reading is occurring in the home between the child and the parent. This information may be used to assist the parent in helping children with reading difficulties.

In sum, neither approach alone portrays the reading competence of the students, but together they provide useful information about students' reading ability and progress. The two approaches provide complementary rather than opposing or even overlapping information about students' reading competence. Furthermore, the alternative assessment approaches appear to be appropriate for both culturally and linguistically diverse students, lending additional credibility to their use in the classroom.

Notes

1. In other analyses not presented here, there do not appear to be systematic differences in students' performance according to which achievement test (APRENDA or SABE) they completed (Lindholm, 1994).
2. English Reading Rubric scores were not collected because, in this educational model, students begin reading instruction in English in third grade; there were only 25 students (18 Spanish speakers, 7 English speakers) for whom there were English Reading Rubric scores.

Chapter 12

Student Outcomes: Content Area Achievement in Mathematics, Science and Social Studies

Introduction to Academic Achievement

Most research with bilingual and immersion programs has been conducted with respect to achievement in language arts and reading, but research suggests that content area achievement in mathematics, science and social studies parallels the findings in language arts and reading. That is, students in various types of high-quality language education programs perform on various measures of achievement in mathematics at least at grade level or at levels comparable to their peers who are not enrolled in the language education program. These results hold true for partial and total immersion as well as for bilingual programs in the United States and many other countries – Australia, Brussels, Canada, Hong Kong, Hungary, South Africa, Spain (both Basque and Catalan programs) (e.g. Artigal, 1995; Baetens Beardsmore & Swain, 1985; Byram & Leman, 1990; Cummins & Swain, 1986; De Courcy, 1997; Dolson & Lindholm, 1995; Duff, 1997; Genesee, 1987; Johnson, 1997; Nuttall & Langhan, 1997; Ramirez *et al.*, 1991; Slaughter, 1997; Willig, 1985).

Academic achievement in the content areas may also be influenced by the level of bilingual proficiency, whereby higher levels of proficiency in the two languages is associated with higher levels of performance on academic achievement tests (e.g. Dawe, 1983; Fernandez & Nielsen, 1986; Lindholm, 1991; Lindholm & Aclan, 1991).

In the United States, performance on academic achievement tests is considered paramount in understanding student outcomes (Linn, 2000). Despite this focus on achievement tests and student performance, the United States does not produce high-achieving students according to international studies in mathematics. In one study of eighth graders in 41 countries (Third International Mathematics and Science Study, 1995), US students lagged behind 20 other countries, scored comparable to 14 countries, and performed higher than students in only six countries. Achievement is even more dismal in certain states in the US, particularly in California, where students scored near the bottom in comparisons of all 50 states (*San Jose News*, 1997). These points are important to keep in mind as the results from the various schools are discussed in this and subsequent chapters.

While there are ethnic differences in mathematics achievement at high school entry, there is an even greater discrepancy between ethnic groups in participation in higher-level mathematics classes, with African American and Hispanics taking many fewer college-track mathematics courses (Davenport *et al.*, 1998).

In addition, gender differences in mathematics and science achievement have diminished over the past few years in the US. Though there are differences in math and science course enrollments at the secondary and college levels, males are significantly more likely to take the highest levels of mathematics and science courses (Davenport *et al.*, 1998).

This literature on achievement leads to some important questions to examine with the DLE students:

- How well do DLE students perform on achievement tests in mathematics, science and social studies?
- Does level of bilingual proficiency relate to DLE students' academic achievement?
- Do student background (ethnicity, SES, gender, language background), school demographic, and program factors (90HI, 90LO, 50:50, TBE, EO) influence achievement performance?

Mathematics Achievement in the Native Language (L1)

The mathematics data derive from the math section of the standardized achievement tests described in Chapter 8. Table 12.1 and Figures 12.1–12.3 present the mathematics achievement scores in NCEs for students, categorized by language background, program type, and grade level. As the table indicates, English speakers in 90HI programs scored at grade level in all grades. Their scores were comparable to statewide averages for English-speaking (non-LEP) students studying in English-only classrooms. English speakers in 90LO and 50:50 programs scored significantly higher than students did in the 90HI programs at grades 1–3. At all grade levels, students in the 90LO and 50:50 programs scored above average to very high (59–79). Students in 50:50 outscored students in the 90LO program only in grade 3. Thus, even though the 90LO students were reading and learning mathematics in Spanish only, they scored similar to 50:50 students who were reading and receiving mathematics instruction in English. Despite the fact that 90:10 students were receiving all their mathematics

Table 12.1 L1 mathematics achievement: NCE scores by grade level and program type, cross-sectional perspective

English speakers in English

Grade level	90HI	90LO	50:50	Calif. state avg.*	Program differences
First	55	68	65		90LO,50>90HI
Second	52	63	63	54	90LO,50>90HI
Third	51	59	79	54	50>90HI,90LO
Fourth	52	61	63	51	None
Fifth		63		52	
Sixth		61		55	

*Based on 1998 California-wide testing; scores provided by the California Department of Education.

Spanish speakers in Spanish

Grade level	90HI	90LO	50:50	TBE	EO	Calif. state avg.	Program differences
First	50	43	44	38			90HI>90LO,TBE
Second	46	39	47	37		53	90HI>90LO,TBE 50:50>90LO
Third	54	36	76	40	31	53	90HI>90LO,TBE,EO 50:50>90HI,90LO, TBE,EO
Fourth	47	41		44	30	52	None
Fifth	44	50	51	52	34	50	90HI>EO
Sixth		42		36		47	None
Seventh		38				47	None

instruction in Spanish and received no English reading instruction until third grade, 90:10 program students achieved scores comparable to state-wide norms, and 90LO students scored similar to 50:50 students.

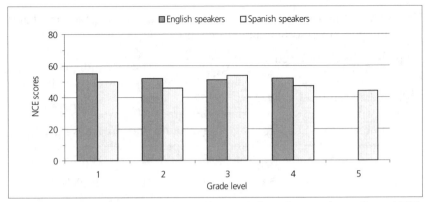

Figure 12.1 L1 mathematics scores for English and Spanish speakers: 90HI

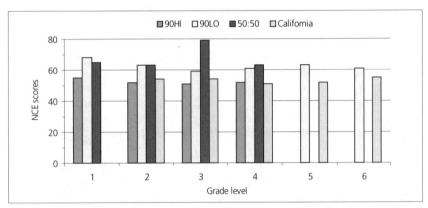

Figure 12.2 L1 mathematics scores for English speakers by program type

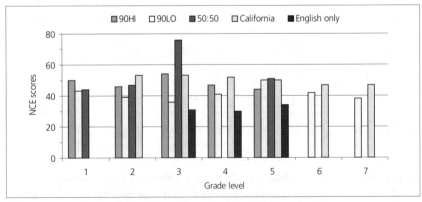

Figure 12.3 L1 mathematics scores for Spanish speakers by program type

Among Spanish-speaking students in their native language, 90HI and 50:50 programs scored average at most grade levels and comparable to statewide averages for Spanish-speaking students tested in Spanish. 90HI students outperformed their 90LO, TBE, and EO peers. Students in 90LO, TBE and EO programs scored below grade level and lower than the statewide averages for LEP students.

Multivariate analyses of variance for grades 1–3 were conducted to determine whether SES, language background and program type influenced students' L1 mathematics achievement. Results showed that, across grade levels, in L1 mathematics achievement there was a significant interaction between program type and language background; these results indicated that 90LO programs were associated with higher mathematics scores for English speakers, while Spanish speakers scored higher in 90HI programs. In addition, English speakers scored higher than Spanish speakers did. There was no significant difference for SES, as low- and mid-SES students performed at similar levels.

A univariate analysis of variance was run at grade 5 to determine whether these effects were still significant. There was no difference between English and Spanish speakers, but there were significant differences for program type and SES: mid-SES students outperformed low-SES students, and 90LO students scored higher than 90HI students.

Analyses were also conducted to determine whether SES and gender significantly affected students' scores in L1 mathematics achievement. There were no significant gender differences at any grade levels.

Tables 12.2 and 12.3 present the longitudinal data for 90:10 students' mathematics achievement for grades 1–5. Table 12.2 and Figure 12.4 show the NCEs for students' mathematics achievement for grades 1–8 (for those students who participated in a 90:10 DLE program from kindergarten or first grade through at least fifth grade and had mathematics achievement scores for each year). As this table illustrates (and as a repeated-measures analysis of variance demonstrated), students made statistically significant growth over time from grade 1 to grade 5. However, there were no differences between English speakers and Spanish speakers. There were no main effects due to SES, but there were significant program-type differences. There was also a significant interaction between program and language background; wherein English speakers scored higher in 90LO programs, while Spanish speakers received higher NCEs in 90HI programs. These results are consistent with the cross-sectional results presented earlier in this section.

In Table 12.3 and Figure 12.5, we see the longitudinal data for fifth graders who had participated since kindergarten or first grade; categorized by language background, program type (90HI vs. 90LO) and SES. Among

Table 12.2 L1 mathematics achievement: NCE scores by grade level and language background, longitudinal perspective

Grade level	*Spanish speakers*	*English speakers*
First	55	60
Second	52	63
Third	55	61
Fourth	60	60
Fifth	58	57
Sixth	58	59
Seventh	67	66
Eighth	59	

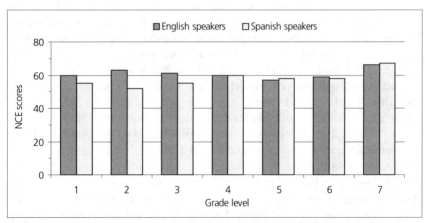

Figure 12.4 L1 mathematics scores for English and Spanish speakers: longitudinal perspective

Spanish speakers, there was some variation (6 NCE points) due to SES (free lunch). For the English-speaking students, mid-SES students scored significantly higher than low-SES in the 90HI program (54 vs. 38); however, mid-SES 90LO students (NCE = 66) outscored their mid-SES peers in the 90HI program (NCE = 54).

English mathematics achievement scores of English speakers according to ethnicity are shown in Table 12.4. African American students scored at grade level in all grades except grades 4 and 5, where they performed

Table 12.3 L1 mathematics achievement for 5th graders: NCE scores by SES and program type, longitudinal perspective

Grade level	Spanish speakers	English speakers
90HI	60	50
Mid SES	64	54
Low SES	58	38
90LO	51	66
Mid SES	—	66
Low SES	51	—
Combined		
Mid SES	57	64
Low SES	51	49

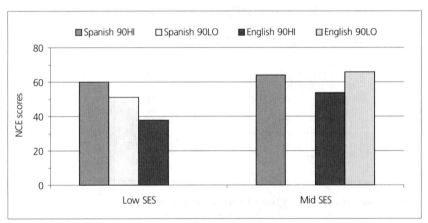

Figure 12.5 L1 mathematics achievement for 5th graders by SES and program type: Longitudinal perspective

slightly below grade level. Asian American students scored the highest in first grade, and similar to Hispanic and African American students in second grade. Hisp-EB students in both programs scored at grade levels, with third and fourth grade 50:50 students above average. These 50:50 participants also performed at a higher level than their 90:10 peers did. Euro American students in both programs scored above grade level. Even though 50:50 students received more English mathematics instruction, their scores were not significantly higher than those of the 90:10 students.

Table 12.4 L1 English mathematics achievement: NCE scores by ethnicity, grade level and program type

English speakers in English: African Americans and Asian Americans

Grade level	90:10 African American	90:10 Asian American
First	55	61
Second	53	54
Third	47	
Fourth	44	
Fifth	40	
Sixth	51	

English speakers in English: Hispanic Americans

Grade level	90:10	50:50	Program differences
First	52	63	50>90:10
Second	46	57	50>90:10
Third	46	80	50>90:10
Fourth	46	66	50>90:10
Fifth	46		

English speakers in English: Euro Americans

Grade level	90:10	50:50	Program differences
First	65	65	None
Second	63	65	None
Third	60	62	None
Fourth	61		
Fifth	59		
Sixth	64		

Table 12.5 L2 mathematics achievement (NCE scores) by grade level and program type: Cross-sectional perspective

English speakers in Spanish

Grade level	90HI	90LO	50:50	State avg. for LEPs	Program differences
First	57	63			None
Second	56	59	54	53	None
Third	61	64		53	None
Fourth	59	55		52	None
Fifth	43	59		50	None

Spanish speakers in English

Grade level	90HI	90LO	50:50	TBE	EO	State avg. for LEPs	Program differences
First	46	45		39			None
Second	41	42	40	41		41	None
Third	38	31	60	38		40	50>90HI,LO,TBE
Fourth	45	42	52	34		36	None
Fifth	36	50	48	46	32	35	EO<90LO,50:50,TBE
Sixth		42				38	None

Mathematics Achievement in the Second Language (L2)

Table 12.5 and Figures 12.6 through 12.8 provide the L2 mathematics NCE scores for English speakers and Spanish speakers. English speakers scored average to slightly above average in all DLE programs. As we can see in Figure 12.7, there were no statistically significant differences between program types.

Spanish-speaking students' scores in all programs ranged from slightly below average to average. The only significant difference was that 50:50 students outperformed 90HI, 90LO, and TBE students at grade 3. Also, English-only students scored lower than all other program types at grade 5 (the only level at which there was sufficient data to analyze). Further, across these different programs, students did not make growth over time;

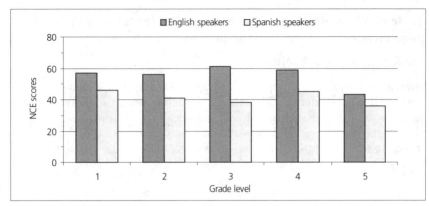

Figure 12.6 L2 mathematics scores for English and Spanish speakers: 90HI

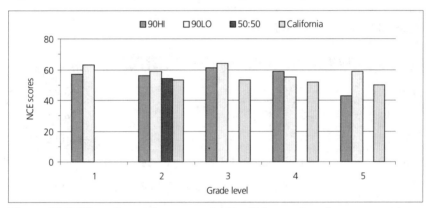

Figure 12.7 L2 mathematics scores for English speakers by program type

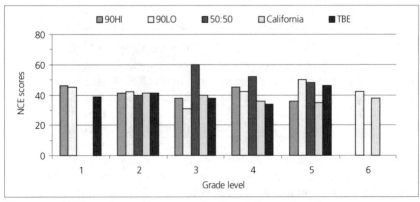

Figure 12.8 L2 mathematics scores for Spanish speakers by program type

as Figure 12.7 illustrates, their scores were fairly stable, neither increasing nor decreasing over time. These findings suggest that both DLE approaches yield equivalent performance in English mathematics achievement.

A multivariate analysis of variance was conducted for grades 1-3[1] to determine whether language background, SES and program type significantly affected students' L2 mathematics achievement scores. From this analysis, language background was statistically significant, with English

Table 12.6 L2 mathematics achievement: NCE scores by grade level and language background, longitudinal perspective

Grade level	Spanish speakers	English speakers
First	43	64
Second	48	65
Third	56	73
Fourth	49	66
Fifth	50	64
Sixth	45	66
Seventh	50	80
Eighth	56	

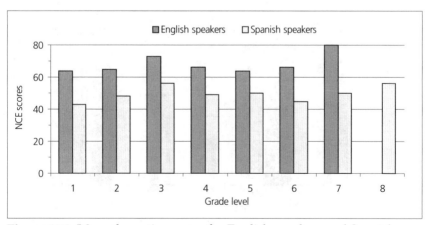

Figure 12.9 L2 mathematics scores for English speakers and Spanish speakers: longitudinal perspective

speakers outperforming Spanish speakers. There was no significant effect for SES. A significant interaction between program type and language background was evident, but only at grade 3 (English speakers scored higher in 90LO programs, while Spanish speakers performed at higher levels in 90HI programs).

Another univariate analysis of variance was conducted at fifth grade to determine whether these variables were still significant. Language back-

Table 12.7 L2 mathematics achievement: NCE scores for 5th graders by SES and program type, longitudinal perspective

Grade level	Spanish speakers	English speakers
90HI	49	63
Mid SES	52	68
Low SES	47	45
90LO	51	61
Mid SES	—	61
Low SES	51	—
Combined	50	62
Mid SES	52	66
Low SES	49	45

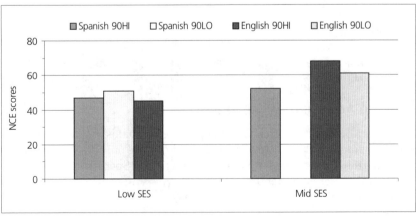

Figure 12.10 Mathematics achievement for 5th graders by SES and program type: longitudinal perspective

ground was not significant, but program type and SES were significant. Thus, mid-SES students outscored low-SES students, and 90LO students outperformed their 90HI peers. There was no significant interaction between program type and language background. Finally, analyses of gender suggested no differences between boys and girls in this respect.

Tables 12.6 and 12.7 (and Figure 12.9) provide the longitudinal L2 mathematics achievement data. As these tables show (and as demonstrated by a repeated measures analysis of variance), the scores of English-speaking students did not vary much over time, while scores of Spanish speakers increased across the grades. Scores of both groups increased up to third grade, then decreased slightly across fourth and fifth grades, and increased again. There was also a significant interaction between language background and program type, wherein Spanish speakers performed at higher levels in 90LO programs while English speakers scored higher in 90HI programs. We can see this difference in Table 12.7 and Figure 12.10, where English-speaking 90HI mid-SES students scored above average (NCE = 68) while their 90LO mid-SES peers scored 7 NCE points lower. The gap between 90HI and 90LO was less for Spanish speakers: free-lunch Spanish speakers scored at grade level (NCE = 51) and slightly above their low-SES peers in 90HI programs (NCE = 47).

The achievement of fifth graders in the two samples (longitudinal versus cross-sectional) was very comparable, with most students scoring close to average. However, 90HI Spanish speakers in the longitudinal sample (NCE = 50) scored much higher than 90HI students in the cross-sectional sample (NCE = 36).

Table 12.8 presents the Spanish mathematics NCE scores according to ethnicity, program type, and grade level. As this table indicates, African American students scored below grade level at grades 1–2, but only slightly below grade level at grades 3–5 (NCE = 42-44). Hisp-EB in 90:10 programs scored about average at most grade levels. Asian American, Hisp-EB in 50:50, and Euro Americans in 90:10 scored above grade level (NCE = 57–80).

Science Achievement in Spanish

Table 12.9 indicates that both English and Spanish speakers scored above average at all grade levels (NCE = 55–78). The only significant difference was the higher scores of English speakers over Spanish speakers at the first-grade level. Neither gender nor SES significantly differentiated students in their achievement.

Table 12.8 L2 Spanish mathematics achievement (NCE scores) in L2 by ethnicity, grade level and program type

English speakers in Spanish: African Americans, Asian Americans, Hispanics, and Euro Americans

Grade level	90:10 African American	90:10 Asian American	90:10 Hispanic-EB	50:50 Hispanic-EB	90:10 Euro Americans
First	38	70	52	63	64
Second	34	63	46	57	62
Third	44		46	80	67
Fourth	43		46	66	61
Fifth	42		46		63

Table 12.9 Science achievement (NCE scores) in Spanish by grade level

Grade level	Spanish speakers	English speakers	Group differences
Third	67	78	English>Spanish
Fourth	65	69	None
Fifth	59	66	None
Sixth	55	62	None
Seventh	65	68	None
Eighth	57		

Social Studies Achievement in Spanish

Table 12.10 presents the students' NCE scores from the social studies portion of the achievement test in Spanish. As this table shows, English speakers outperformed Spanish speakers only at the third grade level. Otherwise, there were no statistically significant differences due to language background, gender or SES. At all grade levels, students performed above average to very high (NCE = 51–80).

Table 12.10 Social studies achievement (NCE scores) in Spanish by grade level

Grade level	Spanish speakers	English speakers	Group differences
Third	68	80	English>Spanish
Fourth	69	65	None
Fifth	66	74	None
Sixth	51	55	None
Seventh	71	77	None
Eighth	66	74	None

Relationships Between Reading Achievement and Mathematics Achievement for DLE Programs

Table 12.11 provides the correlations between L1 and L2 reading achievement and L1 and L2 mathematics achievement, and between mathematics achievement in L1 and L2, categorized by language background and grade level of the student. As this table shows, all of the correlations were statistically significant, and most were fairly high (0.5 or 0.6) to very high (0.7–0.8). Patterns of correlations were similar for both Spanish speakers and English speakers. There was a fairly high correlation between L1 reading achievement and L1 mathematics achievement for both Spanish speakers and English speakers ($r = 0.51$–0.85), though correlations tended to be higher for English speakers. Correlations between reading achievement and mathematics achievement in L2 were higher than those for L1 for both English and Spanish speakers ($r = 0.31$–0.89), except at the third and fifth grade level. The correlations between mathematics scores across the two languages were mostly high ($r = 0.34$–0.85). Once students began reading instruction in grade 3, the correlations between English and Spanish mathematics increased. For the most part, the correlations between reading and mathematics achievement and between mathematics achievement in the two languages were stronger at increasing grade levels (except for grade 5 Spanish speakers in the relationships between reading and mathematics achievement in L2).

Univariate analyses of variance were conducted at grade 5 (the terminating grade level in elementary school), to determine the extent to which various program and student background factors, including level of bilin-

Table 12.11 Correlations between reading and mathematics achievement by grade level and language background

	Spanish speakers *90:10*	*English speakers* *90:10*
Grade 1		
L1 read & L1 math	0.53**	0.56**
L2 read & L2 math	0.55**	0.64**
L1 math & L2 math	0.53**	0.45**
Grade 2		
L1 read & L1 math	0.51**	0.61**
L2 read & L2 math	0.63**	0.64**
L1 math & L2 math	0.49**	0.54**
Grade 3		
L1 read & L1 math	0.65**	0.74**
L2 read & L2 math	0.71**	0.63**
L1 math & L2 math	0.74**	0.67**
Grade 4		
L1 read & L1 math	0.66**	0.69**
L2 read & L2 math	0.68**	0.72**
L1 math & L2 math	0.74**	0.75**
Grade 5		
L1 read & L1 math	0.65**	0.76**
L2 read & L2 math	0.49**	0.31**
L1 math & L2 math	0.79**	0.81**
Grade 6		
L1 read & L1 math	0.79**	0.76**
L2 read & L2 math	0.81**	0.76**
L1 math & L2 math	0.85**	0.74**
Grade 7		
L1 read & L1 math	0.74**	0.62**
L2 read & L2 math	0.74**	0.89**
L1 math & L2 math	0.72**	0.34
Grade 8		
L1 read & L1 math	0.85**	
L2 read & L2 math	0.51	
L1 math & L2 math	0.74**	

Statistical significance: ** = $p < 0.01$

gualism, affected mathematics achievement. The results of these analyses are illustrated in Figures 12.11 (L1 mathematics achievement) and 12.12 (L2 mathematics achievement). In examining L1 mathematics achievement in grade 5, language background and level of bilingualism were not statistically significant, while program type and SES were significant. L2 mathematics achievement was significantly affected by students' level of bilingualism, program type (90:10 vs. 50:50), and SES, and an interaction between program type and language background:

- *For English and Spanish speakers at grade 5, higher mathematics achievement was associated with*: 90LO program type and mid-SES.

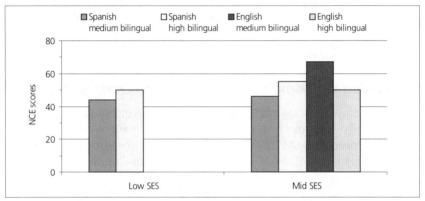

Figure 12.11 Relation between language background, SES, bilingual proficiency and L1 mathematics achievement at grade 5

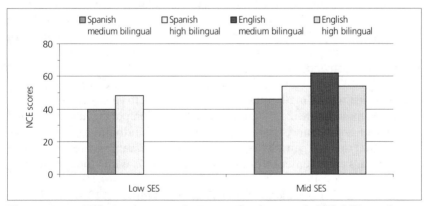

Figure 12.12 Relation between language background, SES, bilingual proficiency and L2 mathematics achievement at grade 5

Table 12.12 Mathematics achievement (NCE scores) in Spanish by grade level and program

Grade level	Lind-holm 90:10	IAMS 80:20	San Diego 90:10		Lindholm 90:10 (longitudinal)		Cali-fornia
	Comb.	Comb.	Eng.	Span.	Eng.	Span.	LEP
Second	48		73	58	65	52	53
Third	44	63	59	61	73	55	53
Fourth	49	62	64	55	66	60	52
Fifth	48	57	69	58	64	58	50
Sixth	48	55	69	59	66	58	47

Comparing Mathematics Achievement to Other Studies

This section compares mathematics achievement data for students in the current study with mathematics achievement outcomes for students in other DLE programs. As Table 12.12 shows for mathematics achievement in Spanish, the IAMS 80:20 combined sample of English and Spanish speakers produced higher scores than my sample of combined English and Spanish speakers in 90:10 programs, though the gap decreased across the grade levels. Comparing the English speakers in the San Diego and Lindholm 90:10 longitudinal samples, indicates that these students performed at fairly comparable levels overall. Similarly, Spanish speakers in the two longitudinal samples also produced very similar scores. What these data clearly show is that the 90:10 DLE model has the potential of promoting average to above-average achievement in Spanish mathematics for both English and Spanish speakers.

Tables 12.13 and 12.14 and Figures 12.13 and 12.14 compare different samples in English mathematics, using normal curve equivalent (NCE) scores from standardized achievement tests. Comparing the combined samples of English and Spanish speakers from Lindholm and IAMS, we can see that the two samples provided very comparable scores in English mathematics achievement from grade 4 to grade 7, with students scoring around grade level.

Among English speakers, Table 12.13 and Figure 12.13 show that all samples scored at or above grade level from second grade (even though students in the 90:10 program did not begin reading in English until grade

Table 12.13 Mathematics achievement in English: NCE scores by grade level and program: Combined and English-speaking samples

Grade level	Cali-fornia norms	Lindholm 90:10	IAMS 80:20	San Diego 90:10	Lind-holm 90:10	Korean 70:30		
	Eng. in EO classes	Comb.	Comb.	Eng.	Eng.	#1 Eng.	#2 Eng.	#3 Eng.
Second	54			53	63	61	47	99
Third	54			56	61	69	44	
Fourth	51	49	48	58	60	67	50	
Fifth	52	48	45	61	57	66		
Sixth	55	48	48	70	59			
Seventh	52	46	47		66			

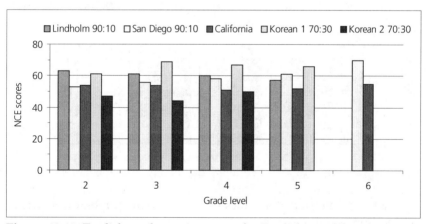

Figure 12.13 English mathematics scores for English speakers: comparison samples

3). The San Diego and Lindholm longitudinal samples of English speakers had scores that were very comparable for grades 3–5, but the San Diego students performed at a higher level in grade 6. In the Korean sample of English speakers, students scored well above average in School #1, average in School #2 and the highest score possible in School #3.

Table 12.14 Mathematics achievement in English: NCE scores by grade level and program, language minority samples

Grade level	California norms	San Diego 90:10	Lindholm longitudinal 90:10	Korean 70:30		
	LEP	*Spanish*	*Spanish*	*#1 Kor.*	*#2 Kor.*	*#3 Kor.*
Second	41	42	48	65	52	80
Third	40	44	56	74	56	80
Fourth	36	49	49	72	56	
Fifth	35	53	50	65		
Sixth	38	56	45			

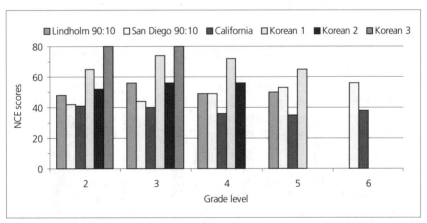

Figure 12.14 English mathematics scores for language minority students: comparison samples

Table 12.14 and Figure 12.14 show the mathematics achievement in English for language minority students (Spanish and Korean speakers) across a variety of samples. As this table shows, the Korean speakers outperformed the Spanish-speaking students in mathematics achievement in English, with scores that were average to very high. As mentioned in the previous chapter, given the difference between the educational backgrounds of Koreans and Hispanics in the US, this difference could be predicted on the basis of social class differences, if the Korean students at the schools are typical of the Korean sample in the US Census.

Comparing the Spanish-speaking samples, we see that the Lindholm sample scored average at all grade levels, while students in the San Diego sample improved their performance across the grade levels, moving toward average performance by fourth grade. Compared to their California state LEP peers, the San Diego and Lindholm samples continued to increase or maintain average scores, while the California norm group diminished in their achievement performance across the grade levels. Thus, at all grade levels for the Lindholm sample and by fourth grade for the San Diego sample, students scored at grade level, but the California state-wide group of LEP students were still performing low, with NCEs of 35–38.

Summary and Conclusions

Mathematics achievement in L1

Both English-speaking and Spanish-speaking students scored on a par with their peers in L1 mathematics achievement using California state norms for English and Spanish speakers. However, results varied somewhat depending on the language background, program type, and grade level of the students:

- Among English speakers, students scored average to above average at all grade levels and in both program types. Also, English speakers performed at levels comparable with or higher than the California statewide norms for English speakers instructed only in English. Students in 90LO programs performed at the same levels as students in 50:50 programs (except at grade 3). These results clearly show that the DLE students were able to keep up with their peers who received English-only instruction. For the most part, students in 90LO and 50:50 programs were scoring about 10 NCE points higher than the state average for English-speaking students educated only in English.
- Spanish speakers in 90HI and 50:50 programs also scored at grade level, and their scores were similar to those for their peers across the state. However, students in 90LO, TBE and EO programs scored below grade level.
- Longitudinal and cross-sectional results were very similar for L1 mathematics achievement.
- In terms of student background characteristics, gender did not affect test scores at any grade level, but language background and SES did

have an effect at different grade levels. In grades 1–3, English speakers outscored Spanish speakers, but this difference evaporated by grade 5. In contrast, SES did not influence math scores at grades 1–3, but was significant by grade 5, where mid-SES students outperformed low-SES students. Further, at grade 5, 90LO students scored higher than 90HI students, regardless of language background. At the lower grade levels (1–3), Spanish speakers scored higher in 90HI programs, while English speakers received higher scores in 90LO programs.

- African American students performed similarly to the other ethnic groups at grades 1–3 and 6, but scored lower and below grade level in grades 4 and 5, though the grade 4 score was only slightly below grade level. These results demonstrate that African American students can perform at or close to grade level in English while being instructed largely in Spanish. Since the great majority of these students were low-SES, these results are encouraging in demonstrating that African American students benefit from DLE programs.

Mathematics achievement in L2

In the second language, students also performed at levels comparable to their peers statewide. However, results also varied according to the language background of the students as well as the program type:

- Among English speakers, students' scores did not vary according to program type. In 90:10 programs, English speakers performed average to above average, and about comparable to statewide norms for Spanish-speaking students.
- Spanish-speaking students also did not differ much by program type. The major program differences were that EO students scored significantly lower than any other program type and that 50:50 students scored higher than 90LO students at grade 3. In both 90HI and 90LO programs, students scored below grade level, but only slightly below grade level by grade 4. However, math achievement scores for Spanish speakers were higher in the longitudinal sample; these students scored at grade level (NCE = 47–52) by grade 5. Students in the 50:50 program outscored students in the 90:10 program at grade 3, but not in grades 4 and 5.
- Social studies and science achievement data were available for a small subset of students in Spanish only. The scores in both areas were average to high for both groups of students at all grade levels.

- For both Spanish and English speakers, mid-SES students scored significantly higher than low-SES students, with both the longitudinal and cross-sectional samples.
- In neither the longitudinal nor the cross-sectional samples did Spanish speakers' scores change much across the grade levels in either language.
- Bilingual proficiency did not influence students' mathematics achievement scores in either language. This result was not expected, as previous studies have shown that higher levels of proficiency in two languages is typically associated with increased performance on academic achievement tests (e.g. Dawe, 1983; Fernandez & Nielsen, 1986; Lindholm, 1991; Lindholm & Aclan, 1991). However, there was a significant correlation between reading and mathematics achievement in the two languages for both English and Spanish speakers. Correlations between reading and mathematics were highly significant (0.5–0.8) in both L1 and L2, and the correlations became stronger across the grade levels. Clearly reading ability was important in mathematics achievement.
- There was also a highly significant correlation between mathematics achievement across the two languages. This result, especially the high correlation in the early grade levels, demonstrates that content learned in one language was available in the other language as well. Despite limited English instruction and no mathematics instruction in English, 90:10 students were able to score at or close to grade level in English.

Finally, these results clearly indicate that DLE students can function at least at grade level in two languages in the content areas. Their scores are on a par with their peers across the state, even when the peers are English monolinguals in English-only classrooms. Further, the lack of differences between students in 90LO and 50:50 programs in English mathematics demonstrates that English and Spanish speakers are not at any disadvantage because of the additional Spanish, and consequently less English, in their instruction.

These students' achievement must also be understood within the context of mathematics achievement in the state of California. During the time of this study, 'California students made little progress in their math skills .. and continued to cling near the bottom of national rankings .. math instruction has been the focus of controversy for at least two years, with conservatives charging that it has strayed too far from the basics' (*San Jose Mercury News*, 1997). The state superintendent of education agreed that

'Clearly, we still have work to do in California to raise these scores.' Thus, the fact that these Spanish-speaking DLE students could perform at or close to grade level by sixth grade, and that English speakers could perform on a par with national peers, is actually quite extraordinary.

Notes

1. Grades 1-3 were selected as the sample size dropped considerably after grade 3 and results were not as robust.

Chapter 13
Student Outcomes: Attitudes

Introduction to Attitudes

Examining student attitudes is important, given the consistent findings that student attitudes affect academic achievement (e.g. Ames & Ames, 1985; Battistich *et al.*, 1995; Snow *et al.*, 1996; Solomon, 1992; Stipek, 1998) and language proficiency (Baetens Beardsmore, 1995; Gardner, 1985; Gardner & Lambert, 1972; Lindholm & Padilla, 1990; Snow, 1990).

Cross-cultural and language attitudes

One important area of attitudinal research involves the investigation of factors that contribute to positive or negative attitudes that members of one community may have toward members of another cultural group and their language. These types of studies are important because attitudes represent an index of intergroup relations, and therefore prove to have important implications for the education of children (Romaine, 1995).

Lambert and his colleagues (Anisfield & Lambert, 1964; Lambert *et al.*, 1960) pioneered the now commonly used 'matched guise' experimental technique to determine students' language attitudes. In these experiments, student judges listened to tape recordings of a number of bilingual speakers and were asked to evaluate the personality characteristics of the speakers in terms of whether they thought the speaker was educated/uneducated, friendly/unfriendly, etc. The judges did not know, however, that they were actually listening to the same speaker, first in French and then in English. As the matched recordings differed only in respect to the language used, differences in students' judgments were attributed to their value judgments of English and French. Results indicated that bilingual students judged the matched guises as more similar than the monolingual students, indicating that bilingual students showed lower frequencies of cultural stereotyping than their monolingual counterparts did.

Similar results were found among younger children as well. In Wales and Hawaii, bilingual school students were found to have more favorable attitudes toward the minority language and culture (Welsh or Hawaiian) than monolingual children (Baker, 1996; Slaughter, 1997). In their study of a DLE program, Cazabon *et al.* (1993) showed that third-grade children enrolled in a DLE program established strong social networks with peers based on the individual characteristics of the person – not their particular racial or ethnic background. In studies of DLE children's attitudes toward bilingualism, DLE Spanish-speakers and English-speakers have favorable attitudes toward being bilinguals (Cazabon *et al.*, 1993; Lindholm, 1994, 1999a, 1999b) and toward children who were different from themselves (Christian *et al.*, 1997; Lindholm, 1994).

Students' attitudes and motivation to learn another language will also affect their ability to learn that language (Baker, 1996). Prejudiced attitudes and stereotypes about another ethno-linguistic group can hinder the motivation needed to learn the other group's language, just as positive attitudes can enhance the language learning process (Lambert, 1987). Generally, reasons to learn a second language fall into two categories: *integrative* or *instrumental* motivation (as discussed in Chapter 7 with regard to parent reasons for enrolling children in a DLE program). Learners are considered to be integratively motivated when they desire to affiliate with and understand another language group. On the other hand, instrumental motivation occurs when a learner has more functional reasons for learning a language, such as advancing a career or passing a test. Most of the research in this area has shown that learners who demonstrate integrative motivation for learning another language have more success in achieving proficiency than students learning for instrumental reasons (Baker, 1996). The reason for this difference may be that integrative motivation involves the development of personal relationships that may be long lasting, whereas instrumental motivation can be short-term and more self-oriented (Lambert & Tucker, 1972).

Gender and age have also been shown to affect students' attitudes and motivation toward learning a second language. For example, girls have been found to hold more favorable attitudes than boys do, and younger children consistently show more favorable attitudes than adolescent-age students (Sharp *et al.*, 1973).

Finally, most students in immersion and bilingual education programs in Australia (De Courcy, 1997) and Germany (Wode, 1998) who were asked about their satisfaction with the program reported high levels of satisfaction and enjoyment.

Self-esteem

Many studies have examined self-esteem or self-concept and have tied students' attitudes toward self to motivation and ultimately to school achievement (for reviews, see Harter, 1983; Skaalvik, 1997). However, there is no general consensus as to a definition of self esteem, how to measure it, and whether measurement instruments accurately assess self esteem across different groups of subjects – males vs. females, or across ethnic groups (Marsh, 1989; Padilla & Lindholm, 1995; Skaalvik, 1997; Snow *et al.*, 1996). While some researchers (e.g. Bandura, 1977; Marsh, 1993) suggest that self-esteem may not be a particularly useful measure, others (e.g. Skaalvik, 1997) argue for its importance because of predictive relationships to students' goal orientation and expectations of failure and success. Skaalvik (1997: 57) notes that 'Research on causes and consequences of self-esteem in educational settings is therefore a neglected, but important task for educational researchers.'

Gender differences in self-esteem have received considerable attention, with most research suggesting that boys have higher self-esteem than girls, particularly from adolescence (Harter, 1983; Marsh, 1989; Skaalvik, 1986, 1997).

Many early studies emphasized low self-esteem levels for minorities, especially for African Americans, though these findings were also generalized to include members from any minority racial or ethnic group (Rosenberg, 1979; Rosenberg & Simmons, 1972). Later studies contradicted these findings by indicating that African American and Hispanic students have at least as high levels of self-esteem as European Americans (Martinez & Dukes, 1987; Powell, 1989; Rosenberg, 1979; Rosenberg & Simmons, 1972; Wylie, 1979), though most studies have not controlled for possible differences due to social class (Padilla & Lindholm, 1995; Portes, 1996).

Researchers also have been interested in the self-concept of children in bilingual programs (e.g. Genesee & Gándara, 1999). Generally, findings indicate that quality bilingual education programs enhance the self-esteem of students (Hernandez-Chavez, 1984) and promote academic achievement (Willig, 1985) because students' home culture and language are valued in the classroom. Findings have shown that Hispanic and European American students in DLE programs showed no difference in their ratings of both their self-worth and their scholastic competence (Lindholm, 1994), and have demonstrated higher levels of optimism than control groups (Cazabon *et al.*, 1993).

As students enter early adolescence, most make the important transition from elementary school to middle or junior high school. The changes in age and school environment have been shown to have a significant impact on students' self-esteem and self-perception (Rosenberg, 1986). Studies have shown that young adolescents have lower self-concepts regarding their ability than do younger students (Wigfield *et al.*, 1991), are more negative about school and themselves (Eccles *et al.*, 1984) and generally are more anxious about school (Harter *et al.*, 1992).

Attitudes toward school and achievement

Various approaches have been used to examine students' attitudes toward school and achievement (see Banks & Banks, 1995; Berliner & Calfee, 1996; Brophy, 1998; Maehr & Pintrich, 1997). These perspectives are primarily concerned with understanding and promoting students' interest in learning, motivation, value of education, and confidence in their own capacities and attributes. Research consistently demonstrates that students who show a strong sense of intrinsic motivation and self efficacy demonstrate positive emotions in the classroom, are generally satisfied with school, enjoy academic work, and experience positive academic performance (Ames & Ames, 1985; Graham & Weiner, 1996; Grolnick _et al._, 1991; Schultz, 1993; Skaalvik, 1997; Vallerand _et al._, 1989).

Few current systematic studies have investigated ethnic differences in achievement-related attitudes. Most studies that have examined ethnic differences have not adequately distinguished between ethnicity and socioeconomic differences, thereby confounding the effects of these two variables (Graham, 1992, 1994; Padilla & Lindholm, 1995; Wigfield _et al._, 1996). Most of the sparse research demonstrates that there are ethnic differences in achievement-related attitudes. Findings indicate that the beliefs of Hispanic, African American, and European American children about academic achievement are similarly positive regarding reading and mathematics, with differences favoring African American and Hispanic students. African American fifth graders like math significantly more than European American and Hispanic students do, and Hispanic and African American students like homework and school in general more than European American students do (Stevenson _et al._, 1990). While African American children may express positive academic self-concepts, by the time they are adolescents, their positive academic-related attitudes have diminished (Hare, 1985).

Several authors have suggested that the depressed academic attitudes of African American adolescents may relate to their understanding of their relatively poorer academic performance compared with European Americans (Hare, 1985). Ogbu (1995) has argued that African American adolescents have developed ambivalent or rejecting attitudes toward school as a means of repudiating negative stereotypes of Euro Americans toward African Americans, or because the achievement attitudes are characteristics of Euro Americans, with which African American students do not identify. While there is little research on the achievement-related attitudes of African American students, there is considerably less on the attitudes of Hispanic students, regardless of whether they are in language education or mainstream education programs.

Research on third-grade and fourth-grade Spanish- and English-speaking children in DLE programs has yielded positive academic attitudes among these students (Cazabon *et al.*, 1993, Lindholm 1994). Both studies also found no ethnic differences in students' academic attitudes.

Studies comparing the achievement attitudes and motivation of students from various socioeconomic status (SES) backgrounds have overwhelmingly supported the hypothesis that a stronger need for achievement and ultimate educational attainment is associated with higher SES (Battistich *et al.*, 1995; Knapp & Woolverton, 1995; Natriello *et al.*, 1990; Rumberger, 1995; Schultz, 1993), regardless of country and sub-population within a country (Knapp & Woolverton, 1995). Further, student outcomes are strongly related to the socioeconomic level of the school (Battistich *et al.*, 1995).

Students' perceptions of their academic ability have also been found to differ by gender (Eccles *et al.*, 1984; Martinez & Dukes, 1987). During their early adolescent years, boys show significantly higher math-ability perceptions than girls, while girls show significantly higher language-related ability perceptions than boys (Wigfield *et al.*, 1991).

Classroom environment and teacher expectations

The classroom environment has also been shown to affect students' achievement and attitudes (e.g. Battistich *et al.*, 1995; Darling-Hammond, 1995; Levine & Lezotte, 1995; Lucas *et al.*, 1990; Minami & Ovando, 1995 ; Slavin, 1995). For example, studies of classrooms that utilize ethnically mixed cooperative-learning techniques with students from different racial and ethnic backgrounds consistently show that the students develop higher levels of achievement and more positive cross-cultural and racial attitudes (Aronson & Gonzalez, 1988; Kagan, 1986; Slavin, 1983) as well as gains in cross-ethnic friendships (Slavin, 1995). Battistich *et al.* (1995) have suggested that students' attitudinal and motivational outcomes are enhanced when they are in school environments where they feel respected, supported and valued by others in their school communities. These findings were consistent across a range of student socioeconomic backgrounds (Knapp & Woolverton, 1995; Levine & Lezotte, 1995), but were especially influential among schools with the most disadvantaged student populations (Battistich *et al.*, 1995).

Home environment and parent expectations

As a child's first teachers, parents set the stage for academic success later in childhood (see Chapter 7). Extensive research has consistently shown that parenting styles, behaviors, expectations, and involvement influence children's cognitive and academic outcomes (Cazden, 1992; Grolnick & Ryan, 1989; Snow *et al.*, 1991; Sternberg & Williams, 1995; see Chapter 7 for a review of this literature), as well as children's self-esteem (Grolnick *et al.*, 1997). As pointed out in Chapter 7, research generally shows that more educated families are more involved with their children's formal education (Levine & Lezotte, 1995). However, families from all situations – regardless of the formal education or income level of the parents, and regardless of the grade level or ability of the student – use strategies to encourage and influence their children's education and development.

This chapter will specifically examine three issues related to student attitudes in DLE programs because, as discussed previously in the literature reviews, these factors influence student achievement and language proficiency:

- Student satisfaction, achievement- and classroom-related attitudes, parent expectations, and self-esteem in DLE programs.
- Student background (ethnicity, SES, gender, grade level) and school demographic characteristics (90HI vs. 90LO) associated with student attitudes.
- Relationships among the attitude categories.

Data Collection

All students completed an 80-item questionnaire in either English or Spanish, comprising nine different categories of student attitudes. Each item was rated on a four-point Likert scale ranging from 1 ('strongly disagree') to 4 ('strongly agree'), with some items reversed scored (see Table 13.2 for the categories and their items, and the Appendix for the questionnaire). Most of the category items had high or acceptable internal consistency[1]:

- Cross-cultural and integrative language attitudes (Cronbach's alpha = 0.72).
- Instrumental language attitudes (0.73).
- Self esteem and appearance (0.73).
- Positive academic attitudes/intrinsic motivation (0.86).
- Work avoidance (0.74).
- Positive academic behaviors (0.67).
- Classroom environment and teacher expectations (0.63).
- Home environment and parent expectations (0.67).
- Satisfaction with program (0.62).

The items for the scales were developed based on the literature and some items were adapted from Johnson (1974).

Student background characteristics

A total of 611 grade 3–8 students from nine DLE schools participated in the study. Students were equally distributed among the genders (50% male, 50% female) and among 90HI (51%) and 90LO (49%) programs. Students' ethnic background, as shown in Table 13.1, was as follows:

- 56% Hispanic-Spanish speaking (60% Hisp-SP in 90HI, 52% in 90LO);
- 11% Hispanic-English speaking (16% Hisp-EB in 90HI, 7% in 90LO);
- 28% European American (18% EURO in 90HI, 39% in 90LO);
- 5% African American (6% African-Am in 90HI, 3% in 90LO).

More than half the students participated in the free school lunch program (63% in 90HI and 48% in 90LO), indicating that about half of the students were from very low income families. Considerably more Hisp-SP students (82%) were on free lunch, followed by African American (57%), Hisp-EB (27%) and lastly Euro Americans (16%). Hisp-SP, Hisp-EB, and African American students were more highly represented in 90HI programs, while EURO pupils were more likely to participate in 90LO programs. Students also varied by grade level, though considerably more students were represented at the elementary level (grades 3–5) than at the middle school (grades 6–8) level.

Table 13.1 Student background characteristics by program type

	90:10 HIHI *(n=314)*	*90:10 LOLO* *(n=297)*	*Group differences*
Ethnicity			$\chi^2(3) = 39.9, p < 0.0001$
Hispanic-Spanish	60%	52%	
Hispanic-English	16%	7%	
European American	18%	39%	
African American	6%	3%	
SES			
Free-lunch program	63%	48%	$\chi^2(1) = 12.5, p < 0.001$
Non-free-lunch program	37%	52%	
Grade level			$\chi^2(1) = 4.1, p < 0.05$
3–5	87%	81%	
6–8	13%	19%	

Table 13.2 Category items and reliabilities

Cross-cultural and integrative language attitudes (0.72)

I think learning another language helps me to understand kids who are different from me

I like to invite kids to my house no matter what skin color they have

I think that all people should be treated equally

I like to play with other kids no matter what they look like

I enjoy meeting and listening to people who speak another language

I believe that learning Spanish is important so I can talk with Spanish-speaking people

I think that learning another language will help me get along better with other people

---

Instrumental language attitudes (0.73)

I think that learning two languages will help me do better in school

I think that knowing two languages will help me get a better job when I grow up

I believe that learning two languages helps me get better grades

I believe that learning two languages will make me smarter than if I learned only one language

I think that learning two languages helps me learn how to think better

---

Self-esteem/appearance (0.73)

I like my body the way it is

I like my physical appearance the way it is

I wish something about my hair or face looked different*

I am pretty pleased with myself

I like the way I am leading my life

I am happy with myself most of the time

I often wish I were someone else*

I wish I were different*

Negative academic attitudes/work avoidance (0.74)

I don't care whether I understand something or not as long as I get the right answer*

I prefer easy work that I am sure I can do*

I don't like difficult school work because I have to work too hard*

I stick to the assignments which are pretty easy to do*

I like school subjects where it's pretty easy to learn the answers*

Some of the work we do in school is too hard for me*

When I do my work, I skip the hard parts*

When doing my schoolwork, I guess a lot so that I can finish quickly*

Positive academic attitudes (0.86)

I like reading

I like mathematics

I like school

I like to learn

I like hard work because it's a challenge

I like difficult problems because I enjoy trying to figure them out

I like school subjects that make me think pretty hard and figure things out

I like difficult schoolwork because I find it more interesting

I do my work because it makes me feel good inside

I can do almost any problem if I keep working at it

I can do even the hardest work in my class

I am good in mathematics

Positive academic behavior (0.67)

I take my time to figure out my work

I go back over schoolwork I don't understand

I spend time thinking about how to do my work before I start it

I ask myself questions while I read to make sure I understand

Classroom environment (0.63)

Our teacher wants us to help each other with our school work

Most kids take part in class discussions

Kids care about each other in my class

Kids treat each other equally in our class

I have someone at school I could talk to if I had a problem

My teacher expects me to do well in school

Home environment (0.67)

My parents make sure I get my homework done

My parents help me when I need it

My parents expect me to do well in school

My parents know who my friends are

At home, I have a place where I can concentrate and study

Satisfaction (0.62)

I want to continue studying and learning in Spanish and English, like I do now

I enjoy studying in Spanish and English the way I do at school

Full scale (0.91)

* Represents items that were recorded.

Findings

Cross-cultural and language attitudes

Cross-cultural and integrative language attitudes

Ratings of cross-cultural and integrative language attitudes (see Table 13.2 for items) were consistently high (mean = 3.5) regardless of the students' backgrounds or the school demographic characteristics. The major program differences were that 90LO students were *more* likely than 90HI students were to feel that all people should be treated equally (mean = 3.7 vs. 3.4). However, 90HI students gave a higher rating than 90LO students did to the item that a second language helps people get along better with others (mean = 3.5 vs. 3.3). Overall, students in 90HI programs did not vary by grade level in their attitudes, but 90LO upper-grade students had slightly lower attitudes (mean = 3.4) than lower-grade students (mean = 3.6).

For the items relating their perceptions and willingness to interact with others who differed in physical characteristics (looks, skin color) or in language background, the attitudes were very high (mean = 3.3–3.6). Similarly, students recognized that speaking another language could help them understand and get along better with other people, and that Spanish is important to talk with others (mean = 3.4–3.6). Students rated enjoyment in meeting people who speak another language fairly high (mean = 3.3). Students did not differ in their cross-cultural and language attitudes according to gender, SES, or ethnicity, except that African American students consistently scored the lowest on every item.

Instrumental attitudes toward language

High scores were also given to the instrumental language attitudes (mean = 3.5). There were no differences in how students rated the items overall according to their background or school demographic characteristics.

A few noteworthy results emerged: students strongly believed that being bilingual would help them get a better job (mean = 3.7), made them smarter (mean = 3.4), helped them do better in school (mean = 3.6), and helped them get better grades (mean = 3.4). While positive, they were not quite as likely to strongly agree that learning two languages helped them think better (mean = 3.2). As with the previous set of items, African American students on free lunch scored lowest on each item, and significantly lower on questions pertaining to whether learning two languages helped them do better in school, or would help them get a better job.

Self-esteem

Self-esteem items assessed students' satisfaction with their physical appearance and with their life in general. Interestingly, the physical-appearance items made this scale more reliable than the self-esteem items alone.

Overall, students were moderately satisfied (mean = 3.2) with their physical appearance and overall life. However, boys rated their self-esteem significantly higher (mean = 3.2) than did girls (mean = 3.1), and younger students had higher self-esteem (mean = 3.2) than older students (mean = 2.9). Self-esteem and appearance items did not vary at all according to program type (90HI vs. 90LO), student ethnicity, or social class.

Attitudes toward school and achievement

Four scales provided information on students' attitudes toward school and on achievement: satisfaction with the DLE program, positive academic attitudes, learning strategies, and negative academic attitudes.

Positive academic attitudes

Positive academic attitudes included students' enjoyment of school, learning, mathematics, reading, and academic challenge, as well as their academic persistence. Overall, students scored an average of 3.2. One important result was that students did not differ according to grade level, gender, ethnicity, SES, or program characteristics, though there was some variation by grade and ethnic/language group combined:

- Hisp-SP and EURO students in grades 3–5 scored higher than in grades 6–8 (Hisp-SP: mean = 3.4 vs. 2.9 and EURO: mean = 3.2 vs. 3.0).
- In contrast, Hisp-EB received lower scores in grades 3–5 than in grades 6–8.

In looking at particular items, the highest ratings were given to:

- Like to learn (mean = 3.6).
- Like reading (mean = 3.4).
- Doing work makes me feel good (mean = 3.4).
- Can do almost any problem (mean = 3.4).
- Like math (mean = 3.3).
- Like school (mean = 3.3).

In contrast, items that students did not rate as highly included:

- Can do hardest work (mean = 2.8) – African American students on free lunch scored highest on this item (mean = 3.2).
- Like hard work because it's a challenge (mean = 3.0).
- Like difficult problems because enjoy trying to figure them out (mean = 3.0).
- Like difficult work because it is more interesting (mean = 3.1).

Just as importantly, though, they did not disagree with these items. Overall, these results suggest that the students like school, and enjoy being challenged.

Satisfaction with DLE program

The satisfaction items had students select, on a scale from 1 (Very Dissatisfied) to 5 (Very Satisfied), whether they enjoyed studying in English and Spanish, and whether they wanted to continue studying in English and Spanish. Students were satisfied with the DLE program (mean = 3.4). Results showed that:

- Students in grades 3–5 (mean = 3.5) were significantly more satisfied than students in grades-6–8 were (mean = 3.3).
- Hisp-EB were most satisfied (mean = 3.6), while African American students were least satisfied (mean = 3.3).
- Actually, African American students varied, with free-lunch participants least satisfied (mean = 3.1) and non-free-lunch students as satisfied as students from the other ethnic groups (mean = 3.5). African American students on free lunch were also less likely to enjoy or want to continue studying in both languages.
- Students rated enjoyment (mean = 3.5) lower than continue (mean = 3.8), indicating that students would continue, even if they did not highly rate enjoyment.
- Students in 90HI programs who were not on free lunch tended to be more satisfied than students in 90HI on free lunch, and these results were more pronounced for African American students.

Negative academic attitudes

Students rated items related to negative academic attitudes and work avoidance (see Table 13.2 for items) with an overall score of 2.4, indicating general *disagreement*. There were variations between grades and ethnic/language groups:

- EURO (mean = 2.5) students scored higher (more negatively) than Hisp-SP students (mean = 2.3).
- Students on free lunch rated these items higher (more negatively) than non-free lunch participants (mean = 2.5 vs. 2.3).

Students were least likely to agree that:

- Some work is too hard (mean = 2.2).
- Prefer easy work I can do (mean = 2.2).
- Stick to easy assignments (mean = 2.3).
- Like subjects where it is easy to learn answers (mean = 2.4)

More neutral responses were given to:

- Skip hard parts of work (mean = 2.8).
- Guess a lot to finish quickly (mean = 3.1).

Learning strategies

In looking at the students' responses to learning strategies, overall students tended to agree that they use these strategies (mean = 3.2). The highest ratings were given to these items:

- Take time to figure out work (mean = 3.4).
- Go back over work I do not understand (mean = 3.3).

Also, encouragingly, students tended to agree to:

- Thinking about work before starting (mean = 3.1).
- Asking self questions while reading (mean = 3.1).

While one might expect to see grade-level differences, we would anticipate that these cognitive strategies would increase rather than decrease across grade levels. Among these students, though, scores were higher among the younger (grades 3–5) students than among the older (grades 6–8) students.

Classroom environment and teacher expectations

Students' perceptions of their classroom environment and teacher expectations were examined according to student ethnicity, SES, grade level and school demographic characteristics.

Students tended to agree that the classroom environment was positive (mean = 3.2). Students clearly agreed that the teacher expected them to do well (mean = 3.6), that they have someone at school with whom they can talk (mean = 3.4), and that the teacher wants students to help each other (mean = 3.4). When it came to rating peers, the students were less optimistic, though they tended to agree that kids care about each other in their class (mean = 2.9) and that kids treat others equally in class (mean = 2.9). Students did not vary in their ratings of the individual classroom environment items by any student background variables. However, students differed in their ratings of classroom environment according to their ethnic background and a combination of program type and grade level:

- Hispanic Spanish speakers perceived a more positive classroom environment (mean = 3.3) than other students (mean = 3.0–3.2).
- 90HI students in grades 6–8 gave higher ratings of classroom environment (mean = 3.3) than 90HI students in grades 3–5 (mean = 3.2). The

opposite was true of students in the 90LO program, with upper-grade students scoring lower (mean = 3.0) than those in grades 3–5 (mean = 3.2).

Home environment and parent expectations

Home environment and parental expectations were highly rated by the students, with average ratings of 3.5. The only difference in student ratings was that the gap between free-lunch and non-free-lunch students was greater in the 90LO program than in the 90HI program. Overall, students felt that their parents:

- Make sure they get their homework done (mean = 3.6).
- Help them with homework (mean = 3.6).
- Expect them to do well in school (mean = 3.7).
- Know who their friends are (mean = 3.4).
- Make sure that they have a place to study at home (mean = 3.3).

African American students on free lunch had consistently the lowest scores on each item, except for having a place to study, where Hisp-SP scored lowest.

Relationships among Different Attitudes

Table 13.3 provides results from the correlations among the attitudinal variables. As Table 13.3 demonstrates, there were highly significant correlations, though low to moderate, between many of the variables. In looking at correlations between the cross-cultural and language attitudes and other attitudinal dimensions, the following relationships were significant:

- Cross-cultural/integrative attitudes with instrumental attitudes ($r= 0.57$).
- Positive academic attitudes with cross-cultural/integrative ($r = 0.45$) and instrumental ($r = 0.41$) attitudes.
- Classroom environment with cross-cultural/integrative ($r = 0.49$) and instrumental ($r = 0.42$) attitudes.
- Home environment with cross-cultural/integrative ($r = 0.56$) and instrumental ($r = 0.43$) attitudes.

There were a number of important relationships between satisfaction and the other categories; satisfaction was positively related to:

- Positive academic attitudes ($r = 0.51$) and behaviors ($r = 0.47$). Positive academic behaviors were more highly related to satisfaction among 90HI than among 90LO students.
- Cross-cultural/integrative language attitudes ($r = 0.46$) as well as

Table 13.3 Correlations among attitudinal components

	Instrumental language attitudes	Self-esteem	Negative academic attitudes	Positive academic attitudes	Positive academic behaviors	Classroom environment	Home environment	Satisfaction
Cross-cult./integrative attitudes	0.57***	0.33***	0.09**	0.45***	0.39***	0.49***	0.56***	0.46***
Instrumental language attitudes		0.22***	0.00	0.41***	0.39***	0.42***	0.43***	0.44***
Self-esteem			0.18***	0.37***	0.23***	0.31***	0.35***	0.30***
Negative academic attitudes				0.31***	0.00	-0.07	0.06	0.07
Positive academic attitudes					0.47***	0.51***	0.52***	0.51***
Positive academic behaviors						0.48***	0.52***	0.47***
Classroom environment							0.57***	0.46***
Home environment								0.49***

** $p < 0.01$, *** $p < 0.001$

instrumental attitudes ($r = 0.44$). The relationship between satisfaction and cross-cultural attitudes was stronger among students in 90LO programs than students in 90HI programs.

- Classroom environment ($r = 0.46$).
- Home environment ($r = 0.49$).
- Satisfaction was *not* related to negative academic attitudes.

Positive academic attitudes were highly correlated with positive academic behaviors ($r = 0.47$), and each were also related to:

- Classroom environment ($r = 0.48–0.51$).
- Home environment ($r = 0.52$).

Summary and Conclusions

This chapter has provided information about the students' attitudes in DLE programs. The results, which will be summarized here, illustrate some important dynamics related to students' attitudes. Overall, students had very positive attitudes toward the program, their teachers, their parents, and the classroom environment, as well as positive learning attitudes and behaviors. Because the attitudes were generally positive, it is not surprising that many of these attitudinal components were significantly correlated.

While students did not differ much from each other according to school or background characteristics, there were some important differences:

- Language attitudes were slightly lower among 90LO than among 90HI students, particularly as they moved into the upper grades. These older 90LO students also gave lower ratings to classroom environment.
- Non-free-lunch participants were more satisfied than were free-lunch students in 90HI programs. Combined with less satisfaction were more negative academic attitudes on the part of these free-lunch participants. In 90LO programs, there was a gap between free-lunch and non-free-lunch participants in the ratings of home environment, with more positive ratings on the part of non-free-lunch students.
- African American students on free lunch were least satisfied with the program, least likely to enjoy the program or want to continue in it; and scored consistently lower on every item in the home environment scale. However, these students rated themselves highest on the item 'I can do the hardest work.'
- African American students not on free lunch were as satisfied with the program as the Hispanic and EURO students.

The findings from this study are important both theoretically and practically. They demonstrate no difference between the Hispanic and EURO students in their ratings of both their scholastic competence and their global self worth. In addition, the students' ratings were comparable to those reported in other studies (e.g. Harter, 1983). In Harter's sample of California middle- to upper-class third graders, the mean scholastic competence score was 3.0, while the mean obtained in the current study was 2.8. Despite the social-class gap between the Harter sample (middle to upper class) and the current sample (lower to middle class), these means are very comparable. Similarly, for self worth, Harter's California students obtained a mean score of 3.0, which is equivalent to the mean rating of the students in the current study (mean = 2.9).

Pedagogically, these results are encouraging for two reasons. One reason is that the findings could be interpreted to suggest that ethnic minority children in a high-quality educational program that incorporates the language and culture of both groups and fosters academic achievement could also enhance the perceived scholastic competence and global self worth of those students. Another reason is that the results show that EURO students who are in a classroom in which Spanish is the language of instruction, and in which they are the minority in terms of the number of students in the class, demonstrate a level of scholastic competence and global self worth that is comparable to middle- and upper-class students who are most likely in an English only program. Thus, these results suggest that both Hispanic and EURO students can benefit psychosocially from their experience of an integrated bilingual classroom.

At a theoretical level, the lack of ethnic differences in student ratings may be particularly important because Harter (1983), among others (e.g. Cortes, 1986; Wylie, 1979), has suggested that perceived competence and academic achievement are related. Harter (1998) has shown that achievement is causally prior to perceived scholastic competence and that perceived competence, in turn, predicts one's motivational orientation, which can then influence academic achievement.

Notes

1. 'Reliability coefficients of 0.7 or above are usually considered respectable, regardless of the type of reliability calculated or the method of calculation used' (Morris *et al.*, 1987: 118).

Part 4

Conclusions and Implications for Language Education Programs

Chapter 14
Summary and Conclusions

The purpose of this chapter is to summarize the findings and to integrate various results across different chapters. This chapter does not repeat the myriad findings reported in this book, but will rather highlight key results, particularly as we can integrate the results and better understand the outcomes from the Dual Language Education[1] (DLE) model. Further, discussions of these results were presented in previous chapters and thus will not be repeated here. Using this chapter's discussion and integration of key findings, implications for language education programs will be examined in the next chapter.

Children and their Parents: Contexts for Language Proficiency and Achievement

Chapter 7 provided an examination of the parents' backgrounds and attitudes in DLE programs. The results summarized here provide a context for better understanding the students' language proficiency and achievement outcomes.

With respect to parent background, there were some important similarities and differences. First, parents differed in terms of ethnicity, language background, and education. Parents were categorized according to their ethnicity and language background as: European American English speaking (EURO), Hispanic-Bilingual (Hisp-Bil), Hispanic-English speaking (Hisp-EB), and Hispanic-Spanish speaking (Hisp-SP). These parents were quite distinct in some important ways:

- *EURO* parents had relatively higher levels of education; half of these parents had earned a university/professional/graduate degree and 82% had at least some college-level education. Almost all parents (94%) were born in the US, though the majority had visited a Spanish-speaking country at some point. Most parents had studied Spanish, though their proficiency was quite limited. The language of the home was almost exclusively English, with parents speaking to the child in English and the child responding in English. Thus, it is not surprising that these children entered school as English monolinguals. About 12% of these children were participating in the free lunch program.

- *Hisp-Bil*: parents were similar in many ways to the EURO parents with respect to their level of education and their attitudes. More than a third of these parents had high levels of education (university/ professional/graduate degree), and a total of 74% had some college-level education. While almost all children were born in the US, about half of the parents were born in the US. All of these parents rated themselves as proficient bilinguals, and close to two thirds had lived in a Spanish-speaking country. Half of these parents used English in conversing with their child, a third used Spanish and the remainder used both languages. Children were more likely to answer back using English with both their parents and siblings. Among these children, 77% began school as English proficient and 23% as limited English proficient (LEP). Over one-third of these children were receiving the free-lunch program at school.
- *Hisp-EB* parents were different from the Hisp-Bil parents in many ways. Only 4% of these parents had high levels of education, and only half had some college-level education. All parents and their children were born in the US, and about half had visited a Spanish-speaking country. Only half had ever studied Spanish, a lower percentage than the other parent groups, and all rated their proficiency in Spanish as limited. These parents were much more likely than EURO or Hisp-Bil parents to agree that they encourage their child to use English. While English was not used exclusively in these homes, most communication between the parents and children took place in English. Given the largely English language background, it was surprising that half of these students began kindergarten as limited English proficient. About 60% of the children were participating in the free-lunch program.
- *Hisp-SP* parents possessed low levels of education; over half had attained only an elementary-level education, and the remainder were split between 7–9 and 10–12 years of schooling. Almost all parents were born outside the US, whereas three-quarters of their children were born in the US. Most parents (83%) had studied English, though all rated their proficiency in English as low. In these homes, parents used mostly Spanish, but some English, with their children. Among children, most used Spanish or both languages with their parents, but children were split between the use of Spanish and both languages with siblings. All of these children entered kindergarten as limited English proficient, and 90% were taking part in the free-lunch program.

As indicated in Chapter 7, these family backgrounds do not represent all students; they represent only a small percentage of students discussed here. However, they do provide some context for understanding student outcomes.

Parents mostly agreed that parental involvement is important. However, parents' ratings of the importance of involvement varied according to their ethnic/language and education backgrounds. Parents who had at least some college education were more likely to agree that parental involvement was important than parents who had only a high school diploma or less. Parents in the lowest educated group, Hisp-SP, were most likely to agree about the importance of parental involvement. Hisp-EB parents with only a high school diploma or less were least likely to agree about the importance of involvement.

EURO and Hisp-Bil parents, who were the most highly educated parents, were more likely to be involved outside of class, to help with the parent club and to assist with or attend school activities/events. About one third of EURO, Hisp-Bil, and Hisp-SP parents reported that they attended the parent group meetings, though only a handful of the Hisp-EB parents attended.

Parent attitudes were very favorable toward bilingualism, as one might expect. Most parents agreed that it was important that their child study Spanish: to be comfortable with other Spanish speakers, to meet and converse with varied people, to understand Hispanic culture, to participate in activities with people of other cultures, and because others will respect the child if s/he is bilingual. Most parents also perceived that studying Spanish would be an asset for their child for career and intellectual benefits. Parents of different ethnic/language backgrounds did not differ in their attitudes except that Hisp-EB (English speaking and Bilingual) parents were more likely than EURO parents to believe in the importance of Spanish for career advantages.

Findings also revealed that parents had different reasons for enrolling their child in the program, and these variations depended on heritage background. Euro American parents identified with both instrumental and integrative reasons. However, for Hispanic parents, for whom the target (non-English) language was their heritage language, the primary purpose was integrative in nature. These results were true regardless of whether the Hispanic parent was a Spanish monolingual or a Bilingual/ English speaker. As we noted earlier, these findings corroborated research in Wales and in the US that showed that Welsh and Chicano parents possessed strong integrative motivation for enrolling their child in a heritage language bilingual program (Bush, 1983, cited in Torres, 1988).

Realistically, most of these parents also possess instrumental motivation in recognizing that bilingual skills will help their children as they enter the job market than were EURO parents.

Parents perceived medium levels of support from the district. Parents with children at 90HI[2] sites and with lower levels of education felt lower levels of district support than parents at 90LO sites and parents with college-level education. Across the different school sites, parents gave staff high ratings for promoting diversity at the school site and for balancing the needs of both groups of students. While most parents believed that staff was successful in promoting diversity, parents with children at 90HI sites gave staff higher scores than parents with children at 90LO sites. Parents were also highly consistent that they would recommend the program to other parents, regardless of their ethnic/language background, education level, child's grade level, or the program type (90HI, 90LO).

In summary, parents differed widely in terms of their ethnic/language background and educational backgrounds. Most parents had positive attitudes toward the program and how it was being implemented; this support and belief in the program was substantiated by their recommendation of the DLE program to other parents.

Language Proficiency

The oral language proficiency results indicate that DLE students scored at or near the top of the SOLOM in their first language, and almost all students were rated as proficient in their two languages, particularly by the upper grade levels. Students made excellent progress in both languages across the grade levels. These data were consistent whether we examined them from a cross-sectional or longitudinal perspective, and regardless of the language measures that were used.

L1 proficiency

English speakers and Spanish speakers were rated as highly proficient in their native language, especially by the time they reached the upper grade levels. English speakers did not vary in their English language development according to the type of program in which they were participating: 90:10 students, who received as little as 10% or 20% of their instruction in English, scored as high as 50:50 students, who spent half their instructional day in English. Both groups of DLE English speakers were rated as high in English as monolingual English speakers in English Only programs. These findings were just as true for African American and Hisp-EB students as they were for EURO students, and the results held whether these students were low-SES or mid-SES.

Significant program differences influenced the Spanish proficiency of Spanish speakers. Students in 90:10 programs obtained higher ratings in Spanish than did students in 50:50 and TBE programs. Thus, Spanish speakers clearly benefited from the additional instructional time in Spanish to improve their Spanish language development.

What follows is a brief synopsis of the influence of each school or student factor in promoting L1 proficiency:

- Program type was influential for Spanish speakers but not for English speakers, with 90:10 programs promoting higher levels of Spanish proficiency.
- Ethnic density/SES need (90HI vs. 90LO) was not a significant factor in L1 proficiency for either group.
- English speakers received higher ratings than Spanish speakers did.
- SES was not a significant factor, though it was important by the final year of elementary school (fifth grade), where mid-SES students were rated higher than low-SES students.
- Students of all ethnic groups made significant progress in developing their L1.
- Girls generally scored higher than boys did, though these differences were not significant at any grade level.

L2 proficiency

There were important program type and school demographic differences in the L2 proficiency ratings of these students. For English speakers, 90:10 students outscored 50:50 students. Thus, receiving a much larger percentage (80–90% compared to 50%) of instruction in Spanish in the early grade levels produced a greater gain in Spanish proficiency. English-speaking students from all ethnic groups made good gains in developing Spanish, even when a significant percentage were low-SES.

Among Spanish-speaking students, there were important program-related findings. DLE students made significant gains across the grade levels, and there was no significant difference between 90:10 and 50:50 participants. Despite receiving only 10–20% of their instructional day in English compared with 50% for 50:50 students, 90:10 students scored similarly to 50:50 students in their proficiency ratings. Thus, receiving less English in their curriculum did not negatively affect the English language proficiency of these students relative to students who received half of their instruction in English.

In summary, the following program/school and student factors were influential in L2 proficiency:

- Program type significantly influenced English speakers (90:10>50:50), but was not important for Spanish speakers (90:10=50:50).
- School ethnic density/SES need was influential at the upper grade levels, where English-speaking 90HI students were rated more proficient in Spanish than were English speakers in 90LO programs.
- Spanish speakers scored higher than English speakers.
- Other student background factors were not significant: students of all ethnicities, both genders and all SES categories made excellent progress in developing proficiency in a second language.

Bilingual proficiency

Students were at different levels of bilingual proficiency: some students were very high in both languages, some were high in one language and moderate or low in the other language. However, at the upper grade levels, there were no students who were low in both languages, though there were a few students who were moderate in one language and low in the other.

Most English speakers were medium bilinguals, though 20–50% of 90:10 students were classified as high bilinguals. Among Spanish-speaking students, by fifth and sixth grades, over half of the 90:10 and 50:50 students were medium bilinguals. However, more 90:10 compared to 50:50 students were categorized as high bilinguals.

Integration of language proficiency with attitudinal data

In Chapter 9, we noted that several attitudinal factors have been found to influence language proficiency. The following parent factors and student attitudes were associated with language proficiency:

- Among English speakers, neither integrative motivation orientation (motivation to learn a second language in order to socially engage or integrate with people of another group) nor instrumental motivation (in which the learner sees some academic, intellectual or career gain in becoming proficient in the second language) was associated with Spanish language proficiency in grade 5.
- Among Spanish speakers, proficiency in English was significantly correlated with both integrative motivation and instrumental motivation.
- Another variable was highly correlated with Spanish language proficiency for Spanish speakers – how often students translated for their family or friends. The more they translated, the higher were their scores in Spanish language proficiency.

- No other attitudinal factors were related to language proficiency for English and Spanish speakers.
- There was a significant association between the number of Hispanic cultural activities to which a parent took his/her child and the level of bilingualism. Of parents who took their grades 5–7 children to at least 2–3 cultural activities per year, 75% of their children were high bilinguals compared to only 30% high bilinguals among parents who took their children to 0–1 cultural activities per year.
- Students whose parents attended the parent club meetings were more likely to be high bilinguals than were students whose parents did not attend the parent meetings (100% of children whose parents attended were high bilinguals, compared with only 52% of children whose parents did not attend).
- In looking at whether students' scores differed according to the ethnic/language group of their parents (EURO, Hisp-EB, Hisp-Bil, Hisp-SP), there were no significant differences by grades 3–5 between the English speakers (EURO, Hisp-EB, Hisp-Bil) in their English proficiency, though among these three groups the Hisp-Bil children had slightly higher scores, and the Hisp-EB students had lower scores. The EURO and Hisp-EB students had the same scores in Spanish proficiency, one point lower than the Hisp-Bil students. Overall, though, there were no significant differences between these groups.

Summary

These results show that both DLE models, 90:10 and 50:50, promoted proficiency in two languages. Students in 90:10 programs developed higher levels of bilingual proficiency than students in the 50:50 program. In developing proficiency in the English language, both English speakers and Spanish speakers benefited equally from 90:10 and 50:50 programs. Thus, whether they spent 10–20% or 50% of their instructional day in English, students were equally proficient in English. In contrast, developing high levels of Spanish proficiency was much more likely to occur in 90:10 than in 50:50 programs for both English and Spanish speakers. Further, for English speakers, 90HI programs augmented Spanish proficiency even more than 90LO programs did.

Clearly, there is no evidence to suggest that participation in DLE programs retards the native language development of Spanish or English speakers. Almost all students, regardless of their student characteristics, were proficient in English and Spanish. These results, as noted earlier and as we will further discuss in Chapter 15, were consistent with the literatures on immersion education and bilingual education, which show that students develop high levels of proficiency in their two languages. The implications of these results for program development, program planning, and parent recruitment and training are examined in Chapter 15.

Reading and Language Achievement

Reading and Language Achievement in L1

Students made significant progress in reading and language achievement in their first language, and they performed as well as their peers using California state norms for English and Spanish speakers. Longitudinal and cross-sectional results were very consistent for L1 reading achievement. Also, language achievement results paralleled the reading achievement results. Results did vary somewhat depending on the program type, school characteristics and student background factors:

- By the time English speakers began English reading instruction in grade 3, they performed at grade level and at least as high as the California statewide norms for English speakers instructed only in English. Students in 90LO programs performed at levels similar to students in 50:50 programs. These results clearly show that the DLE English-speaking students were able to catch up to and surpass their peers in English-only instruction. At all but the third grade level, the 90LO and 50:50 students had similar scores.
- Spanish-speaking students participating in 90HI and 50:50 programs also scored average and at least as high as their peers across the state of California, while students in 90LO, TBE and EO programs performed below grade level.
- Mid-SES students scored significantly higher than low-SES students did.
- Girls outscored boys in grades 3 and 4, but at no other grade levels.
- Students of all ethnic groups made good progress in L1 reading achievement. African American students scored similarly to the other ethnic groups at grades 1 and 2, but their scores were below grade level in grades 3 and 5, though the grade 5 score was only slightly below grade level. These results demonstrate that African American students can perform at or close to grade level in English while being instructed largely in Spanish. Since the great majority of these students were low-SES, these results are encouraging in demonstrating that African American students of different economic backgrounds can benefit from DLE programs.

Reading and language achievement in L2

Students also demonstrated growth in reading and language achievement in their second language. Where language achievement data were available, the scores and results tended to mirror the reading achievement outcomes. Similar to L1 achievement, results varied according to the program type, school characteristics, and student background factors:

- The scores of English-speaking students in Spanish reading achievement differed depending on the program. In 90HI programs, English speakers scored average to high, and about comparable to statewide norms for Spanish-speaking students. In 90LO programs, though, these students' scores were average to below average and they did not reach the statewide norms for Spanish speakers.
- Spanish speakers also differed in their English reading achievement according to the school demographic characteristics, with 90LO students scoring higher than 90HI students in grades 1, 2 and 5. In both 90HI and 90LO programs, students scored below grade level, but only slightly below grade level by grade 7. However, Spanish speakers in the 90LO program who were mid-SES scored at grade level. Students in the 50:50 program performed higher than students in the 90:10 program at grades 3 and 4, but not in grades 5 and 6. By grade 6, Spanish-speaking students in all DLE program types (50:50, 90LO, 90HI) scored comparably.
- For both Spanish and English speakers, mid-SES students scored significantly higher than low-SES students did.
- Other than SES, there were no student background characteristics that differentiated students.

Other influences on reading achievement: bilingual proficiency and attitudes

Results demonstrated that bilingual proficiency influenced students' reading achievement scores in both L1 and L2. This finding did not hold for English speakers in English reading, but bilingual proficiency was clearly an important factor for English speakers in Spanish reading and for Spanish speakers in English and Spanish reading. Higher levels of bilingual proficiency were associated with higher levels of reading achievement.

Students' reading achievement in Spanish and English was examined with respect to other student and parent attitudes and to parent ethnic/language background. Results from these analyses indicated that:

- L1 and L2 reading achievement was not related to whether students like to read, whether they like school, or whether they like to learn.
- While reading achievement in L1 was positively and significantly correlated with the students' assessment of their reading competence in L1 for English speakers, the correlation was negative, though barely significant, for Spanish speakers. There was no significant correlation between students' perceived ability to read in their L2 and their actual performance.
- Among English speakers, but not Spanish speakers, overall academic competence was linked to reading achievement in both L1 and L2.
- Reading achievement was also significantly correlated with positive academic attitudes, but not with classroom environment.
- For Spanish speakers, but not for English speakers, reading achievement was also associated with positive academic behaviors.
- In addition, for L2 reading achievement for Spanish speakers, reading was correlated with students' perceptions of whether they were ahead of or behind their peers. Higher achievement was associated with the perception that they were ahead of their peers, while lower achievement was linked to feeling that they were behind their peers.
- While home environment was not significantly associated with reading achievement according to student ratings, parents and the home environment were significant factors in students' reading performance:
  —From the portfolio assessment in Chapter 11, we saw that the frequency with which parents read to their child was significantly associated with the child's standardized reading achievement score and the teacher's assessment of the child's reading skills.
  —Parents who attended the parent meetings had students with higher (though not significantly higher) achievement scores in both L1 and L2.
  —Parents who took their children to 2–3 Hispanic cultural activities per year had children with higher *English reading* achievement scores than did parents who took their children 0–1 times per year.
- Parent ethnic/language background also influenced students' reading achievement scores in English, but not in Spanish. While children of Hisp-SP and Hisp-Bil parents scored higher in *Spanish reading* achievement (NCE = 61–62), their scores were not significantly higher than those of offspring of EURO and Hisp-EB (NCE = 54–56) parents. However, in *English reading* achievement, children of EURO and Hisp-Bil parents scored highest, and much higher (10–15 NCE points)

than Hisp-EB students, who scored only 10 points higher than the Hisp-SP students.

- Another analysis was conducted to determine how students' scores in reading achievement varied according to student language background and the educational level of their parents. Above, we noted that student SES (measured by free-lunch participation) influenced reading achievement. In looking at *reading achievement in Spanish*, there was no difference between English speakers whose parents had an elementary/high school education versus some college education (NCE = 55 vs. 56). While the difference was not statistically significant, Spanish speakers whose parents completed elementary/high school scored lower than did students whose parents had some college education (NCE = 62 vs. 69). In *English reading achievement*, this difference was much more dramatic, and highly statistically significant for both English speakers (NCEs: elementary/high school = 42; college = 57) and Spanish speakers (NCEs: elementary/high school = 29; college = 50).

Summary of reading achievement

In comparing the results obtained from a traditional standardized achievement approach with an alternative assessment approach in evaluating the progress of native English-speaking and native Spanish-speaking students in Spanish reading achievement, neither approach alone represented the reading competence of the students, but together the approaches provided useful information about students' reading ability and progress. These two approaches provide complementary rather than opposing or even overlapping information about students' reading competence.

When we compared the performance of the DLE students in the samples reported here with the results from other DLE programs, there were many parallels in the findings. DLE students' Spanish reading achievement was similar to those of another site across the country, though slightly lower than a comparable 90:10 site in California. Overall, though, the trends were comparable, with average to above-average performance across the grade levels.

In examining the reading achievement of limited English proficient (LEP) students from a variety of DLE samples, there were very compatible trends of increasing performance, from very low NCE scores in the primary grades to about average performance by seventh grade. DLE former-LEP students also outscored their peers across the state. Among English speakers, students scored average to above average by the time they received reading instruction in English. They also performed as well as or superior to their English monolingual peers in English-only instruction in tests of English reading and language achievement. Further, they could read and write in Spanish, which their English monolingual peers could not!

In sum, these results clearly show that both English-speaking and Spanish-speaking students benefited from instruction in DLE programs. These findings were true regardless of the students' background characteristics (ethnicity, socioeconomic class, gender, language background, grade level), program type (90:10, 50:50), or school characteristics (90LO, 90HI). The fact that the results from these samples were similar to those from other DLE programs lends further credence to the conclusion that DLE programs are successful in promoting reading achievement in two languages for language-majority and language-minority students from a variety of program types and student backgrounds.

Content Area Achievement

Mathematics achievement in L1

Both English-speaking and Spanish-speaking students scored on a par with their peers in L1 mathematics achievement using California state norms for English and Spanish speakers. Longitudinal and cross-sectional results were very similar for L1 mathematics achievement. However, results varied somewhat depending on the student background, program type, and school demographic characteristics:

- Among English speakers, students performed average to above average at all grade levels and in both program types. Also, English speakers performed at levels comparable to or higher than the California statewide norms for English speakers instructed only in English. Students in 90LO programs performed at the same levels as students in 50:50 programs (except at the third-grade level). These results clearly show that the DLE students were able to keep up with their peers in English-only instruction. For the most part, students in 90LO and 50:50 programs were scoring about 10 NCE points higher than the state average for English-speaking students educated only in English.
- Spanish speakers in 90HI and 50:50 programs also scored at grade level, and their scores were similar to those for their peers across the state. However, students in 90LO, TBE and EO programs scored below grade level.

In terms of student background characteristics:

- Gender was not significant at any grade level.

- Language background was significant at different grade levels. In grades 1–3, English speakers outscored Spanish speakers, but this difference disappeared by grade 5.

- SES was not significant at grades 1–3, but was significant by grade 5, where mid-SES students outperformed low-SES students. Further, in grade 5, 90LO students scored higher than 90HI students, regardless of language background. At the lower grade levels (1–3), Spanish speakers scored higher in 90HI programs while English speakers received higher scores in 90LO programs.

- African American students performed similarly to the other ethnic groups in grades 1–3 and 6, but scored lower and below grade level in grades 4 and 5, though the grade 4 score was only slightly below grade level. These results demonstrate that African American students can perform at or close to grade level in English while being instructed largely in Spanish. Since the great majority of these students were low-SES, these results are encouraging in demonstrating that African American students benefit from DLE programs.

Mathematics achievement in L2

In the second language, students also performed at levels comparable to their peers statewide. In neither the longitudinal nor the cross-sectional samples did Spanish speakers' scores change much across the grade levels in either language. However, results did fluctuate according to the language background of the students as well as the program type:

- Among English speakers, students' scores did not vary according to program type. In 90:10 programs, English speakers performed average to above average, and about comparable to statewide norms for Spanish-speaking students.

- Spanish-speaking students also did not differ much by program type. The major program differences were that EO students scored significantly lower than any other program type, and that 50:50 students scored higher than 90LO students at grade 3. In both 90HI and 90LO programs, students scored below grade level, but only slightly below grade level by grade 4. However, math achievement scores for Spanish speakers were higher in the longitudinal sample; these students scored at grade level by grade 5. Students in the 50:50 program outscored students in the 90:10 program at grade 3, but not in grades 4 and 5.

- Social studies and science achievement data were available for a small subset of students in Spanish only. The scores in both areas were average to high for both groups of students at all grade levels.

- For both Spanish speakers and English speakers, mid-SES students scored significantly higher than low-SES students, in both the longitudinal and cross-sectional samples.

Other influences on mathematics achievement: bilingual proficiency and attitudes

- Bilingual proficiency did not influence students' mathematics achievement scores in either language.
- There was a significant correlation between reading and mathematics achievement in the two languages for both English speakers and Spanish speakers. Correlations between reading and mathematics were highly significant in both L1 and L2, and the correlations became stronger across the grade levels. Thus, reading ability was important in mathematics achievement.

Students' mathematics achievement in Spanish and English was examined with respect to other student and parent attitudes and parent ethnic/language background. Results from these analyses indicated that:

- L1 and L2 mathematics achievement were not related to whether students like math, whether they like school, or whether they like to learn.
- There was no significant difference between students' perceived mathematics ability and their actual performance for either Spanish or English speakers, in L1 or L2.
- Among both English speakers and Spanish speakers, overall academic competence was linked to mathematics achievement in both L1 and L2. The correlation was much higher for the relation between academic competence and L2 than with L1 mathematics achievement.
- Mathematics achievement was also significantly correlated with positive academic attitudes, but not with classroom environment.
- For Spanish speakers, but not for English speakers, mathematics achievement was also associated with positive academic behaviors.
- Parent ethnic/language background significantly affected students' mathematics achievement scores in English and Spanish. Children of Hisp-SP and Hisp-EB parents scored lower in *Spanish mathematics* achievement (NCE = 61–63) than the offspring of EURO and Hisp-Bil (NCE = 71–75) parents. In *English mathematics* achievement, children

of Hisp-EO parents scored lowest (NCE = 35), and even lower than Hisp-SP students.

- Students' scores in mathematics achievement were next examined to determine whether they varied according to the educational level of their parents, since Chapter 12 had shown that student SES (measured by free lunch participation) influenced mathematics achievement. In looking at *mathematics achievement in Spanish*, there was no difference between English speakers whose parents had elementary/high school education versus some college education (NCE = 73 vs. 72). While the difference was not statistically significant, Spanish speakers whose parents completed elementary/high school scored much lower than students whose parents had some college education (NCE = 64 vs. 80). In *English mathematics achievement*, this difference was statistically significant for both English speakers (NCEs: elementary/high school = 45; college = 56) and Spanish speakers (NCEs: elementary/high school = 45; college = 53).

Summary of mathematics achievement

Mathematics achievement was highly related across the two languages. This result, especially the high correlation in the early grade levels, demonstrates that content learned in one language was available in the other language as well. Despite limited English instruction and no mathematics instruction in English, 90:10 students were able to score at or close to grade level in English.

These results clearly indicate that DLE students can function at least at grade level in two languages in the content areas. Their scores are on a par with their peers across the state, even when the peers are English monolinguals in English-only classrooms. Further, the lack of differences between students in 90LO and 50:50 programs in English mathematics demonstrates that English and Spanish speakers are not at any disadvantage because of the additional Spanish, and consequently less English, in their instruction.

As mentioned in Chapter 12, the achievement of these students must also be understood within the context of mathematics achievement in the state of California. At the time of this study, California students were scoring very poorly in their mathematics achievement, with scores near the bottom of national rankings. Thus, the fact that these Spanish-speaking DLE students could perform at or close to grade level by sixth grade and that English speakers could perform on a par with their English-speaking peers in English-only classrooms nationwide is actually quite amazing.

Student Attitudes

Students had very positive attitudes toward the program, their teachers, their parents, and the classroom environment, as well as positive learning attitudes and behaviors. While students did not differ much from each other according to school or background characteristics, there were some important differences:

- Language attitudes were slightly lower among 90LO than among 90HI students, particularly as they moved into the upper grades. These older 90LO students also gave lower ratings to classroom environment.
- Non-free-lunch participants were more satisfied than free-lunch students in 90HI programs were. Combined with less satisfaction were more negative academic attitudes on the part of these free-lunch participants. In 90LO programs, there was a gap between free lunch and non-free-lunch participants in the ratings of home environment, with more positive ratings on the part of non-free-lunch students.
- African American students on free lunch were least satisfied with the program, least likely to enjoy the program or want to continue in it; and scored consistently lower on every item in the home environment scale. However, these students rated themselves highest on the item 'I can do the hardest work.'
- African American students not on free lunch were as satisfied with the program as the Hispanic and EURO students were.

The results suggest that ethnic minority children in a high-quality educational program that incorporates the language and culture of both groups and fosters academic achievement can also enhance the perceived scholastic competence and global self-worth and motivation of ethnic minority students. The results also demonstrate that EURO students who are in a classroom in which Spanish is the language of instruction and in which they are the minority in terms of the number of students in the class, also demonstrate a level of scholastic competence and global self-worth comparable to middle- and upper-class students who are most likely in an English only program. Thus, the results suggest that Hispanic, African American and EURO students of different economic backgrounds can all benefit psychosocially from their integrated bilingual classroom experience.

Teacher Attitudes, Classroom and School Environment

Results related to the teachers' backgrounds and attitudes in the DLE programs illustrate some important issues about teachers' perceptions of support, program development, classroom instruction issues, and satisfaction and how teacher attitudes may vary according to the teacher's background, the school demographic characteristics or the type of program that is implemented (90:10, 50:50, TBE).

With respect to teacher background, there were some important similarities and differences:

- Teaching experience and educational background did not vary in the teachers from the four program types (90LO, 90HI, 50:50, TBE).
- Hispanic teachers were more likely to be hired in 90HI and 50:50 programs than in 90LO and TBE programs, Hispanic teachers were more likely to possess both the bilingual and ESL certificates, and they were more proficient in Spanish. However, there were more teachers in the 50:50 program with both credentials than in the other programs.
- 90:10 teachers were more likely to agree that they understood the model than were 50:50 teachers.

With respect to teachers' attitudes and perceptions:

- Teachers perceived medium levels of support from the district and staff, and medium-high levels of support from the principal and parents. While they did not differ much in their opinions about the support they received in the program according to their backgrounds, there were important differences across the various programs and schools in terms of the support they felt. District support did not vary depending on the type of program, but teachers at different schools experienced quite distinct levels of support from the district. These results suggest that district administrators and boards of education were no more likely to support one model over another, at least from the perspective of teachers. Rather, support varied according to the particular concerns and needs of each district.
- At the school site level, teachers perceived medium staff support and unity. Teachers in 90LO programs felt much less support than did teachers in TBE and 50:50 programs. Ratings of support were much higher for the principal, who was viewed as highly supportive – except in 90LO programs. It is interesting, but not surprising, that 90LO teachers experienced little support at their school site. At these school sites, there were typically fewer ethnic-minority students, a smaller percentage of students on free lunch, and fewer students who were rated as limited English proficient (LEP). However, there was considerable variability at the different 90HI school sites in how much support they felt from their principal. These results are further

discussed in the next chapter with respect to the implications for program planning.

- Teachers perceived parents as very supportive of the program. While DLE teachers rated both groups of parents as supportive, they felt that Spanish-speaking parents were more supportive and less worried about their children learning to read in English than English-speaking parents were. Hispanic teachers were also more optimistic about parent support than were European American teachers.
- Ratings of multicultural equity concerns varied widely depending on the background of the teacher, program type, and school site. With more teaching experience and more credential training, teachers were more likely to agree that the model at their site was equitable, effective for both groups of students, valued both student groups, and provided an integrated approach to multicultural education. Furthermore, 90HI teachers gave consistently higher ratings to meeting these needs than did the teachers from the other program types.

These findings will be further discussed in the next chapter as they relate to important program planning issues around assuring that the program is operating with the absolutely essential core foundation of educational equity.

Classroom language

The studies examining the teacher instructional language and teacher–student interaction patterns yielded some very important results:

- Teachers did not mix the two languages at all.
- Students typically responded to the teacher in the language that the teacher used with them. Further, almost all responses were accurate in English, though students were able to respond correctly regardless of the language of instruction.
- There was little variety in verb forms and in sentence complexity.

In sum, these results are consistent with reports by Swain and Lapkin (1986), who point out that only a limited variety of verb forms is used in immersion classrooms, which restricts opportunities for students to learn how to use the language as a native speaker. On the other hand, the results also indicated that the teacher utterances were similar in function to teacher utterances in EO classrooms. Thus, these teachers may be teaching content as they would in any classroom, and they have provided students with the basic academic and cognitive skills. However, as in most monolingual classrooms, the cognitive complexity could certainly be higher. Finally, the findings are encouraging in demonstrating that students were responsive to the language of the classroom and attempted to respond in the language appropriate to the task.

Conclusions

In summary, the results show that the DLE model is successful in promoting high levels of first-language, second-language and at least medium levels of bilingual proficiency among both language-minority and language-majority students. Further, students can achieve at least as well as their peers who are not in DLE classrooms. By the upper grade levels (grades 6 and 7), students on the average can perform at least at grade level in achievement tests of reading, language and the content areas.

Teachers have positive attitudes toward the DLE model, and enjoy teaching in the program. Further, they appear to understand the model and are following the same patterns as teachers in monolingual classrooms with respect to their instructional language and interactions with students. Also, parents have positive attitudes toward the program and highly recommend it to other parents.

In sum, while there are some important student background, program type and school characteristic differences in the various student, parent and teacher outcomes, considerable evidence demonstrates that this model is highly successful for students from diverse cultural, linguistic and economic backgrounds. This conclusion is further bolstered by the great extent to which these results are consistent with other studies in bilingual education, immersion education, dual language education, and with literature in a variety of educational arenas.

Notes

1. Dual Language Education is used here to refer to two-way bilingual immersion/ two-way immersion programs that integrate language-majority and language-minority students for instruction through two languages. See Chapter 1 for a more detailed definition. This term, as used here, does not include other language education models.
2. In Chapter 4, school sites were distinguished according to program type (90:10, 50:50) and school demographic characteristics (HI = high ethnic diversity and high proportion of students on free lunch; LO = low ethnic diversity and relatively few students on free lunch). Thus, 90HI programs were 90:10 programs with high ethnic diversity and a high proportion of students on free lunch.

Chapter 15

Implications

Introduction

As pointed out in Chapter 1, many programs have been designed to meet the language and educational needs of language minority and language majority students in various countries around the world. The realities of living in multicultural communities and an ever-shrinking global community with a variety of languages requires training students with high levels of multilingual and multicultural competencies. There are many findings from previous chapters that have implications for promoting high levels of bilingual proficiency and academic achievement among culturally, economically and linguistically diverse students.

The purpose of this final chapter is to use the findings to discuss implications for language education programs. Using the summary and integration from the previous chapter, several issues that have been consistently important to dual language education, and which may influence language education programs in general, will be discussed:

- Design and implementation, including decisions about model selection, resources, leadership;
- Teachers and training;
- Parent Recruitment and education;
- Student characteristics;
- Evaluation and assessment;
- Transition to secondary school.

Program Design and Implementation

Many successful language education models have been described here and in the literature. However, politics, human and material resources and student population are examples of issues that may restrict which model one can ultimately select. One might prefer to implement a particular model, but the realities under which a school site operates may not allow implementation of that model. Or, it may be that one model may work more effectively for a particular population of students than another (e.g. immersion for language majority vs. language minority students). Or, there may not be the student population characteristics for a model that is deemed more desirable (e.g. there may not be enough language minority students to implement a DLE program, so the school site must implement a one-way immersion model). In selecting a model, it is important to examine the various models, assess the fit of the particular model to a local population and the political realities of implementing that model in the particular school and community.

Which DLE model: 90:10 or 50:50?

Many administrators and educators must decide on whether to implement a 90:10 model (a language education model with a significantly greater proportion of the minority language), a 50:50 model (a language education model with equal amounts of the majority and minority language), or a model in between (e.g. 80:20, 70:30). Results from previous chapters that address similarities and differences in student outcomes for 90:10 versus 50:50 programs will be highlighted here.

Language proficiency outcomes

For Spanish speakers, there were significant program differences associated with their *Spanish* proficiency. Students in 90:10 programs received higher ratings than did students in 50:50 programs. Thus, Spanish speakers clearly benefited from the additional instruction in Spanish to promote their Spanish language development. With respect to *English* proficiency, there was no significant difference between 90:10 and 50:50 participants. Despite receiving only 10–20% of their instructional day in English compared to 50% for 50:50 students, 90:10 students achieved scores similar to those of 50:50 students in their English proficiency ratings. Thus, receiving less English in their curriculum did not negatively affect the English language proficiency of these students relative to students receiving half of their instruction in English. These results for Spanish-speaking students are consistent with findings reported in the bilingual education literature. Additional instruction in Spanish is typically associated with higher levels of proficiency in Spanish, and with no loss to English proficiency; LEP students in late-exit programs (like the 90:10 program) acquire higher levels of proficiency in English than do students in early-exit (TBE) programs (August & Hakuta, 1997; Escamilla & Medina, 1993; Medina & Escamilla, 1992; Padilla *et al.*, 1991; Ramirez *et al.*, 1991; Willig, 1985).

English speakers did not vary in their *English* language development according to the type of program in which they were participating. Students receiving as little as 10–20% of their instructional day in English scored as well as students spending half their instructional day in English, and both of these bilingual participants were rated as high as monolingual English speakers in English-only programs. With respect to proficiency in *Spanish* for English speakers, 90:10 students outscored 50:50 students. Thus, receiving a much larger percentage of instruction in Spanish (80–90% compared to 50%) in the early grade levels produced a larger gain in Spanish proficiency. These findings for L1 and L2 proficiency are similar to results obtained from immersion research, in which English speakers develop high levels of proficiency in their *first language*, regardless of whether they participate in a partial (50:50 type) or full (90:10 type) immersion program (Genesee, 1987; Swain & Lapkin, 1982). Further, immersion students develop high levels of *L2* proficiency in both partial and full immersion programs (Campbell *et al.*, 1985; Genesee, 1987), though their proficiency is higher in full immersion programs (Campbell *et al.*, 1985).

With respect to *bilingual proficiency*, most English speakers were medium bilinguals, with one fifth to one half of 90:10 students classified as high bilinguals. By fifth and sixth grades, over half of the Spanish-speaking 90:10 and 50:50 students were medium bilinguals. However, over 20% more 90:10 Spanish speakers were high bilinguals compared to 50:50 Spanish-speaking students. Students in 90:10 programs developed higher levels of bilingual proficiency than did the students in the 50:50 program.

In sum, with respect to developing proficiency in the English language, both English speakers and Spanish speakers benefited equally from 90:10 and 50:50 programs. Thus, whether they spent 10–20% or 50% of their instructional day in English, the students were equally proficient in English. In contrast, for both English and Spanish speakers, developing high levels of Spanish proficiency and bilingual proficiency was much more likely to occur in 90:10 than in 50:50 programs.

Academic achievement

By the time English-speaking DLE students began English reading instruction in grade 3, in both *English reading and mathematics* they scored average and at least as high as the California statewide norms for English speakers instructed only in English. In L1 reading and mathematics achievement, students in 90LO programs performed at levels similar to those of students in 50:50 programs.

There was little data available on the *Spanish reading and mathematics* achievement of English-speaking 50:50 students. Thus, comparisons could not be made across programs. However, English speakers in 90:10 programs scored average to above average in Spanish reading and mathematics.

In *Spanish reading and mathematics*, Spanish speakers in 90HI and 50:50 programs also scored at grade level, and at least as high as their peers did across the state of California achievement. However, in Spanish reading and mathematics, students in 90LO, TBE and EO programs scored below average. At sixth grade, Spanish-speaking students in all DLE program types (50:50, 90LO, 90HI) scored comparably in *English reading and mathematics*.

These results clearly indicate that DLE students can function at least at grade level in two languages in the content areas. Their scores are on a par with their peers across the state, even when the peers are English monolinguals in English-only classrooms. Further, the lack of differences between students in 90LO and 50:50 programs in English reading and mathematics at the upper grade levels demonstrates that English and Spanish speakers in 90:10 programs are not at any disadvantage because of the additional Spanish, and consequently less English, in their instruction.

Influence of bilingual proficiency on achievement

As pointed out previously, students in 90:10 programs were more likely to possess higher levels of bilingual proficiency than were students in 50:50 programs. However, let's review the influence that bilingualism might have on reading and mathematics achievement.

Chapter 10 provided data that demonstrated the important influence of bilingual proficiency on the reading achievement scores of students. While this finding was not as strong for English speakers in English reading, it was certainly true for English speakers in Spanish reading, and for Spanish speakers in English and Spanish reading. Thus, higher levels of bilingual proficiency were associated with higher levels of reading achievement. Further support for this interpretation is that, across the grade levels, as students became more proficient in both languages, the correlation between reading achievement in English and Spanish increased. These results are consistent with previous studies showing that a higher level of proficiency in two languages is associated with increased performance on academic achievement tests (e.g. Dawe, 1983; Fernandez & Nielsen, 1986; Lindholm, 1991; Lindholm & Aclan, 1991). Such an interpretation is also congruent with bilingual research demonstrating that higher levels of bilingual language proficiency are related to elevated academic and cognitive functioning (Cummins, 1979, 1987; Toukomaa & Skutnabb-Kangas, 1977).

Bilingual proficiency did not directly influence students' mathematics achievement scores in either language. This result was unexpected, as previous studies have shown that a higher level of proficiency in two languages is typically associated with increased performance on academic achievement tests (e.g. Dawe, 1983; Fernandez & Nielsen, 1986; Lindholm,

1991; Lindholm & Aclan, 1991). However, for both English and Spanish speakers, there was a significant correlation between reading and mathematics achievement in the two languages. Correlations between reading and mathematics were highly significant in both L1 and L2, and the correlations became stronger across the grade levels. Thus, clearly reading ability was important in mathematics achievement. Further, reading achievement was highly associated with bilingual proficiency (except for English speakers reading in English). Thus, bilingual proficiency was indirectly related to mathematics achievement, as bilingual proficiency was associated with reading achievement: students with greater bilingual proficiency scored higher in reading achievement, and those who scored higher in reading achievement performed at a higher level in mathematics achievement.

Summary

What these results show is that academic achievement scores were similar for English-speaking and Spanish-speaking students in both 90:10 and 50:50 programs. On this basis alone, it would not make much difference whether a school implemented a 90:10 or a 50:50 program. By the time students were in the upper grade levels, they scored as well in English reading and mathematics regardless of whether initially they received a smaller amount of instruction through English (90:10 model) or half their day in English (50:50 model). Similarly, their scores in Spanish reading and mathematics were comparable whether they studied half of their day in Spanish (50:50) or a significant amount in Spanish (90:10). These results hold true because these models are based on the important theoretical premise discussed in Chapter 2, that students will learn the content regardless of which language they learn it through.

Also, in looking at the language proficiency of students, for English language proficiency it made no difference whether they participated in the 90:10 or 50:50 program. Whether students spent half or a lesser amount of their instructional day in English, they were just as proficient in English. Program type did have a large effect on Spanish and bilingual proficiency. Both English and Spanish speakers in 90:10 programs were more proficient in Spanish than students in 50:50 programs. Further, more Spanish speakers were high bilinguals if they participated in 90:10 than in 50:50 programs.

Thus, clearly 90:10 programs have the advantage of promoting higher Spanish and bilingual proficiency. However, it is important to remember that higher levels of bilingual proficiency were associated with increased performance in reading, and higher scores in reading were linked with better performance in mathematics.

Because the sample was limited to elementary students and a small number of students with scores two years into secondary school, we have probably not fully tapped the advantages that bilingualism may play on the reading and mathematics achievement of students. According to research presented earlier, it takes 5–7 years to fully acquire a second language (Collier, 1989; Cummins, 1981; National Commission on Excellence in Education, 1983; Swain, 1984; Troike, 1978). Further the cognitive and academic advantages of bilingualism do not accrue until students reach a sufficiently high level of bilingual proficiency (Cummins, 1979, 1987; Toukomaa & Sknutnabb-Kangas, 1977). Thus, one might expect the 90:10 students to continue to perform at higher levels than their 50:50 peers because of their higher levels of bilingualism and associated cognitive advantages.

Political/community concerns

Political and community pressure can influence a decision on which type of language education model to choose. As mentioned in Chapter 1, the passage of an anti-bilingual education law (Proposition 227) in California resulted in an erosion of bilingual programs for language minority students and forced some programs to add English time to (and thus subtract Spanish time from) the instructional day. While many educators may not have to deal with such a high level of political pressure in deciding on or planning for a language education program, other pressures may come to bear. Parents or administrators may voice concern for a program (like the 90:10 design) that includes a significant amount of the instructional day in the target language. In these cases, if parents and educators cannot be convinced by the research findings, then a school may have to implement a model with more time (70:30 or 50:50) devoted to the societal language. In some cases, so little of the target language is allowed during the instructional day that the program may need to resemble a foreign language program. While the research shows that the proficiency in the non-societal language and bilingual proficiency will be lower, and there will not likely be cognitive advantages associated with bilingualism, students can still benefit from language education models with small amounts of the second language. We are currently seeing some schools running Spanish clubs because they were no longer allowed to introduce Spanish into the instructional day. While this type of program will not lead to much Spanish proficiency, students may acquire the positive attitudes and interest in later studying Spanish. In essence, though, political pressure can have serious implications for decisions about selecting and implementing a particular program model.

Human and material resource concerns

Selecting a language education model may also hinge on the resources a school may have available. Such resources include: finances, curriculum materials, teachers, and students.

DLE and other language education models do not typically cost more to implement than the mainstream program does. Students need a teacher, classroom and instructional materials in a DLE program just as they do in any program. Some schools have opted to add resources to the program, including additional teachers, resource specialists (e.g. reading specialist), and teacher aides. Some districts have funded a program coordinator for the DLE program to oversee program development, teacher training, parent recruitment, and material acquisition. However, most schools operate without these additional resources. That is not to say that these additional resources are not helpful or even important, just that they are not absolutely essential.

Technically, though, there are some extra costs associated with beginning a new language education program. One cost is in training the teachers so that they understand the model they are supposed to implement. Other start-up costs include acquiring: instructional materials in the second language, resource materials for the library so students can conduct research in the target language, and pleasure reading materials to promote literacy in the second language.

Another resource factor to consider is whether there are sufficient teachers with high enough levels of language proficiency to teach in the program. Also, is there an appropriate administrator who can and is willing to provide leadership for the program?

Finally, program decisions must include considerations of the student population and whether there are sufficient students to implement the desired model. If a DLE program is desired, is there an adequate population of majority and language minority students? A continuous shortage of one or the other group of students will not meet the definition of a DLE program (see Chapter 3 for further information about student issues).

One question some educators ask is: What is the minimum number of students necessary from one group or the other to implement a program, if there is a small number of one group and a large majority of the other group? Research has not been conducted on this issue. However, Chapter 3 pointed out that a ratio of 33:67 was probably a minimum, but a ratio of 50:50 was an ideal. There must be enough students to serve as role models for the other group. We have observed that, if there are too few students of one group, then those students tend to cluster together and do not mix appropriately with the other students, which has deleterious effects on both groups. The major consideration should be whether the program model can meet the educational and language needs of both groups of students in an equitable classroom environment.

Program Planning

Program planning occurs at different levels, involving the educational curriculum, language curriculum, and school/classroom environment.

Educational curriculum

In the study reported in Chapter 5, teachers were in general agreement that they have articulated the program across grade levels. It is not clear how this planning has occurred without spending time as a group to plan, which was generally their response. However, the extent to which planning occurred varied considerably by school site.

Research on effective schools demonstrates the importance of planning, especially coordinating across the grade levels (Levine & Lezotte, 1995). In addition, students need a high-quality curriculum that is not simplified and replete with lowered expectations.

Ethnic density and SES need affected student outcomes in the following ways:

- For English speakers, 90HI programs augmented *Spanish proficiency* even more than 90LO programs did.
- Reading achievement varied according to school demographic factors, but the results were similar for both English speakers and Spanish speakers: 90HI programs promoted higher levels of *Spanish reading achievement* than 90LO programs did.
- 90LO programs led to higher levels of *English reading achievement* than 90HI programs did.

By understanding that these school demographic characteristics influence language proficiency and academic achievement, schools can use this information to identify and strengthen areas of weakness. For example, 90HI programs promote higher levels of language proficiency and reading achievement in the target language, but need to work harder to improve English reading achievement. In like manner, 90LO programs typically produce higher achievement in English reading and mathematics, but lower levels of Spanish proficiency and reading achievement, and schools could develop their program to focus more on boosting these areas of weakness.

Linguistic curriculum and planning

The classroom language results were consistent with Swain and Lapkin's (1986) contention that there is a limited variety of verb and syntactic forms used in Canadian immersion classrooms, and this restricts opportunities for students to learn how to use the language as native speakers. Thus, the results of this study concur with the results of other immersion studies that there needs to be planning around integrating direct instruction of language structure into classroom teaching so that students will hear a variety of verb forms and complex structures in their teachers' speech. Such advice is clearly consistent with immersion researchers and practitioners, particularly Day and Shapson (1996), Lyster (1987, 1990, 1994), and Swain (Lapkin _et al._, 1990; Tarone & Swain, 1995), who advocate integrating the teaching of language structure with content in a meaningful context. A 'linguistic syllabus' (Lyster, 1987), which consists of a systematic and graded presentation of grammar, must be developed. Lyster (1987) points out that the development of the linguistic syllabus would not be the responsibility of individual teachers, but rather the domain of the school board, or those who plan the immersion curriculum. Lyster (1990, 1994) and Day and Shapson (1996) have provided excellent frameworks for understanding analytic language teaching and for incorporating such teaching in an immersion classroom at the secondary level.

Several DLE schools have begun to develop language objectives in English and Spanish. In fact, teachers in this study tended to state that they were developing such language objectives. However, this area of academic language development has been very weak, especially regarding English language development for Spanish speakers, which shows up in students' somewhat diminished achievement scores in English. However, this weakness resulted from the initial belief that an immersion program must not teach language formally, but that students would learn about language through using it. After a couple of decades of immersion proficiency, many educators (Kowal & Swain, 1997) recognize that we must formally teach the language if students are to develop it to a high level.

For years, the task of translation has been taught to foreign language students. We found that students in the present study who translated for their parents developed higher levels of proficiency. Clearly, there ought to be a place for inserting translation and the study of semantic, syntactic and lexical similarities and differences across the two languages into the linguistic syllabus.

Another observation verified by this study is that teachers adjusted their speech according to the subject area taught. Cazden (1979) pointed out that science and mathematics provide different opportunities for learning; at the elementary school level, science was characterized by active participation where talk was necessary during data collection, laboratory investigation, and interpretation of the results. By contrast, mathematics was often a silent and solitary activity. Science, therefore, provided more of an occasion for verbal interaction. Indeed, science lessons observed for this study produced higher levels of teacher modeling and higher-order questioning, whereas mathematics lessons yielded more directives and information presentation. Swain and her colleagues (Lapkin *et al.*, 1990; Swain & Carroll, 1987) have also pointed out that different subject areas provide distinct opportunities for a greater variety of verb forms and grammatical structures.

School/classroom environment

Normally, language education programs are not discussed with respect to any student background characteristics other than language background. However, because DLE programs required two distinct populations, student characteristics become an important concern. Previous literature has clearly shown that the socioeconomic characteristics and ethnic density of the school influence many aspects of the students' educational experience (e.g. Darling-Hammond, 1995; Knapp & Woolverton, 1995; Levine & Lezotte, 1995). It was still surprising to this author to witness the extent to which the ethnic density/SES need variable (distinguishing 90HI from 90LO) influenced language proficiency, achievement and attitudinal outcomes among students, teachers and parents.

Program planning around multicultural equity concerns for the school and classroom is critical for the DLE and other language education models. At the core of the DLE and even TBE program model is the necessity for assuring that the program meets the needs of the culturally and linguistically diverse populations. In the current study of teachers, ratings of multicultural equity concerns differed widely depending on the background of the teacher, program type, and school site. 90HI teachers gave consistently higher ratings to meeting these needs than did the teachers from the other program types.

Parents with children at 90HI sites and with lower levels of education felt lower levels of district support than parents at 90LO sites and parents with college-level education. This lower level of district support is consistent with literature reporting that low-income parents and minority parents feel alienation, distrust and discrimination from school personnel (Comer, 1986; Garcia, 1990; Hidalgo *et al.*, 1995; Kozol, 1995; Ogbu, 1987). While most parents believed that the staff was successful in promoting diversity, parents with children at 90HI sites gave staff higher scores than did parents with children at 90LO sites.

Among students, language attitudes were more positive among 90HI than among 90LO students, particularly as they moved into the upper grades. Older 90LO students also gave lower ratings to classroom environment.

These support items show an important and potentially negative impact on 90LO programs. 90LO programs are distinct from 90HI programs because the population of students served in 90LO programs is not particularly diverse, nor is it particularly needy. Thus, some of these schools have not had bilingual programs before and staff perceive no need for bilingual programs, especially since, as noted in previous chapters, bilingual programs are typically not valued. Therefore, 90LO program teachers report that their principals are less supportive, knowledgeable and interested in the program, and do not see the need for the minority language. They do not work to integrate the program on the site or to bring the staff together. Because the non-DLE teachers are not informed about the program nor encouraged to see it as an important strand within the school, they may feel disdain for the program. This is particularly the case if they believe that their jobs may be threatened at the school site as the program grows across the grade levels. If this perception exists at the school site, then it is no surprise that the 90LO teachers feel alienated from the staff and perceive little support from the principal.

These are important findings because they indicate that some DLE programs, particularly 90LO programs, are operating without the absolutely essential core foundation of educational equity. This conclusion is bolstered by a variety of perspectives in 90LO programs. These include: the teachers' strong agreement that they have *not* received enough training in the DLE model and in how to treat students equitably, their beliefs that the students were not equitably treated, and their lower levels of perceived support from the principal and other staff at their school; and students' less positive ratings of the classroom environment.

Consistent research findings show that effective schools have high expectations for all students and are marked by a commitment to ethnic and cultural pluralism (Darling-Hammond, 1995; Levine & Lezotte, 1995). So it is vitally important to plan for school and classroom environments that meet the educational and linguistic needs of the linguistic and cultural groups that are represented in the school and classroom.

Leadership

In Chapter 7, we noted that teachers in 90LO programs felt much less support than did 90HI or 50:50 teachers. Ratings of support were much higher for the principal, who was viewed as highly supportive in 90HI but not in 90LO programs. The findings that teaching efficacy and satisfaction were highly related to principal support are consistent with the significance of leadership in the literatures on school effectiveness and bilingual education effectiveness (Bullard & Taylor, 1993; Cortes, 1986; Levine & Lezotte, 1995; Levine & Stark, 1981; Troike, 1986). Principals of language education programs need to integrate the program within the school, understand the language education model so that they can defend it to the school board and parents, promote staff unity, support the program's implementation, and show support and concern for teachers.

Teachers and Training

High quality instructional personnel

Any educational program benefits from knowledgeable teachers, and this is just as true in different language education or DLE programs. However, teachers in language education programs need to possess high levels of language proficiency in two languages (see Chapter 3). Years of teaching experience are not as important in terms of their relation to other teacher attitudes as the teaching credentials they had earned. Teachers with more credentials (none vs. bilingual or ESL vs. both) had higher levels of: language proficiency, understanding the DLE model, perceived support, planning with other teachers, and concern for the multicultural environment of students. These results show that teachers with both credentials are highly desirable. If such teachers are not available, then considerable training is necessary.

Training

To have an effective program with good teachers requires training. Researchers in immersion education have discussed the importance of specialized training in immersion pedagogy and curriculum, as well as materials and resources (Day & Shapson, 1996). In the dual language education program, there must be training in:

- the dual language education model, including bilingual and immersion research and theory;
- second language development;
- instructional strategies in second language development, including how to implement a linguistic syllabus in their teaching;
- multicultural and educational equity training;
- cooperative learning.

According to Levine and Lezotte (1995: 536), training should be focused to avoid teacher and school overload: 'One of the most common reasons why effective schools projects fail is because they try to do too much in too short a time ... Priorities should be determined and resources allocated as part of a realistic plan that takes account of constraints and overload.' This is an important recommendation, as many schools try to take on too much when they begin a program: the DLE model, second language development, cooperative learning, computers, mathematics and language arts. That is far too much. I usually recommend to schools that they select one area of focus and work on that area all year, with professional development, faculty meetings and grade-level or team meetings oriented toward that area of focus. For new programs, the first area of focus needs to be an understanding of the model, including the key components of educational equity, second language development and grouping strategies.

Parent Recruitment and Education

The results presented in Chapter 7 have important implications for understanding parental backgrounds, for parent recruitment and for parent education.

First, parents differed significantly in terms of ethnicity, language background, and education. These parents' backgrounds were described in Chapter 7 and the results summarized in Chapter 14. Understanding these parents in terms of their educational and language backgrounds could be very helpful in parent recruitment and education.

Parent attitudes toward bilingualism were very favorable, as one might expect. Most parents agreed that it was important that their child study Spanish in order to: be comfortable with other Spanish speakers, meet and converse with varied people, understand Hispanic culture, participate in activities with people of other cultures, and because others will respect the child if s/he is bilingual. Most parents also perceived that studying Spanish would be an asset for their children for career and intellectual benefits.

The findings are also important in validating the different reasons that parents, according to their heritage background, enrolled their children in the program. European American parents identify with both instrumental and integrative reasons. However, for Hispanic parents, for whom the target (non-English) language is their heritage language, the primary purpose is integrative in nature. These results hold true regardless of whether the Hispanic parent is a Spanish monolingual or a bilingual/English speaker. The findings from this study are also consistent with research in Wales and in the US that shows that Welsh and Chicano parents communicated strong integrative motivation for putting their child in a heritage language bilingual program (Bush, 1983, cited in Torres, 1988).

Parents were very satisfied with the program, and would recommend it to other parents. Parents differed somewhat in their satisfaction that their child was receiving access to the subject matter, with EURO parents less satisfied than Hispanic parents were. Parent satisfaction also varied considerably according to the children's grade level. While all parents were satisfied, parents of kindergartners were most satisfied, followed by parents who had older children in grades 6–8. Parents of children in grades 3–5 were least satisfied. Similarly, in looking at parents' satisfaction with their child's progress in English reading, there was also a clear difference according to the children's grade level. Parents of kindergartners or upper graders (6–8) were most satisfied, parents of first and second graders were least satisfied, and those with children in grades 3–5 were in between.

We might expect parents who enroll their kindergartners to be optimistic about the program, especially toward the end of the year when both groups of children are beginning to use the second language and to demonstrate preliteracy skills in Spanish. By grade 2, we typically see the lowest levels of satisfaction. Since children do not begin formal English reading until grade 3, parents see their children reading in Spanish but not in English, and become concerned that their children will fall behind. This is a typical outcome observed among parents, particularly English-speaking parents, in 90:10 programs. In fact, this phenomenon is typically referred to as the 'Second-Grade Panic.' When children begin English reading instruction in grade 3 and become competent readers in English by grade 5, there is less concern. By grades 6–8, parents are not at all concerned; they know their children can do all of their academic work in English.

Ethnic/language and school demographic differences did influence how parents felt about the success of staff in balancing the needs of Spanish bilingual and English bilingual students. Parents at 90HI sites gave higher ratings to staff than did parents at 90LO schools. While the scores of Hisp-SP and Hisp-Bil were very positive, the ratings of Hisp-EO and EURO parents were also similar and much lower. Thus, these results would suggest that English-speaking and the most culturally assimilated parents (Hisp-EO) were less confident that the program is successful in meeting the needs of their English-speaking children.

Several implications for parent training follow from these results:

- Teach parents about the model, the educational equity underlying the model that balances meeting the educational needs of both groups of students. Also, parents need to understand the model so they can defend their decisions to put their children in the program to family, friends and neighbors who do not understand the advantages of bilingual education.

- Provide training about what to expect from children's development at each of the grade levels. Tell parents about the 'second-grade panic' so they know the program has planned for this already. Provide research to show how children progress across the grade levels, and include research from the school site to show parents that the student outcomes are occurring as expected. If the outcomes are well below what would be expected, then there should be some serious planning about how to improve the student performance.
- Teach parents how to promote language proficiency; take children to cultural activities, especially activities in which the target language is used; have older children translate if they feel comfortable doing so.
- Provide language training for parents. Parents who are well trained are primed to help with recruitment. Since many parents were recruited through friends and family, it is important to have many parents who can talk to other parents about the model.

Finally, in many school sites, particularly 90LO schools, the EURO parents are used to running parent committees, making decisions affecting their children, and pushing for various remedies to improve the school climate or instruction. When Hispanic parents, especially Spanish-speaking parents who are not well educated, try to join in these activities, EURO parents often take over and leave Hispanic parents feeling alienated from decision-making and school events. DLE programs will run much more effectively if the total school environment supports both groups of parents rather than one group over another. Thus, it is vital to unify these parents and not allow EURO parents an inequitable share of power and resources with which to influence the program. This is not a criticism of caring parents, but a note of caution to program coordinators or principals.

Student Characteristics

There is no evidence to suggest that participation in DLE programs retarded the native language development of Spanish or English speakers. In contrast, almost all students, regardless of their student characteristics, were proficient in English and Spanish. These students were also able to score at or above grade level and at least as well as their non-DLE peers by the upper grade levels. However, there are some educators who believe that certain student characteristics ought to limit participation in dual-language programs, and thus, some of the findings from the research discussed will be highlighted here to determine whether there is any validity to such concerns.

Language background

In terms of student background characteristics, English speakers received higher ratings than Spanish speakers in L1 proficiency, while Spanish speakers outscored English speakers in L2 proficiency. At the early grade levels, English speakers tended to perform at higher levels in L1 reading and mathematics achievement, but these differences diminished by the upper grade levels. Further, because language background was confounded with SES, most of these differences were probably due to social class. Data do not support any limitations for language education participation for either English speakers or Spanish speakers.

Socioeconomic status

Overall, SES was not a significant factor in L1 proficiency or mathematics, though it was important by the final year of elementary school (fifth grade), where mid-SES students scored higher than low-SES students did. In L2 reading and mathematics, for both Spanish and English speakers, mid-SES students scored significantly higher than low-SES students did, in both the longitudinal and cross-sectional samples.

While some results support higher performance on the part of mid-SES students over low-SES students and these results are highly consistent with the literature, other results showed no difference. One could argue that, even if there are differences associated with SES, the low-SES students are more challenged and cognitively stimulated in a DLE classroom than their peers are in a monolingual English classroom. Thus, these low-SES students may have more opportunity to develop high proficiency and achievement, and will be bilingual and biliterate as well.

Ethnicity

The objective in including ethnicity in analyses was not to determine which groups scored higher than other groups. Rather, the focus was on determining whether the DLE program seemed inappropriate for certain groups – that is, such students did not develop high levels of L1 proficiency, at least medium levels of L2 proficiency, and achievement comparable to their peers. I should point out that not all ethnic groups were represented, and even some groups that were included had very few students (African American, Asian American).

These results showed that students from European American, Hispanic, African American and Asian American (though there were few students) backgrounds all benefited from the DLE program. This was true regardless of the students' social class backgrounds, though middle-class students typically outperformed lower-class students.

Some administrators fear that any instruction involving two languages is inappropriate for African American students, especially bi-dialectal African American students from working class families. However, analyses presented here show that these students performed similarly to the other ethnic groups at most grade levels in L1 reading and mathematics. These results demonstrate that African American students can perform at or close to grade level in English while they are being instructed largely in Spanish. Since the great majority of these students were low-SES, these results are encouraging in demonstrating that even low-income African American students benefit from DLE programs. However, because the results indicated strong influences due to student SES and parent educational background, programs with many low-income African American students should develop tutorial programs to facilitate their academic achievement. This conclusion is true for *any educational program* that includes low-income culturally diverse student populations.

Gender

The only gender differences were that:

- In L1 reading, girls outscored boys in grades 3–4, but at no other grade levels.
- Boys rated their self esteem significantly higher than did girls.

These results lend further credence to the growing literature suggesting that there are few significant differences in educational outcomes between girls and boys, except in the area of self esteem and self confidence, where boys outscore girls (Eisenberg *et al.*, 1996).

Students with special learning needs

This research did not examine the language proficiency and achievement of students with special learning needs, because we did not have this information available. Nor did we exclude such students from the data set. Thus, analyses were based on an average classroom containing some special needs students. At some sites, there were many special needs students, as the DLE program was considered the best program for them. This decision was consistent with immersion education (Cloud *et al.*, 2000; Genesee, 1987), in which students with special education needs or learning disabilities are typically accepted in the program. The only caveat is the situation in which students have a serious speech delay in their native language; in these cases, the decision for admittance is carefully conducted on an individual basis.

Thus, students are typically not moved from the DLE program because of special education or learning disability needs. We have observed many instances in which children were identified with special education needs and the DLE program was blamed for the problem. The student was then pulled from the program and put into an English mainstream program, and the parent returned the following year asking for re-admittance into the DLE program because the children had the same problems in English. The parent then felt that the child received more stimulation and a better learning environment in the DLE program. Unfortunately, an English-speaking child cannot be readmitted at this point because, after a year out of target-language instruction, the child has fallen too far behind.

Evaluation and Assessment

The results in all outcomes are based on various forms of assessment – norm-referenced standardized achievement tests, rubrics, individually administered tests, and surveys.

In examining language proficiency, we relied largely on teacher ratings of students' proficiency using the SOLOM and the FLOSEM instruments (see Chapter 9). There was considerable agreement between the ratings that these two instruments provided. For both Spanish speakers and English speakers, correspondence between these two ratings was higher in evaluating proficiency in L1 than L2. One objection to using these teacher-rated instruments is that teachers may not provide reliable scores. However, if teachers are trained, the consistency between these two measures indicates that the teachers can be very reliable raters. Further, when we compared ratings of the teacher judgments with scores from individually administered tests of language proficiency, there was considerable correspondence in the outcomes. When the ratings did not agree, the other language proficiency measures produced higher scores than the SOLOM ratings did. Thus, I would argue that these teacher ratings are quite reliable. Further, they are economical and quick to score.

Achievement data were based largely on norm-referenced standardized achievement tests. There have been many criticisms of the validity of these tests for language and ethnic minority students (see Chapter 2), but they have become more rather than less important in the US, because of national and state goals targeting higher educational standards and more academic accountability. Whether we agree with or like these tests or not, outcomes from them are considered vital in the US (US Department of Education, 2001).

Because standardized tests have questionable validity for ethnic and language minority students (AERA *et al.*, 1999; California Council on the Education of Teachers, 2001), it is helpful to have other measures of student progress (Linn, 2000). In Chapter 11, results from an alternative assessment were presented and then compared to the results obtained from a traditional standardized achievement approach. It is important to ensure that alternative assessments are at least as valid as traditional tests, and that alternative assessment procedures are appropriate for culturally and linguistically diverse student populations (Cloud *et al.*, 2000; Darling-Hammond, 1995; Lacelle-Peterson & Rivera, 1994; Linn, 2000). In sum, neither approach alone portrayed the reading competence of the students, but together they provided useful information about students' reading ability and progress. These two approaches afforded complementary rather than opposing or even overlapping information about students' reading competence. Furthermore, the alternative assessment approaches appeared to be appropriate for both culturally and linguistically diverse students, lending additional credibility to their use in the classroom. Linn *et al.* (1991) have encouraged educators to consider the complementary roles that traditional testing and alternative assessment can serve in understanding student achievement.

What are largely absent from this research are observational and ethnographic studies of dual language education programs. This research focus (e.g. Bernhardt, 1992; Day & Shapson, 1996; Freeman, 1998; Hornberger & Micheau, 1993; McCollum, 1994; Pease-Alvarez, 93) would add considerable depth to understanding children's language development within various contexts, their use of language with each other and how they learn language from each other, the types of conversations in which children engage with each other, how they use reading in context, and a whole variety of other topics.

Transition to Secondary School

In the US, most secondary school language education programs consist of a foreign language program for language majority students and an English as a Second Language (ESL) program for language minority students who do not have the proficiency in English to participate in mainstream classes. See Chapter 1 for a synthesis of foreign language programs in California, which are representative of foreign language teaching in the US and many other countries as well.

Secondary DLE programs are becoming more popular as students graduate from the elementary program, and parents want their children to continue at the middle and high school levels. A secondary DLE program typically includes a language arts class and one or two content courses that are offered in the target language at each grade level. Some of these content courses are classes the student needs for graduation requirements, and others are electives. At some sites, the DLE program has enabled the schools to expand or develop a program for immigrant Spanish-speaking students who are new to the school. These classes, which integrate the DLE students with recently arrived immigrants, can serve to strengthen the need to use the target language and revitalize language development for the DLE students, especially English speakers. See Montone and Loeb (2000) for more information on implementing dual language education programs at the secondary level.

In a follow-up study I am conducting with students who are now in high school, but were enrolled in a DLE elementary program, results indicate that many of these students are taking the Advanced Placement examinations in Spanish for college credit, and the majority of students are passing their exams. Findings also show that: these students would recommend that other students take the DLE program, that the students are not dropping out of school, that they expect to attend college, and they know that getting good grades and going to college are important. This study is pointing to one area that we need to work on with language minority students from families with very limited educational backgrounds. That area involves understanding what it means to go to college:

- What do good grades mean?
- How does one apply to college?
- What are the requirements?

There are a couple areas of socialization that require more attention:

- Working with parents and children to help particularly low-income parents understand the pathways that lead to successful entrance to and graduation from college.
- Educating secondary teachers and administrators who still think that Latino children who have been in a bilingual program are limited English proficient, and place them in lower academic tracks.

It is in these areas of parent education and administrator training that there is still substantial work to do.

Final Conclusions

Previous chapters have presented a considerable amount of data collected in DLE programs relating to student, parent, and teacher outcomes. The general conclusions are that:

- DLE programs can be effective in promoting high levels of language proficiency, academic achievement, and positive attitudes in students.
- Teachers enjoy teaching in DLE programs.
- Parents are satisfied with the DLE program, and recommend it to other parents.

This chapter has highlighted the various results and examined issues of design and implementation, student population characteristics, teacher training, parent recruitment and education, evaluation and assessment, and transition to secondary school. While these issues are discussed largely with respect to DLE programs, they also relate to other types of language education programs.

In conclusion, probably the most important consideration for any language education program with regard to program planning and implementation, assessment, and training parents and teachers is in considering the education and linguistic needs of the various populations of culturally, linguistically, and economically diverse students in the language education program. By meeting the needs of these various students, any language education program can be successful.

Appendix

This appendix reproduces the following questionnaires:

- Teacher background
- Parent background
- Student background

TITLE VII DBE PROJECT

TEACHER BACKGROUND

QUESTIONNAIRE

Name: _____   School: _____   Grade: _____

Date: _____   Social Security Number: _____

PLEASE WRITE IN AND BUBBLE IN YOUR NAME & SOCIAL SECURITY NUMBER ON THE ANSWER SHEET NOW. ALSO, WRITE IN THE SCHOOL NAME where it says COURSE and bubble in your GRADE LEVEL where it says COURSE I.D. (Kinder=0).

This questionnaire asks for information about the educational and professional background of teachers, as well as teaching practices and beliefs, in projects supported by Title VII Bilingual Education. The information is required of all instructional projects receiving support from Title VII. The information you provide will help the project respond to the requirements in a timely and comprehensive manner. Responses will not be reported individually.

THESE ANSWERS ARE CONFIDENTIAL. PLEASE RETURN THE COMPLETED QUESTIONNAIRE AND ANSWER SHEET IN THE ENVELOPE PROVIDED

PLEASE ANSWER THE FOLLOWING QUESTIONS DIRECTLY ON THIS SHEET.

What is the total number of years of general teaching experience (not necessarily with LEP students) that you have? _____ years
How many years have you taught in a bilingual classroom? _____ years
How many years have you taught in the bilingual or bilingual immersion program at your current school? _____ years

What is your instructional role as a teacher for Title VII students?
___ Teach in Spanish only (Spanish language model)
___ Teach in English only (English language model)
___ Teach in English and Spanish (Spanish and English language model)

What do you believe is the bilingual or bilingual immersion program's greatest strength in your school?

_____

_____

What is the bilingual or bilingual immersion program's greatest weakness?

_____

OTHER COMMENTS:
Please mark on the attached answer sheet the extent to which you agree or disagree with the following statements. Please answer as carefully and truthfully as you can, as there is not a particular right or wrong answer; many responses may vary a lot by grade level. These responses will tell us about the children's instruction as a whole; we will not evaluate how *you* as an *individual* answer the questions. Be sure to bubble in each response clearly. Make only one choice for each item.

1	2	3	4	5
STRONGLY DISAGREE	DISAGREE	NEITHER AGREE NOR DISAGREE	AGREE	STRONGLY AGREE

1.   Our principal (on-site administrator) agrees with the idea that the minority language should be used for classroom instructional purposes.

Teacher questionnaire (page 1 of 5)

8. Our principal is assertive about pushing for the needs of our students and school with the district.

9. Our principal expects high performance from the teachers.

10. Our principal communicates high expectations for our students.

11. The non-bilingual or bilingual immersion teachers in my school are well informed about the bilingual or bilingual immersion program.

12. The non-bilingual or bilingual immersion teachers in my school are critical of the bilingual or bilingual immersion program.

13. The Board of Education is supportive of the bilingual or bilingual immersion program.

14. The Board of Education and/or administrative leadership (off site) have helped in recruitment, obtaining funds, etc. for the bilingual or bilingual immersion program.

15. Our district is pushing to make our bilingual or bilingual immersion program exemplary.

16. Our program better serves the needs of English speakers than Spanish speakers.

17. Our district seems to have conflicting ideas about the best way to implement bilingual or bilingual immersion or bilingual education.

18. Our district is really committed to serving the needs of our Spanish speaking students.

19. The bilingual or bilingual immersion program has a sufficient supply of non-English language materials and necessary instructional resources.

20. There is a sufficient number of bilingual teacher aides.

21. There are too few language minority students in my classroom.

22. There are too few language majority students in my classroom.

23. Teachers are not given enough training in how to properly implement the bilingual or bilingual immersion program.

24. Bilingual or bilingual immersion teachers are given so much training that it is difficult to incorporate what we have learned into our teaching.

25. While teachers have received training in many areas (e.g., cooperative learning, whole language), there has not been the follow-through that would help us correctly implement these strategies in the classroom.

26. I am overwhelmed with all the extra work I have to do in bilingual or bilingual immersion.

27. I enjoy teaching in the bilingual or bilingual immersion program.

28. We have a very effective bilingual or bilingual immersion program on our campus--for Spanish speaking students.

29. We have a very effective bilingual or bilingual immersion program on our campus--for English speaking students.

30. I know that it is difficult to *really* treat students of different genders, ethnicities, language backgrounds, social classes equitably, but I have not received enough instruction to know how to really treat students equitably.

31. I find that I tend to expect more of my English speakers than I do of my Spanish speakers.

32. When it comes right down to it, a teacher can't do much because most of a student's motivation and performance depend on his or her own environment.

33. Hispanic students, parents, staff and community members are made to feel like a valuable part of our school culture.

34. We have developed language objectives by grade level for the bilingual or bilingual immersion program.

35. We have discussed how to articulate the bilingual or bilingual immersion program across the grade levels.

36. Bilingual or bilingual immersion teachers work together in teams or as a group to plan for instruction.

37. I team teach with another colleague.

38. Bilingual or bilingual immersion teachers do not spend enough time as a group or team to plan for instruction.

39. Competition in school is an important preparation for life.

40. At-risk students should be given assignments that require problem solving aptitude.

41. I give special privileges to students who do the best academically.

Teacher questionnaire (page 2 of 5)

42. I encourage my students to take risks academically.

43. Some students are not going to make a lot of progress this year, no matter what I do.

44. Competition among students enhances learning.

45. It is better to give students work that is too easy than work that is too hard.

46. I try to teach in a way that minimizes the number of mistakes students make.

47. I encourage my students to monitor their own progress.

48. There is little I can do to ensure that all my students make significant progress this year.

49. Contests between students are a useful way of increasing motivation.

50. Grouping students by ability increases the gap between the highs and the lows.

51. I give my students lots of choices.

52. I can deal with almost any learning problem.

53. Parents should be told how their child is doing compared to others in the class.

54. At-risk students should be given assignments that require creativity.

55. I display the work of the highest achieving students as an example.

56. I encourage students to ask other students to help them with their work.

57. I am certain I am making a difference in the lives of my students.

58. Grades are a necessity; students have to have a realistic view of their ability.

59. Most students are capable of setting their own learning goals.

60. I integrate multicultural themes and literature throughout the year.

61. I help students understand how their performance compares to others.

62. I encourage students to suggest topics to study.

63. If I try really hard, I can get through to even the most difficult student.

64. Students should not be penalized for making errors.

65. I point out those children who do well academically, as a model for the other students.

66. I tell students that making mistakes is an essential part of learning.

67. I am good at helping all the students in my class make significant improvement.

68. Students should be given the opportunity to redo tests and improve their scores.

69. At-risk students should be given assignments they can learn from even if they will have difficulty.

70. I use competitive academic games or contests.

71. I analyze mistakes in class in order to promote understanding.

72. Sometimes I have difficulty in helping my LEP/ELL students because they are a little behind the EO students.

73. Grouping students by ability promotes learning.

74. I use language that is slightly below my students' abilities so they will be sure to understand.

75. Students shouldn't worry about failure.

76. I use cooperative academic activities or games with mixed ability level groups.

77. I accept all students' attempts at communication even if they are expressed incorrectly.

78. I rarely or never explain points of grammar to my students.

79. During content instruction, I respond to students' questions and answers even if they use the other language.

Teacher questionnaire (page 3 of 5)

80.   I think it makes more sense to students to discuss multiethnic themes around holidays or social studies units that discuss the particular ethnic group.

81.   (Grades 3 and above only) I have students do research where they observe, gather evidence (such as interviews) and write descriptions, generalizations, conclusions, and so on.

82.   I have developed specific language objectives that I incorporate into content.

83.   I fairly often, but not always, correct students' grammatical errors.

84.   During content instruction, I use both languages to reinforce certain concepts.

85.   When teaching in English, I often have to find a way to make the lesson <u>less</u> difficult for my students so they don't become frustrated.

86.   I adjust my lesson plans based on the student feedback that I receive.

87.   I often try to relate new vocabulary and knowledge to information the students have previously learned.

88.   I correct students' pronunciation errors.

89.   (Grades 3 and above only) I expect correct spelling, punctuation, and grammar on most written assignments.

90.   I provide many activities and opportunities for students to work in pairs or groups.

91.   I provide many activities and opportunities for students to talk with one another (especially LEP with EO).

92.   I provide my students with *considerable* time to think about answers when I ask them questions.

93.   I develop activities to address consistent language errors that students make.

94.   I think it is important to teach students social skills so that they can interact more appropriately with one another.

95.   I model writing in the classroom through journals and other activities.

96.   My students ask a lot of content-related questions in class.

97.   Sometimes I feel that my Spanish proficiency isn't at a high enough level to really provide students with different ways of expressing or understanding concepts or vocabulary items.

98.   I organize my lessons around themes appropriate to the grade level.

99.   I feel that math is a weak point in my instruction.

100.   All language that is displayed in my classroom is free of errors (including accents in Spanish).

101.   My students are almost always on task.

102.   My English speaking parents do not know how to assist their children at home with homework or school activities.

103.   My Spanish speaking parents do not know how to assist their children at home with homework or school activities.

104.   I tend to call on smart kids more than other kids, so they can model the correct answers.

105.   I don't really understand all that I should about the bilingual or bilingual immersion program.

106.   Sometimes I feel uncomfortable interacting with the Spanish speaking parents.

107.   Sometimes I feel uncomfortable interacting with the English speaking parents.

108.   Parents volunteer in my class.

109.   English speaking parents in my classroom are supportive of the bilingual or bilingual immersion program.

110.   Spanish speaking parents in my classroom are supportive of the bilingual or bilingual immersion program.

111.   English speaking parents in my classroom complain about the bilingual or bilingual immersion program.

112.   Spanish speaking parents in my classroom complain about the bilingual or bilingual immersion program.

113.   English speaking parents in my classroom are worried about their children learning to read in English.

114.   Spanish speaking parents in my classroom are worried about their children learning to read in English.

115.   In teaching, I usually:

Teacher questionnaire (page 4 of 5)

1) Make sure I keep the two languages separate
2) Try to keep the two languages separate, but sometimes mix or switch
3) Switch languages when children don't understand me
4) Switch languages frequently

116.   In general, how satisfied are you with the way the current bilingual or bilingual immersion program is operating?

1	2	3	4	5
Very Satisfied	Satisfied	Not Sure	Dissatisfied	Very Dissatisfied

Please bubble in the most accurate response for each question.

Using the categories below, what is your proficiency in the two languages of students in this project?
117.   Spanish
118.   English

(1)   **No practical proficiency:** Proficiency is not adequate for even most elemental communicative needs
(2)   **Minimal communicative proficiency:** Conversation with native speakers is possible to a limited degree for brief and simple interactions. No sustained conversation on school-related topics is possible.
(3)   **Basic communicative proficiency:** Sustained conversation on school issues is possible with students and parents. Proficiency is not adequate to handle more than limited subject matter instruction.
(4)   **Professional proficiency:** With some preparation, usually minor in nature, proficiency is adequate to provide a wide range of classroom instruction.
(5)   **Full professional proficiency or Native Speaker:** Proficiency is adequate to provide the complete range of educational services without need for special preparation.

119.   Which racial/ethnic code most closely describes your background?
        (1)   Native American/Eskimo/Aleut
        (2)   Asian American/Pacific Islander
        (3)   Hispanic/Latino
        (4)   Black/African American, other than Hispanic
        (5)   White, other than Hispanic

Which, if any, certificates or endorsements do you have? (Answer **1** for all that apply.)
120.   Administration
121.   Bilingual
122.   ESL/LDS/CLAD

123.   What is the <u>highest</u> degree you have received?
        (1) High School Diploma
        (2) Associate of Arts Degree
        (3) Bachelor's Degree
        (4) Master's Degree
        (5) Doctoral Degree or Professional Degree

Rate your training/understanding/use of the following concepts using the scale below.
        1   No training, no understanding
        2   No training, but some understanding
        3   Training, but still don't understand
        4   Training, and incorporate to some extent
        5   Training, and feel very comfortable

124.   Cooperative learning
125.   Educational Equity (How to treat students equally)
126.   Integrating multicultural content
127.   Second language development
128.   Literacy
129.   Writing process
130.   Manipulatives
131.   Computer
132.   Critical thinking
133.   Classroom management
134.   English language development

Rate the frequency with which you integrate or use the folllowing concepts
        1   Never
        2   Once in a while
        3   Weekly
        4   Few times a week
        5   Daily

135.   Cooperative learning
136.   Educational Equity (How to treat students equally)
137.   Integrating multicultural content
138.   Second language development
139.   Literacy
140.   Writing process
141.   Manipulatives
142.   Computer
143.   Critical thinking
144.   Classroom management
145.   English language development

Teacher questionnaire (page 5 of 5)

Parent Questionnaire

Important: YOU DO NOT NEED TO WRITE YOUR NAME OR CHILD'S NAME ON THIS QUESTIONNAIRE!

Part 1. Background

1.1 Your relationship to child(ren) enrolled in the program: Mother_____ Father_____ Other_____
Child(ren)=s grade level: K ___ 2nd ___ 4th ___

1.2 What is your and your spouse's ethnic background?
You Your spouse
___ ___ Hispanic/Latino
___ ___ Caucasian/Anglo
___ ___ African-American
___ ___ Asian-American
___ ___ American Indian/Alaskan Native

1.3 What is the highest level of education that you and your spouse have completed?
You Your spouse   You Your spouse
___ ___ Elementary   ___ ___ Community College/Vocational School
___ ___ Junior High/Middle School   ___ ___ 4-year College/University Degree
___ ___ High School or equivalent   ___ ___ Professional Degree/Graduate School

1.4 What language(s) do you and your spouse speak? You:_____ Your Spouse:_____

1.5 What language did you first learn as a child before entering school? You:_____ Your Spouse:_____

1.6 Please list the language(s) most often used in the home by the:
Mother to child_____
Father to child_____
Parents to each other_____

1.7 Please check below **your own** and **your spouse's** ability to communicate in Spanish.
You Your spouse
___ ___ No ability; cannot understand or speak the language at all.
___ ___ Can understand somewhat but cannot speak the language.
___ ___ Can understand and speak the language somewhat.
___ ___ Can understand and speak the language very well.
___ ___ Native speaker, or native-like ability in the language.

1.8 Have you ever studied Spanish? _____ Yes _____ No   ----   If **yes**, for how long?_____

1.9 What are the **three most important** reasons for enrolling your child in the immersion program? (Put a **1** next to the MOST IMPORTANT, a **2** next to the SECOND MOST IMPORTANT, a **3** next to the THIRD MOST IMPORTANT)
_____ it is our neighborhood school
_____ it is a high quality academic program
_____ my child will be able to communicate with family, friends, or other Spanish speaking people
_____ my child will have an academic or career advantage
_____ my child will have a stronger identity as a bilingual-bicultural/multicultural individual

Part 2.

2.1 How did you learn about the program? (Please mark **all** that apply)
___Parent handbook from district
___Recruited by school staff
___Friend/family member who has a child enrolled in the program
___Newspaper articles or advertisements about school
___Other _____

2.2 Please mark **all** of the following activities in which you participate:
___None   ___Serve on school and/or district committees
___Volunteer in classroom at least once   ___Help with parent club
___Volunteer in classroom frequently   ___Help with or attend school activities or events

Parent questionnaire (page 1 of 3)

___Help outside of class (e.g., field trips)   ___Other _____

2.3   I am unable to help at school because: (Check <u>all</u> that apply)
       ___Employment and school schedules conflict   ___Lack of classroom skills   ___Can help child better at home
       ___Transportation difficulties   ___Lack of language skills
       ___Lack of child care   ___Lack of school encouragement

2.4   Please mark the following types of school activities you have attended:
       ___None   ___English language class   ___Parent Workshops/Conferences
       ___Spanish language class   ___Teacher/parent communication meetings___ Other _____

2.5   How often do you attend parent group meetings and school-related activities?
       ___ Not at all   ___ Occasionally   ___ Frequently

2.6   I do not become involved with parent group activities because:
       ___Employment schedule conflicts with meeting times   ___Lack of encouragement from group
       ___Lack of child care   ___Lack of knowledge about school affairs

2.7   Check two (2) strategies frequently used to help with your child=s homework or reading.
       ___I give answers when work is difficult for my child.   ___I suggest different ways to solve problems.
       ___My child rarely asks for help with homework.   ___I encourage my child to complete work on his/her own.

Part 3. Please indicate how strongly you agree or disagree with the following statements about the Bilingual Immersion Program. (CIRCLE ONE ANSWER FOR EACH STATEMENT.) If more than one child is enrolled, answer questions using the oldest child as the example.

		Strongly Disagree	Disagree	Not Sure	Agree	Strongly Agree
3.1	I am satisfied that the Two-Way Immersion Program is giving my child access to the subject matter that s/he needs	1	2	3	4	5
3.2	I am <u>not</u> satisfied that the program is effective in developing my child=s ability to communicate in *Spanish.*	1	2	3	4	5
3.3	I am satisfied that the program is effective in developing my child=s ability to read in *English.*	1	2	3	4	5
3.4	I am <u>not</u> satisfied that the program is effective in developing my child=s ability to write in *English.*	1	2	3	4	5
3.5	Hispanic students, parents, staff and community members are made to feel like a valuable part of our school culture.	1	2	3	4	5
3.6	The faculty and staff have been successful in promoting diversity and understanding among the school community.	1	2	3	4	5
3.7	The faculty and staff are successful in balancing the needs and concerns of both English and Spanish speaking communities.	1	2	3	4	5
3.8	The administration in our school district office is <u>not</u> supportive of the needs and concerns of the school community.	1	2	3	4	5
3.9	I would recommend this program to other parents.	1	2	3	4	5
3.10	Studying Spanish is important for my child (oldest child) because it will allow him/her to be more comfortable with other Spanish speakers.	1	2	3	4	5

Parent questionnaire (page 2 of 3)

3.11	Studying Spanish is important for my child because it will allow him/her to meet and converse with more and varied people.	1	2	3	4	5
3.12	Studying Spanish is important for my child because it will enable him/her to better understand and appreciate Hispanic culture.	1	2	3	4	5
3.13	Studying Spanish is important for my child because s/he will be able to participate more freely in the activities of other cultural groups.	1	2	3	4	5
3.14	Studying Spanish is important for my child because s/he will need it for his/her future career.	1	2	3	4	5
3.15	Studying Spanish is important because it will make my child smarter.	1	2	3	4	5
3.16	I have the academic skills to help my child (oldest child) with homework.	1	2	3	4	5
3.17	I have the language skills to help my child with homework.	1	2	3	4	5
3.18	My involvement as a parent is important to the school community.	1	2	3	4	5
2.19	As a Spanish speaker, I feel there is more opportunity for program involvement.	1	2	3	4	5
2.20	As an English speaker, I feel there is more opportunity for program involvement.	1	2	3	4	5

Part 4. Please indicate how often you participate in the following activities.

		Almost Never	1-2 times per year	1-2 times per month	1-2 times per week	Usually Daily
4.1	I/My spouse read with my child in Spanish.	1	2	3	4	5
4.2	I/My spouse read with my child in English.	1	2	3	4	5
4.3	I/My spouse check out library books or buy books in Spanish	1	2	3	4	5
4.4	Spanish speaking children come to our house to play with my child	1	2	3	4	5
4.5	My child goes to the homes of other Spanish speaking children	1	2	3	4	5

THANK YOU FOR PARTICIPATING IN THIS SURVEY!
COPIES OF THE RESULTS WILL BE SENT TO YOUR SCHOOL

Parent questionnaire (page 3 of 3)

WHAT I BELIEVE--1

1	2	3	4
strongly disagree	**disagree**	**agree**	**strongly agree**

1. I am pretty good at my school work.
2. I find it easy to make friends.
3. I am <u>not</u> happy with the way I look.
4. I am pretty pleased with myself.
5. I like the way I am leading my life.
6. I am pretty slow in finishing my school work.
7. I am happy with myself most of the time.
8. I often wish I were someone else.
9. I like my body the way it is.
10. I don't do very well at my classwork.
11. I like my physical appearance the way it is.
12. I wish something about my face or hair looked different.
13. I wish I were different.
14. I think that learning another language helps me understand kids who are different from me.
15. I like to invite kids to my house no matter what color skin they have.
16. I think that learning two languages will help me do better in school.
17. I enjoy meeting and listening to people who speak another language.
18. I think that knowing two languages will help me get a better job when I grow up.
19. I believe that learning Spanish is important so I can talk with Spanish-speaking people.
20. I think that all people should be treated equally.
21. I think that learning two languages will help me really know my first language better.
22. I think that learning another language will help me get along better with other people.
23. I like to play with other kids no matter what they look like.
24. I believe that learning two languages helps me get better grades.
25. I believe that learning two languages will make me smarter than if I learned only one language.
26. I think that learning two languages helps me learn how to think better.
27. Kids care about each other in my class.
28. Kids treat each other pretty equally in our class.
29. I like hard work because it's a challenge.
30. I like difficult problems because I enjoy trying to figure them out.
31. I like school subjects that make me think pretty hard and figure things out.
32. I prefer easy work that I am sure I can do.
33. I don't like difficult schoolwork because I have to work too hard.
34. I stick to the assignments which are pretty easy to do.
35. I like school subjects where it's pretty easy to just learn the answers.
36. I like difficult schoolwork because I find it more interesting.
37. I can do almost any problem if I keep working at it.
38. I can do even the hardest work in my class.

Student questionnaire (page 1 of 3)

WHAT I THINK--2

1	2	3	4
strongly disagree	**disagree**	**agree**	**strongly agree**

41. I like reading.
42. I like mathematics.
43. I like school.
44. I enjoy studying in Spanish and English the way I do at school.
45. I read well in English.
46. I read well in Spanish.
47. I am good in mathematics.
48. I have someone to help me with my homework.
49. At home, I have a place where I can concentrate and study.
50. My parents make sure I get my homework done.
51. At home, I sometimes get to help make decisions about things that affect me.
52. My parents help me when I need it.
53. My parents expect me to do well in school.
54. My parents know who my friends are.
55. I spend a lot of time watching TV after school.
56. My teacher expects me to do well in school.
57. I have someone at school I could talk to if I had a problem.
58. I like to learn.
59. Some of the work we do in school is too hard for me.
60. I do my work because it makes me feel good inside.
61. Doing better than other kids in my class is important to me.
62. I like to show my teacher that I'm smarter than the other kids.
63. I don't care whether I understand something or not as long as I get the right answer.
64. Our teacher wants us to help each other with our schoolwork.
65. Most kids take part in class discussions.
66. I feel badly when I don't do as well as other kids.
67. We know who the smart kids are in our class because they are treated differently.
68. It is very important to get good grades.
69. Only a few kids do really well in our class.
70. It's more important to get the right answers than to know why they are right.
71. When I do my work, I skip the hard parts.
72. When doing my schoolwork, I guess a lot so that I can finish quickly.
73. I take my time to figure out my work.
74. I go back over schoolwork I don't understand.
75. I spend some time thinking about how to do my work before I start it.
76. I ask myself questions while I read to make sure I understand.
77. Our teacher tells us how we compare with other kids.
78. I want to continue studying and learning in Spanish and English, like I do now.

Student questionnaire (page 2 of 3)

MY FEELINGS ABOUT SPANISH AND ENGLISH--3   Form C

81. In speaking, I am:
     1)   Much better in Spanish than in English
     2)   A little better in Spanish than in English
     3)   About as good in Spanish as in English
     4)   A little better in English than in Spanish
     5)   Much better in English than in Spanish

82. In understanding spoken English or Spanish, I am:
     1)   Much better in Spanish than in English
     2)   A little better in Spanish than in English
     3)   About as good in Spanish as in English
     4)   A little better in English than in Spanish
     5)   Much better in English than in Spanish

83. In reading, I am:
     1)   Much better in Spanish than in English
     2)   A little better in Spanish than in English
     3)   About as good in Spanish as in English
     4)   A little better in English than in Spanish
     5)   Much better in English than in Spanish

84. In writing, I am:
     1)   Much better in Spanish than in English
     2)   A little better in Spanish than in English
     3)   About as good in Spanish as in English
     4)   A little better in English than in Spanish
     5)   Much better in English than in Spanish

85. How often have you translated from Spanish to English or English to Spanish for your family or friends?
     1) Never   2) Hardly at all   3) A few times   4) Many times

86. At home, with your parents or brothers or sisters, how often do you speak in Spanish and English?
     1)   I speak Spanish all of the time
     2)   I speak Spanish most of the time; sometimes I speak in English
     3)   I speak English most of the time; sometimes I speak in Spanish
     4)   I speak English all of the time

87. When you talk with your school friends who are Spanish-speaking at home, which language do you use when you meet after school or on the way home?
     1)   We speak Spanish all of the time
     2)   We speak Spanish most of the time; sometimes we speak in English
     3)   We speak English most of the time; sometimes we speak in Spanish
     4)   We speak English all of the time

88. Now that you are learning to speak and understand Spanish and English, who do you most play with?
     1)   I always play with my Spanish-speaking friends
     2)   I play mostly with Spanish-speaking friends, but also a few English-speaking friends
     3)   I play mostly with English-speaking friends, but also a few Spanish-speaking friends
     4)   I always play with my English-speaking friends

89. Would you rather go to an all-English school?
     1) Yes, I would very much   2) I'm not sure   3) No, I enjoy school as it is

90. Do you think you are behind or ahead in English compared to children at other schools who do not study Spanish?
     1)   I am definitely behind in English
     2)   I may be a bit behind, but not very much
     3)   I don't think I'm behind in English at all
     4)   I may be ahead in English
     5)   I am definitely ahead in English

Student questionnaire (page 3 of 3)

References

Adorno, T.W., Frenkel-Brunswick, F., Levinson, D.J. and Sanford, R.H. (1950) *The Authoritarian Personality*. New York: Harper & Row.

AERA, APA and NCME (1999) *Standards for Educational and Psychological Testing*. A joint publication of the AERA, APA and NCME. Washington, DC: AERA, APA or NCME.

Aguirre, A. Jr. (1984) Parent and teacher opinions of bilingual education: Comparisons and contrasts. *Journal of the National Association for Bilingual Education* 9, 41–51.

Allen, J.P. and Turner, E.J. (1988) Immigrants. *American Demographics* 10 (22–27), 59–60.

Allport, G. (1954) *The Nature of Prejudice*. Cambridge, MA: Addison-Wesley.

Ames, C. and Ames, R. (1985*) Research on Motivation In Education (2): The Classroom Milieu*. New York: Academic Press.

Anisfield, E. and Lambert, W.E. (1964) Evaluative reactions of bilingual and monolingual children to spoken language. *Journal of Abnormal and Social Psychology* 69, 89–97.

Aronson, E. and Gonzalez, A. (1988) Desegregation, jigsaw and the Mexican-American experience. In P.A. and D.A. Taylor (eds) *Eliminating Racism: Profiles in Controversy*. New York: Plenum Press.

Artigal, J.M. (1995) Multilingualism for all: A Catalan perspective. In T. Skutnabb-Kangas (ed.) *Multilingualism for All*. Netherlands: Swets & Zeitlinger B.V.

Artigal, J.M. (1997) The Catalan immersion program. In R.K. Johnson and M. Swain (eds) *Immersion Education: International Perspectives*. New York: Cambridge University Press.

Ascher, C. and Flaxman, E. (1987) Parent participation and the achievement of disadvantaged students. In D.S. Strickland and E.J. Cooper (eds) *Educating Black Children: America's Challenge*. Washington, DC: Howard University Press.

August, D. and Hakuta, K. (1997) *Improving Schooling for Language-Minority Children: A Research Agenda*. Washington, DC: National Academy Press.

Au, K.H. (1993) *Literacy Instruction in Multicultural Settings*. Fort Worth: Harcourt Brace Jovanovich.

Baetens Beardsmore, H. (ed.) (1993) *European Models of Bilingual Education*. Clevedon: Multilingual Matters.

Baetens Beardsmore, H. (1995) The European School experience in multilingual education. In T. Skutnabb-Kangas (ed.) *Multilingualism for All*. Netherlands: Swets & Zeitlinger B.V.

Baetens Beardsmore, H. and Swain, M. (1985) Designing bilingual education: Aspects of immersion and 'European School Models'. *Journal of Multilingual and Multicultural Development* 6, 1–15.

Baca, L.M. and Cervantes, M.T. (1998) *The Bilingual Special Education Interface* (3rd edn). Columbus, OH: Merrill Publishing.

Baecher, R.E. and Coletti, C.D. (1986) Two-way bilingual programs: Implementation of an educational innovation. *SABE Journal* 2, 42–58.

Baker, C. (1996) *Foundations of Bilingual Education and Bilingualism* (2nd edn). Clevedon: Multilingual Matters.

Baker, C. and Jones, S.P. (1998) *Encyclopedia of Bilingualism and Bilingual Education*. Clevedon: Multilingual Matters.

Baker, K. (1987) Comment on Willig's 'A meta analysis of selected studies of bilingual education'. *Review of Educational Research* 57, 351–62.

Baker, K. and de Kanter, A.A. (1981) *Effectiveness of Bilingual Education: A Review of Literature*. Washington, DC: Office of Planning, Budget and Evaluation, US Department of Education.

Baker, K. and de Kanter, A.A. (1983) *Bilingual Education: A Reappraisal of Federal Policy*. Lexington, MA: Lexington Press.

Baker, S. (1996) Look at students' use of the target language in two-way immersion programs. Master's thesis, Stanford University, Stanford CA.

Bandura, A. (1977) Self-efficacy: Toward a unifying theory of behavioral change. *Psychological Bulletin* 84, 191–215.

Banks, J.A. and Banks, C.M. (eds) (1995) *Handbook of Research on Multicultural Education*. New York: Macmillan.

Baron, J. (1991) Beyond the promise: Design, data and measurement in new forms of assessment. Symposium conducted at the annual meeting of the National Council on Measurement in Education and the American Education Research Association, Chicago IL.

Baron, R.M., Tom, D.Y. and Cooper, H.M. (1985) Social class, race, and teacher expectations. In J. Dusek (ed.) *Teacher Expectancies* (pp. 251–69). Mahwah, NJ: Lawrence Erlbaum.

Battitstich, V., Solomon, D., Kim, D., Watson, M. and Schaps, E. (1995) Schools as communities, poverty levels of student populations, and students' attitudes, motives and performance: A multi-level analysis. *American Educational Research Journal* 32, 627–58.

Ben-Zeev, S. (1977) The influence of bilingualism on cognitive strategy and cognitive development. *Child Development* 48, 1009–18.

Berliner, D.C. and Calfee, R.C. (1996) *Handbook of Educational Psychology*. New York: MacMillan .

Bermudez, A.B. and Marquez, J.A. (1996) An examination of a four-way collaborative to increase parental involvement in the schools. *The Journal of Educational Issues of Language Minority Students* 16, 1–16.

Bermudez, A.B. and Padròn, Y.N. (1990) Improving language skills for Hispanic students through home–school partnerships. *Journal of Educational Issues of Language Minority Students* 6, 33–43.

Bernhardt, E.B. (ed.) (1992) *Life in Language Immersion Classrooms*. Clevedon: Multilingual Matters.

Bialystok, E. (1999) Cognitive complexity and attentional control in the bilingual mind. *Child Development* 70, 636–44.

Bialystok, E. and Hakuta, K. (1994) *In Other Words: The Science and Psychology of Second-Language Acquisition*. New York: Basic Books.

Binet, A. and Simon, T. (1916) *The Development of Intelligence in Children (The Binet-Simon Scale)* (E.S. Kite, trans.) Baltimore: Williams and Wilkins.

Björklund. S. (1995) Development of the second language lexicon and teacher work in immersion. In J. Arnau and J.M. Artigal (eds) *Els Programes d'immersió: Una Perspectiva Europea Immersion Programmes: A European Perspective.* Barcelona, Spain: Universitat de Barcelona.

Black, S. (1993) Learning languages. Research report. *The Executive Educator* 33–36.

Bloom, B.S. (ed.) (1956) *Taxonomy of Educational Objectives: Handbook I: Cognitive Domain.* New York: Green and Co.

Bright, J.A. (1992) High-achieving, low-achieving, low-income black children: What makes the difference? Unpublished doctoral dissertation, Syracuse University, Syracuse, NY.

Brisk, M.E. (1998) *Bilingual Education: From Compensatory to Quality Schooling.* Mahwah, NJ: Lawrence Erlbaum Associates.

Brittingham, A. (1999) *The Foreign-Born Population in the United States.* Report PPL-123. Washington, DC: US Census Bureau.

Brophy, J. (1986) Teacher influences on student achievement. *American Psychologist* 41, 1069–77.

Brophy, J. (ed.) (1998) *Advances in Research on Teaching* (Vol. 7). Greenwich, CT: JAI Press Inc.

Brophy, J. and Good, T. (1986) Teacher behavior and student achievement. In M. Wittrock (ed.) *Third Handbook of Research on Teaching* (pp. 328–75). New York: Macmillan.

Bullard, P. and Taylor, B.O. (1993) *Making School Reform Happen.* Boston: Allyn and Bacon.

Bus, A.G. Van Ijzendoorn, M.H. and Pellegrini, A. (1995) Joint book reading makes for success in learning to read: A meta-analysis on intergenerational transmission of literacy. *Review of Educational Research* 65 (1), 1–21.

Buss, M. and Lauren, C. (eds) (1995) *Language Immersion: Teaching and Second Language Acquisition. From Canada to Europe.* Vaasa/Vasa: University of Vaasa.

Byram, M. and Leman, J. (eds) (1990) *Bicultural and Trilingual Education: The Foyer Model in Brussels.* Clevedon: Multilingual Matters.

California Council on the Education of Teachers (2001) Success for English language learners: Teacher preparation policies and practices. *Teacher Education Quarterly* 28, 1–7.

California State Board of Education (1998) *English-Language Arts Content Standards for California Public Schools: Kindergarten through Grade Twelve.* Sacramento, CA: California State Board of Education.

California State Department of Education (1982) *Basic Principles for the Education of Language Minority Students: An Overview.* Sacramento: Office of Bilingual Bicultural Education.

California State Department of Education (1984) *Studies on Immersion Education: A Collection for US Educators.* Sacramento: Office of Bilingual Bicultural Education.

California State Department of Education (1991) *Remedying the Shortage of Teachers for Limited-English-Proficient Students.* Sacramento: Office of Bilingual Bicultural Education.

California State Department of Education (1996a) *1996 LEP Ed Services Little Changed from 1995.* Sacramento: Office of Bilingual Bicultural Education.

California State Department of Education (1996b) *Teacher Reading: A Balanced Comprehensive Approach to Teaching Reading in Prekindergarten through Grade Three.* Sacramento: State Superintendent of Public Instruction.

Campbell, R.N. (1984) The immersion education approach to foreign language teaching. In *Studies on Immersion Education: A Collection for US Educators.* Sacramento, CA: California State Department of Education.

Campbell, R.N., Gray, T.C., Rhodes, N.C. and Snow, M.A. (1985) Foreign language learning in the elementary school: A comparison of three programs. *Modern Language Journal* 69, 44–54.

Carrasquillo, A.L. and Carrasquillo, C. (1979) Bilingual parents can help you teach reading and language arts in English. *Journal of the National Association for Bilingual Education* 3, 83–91.

Cazabon, M., Lambert, W.E. and Hall, G. (1993) Two-way bilingual education: A progress report on the Amigos Program. Research Report No. 7, The National Center for Research on Cultural Diversity and Second Language Learning. Santa Cruz, CA: University of California.

Cazden, C.B. (1979) Curriculum/language contexts for bilingual education. *Language Development in a Bilingual Setting.* Los Angeles: National Dissemination and Assessment Center.

Cazden, C.B. (1988) *Classroom Discourse: The Language of Teaching and Learning.* Portsmouth, NH: Heinemann Education Books.

Cazden, C.B. (ed.) (1992) *Whole Language Plus.* New York: Teachers' College Press.

Chaudron, C. (1983) A descriptive model of discourse in the corrective treatment of learners' errors. In B.W. Robinett and J. Schachter (eds) *Second Language Learning: Contrastive Analysis, Error Analysis and Related Aspects* (pp. 428–45). Ann Arbor: University of Michigan Press.

Choy, V.K.S. (1993) Parents' critical reflections on an elementary Japanese bilingual bicultural public school program: A participatory research study. Unpublished doctoral dissertation. University of San Francisco.

Chrispeels, J.H. (1992) *Purposeful Restructuring.* Bristol, PA: Falmer.

Christian, D. and Mahrer, C. (1992) *Two-Way Bilingual Programs in the United States 1991–1992.* Washington, DC: The National Center for Research on Cultural Diversity and Second Language Learning, Center for Applied Linguistics.

Christian, D. and Mahrer, C. (1993) *Two-Way Bilingual Programs in the United States, 1992–1993.* Washington, DC, and Santa Cruz, CA: National Center for Research on Cultural Diversity and Second Language Learning.

Christian, D. and Montone, C. (1994) *Two-way Bilingual Programs in the United States 1991-1994.* Washington, DC: The National Center for Research on Cultural Diversity and Second Language Learning, Center for Applied Linguistics.

Christian, D., Montone, C., Lindholm, K. and Carranza, I. (1997) *Profiles in Two-Way Bilingual Education.* McHenry, IL: Delta Systems.

Christian, D. and Whitcher, A. (1995) *Directory of Two-Way Bilingual Programs in the United States,* Washington, DC: Center for Applied Linguistics, The National Center for Research on Cultural Diversity and Second Language Learning.

Clancy, P.L. (1982) *19 Improving Schools and Why.* Ypsilanti: Eastern Michigan University Press.

Cloud, N., Genesee, F. and Hamayan, E. (2000) *Dual Language Instruction.* Boston, MA: Heinle and Heinle.

Cohen, A. (1974) The Culver City Spanish immersion program: The first two years. *Modern Language Journal* 58, 95–103.

Cohen, E.G. (1994) *Designing Groupwork: Strategies for the Heterogeneous Classroom*, 2nd edn., New York: Teachers College Press.

Cohen, E.G. and Lotan, R.A. (1995) Producing equal-status interaction in the heterogeneous classroom. *American Educational Research Journal* 32 (1), 99–120.

Collier, V. (1989) How long? A synthesis of research on academic achievement in a second language. *TESOL Quarterly* 23 (3), 509–31.

Comer, J.P. (1986) Parent participation in the schools. *Phi Delta Kappan*, 442–46.

Cortés, C.E. (1986) The education of language minority students: A contextual interaction model. In *Beyond Language: Social and Cultural Factors in Schooling Language Minority Students* (pp. 3–33). Los Angeles, CA: Evaluation, Dissemination and Assessment Center, California State University.

Crawford, J. (1999) *Bilingual Education: History, Politics, Theory and Practice*, 4th edn. Los Angeles, CA: Bilingual Education Services, Inc.

Cummins, J. (1979) Linguistic interdependence and the educational development of children. *Review of Educational Research*, 49, 222–51.

Cummins, J. (1980) The cross-lingual dimensions of language proficiency: Implication for bilingual education and the optimal age issue. *TESOL Quarterly* 14, 175–87.

Cummins, J. (1981) The role of primary language development in promoting educational success for language minority students. In California State Department of Education (ed.) *Schooling and Language Minority Students. A Theoretical Framework*. Los Angeles: California State Department of Education.

Cummins, J. (1983) *Heritage Language Education: A Literature Review*. Toronto: Ministry of Education.

Cummins, J. (1984) Wanted: A theoretical framework for relating language proficiency to academic achievement among bilingual students. In C. Rivera (ed.) *Language Proficiency and Academic Achievement*. Clevedon: Multilingual Matters.

Cummins, J. (1986) Empowering minority students: A framework for intervention. *Harvard Educational Review* 56, 18–36.

Cummins, J. (1987) Bilingualism, language proficiency, and metalinguistic development. In P. Homel, M. Palij and D. Aaronson (eds) *Childhood Bilingualism: Aspects of Linguistic, Cognitive and Social Development* (pp. 57–73). Hillsdale, NJ: Lawrence Erlbaum Associates.

Cummins, J. (1989) *Empowering Minority Students*. Sacramento: California Association of Bilingual Education.

Cummins, J. (1991) Interdependence of first- and second-language proficiency in bilingual children. In E. Bialystok (ed.) *Language Processing in Bilingual Children* (pp. 70–89). New York: Cambridge University Press.

Cummins, J. (2000) Biliteracy, empowerment, and transformative pedagogy. In J.V. Tinajero and R.A. DeVillar (eds) *The Power of Two Languages 2000: Effective Dual-Language Use Across the Curriculum*. New York: McGraw-Hill.

Cummins, J. and Swain, M. (1986) *Bilingualism in Education: Aspects of Theory, Research and Practice*. London: Longman.

Darling-Hammond, L. (1995) Inequality and access to knowledge. In J.A. Banks and C.A. McGee Banks (eds) *Handbook of Research on Multicultural Education*. New York: Macmillan.

Dash Moore, D. (1981) *At Home in America: Second Generation New York Jews*. New York: Cambridge University Press.

Davenport, E.C., Davison, M.L,. Kuang, H., Ding, S., Kim, S. and Kwak, N. (1998) High school mathematics course-taking by gender and ethnicity. *American Educational Research Journal* 35, 497–514.

Dawe, L.C. (1983) Bilingualism and mathematical reasoning in English as a second language. *Educational Studies in Mathematics* 14, 325–53.

Day, E.M. and Shapson, S.M. (1996) *Studies in Immersion Education*. Clevedon: Multilingual Matters.

De Courcy, M. (1997) Benowa High: A decade of French immersion in Australia. In R.K. Johnson and M. Swain (eds) *Immersion Education: International Perspectives*. New York: Cambridge University Press.

Diaz, R.M. (1983) Thought and two languages: The impact of bilingualism on cognitive development. In E. Gordon (ed.) *Review of Research in Education*, Vol. 10. Washington, DC: American Educational Research Association.

Dillon, J.T. (1985) Using questions to foil discussion. *Teaching and Teacher Education* 1, 109–21.

Dolson, D. (1985) Bilingualism and scholastic performance: The literature revisited. *NABE Journal* 10, 1–35.

Dolson, D. and Lindholm, K.J. (1995) World class education for children in California: A comparison of the bilingual immersion and European schools models. In T. Skutnabb-Kangas (ed.) *Multilingualism for All*. The Netherlands: Swets & Zeitlinger B.V.

Dolson, D. and Mayer, J. (1992) Longitudinal study of three program models for language minority students: A critical examination of reported findings. *Bilingual Research Journal* 16, 105–58.

Dorian, N.C. (1982) Language loss and maintenance in language contact situations. In W.E. Lambert and B.G. Freed (eds) *The Loss of Language Skills* (pp. 44–59). Rowley, MA: Newbury House.

Duff, P.A. (1995) An ethnography of communication in immersion classrooms in Hungary. *TESOL Quarterly* 29 (3), 505–37.

Duff, P.A. (1997) Immersion in Hungary: An EFL experiment. In R.K. Johnson and M. Swain (eds) *Immersion Education: International Perspectives*. New York: Cambridge University Press.

Dulay, H. and Burt, M. (1978) From research to method in bilingual education. In J. Alatis (ed.) *International Dimensions in Bilingual Education*. Washington, DC: Georgetown University Press.

Dusek, J.B. (1985) *Teacher Expectancies*. Hillsdale, NJ: Lawrence Erlbaum Associates.

Eccles, J.S. Midgley, C. and Adler, T. (1984) Grade-related changes in the school environment: Effects on achievement motivation. In J.G. Nicholls (ed.) *The Development of Achievement Motivation* (pp. 283–331). Greenwich, CT: JAI Press.

Edmonds, R.R. (1983) *Search for Effective Schools: The Identification and Analysis of City Schools that are Instructionally Effective for Poor Children* (Final report). East Lansing: Michigan State University.

Education Trust (1998) *Education Watch: The 1998 State and National Data Book* (Vol. II). Washington, DC: Education Trust.

Edwards, J.R. (1977) Students' reactions to Irish regional accents. *Language and Speech* 20, 280–86.

Eisenberg, N., Martin, C.L. and Fabes, R.A. (1996) Gender development and gender effects. In D.C. Berliner and R.C. Calfee (eds) *Handbook of Educational Psychology* (pp. 358–96). New York: Simon and Schuster Macmillan.

Escamilla, K. (2000) Teaching literacy in Spanish. In J.V. Tinajero and R.A. DeVillar (eds) *The Power of Two Languages 2000: Effective Dual-Language Use Across the Curriculum*. New York: McGraw-Hill.

Escamilla, K. and Medina, M. Jr. (1993) English and Spanish acquisition by limited-language-proficient Mexican Americans in a three-year maintenance bilingual program. *Hispanic Journal of Behavioral Sciences* 15, 108–20.

ESEA Title VII Bilingual Demonstration Project (1982) *An Exemplary Approach to Bilingual Education: A Comprehensive Handbook for Implementing an Elementary-Level Spanish–English Language Immersion Program*. San Diego Unified School District, San Diego, CA: Publication #I-B-82–58.

Fernandez, R.M. and Nielsen, F. (1986) Bilingualism and Hispanic scholastic achievement: Some baseline results. *Social Science Research* 15, 43–70.

Fisher, C.W. and Guthrie, L. (1983) *Executive Summary: The Significant Bilingual Instructional Features Study*. San Francisco: Far West Laboratory for Educational Research and Development

Fishman, J.A. (1989) *Language and Ethnicity in Minority Sociolinguistic Perspective*. Clevedon: Multilingual Matters.

Florio, S. (1978) Learning how to go to school: An ethnography of interaction in a kindergarten/first grade classroom. Unpublished doctoral dissertation, Harvard University.

Ford, D.Y. and Harris III, J.J. (1996) Multicultural gifted education: A wake-up call to the profession. *Roeper Review* 19, 72–78.

Fordham, S. and Ogbu, J.U. (1986) Black students' school success: Coping with the burden of 'acting White'. *The Urban Review* 18, 176–206.

Fortune, T. and Jorstad, H.L. (1996) US immersion programs: A national survey. *Foreign Language Annals* 29(2), 163–90.

Foster, M. (1995) African American teachers and culturally relevant pedagogy. In J.A. Banks and C.A. McGee Banks (eds) *Handbook of Research on Multicultural Education* (p. 575). New York: Macmillan.

Freeman, R. (1998) *Bilingual Education and Social Change*. Clevedon: Multilingual Matters.

Fruhauf, G., Coyle, D. and Christ, I. (1996) *Teaching Content in a Foreign Language*. Alkmaar, The Netherlands: Stichting Europrint.

Galindo, R. and Escamilla, K. (1995) A biographical perspective on Chicano educational success. *The Urban Review* 27 (1).

Gándara, P. (1995) *Over the Ivy Walls: The Educational Mobility of Low-Income Chicanos*. Albany: State University of NewYork Press.

Gándara, P., Larson, K., Rumberger, R. and Mehan, H. (1998) Capturing Latino students in the academic pipeline. *California Policy Seminar Brief Series* [On-line], 10. Available http://www.ucop.edu/crpc/pipeline.html.

Garcia, D.C. (1990) *Creating Parental Involvement: A Manual for School Children and Parents Interacting Program*. Miami: Florida University, School of Education. (ERIC Document Reproduction Service No. ED 323 273)

Garcia, E.E. (1988) Attributes of effective schooling for language minority students. *Education and Urban Society* 20, 387–98.

Garcia, E.E. (1991) Effective instruction for language minority students: The teacher. _Journal of Education_ 173 (2), 130–41.

Garcia, O. and Baker, C. (eds) (1995) _Policy and Practice in Bilingual Education: A Reader Extending the Foundations_. Clevedon: Multilingual Matters.

Gardner, R.C. (1985) _Social Psychology and Second Language Learning: The Role of Attitudes and Motivation_. London: Edward Arnold (Publishers) Ltd.

Gardner, R.C. and Lambert, W.E. (1972) _Attitudes and Motivation in Second-Language Learning_. Rowley, MA: Newbury House Publishers, Inc.

Gass, S.M. and Madden, C.G. (eds) (1985) _Input in Second Language Acquisition_. Rowley, MA: Newbury House Publishers, Inc.

Genesee, F. (1983) Bilingual education of majority language children: The immersion experiments in review. _Applied Psycholinguistics_, 4, 1–46.

Genesee, F. (1984) Historical and theoretical foundations of immersion education. In _Studies on Immersion Education: A Collection For US Educators_ (pp. 32–57). Sacramento: California State Department of Education.

Genesee, F. (1985) Second language learning through immersion: A review of US programs. _Review of Educational Research_, 55 (4), 541–61.

Genesee, F. (1987) _Learning Through Two Languages_. Cambridge: Newbury House Publishers.

Genesee, F. (1989) Early bilingual development: One language or two? _Journal of Child Language_ 16, 267–80.

Genesee, F. and Gándara, P. (1999) Bilingual education programs: A cross-national perspective. _Journal of Social Issues_ 55, 665–85.

Glenn, B. (1981) _What Works? An Examination of Effective Schools for Poor Black Children_. Cambridge, MA: Harvard University Center for Law and Education.

Glenn, C.L. (1990) _Introduction, Two-way Integrated Bilingual Education_. Boston: Department of Education, Office of Educational Equity.

Glenn, C. and Lalyre, I. (1991) Integrated bilingual education in the USA. In K. Jaspaert and S. Kroon (eds) _Ethnic Minority Languages and Education_ (pp. 37–55). Amsterdam: Swets & Zeitlinger B.V.

Goals 2000 (1994) _Educate America Act of 1994_, Pub. L. no. 103–227, 108 Stat. 125.

Goldenberg, C. (2000) Promoting early literacy development among Spanish-speaking children: Lessons from two studies. In J.V. Tinajero and R.A. DeVillar (eds) _The Power of Two Languages 2000: Effective Dual-Language Use Across the Curriculum_. New York: McGraw-Hill.

Good, T.L. and Weinstein, R.S. (1986) Schools make a difference: Evidence, criticisms, and new directions. _American Psychologist_ 41, 1090–97.

Graham, S. (1992) Most of the subjects were white and middle class: Trends in published research on African Americans in selected APA Journals 1970–1989. _American Psychologist_ 47, 629–39.

Graham, S. (1994) Motivation in African Americans. _Review of Educational Research_ 64, 55–117.

Graham, S. and Weiner, B. (1996) Theories and principles of motivation. In D.C. Berliner and R.C. Calfee (eds) _Handbook of Educational Psychology_. New York: MacMillan.

Grolnick, W.S., Deci, E.L. and Ryan, R.M. (1997) Internalization within the family: The self-determination theory perspective. In J.E. Grusec and L. Kuczynski (eds) _Parenting and Children's Internalization of Values_. New York: John Wiley & Sons.

Grolnick, W.S. and Ryan R.M. (1989) Parent styles associated with children's self-regulation and competence in school. *Journal of Educational Psychology* 81, 143–54.

Grolnick, W., Ryan, R.M. and Deci, E.L. (1991) Inner resources for school achievement: Motivational mediators of children's perceptions of their parents. *Journal of Educational Psychology* 83, 508–17.

Gumperz, J.J., Cook-Gumperz, J. and Szymanski, M.H. (1999) Collaborative practices in bilingual cooperative learning classrooms. Research Report #7. Santa Cruz, CA: Center for Research on Education, Diversity and Excellence.

Hakuta, K. (1986) *Mirror of Language*. New York: Basic Books.

Hakuta, K. and D'Andrea, D. (1992) Some properties of bilingual maintenance and loss in Mexican background high-school students. *Applied Linguistics* 13, 72–99.

Hakuta, K. and Diaz, R. (1985) The relationship between degree of bilingualism and cognitive ability: A critical discussion and some new longitudinal data. In K.E. Nelson (ed.) *Children's Language* (Vol. 5). Hillsdale, NJ: Lawrence Erlbaum Associates.

Hakuta, K. and Garcia, E.E. (1989) Bilingualism and education. *American Psychologist* 44, 374–79.

Hakuta, K. and Gould, L.J. (1987) Synthesis of research on bilingual education. *Educational Leadership*, March, 38–45.

Hamers, J. and Blanc, M. (1989) *Bilinguality and Bilingualism*. New York: Cambridge University Press.

Hare, B.R. (1985) Stability and change in self-perceptions and achievement among black adolescents: A longitudinal study. *Journal of Black Psychology* 11, 29–42.

Hargie, O.D.W. (1978) The importance of teacher questions in the classroom. *Educational Research* 20, 99–102.

Harley, B. (1984) How good is their French? *Language and Society* 10, 55–60.

Harley, B. (1986) *Age in Second Language Acquisition*. Clevedon: Multilingual Matters.

Harley, B. (1989) Functional grammar in French immersion: A classroom experiment. *Applied Linguistics* 10, 331–59.

Harley, B., Allen, P., Cummins, J. and Swain, M. (1990) *The Development of Second Language Proficiency*. New York: Cambridge University Press.

Harter, S. (1983) Developmental perspectives on the self-system. In P.H. Mussen (ed.) *Handbook of Child Psychology (Volume IV): Socialization, Personality, and Social Development* (pp. 320–35). New York: John Wiley and Sons.

Harter, S. (1998) The development of self-representations. In W. Damon and N. Eisenberg (eds) *Handbook of Child Psychology: Social, Emotional, and Personality Development* (5th edn, Vol. 3). New York: Wiley.

Harter, S., Whitesell, N. and Kowalski, P. (1992) Individual differences in the effects of educational transitions on children's perceptions of competence and motivational orientation. *American Educational Research Journal* 29, 777–808.

Heath, S.B. (1983) *Ways with Words: Language, Life, and Work in Communities and Classrooms*. Cambridge: Cambridge University Press.

Heath, S.B. (1986) Sociocultural contexts of language development. In California State Department of Education, *Beyond Language: Social and Cultural Factors in Schooling Language Minority Students*. Los Angeles, CA: Evaluation, Dissemination and Assessment Center.

Heath, S.B. (1995) Ethnography in communities: Learning the everyday life of America's subordinated youth. In J.A. Banks and C.A. McGee Banks (eds) *Handbook of Research on Multicultural Education* (pp. 114–28). New York: Macmillan.

Henderson, A.T. (1987) *The Evidence Continues to Grow.* Columbia, MD: National Committee for Citizens in Education.

Henderson, A.T. (1989) *The Evidence Continues to Grow: Parent Involvement Improves Student Achievement.* Columbia, MD: National Committee for Citizens in Education.

Henze, R.C. and Haliser, M.E. (1999) Personalizing culture through anthropological and educational perspectives. Educational Practice Report #4. Santa Cruz, CA: Center for Research on Education, Diversity and Excellence.

Herbert, C.H. (1986) *Final Evaluation Report, Bilingual Basic Grant Project.* ESEA Title VII, San Diego City Schools, San Diego, CA.

Herman, J.L. and Yeh, J.P. (1980) Some effects of parent involvement in schools (Report No. CSE-R-138). Boston, MA: Annual Meeting of the American Educational Research Association. (ERIC Document Reproduction Service No. ED 206 963)

Hernandez-Chavez, E. (1984) The inadequacy of English immersion education as an educational approach for language minority students in the United States. In *Studies on Immersion Education: A Collection for US Educators.* Sacramento: Office of Bilingual Bicultural Education.

Hidalgo, N.M., Bright, J.A., Siu, S., Swap, S.M. and Epstein, J.L. (1995) Research on families, schools, and communities: A multicultural perspective. In J.A. Banks and C.A. McGee Banks (eds) *Handbook of Research on Multicultural Education.* New York: Macmillan.

Holm, A. and Holm, W. (1990) Rock Point, a Navajo way to go to school: A valediction. *The Annals of the American Academy of Political and Social Science* 508, 170–84.

Holobow, N., Genesee, F. and Lambert, W.E. (1991) The effectiveness of a foreign language immersion program for children from different ethnic and social class backgrounds: Report 2. *Applied Psycholinguistics* 12, 179–98.

Homel, P., Palij, M. and Aaronson, D. (1987) *Childhood Bilingualism: Aspects of Linguistic, Cognitive and Social Development.* Hillsdale, NJ: Lawrence Erlbaum Associates Publishers.

Hornberger, N. and Corson, D. (eds) (1997) *Research Methods in Language and Education.* Boston: Kluwer.

Hornberger, N. and Micheau, C. (1993) Getting far enough to like it: Biliteracy in the middle school. *Peabody Journal of Education* 69, 30–53.

Huddy, L. and Sears, D.O. (1990) Qualified public support for bilingual education: Some policy implications. *The Annals of the American Academy of Political and Social Science* 505 (March), 119–34.

Ianco-Worrall, A.D. (1972) Bilingualism and cognitive development. *Child Development* 43, 1390–400.

Imhoff, G. (1990) The position of US English on bilingual education. *The Annals of the American Academy of Political and Social Science* 505 (March), 48–61.

Jaspaert, K. and Kroon, S. (eds) (1991) *Ethnic Minority Languages and Education.* Amsterdam: Swets & Zeitlinger B.V.

Johnson, D.L. (1974) Teacher–pupil interaction in bilingual elementary school classrooms. Paper presented at the meeting of Southwestern Social Science Association.

Johnson, D.W. and Johnson, R.T. (1990) Social skills for successful group work: Interpersonal and small-group skills are vital to the success of cooperative learning. *Educational Leadership* 47, 29–33.

Johnson, D.W., Johnson, R.T. and Holubec, E.J. (1986) *Circles of Learning: Cooperation in the Classroom*. Edina, MN: Interaction Book Company.

Johnson, R. (1994) Case studies of teacher expectations at bilingual education schools. Paper presented at the Annual Meeting of the American Educational Research Association, New Orleans, LA.

Johnson, R.K. (1997) The Hong Kong education system: Late immersion under stress. In R.K. Johnson and M. Swain (eds) *Immersion Education: International Perspectives*. New York: Cambridge University Press.

Johnson, R.K. and Swain, M. (eds) (1997) *Immersion Education: International Perspectives*. New York: Cambridge University Press.

Jones, D. (1995) An assessment of the communicative competence of children in Welsh immersion programmes. In J. Arnau and J.M. Artigal (eds) *Els Programes d'immersió: Una Perspectiva Europea [Immersion Programmes: A European Perspective]*. Barcelona, Spain: Universitat de Barcelona.

Julian, T.W., McKenry, P.C. and McKelvey, M.W. (1994) Cultural variations in parenting: Perceptions of Caucasian, African-American, Hispanic and Asian-American parents. *Family Relations* 43, 30–37.

Kagan, S. (1986) Cooperative learning and sociocultural factors in schooling. *Beyond Language: Social and Cultural Factors in Schooling Language Minority Students*. California State University, Los Angeles: Evaluation, Dissemination, and Assessment Center.

Kaufman, J.E. and Rosenbaum, J.E. (1992) Education and employment of low-income Black youth in White suburbs. *Educational Evaluation and Policy Analysis* 14, 229–40.

Kerman, S. Kimball, T. and Martin, M. (1980) *Teacher Expectations and Student Achievement*. Downey, CA: Office of Los Angeles County Superintendent of Schools.

Kim, Y.G. (1992) The role of attitudes and motivation in learning a heritage language: A study of Korean language maintenance in Toronto. Unpublished doctoral dissertation. University of Toronto.

Knapp, M.S. and Woolverton, S. (1995) Social class and schooling. In J. Banks and C.A. McGee Banks (eds) *Handbook of Research on Multicultural Education* (pp. 8–569). New York: Macmillan.

Kowal, M. and Swain, M. (1997) From semantic to syntactic processing: How can we promote it in the immersion classroom? In R.K. Johnson and M. Swain (eds) *Immersion Education: International Perspectives*. New York: Cambridge University Press.

Kozol, J. (1991) *Savage Inequalities: Children in America's Schools*. New York: Harper Perennial.

Kozol, J. (1995) *Amazing Grace: The Lives of Children and the Conscience of a Nation*. New York: Harper Perennial.

Kraft, C.L. (1991) What makes a successful black student on a predominantly white campus? *American Educational Research Journal* 28, 423–43.

Krashen, S. (1981) Bilingual education and second language acquisition theory. In D.P. Dolson (ed.) _Schooling and Language Minority Students: A Theoretical Framework._ Los Angeles, CA: Evaluation, Dissemination and Assessment Center.

Krashen, S. (2000) The two goals of bilingual education: Development of academic English and heritage language development. In J.V. Tinajero and R.A. DeVillar (eds) _The Power of Two Languages 2000: Effective Dual-Language Use Across the Curriculum._ New York: McGraw-Hill.

Lacelle-Peterson, M.W. and Rivera, C. (1994) Is it real for all kids? A framework for equitable assessment policies for English language learners. _Harvard Educational Review_ 64, 55–75.

Lambert, W.E. (1984) An overview of issues in immersion education. In _Studies in Immersion Education: A Collection for US Educators_ (pp. 8–30). Sacramento: California State Department of Education.

Lambert, W.E. (1987) The effects of bilingual and bicultural experiences on children's attitudes and social perspectives. In P. Homel, M. Palij and D. Aaronson (eds) _Childhood Bilingualism: Aspects of Linguistic, Cognitive and Social Development_ (pp. 197–221). Hillsdale, NJ: Lawrence Erlbaum Associates.

Lambert, W.E., Hodgson, R., Gardner, R. and Fillenbaum, S. (1960) Evaluative reactions to spoken language. _Journal of Abnormal and Social Psychology_ 60, 44–51.

Lambert, W.E, Genesee, F., Holobow, N. and Chartrand, L. (1993) Bilingual education for majority English-speaking children. _European Journal of Psychology of Education_ 8 (1), 3–22.

Lambert, W.E. and Taylor, D.M. (1990) _Coping with Cultural and Racial Diversity in Urban America._ New York: Praeger.

Lambert, W.E. and Tucker, G.R. (1972) _Bilingual Education of Children: The St. Lambert Experiment._ Rowley, MA: Newbury House.

Lapkin, S. and Swain, M. with Shapson, S. (1990) French immersion research agenda for the 90s. _The Canadian Modern Language Review_ 46 (4), 638–74.

Lasagabaster, D. and Cenoz, J. (1995) Language learning in the Basque Country: Immersion vs. non-immersion programs. In J. Arnau and J.M. Artigal (eds) _Els Programes d'immersió: Una Perspectiva Europea [Immersion Programmes: A European Perspective]._ Barcelona, Spain: Universitat de Barcelona.

Laurén, U. (1998) Narrative structures in the stories of immersion pupils in their second language. In J. Arnau and J.M. Artigal (eds) _Els Programes d'immersió: Una Perspectiva Europea [Immersion Programmes: A European Perspective]._ Barcelona, Spain: Universitat de Barcelona.

Lee, Y. (1991) Koreans in Japan and the United States. In M.A. Gibson and J.U. Ogbu (eds) _Minority Status and Schooling: A Comparative Study of Immigrant and Involuntary Minorities._ New York: Garland Publishing Company.

Legaretta, D. (1979) The effects of program models on language acquisition by Spanish-speaking children. _TESOL Quarterly_ 8, 521–34.

Legaretta, D. (1981) Effective use of the primary language in the classroom. In Office of Bilingual Bicultural Education, California Department of Education, _Schooling and Language Minority Students; A Theoretical Framework_ (pp. 83–116). Los Angeles: California State University, Evaluation, Dissemination, and Assessment Center.

Levine, D.U. and Lezotte, L.W. (1995) Effective schools research. In J.A. Banks and C.A. McGee Banks (eds) _Handbook of Research on Multicultural Education_ (pp. 525–47). New York: Macmillan.

Levine, D.U. and Stark, J.C. (1981) *Instructional and Organizational Arrangements and Processes for Improving Academic Achievement Inner-City Elementary Schools*. Kansas City: University of Missouri, Kansas City.

Lindholm, K.J. (1981) Communicative socialization: Parent–child and sibling interactions. Unpublished doctoral dissertation, University of California, Los Angeles.

Lindholm, K. J. (1987) *Directory of Bilingual Immersion Programs*. Educational Report No. 8 of the Center for Language Education and Research, UCLA.

Lindholm, K.J. (1990a) Bilingual immersion education: Criteria for program development. In A.M. Padilla, H.H. Fairchild, and C. Valadez (eds) *Bilingual Education: Issues and Strategies*. Beverly Hills, CA: Sage Publications.

Lindholm, K.J. (1990b) Language proficiency and academic achievement in two languages: Theoretical assumptions and empirical evidence in two-way bilingual immersion education. Paper presented at the Annual National Association for Bilingual Education Conference, Tucson, Arizona.

Lindholm, K.J. (1990c) Bilingual immersion education: Educational equity for language-minority students. In A. Barona and E. Garcia (eds) *Children At Risk: Poverty, Minority Status and Other Issues in Educational Equity*. Washington, DC: National Association of School Psychologists.

Lindholm, K.J. (1991) Theoretical assumptions and empirical evidence for academic achievement in two languages. *Hispanic Journal of Behavioral Sciences* 13, 3–17.

Lindholm, K.J. (1992) Two-way bilingual/immersion education: Theory, conceptual issues, and pedagogical implications. In R.V. Padilla and A. Benavides (eds) *Critical Perspectives on Bilingual Education Research*. Tucson, AZ: Bilingual Review/ Press.

Lindholm, K.J. (1994) Promoting positive cross-cultural attitudes and perceived competence in culturally and linguistically diverse classrooms. In R.A. Devillar, C.J. Faltis and J.P. Cummins (eds) *Cultural Diversity in Schools: From Rhetoric to Practice*. Albany, NY: State University of New York Press.

Lindholm, K.J. (1997) Two-way bilingual education programs in the United States. In J. Cummins and D. Corson (eds) *Encyclopedia of Language and Education, Volume 5: Bilingual Education*. The Netherlands: Kluwer Academic Publishers.

Lindholm, K.J. and Aclan, Z. (1991) Bilingual proficiency as a bridge to academic achievement: Results from bilingual/immersion programs. *Journal of Education* 173, 99–113.

Lindholm, K.J. and Baker, S. (1997) *Sí o No*: Students' limited use of language during Spanish instruction in two-way bilingual immersion programs. Paper presented at the American Educational Research Association annual meeting, Chicago, Illinois.

Lindholm, K.J. and Cava, G. (1997) Parent satisfaction and attitudes in a bilingual immersion program: Comparing Euro-American and Hispanic parents. Paper presented at the American Educational Research Association annual meeting, Chicago, Illinois.

Lindholm, K.J. and Fairchild, H.H. (1989) Evaluation of an 'exemplary' bilingual immersion program. Technical Report No. 13 of the Center for Language Education and Research, UCLA.

Lindholm, K.J. and Fairchild, H.H. (1990) First year evaluation of an elementary school bilingual immersion program. In A.M. Padilla, H.H. Fairchild and C. Valadez (eds) _Bilingual Education: Issues and Strategies_. Beverly Hills, CA: Sage Publications.

Lindholm, K.J. and Molina, R. (1998) Learning in dual language education classrooms in the US: Implementation and evaluation outcomes. In J. Arnau and J.M. Artigal (eds) _Immersion Programmes: A European Perspective_. Barcelona, Spain: Universitat de Barcelona.

Lindholm, K.J. and Molina, R. (2000) Two-way bilingual education: The power of two languages in promoting educational success. In J.V. Tinajero and R.A. DeVillar (eds) _The Power of Two Languages 2000: Effective Dual-Language Use Across the Curriculum_ (pp. 163–174). New York: McGraw-Hill.

Lindholm, K.J. and Padilla, A.M. (1990) The Mount Miguel High School partial immersion program. In A.M. Padilla, H.H. Fairchild and C. Valadez (eds) _Foreign Language Education: Issues and Strategies_. Beverly Hills, CA: Sage Publications.

Lindsay, J.S. (1990) Classroom discourse analysis: A review of the literature with implications for educational evaluation. _Educational Research_ 23, 107–16.

Linn, R.L. (2000) Assessments and accountability. _Educational Researcher_ 29, 4–16.

Linn, R.L., Baker, E.L. and Dunbar, S.B. (1991) Complex, performance-based assessment: Expectations and validation criteria. _Educational Researcher_ 20, 15–21.

Linney, J.A. and Seidman, A. (1989) The future of schooling. _American Psychologist_ 44, 336–340.

Lipton, G.C. (1985) _The Many Faces of Foreign Language in the Elementary School: FLES, FLEX, and Immersion_. American Association of Teachers of French. (ERIC Document Reproduction Service no. ED 264 727)

Liu, K. (1999) Affirming cultural diversity in the classroom: A collaborative inquire Project between Indiana State University and a rural professional development school. UNITE Monograph, Indiana State University.

Long, M.H. (1980) Input, interaction, and second language acquisiton. Unpublished Ph.D. dissertation, University of California, Los Angeles.

Long, M.H. (1981) Input, interaction and second language acquisition. In H. Winitz (ed.) _Native Language and Foreign Language Acquisition_ (p. 379). New York: Annals of The New York Academy of Sciences.

Long, M.H. (1983) Native speaker/non-native speaker conversation in the second language classroom. In M. Clarke and J. Handscombe (eds) _On TESOL 82: Pacific Perspectives on Language, Learning and Teaching_ (pp. 2207–225). Washington, DC: TESOL.

Long, M. H. and Porter, P.A. (1985) Group work, interlanguage talk, and second language acquisition. _TESOL Quarterly_ 19, 207–28.

Lucas, T., Henze, R. and Donato, R. (1990) Promoting the success of Latino language-minority students: An exploratory study of six high schools. _Harvard Educational Review_ 60(3), 315–340.

Luster, T. and McAdoo, H.P. (1994) Factors related to the achievement and adjustment of young African American children. _Child Development_ 65, 1080–94.

Lyster, R. (1987) Speaking immersion. _The Canadian Modern Language Review_ 43 (4), 701–17.

Lyster, R. (1990) The role of analytic language teaching in French immersion programs. _The Canadian Modern Language Review_ 47(1), 159–75.

Lyster, R. (1994) The effect of functional-analytic teaching on aspects of French immersion students' sociolinguistic competence. *Applied Linguistics* 15, 263–87.

Maccoby, E.E. and Martin, J.A. (1983) Socialization in the context of the family: Parent–child interaction. In P.H. Mussen (ed.) *Handbook of Child Psychology, Volume IV: Socialization, Personality, and Social Development.* New York: John Wiley and Sons.

MacKaye, S.D.A. (1990) California Proposition 63: Language attitudes reflected in the public debate. *The Annals of the American Academy of Political and Social Science*, 505 (March) 135–46.

Maehr, M.L. and Pintrich, P.R. (eds) (1997) *Advances in Motivation and Achievement* (Vol. 10). Greenwich, CT: JAI Press Inc.

Marsh, H.W. (1989) Sex differences in the development of verbal and mathematics constructs: The High School and Beyond study. *American Educational Research Journal* 26, 191–225.

Marsh, H.W. (1993) Academic self-concept: Theory measurement and research. In J. Suls (ed.) *Psychological Perspectives on the Self* (Vol. 4). Hillsdale, NJ: Erlbaum.

Martinez, R. and Dukes, R.L. (1987) Race, gender, and self-esteem among youth. *Hispanic Journal of Behavioral Sciences* 9, 427–43.

McCargo, C. and Christian, D. (1998) *Two-way Bilingual Immersion Programs in the United States: 1997–1998 Supplement.* Santa Cruz, CA and Washington, DC: Center for Research on Education, Diversity, and Excellence.

McCollum, P.A. (1993) Learning to value English: Cultural capital in a two-way bilingual program. Paper presented at the annual meetings of the American Educational Research Association, Atlanta, Georgia.

McCollum, P.A. (1994) Language use in two-way bilingual programs. *Intercultural Development Research Association Newsletter* 21, 9–11.

Medina, M., Jr. and Escamilla, K (1992) English acquisition by fluent and limited Spanish proficient Mexican Americans in a three-year maintenance bilingual program. *Hispanic Journal of Behavioral Sciences* 14, 252–67.

Mehan, H. (1978) Structuring school structure. *Harvard Educational Review* 48, 32–64.

Mehan, H. (1979) *Learning Lessons.* Cambridge, MA: Harvard University Press.

Mehan, H. Okamoto, D. Lintz, A. and Wills, J.S. (1995) Ethnographic studies of multicultural education in classrooms and schools. In J.A. Banks and C.A. McGee Banks (eds) *Handbook of Research on Multicultural Education* (pp. 129–44). New York: Macmillan.

Met. M. (1987) Parent involvement in foreign language learning. (ERIC/CLL News Bulletin 11, 2–3, 7–8)

Met, M. (1998) Curriculum decision-making in content-based second language teaching. In F. Genesee and J. Cenoz (eds) *Beyond Bilingualism: Multilingualism and Multilingual Education.* Clevedon: Multilingual Matters.

Met, M. and Lorenz, E.B. (1997) Lessons from US immersion programs: Two decades of experience. In R.K. Johnson and M. Swain (eds) *Immersion Education: International Perspectives* (pp. 243–64). Cambridge: Cambridge University Press.

Minami, M. and Ovando, C.J. (1995) Language issues in multicultural contexts. In J.A. Banks and C.A. McGee Banks (eds) *Handbook of Research on Multicultural Education.* New York: Macmillan.

Molina, R. (2000) Building equitable two-way bilingual programs: Voices from the field. In N. Cloud, F. Genesee and E. Hamayan (eds) *Dual Language Instruction.* Boston, MA: Heinle and Heinle.

Moll, L.C. (1992) Bilingual classrooms studies and community analysis: Some recent trends. *Educational Researcher* 21, 20–24.

Moll, L.C., Amanti, C., Neff, D. and Gonzalez, N. (1992) Funds of knowledge for teaching: Using a qualitative approach to connect homes and classrooms. *Theory into Practice* 31, 132–41.

Moll, L.C. and Diaz, S. (1985) Ethnographic pedagogy: Promoting effective bilingual instruction. In E. Garcia and R. Padilla (eds) *Advances in Bilingual Education Research* (pp. 127–49). Tucson, AZ: The University of Arizona Press.

Montone, C.L. and Loeb, M.I. (2000) Implementing two-way immersion programs in secondary schools, Educational Practice Report No. 5. Santa Cruz, CA: Center for Research on Education, Diversity and Excellence.

Moran, C. and Hakuta, K. (1995) Bilingual education: Broadening research perspectives. In J.A. Banks and C.A. McGee Banks (eds) *Handbook of Research on Multicultural Education* (pp. 97–113). New York: Macmillan.

Morris, L.L., Fitz-Gibbon, C.T. and Lindheim, E. (1987) *How to Measure Performance and Use Tests*. Newbury Park, CA: Sage Publications.

Mortimore, P., Sammons, P., Stoll, L., Lewis, D. and Ecob, R. (1988) *School Matters*. Berkeley: University of California Press.

Náñez, J.E., Padilla, R.V. and Máez, B. (1992) Bilinguality, intelligence, and cognitive information processing. In R.V. Padilla and A.H. Benavides (eds) *Critical Perspectives on Bilingual Education Research*. Tempe, AZ: Bilingual Press.

National Assessment of Educational Progress (1990) *The Reading Report Card 1976–1988*. Princeton, NJ: Educational Testing Service.

National Assessment of Educational Progress (1998) Long-term trends in student reading performance. *NAEP Facts* 3, 1–4.

National Center for Education Statistics (2000) *Dropout Rates in the United States: 1999*, NCES 2001022, by P. Kaufman, J. Kwon, S. Klein and C. Chapman. Washington, DC: US Government Printing Office.

National Commission on Excellence in Education (1983) *A Nation at Risk: The Imperative for Educational Reform*. Washington, DC: United States Government Printing Office.

National Council on Education Standards and Testing (1992) *Raising Standards for American Education: A Report to Congress, the Secretary of Education, the National Education Goals Panel, and the American People*. Washington, DC: Government Printing Office.

National Research Council (1999) *High Stakes: Testing for Tracking, Promotion, and Graduation*. Washington, DC: National Academy Press.

Natriello, G., McDill, E.L. and Pallas, A.M. (1990) *Schooling Disadvantaged Children: Racing Against Catastrophe*. New York: Teachers College Press.

Nuttall, C. and Langhan, D. (1997) The Molteno Project: A case study of immersion for English-medium instruction in South Africa. In R.K. Johnson and M. Swain (eds) *Immersion Education: International Perspectives*. New York: Cambridge University Press.

Odlin, T. (1989) *Language Transfer: Cross-Linguistic Influence in Language Learning*. Cambridge, MA: Cambridge University Press.

Ogbu, J.U. (1987).Variability in minority school performance: A problem in search of an explanation. *Anthropology and Education Quarterly* 18, 312–34.

Ogbu, J.U. (1995) Understanding cultural diversity and learning. In J.A. Banks and C.A. McGee Banks (eds) *Handbook of Research on Multicultural Education* (pp. 582–96). New York: Macmillan.

Okagaki, L., Frensch, P.A. and Gordon, E.W. (1995) Encouraging school achievement in Mexican American children. *Hispanic Journal of Behavioral Sciences* 17, 160–79.

Olneck. M.R. (1995) Immigrants and education. In J.A. Banks and C.A. McGee Banks (eds) *Handbook of Research on Multicultural Education*. New York: Macmillan.

Orfield, G.F., Monfort, F. and Aaron, M. (1989) *Status of School Desegregation: 1968–1986*. Alexandria, VA: National School Boards Association.

Ortiz, A. and Yates, J. (1989) Staffing and the development of individualized educational programs for the bilingual exceptional student. In L. M. Baca and H.T. Cervantes (eds) *The Bilingual Special Education Interface* (2nd edn) Columbus, OH: Merrill Publishing Company

Orum, L.S. (1986) *The Education of Hispanics: Status and Implications*. Washington DC: National Council of La Raza.

Padilla, A.M. and Lindholm, K.J. (1984) Child bilingualism: The same old issues revisited. In J.L. Martinez, Jr. and R.H. Mendoza (eds) *Chicano Psychology* (2nd edn). New York: Academic Press.

Padilla, A.M. and Lindholm, K.J. (1995) Quantitative educational research with ethnic minorities. In J.A. Banks and C.A. McGee Banks (eds) *Handbook of Research on Multicultural Education* (pp. 97–113). New York: Macmillan.

Padilla, A.M., Lindholm, K. J., Chen, A., Duran, R., Hakuta, K., Lambert, W.E. and Tucker, G.R. (1991) The English-only movement: Myths, reality, and implications for psychology. *American Psychologist* 46, 120–130.

Padilla, A.M. and Sung, H. (1995) Study of Asian languages in the United States: Students' motivation, parents' attitudes and parental involvement. Paper presented at the 5th International Conference on Cross-Cultural Communications, August 17, 1995, Harbin, China.

Peal, E. and Lambert, W.E. (1962) The relation of bilingualism to intelligence. *Psychological Monographs* 76, 1–23.

Pease-Alvarez, L. (1993) Moving in and out of bilingualism: Investigating native language maintenance and shift in Mexican-descent children. Research Report 6. Santa Cruz, California: National Center for Research on Cultural Diversity and Second Language Learning.

Pecheone, R. and Shoemaker, J. (1984) *An Evaluation of the School Effectiveness Program in Connecticut*. Hartford: Connecticut State Department of Education.

Peirce, B.N. (1995) Social identity, investment and language learning. *TESOL Quarterly* 29, 9–31.

Pellerin, M. and Hammerly, H. (1986) L'expression orale apres treize ans d'immersion Francaise [Oral expression after thirteen years of French immersion]. *Canadian Modern Language Review* 42 (3), 592–606.

Percell, C.H. (1993) Social class and educational equality. In J. Banks and C.A. McGee Banks (eds) *Multicultural Education: Issues and Perspectives* (2nd edn, pp. 71–89). Boston: Allyn and Bacon.

Petersen, C.I. and Warnsby, E. (1992) Reaching disengaged parents of at-risk elementary schoolers. *The School Community Journal* 2, 56–61.

Phillips, S. (1983) *The Invisible Culture: Communication in the Classroom and Community on the Warm Springs Indian Reservation*. White Plains, NY: Longman.

Piatt, B. (1990) *Only English: Law and Language Policy in the United States.* Albuquerque, NM: University of New Mexico Press.

Poole, D. (1992) Language socialization in the second language classroom. *Language Learning* 42, 593–616.

Popham, W.J. and Sirotnik, K.A. (1992) *Understanding Statistics in Education.* Itasca, IL: F.E. Peacock Publishers.

Portes, A. and Rumbaut, R.G. (1990) *Immigrant America: A Portrait.* Berkeley: University of California Press.

Portes, P.R. (1986) Ethnicity and culture in educational psychology. In D.C. Berliner and R.C. Calfee (eds) *Handbook of Educational Psychology* (pp. 331–57). New York: Simon and Schuster Macmillan.

Powell, G.J. (1989) Defining self-concept as a dimension of academic achievement for inner city youth. In G.L. Berry and J.K. Asamen (eds) *Black Students: Psychosocial Issues and Academic Achievement* (pp. 69–82). Newbury Park, CA: Sage.

Purkey, S.C. and Smith, M.S. (1983) Effective schools: A review. *Elementary School Journal* 86 (4), 427–52.

Qin, Z., Johnson, D.W. and Johnson, R.G. (1995) Cooperative versus competitive efforts and problem solving. *Review of Educational Research* 65 (2), 129–144.

Ramirez, J.D., Pasta J.J., Yuen, S.D., Billings, D.K. and Ramey, D. (1991) Longitudinal study of structured immersion strategy, early-exit, and late-exit bilingual education programs for language minority children (Vols. 1–2). Report No. 300–87–0156. Washington, DC: US Department of Education.

Ramirez, J.D., Yuen, S.D. and Ramey, D.R. (1991) Final report: Longitudinal study of structured English immersion strategy, early-exit and late-exit programs for language-minority children. Report submitted to the US Department of Education. San Mateo, CA: Aguirre International.

Reynolds, D. (ed.) (1985) *Studying School Effectiveness.* Lewes, East Sussex: Falmer.

Rhodes, N.C. (1992) Improving elementary school foreign language teacher education 1989–1992. Final report. Washington, DC: Center for Applied Linguistics. (ERIC Document Reproduction Service No. ED 352 835)

Rhodes, N.C. and Oxford, R.L. (1988) Foreign languages in elementary and secondary schools: Results of a national survey. *Foreign Language Annals* 21 (1) 51–69.

Rhodes, N. and Schreibstein, A. (1983) Foreign language in the elementary school: A practical guide. Washington, DC: Center for Applied Linguistics. (ERIC Document Reproduction Service No. ED 225 403)

Rice, J.M. (1893) *The Public-School System of The United States.* New York: Century.

Riley, R. (2000) *Excelencia para todos* – Excellence for all: The progress of Hispanic Education and the challenges of a new century. Remarks prepared for delivery by US Secretary of Education Richard Riley, Bell Multicultural High School, Washington DC.

Ritts, V. Patterson, M.L. and Tubbs, M.E. (1992) Expectations, impressions, and judgments of physically attractive students: A review. *Review of Educational Research* 62, 413–26.

Rosenberg, M. (1979) *Conceiving the Self.* New York: Basic Books.

Rosenberg, M. (1986) *Conceiving the Self.* Malabar, FL: Robert E. Krieger Publishing Company.

Rosenberg, M. and Simmons, R.G. (1972) *Black and White Self-Esteem: The Urban School Child.* Washington, DC. American Sociological Association.

Romaine, S. (1995) *Bilingualism* (2nd edn). Oxford: Blackwell.

Rosenholtz, S.J. (1985) Effective schools: Interpreting the evidence. *American Journal of Education* 93, 352–88.

Rossmiller, R.A., Holcomb, E.L. and McIsaac, D.N. (1993) *The Effective Schools Process*. Madison, WI: National Center for Effective Schools Research and Development.

Rowe, M.B. (1986) Wait time: Slowing down may be a way of speeding up! *Journal of Teacher Education* 37, 101–8.

Royer, J.M. and Carlo, M.S. (1991) Transfer of comprehension skills from native to second language. *Journal of Reading* 34 (1), 450–55.

Rumberger, R.W. (1995) Dropping out of middle school: A multilevel analysis of students and schools. *American Educational Research Journal*, 32, 583–562.

Salomone, A. (1992a) Immersion teachers' pedagogical beliefs and practices: Results of a descriptive analysis. In E.B. Bernhardt (ed.) *Life in Language Immersion Classrooms*. Clevedon: Multilingual Matters.

Salomone, A. (1992b) Student–teacher interactions in selected French immersion classrooms. In E.B. Bernhardt (ed.) *Life in Language Immersion Classrooms*. Clevedon: Multilingual Matters.

Samimy, K.K. and Tabuse, M. (1992) Affective variables and a less commonly taught language: A study in beginning Japanese classes. *Language Learning* 42, 377–98.

San Jose Mercury News (1996) Race spurred 60% of hate crimes in 95. November 5, p. 4a.

San Jose Mercury News (1997) The sad state of math skills: California students again score near bottom in US. February 28. Michael Bazeley, p. A1.

Santos, S.L. (1985) Parental perceptions of bilingual education in northeast Texas: Implications for administrators. *NABE* 9, 57–67.

Saville-Troike, M. (1987) Bilingual discourse: The negotiation of meaning without a common code. *Linguistics* 25, 81–106.

Schofield, J.W. (1991) School desegregation and intergroup relations. In G. Grant (ed.) *Review of Research in Education* (Vol. 17, pp. 335–409). Washington, DC: American Educational Research Association.

Schultz, G.F. (1993) Socioeconomic advantage and achievement motivation: Important mediators of academic performance in minority children in urban schools. *Urban Review* 25, 221–32.

Secada, W.G. (1987) This is 1987, not 1980: A comment on a comment. *Review of Educational Research* 57, 377–84.

Sharp, D. (1973) *Language in Bilingual Communities*. London: Edward Arnold.

Shin, F. and Gribbons, B. (1996) Hispanic parents' perceptions and attitudes of bilingual education. *AMAE Journal* 16–22.

Singleton, D. (1989) *Language Acquisition: The Age Factor*. Clevedon: Multilingual Matters.

Skaalvik, E.M. (1986) Sex differences in global self-esteem. A research review. *Scandinavian Journal of Educational Research* 30, 167–79.

Skaalvik, E.M. (1997) Issues in research on self-concept. In M.L. Maehr and P.R. Pintrich (eds) *Advances in Motivation and Achievement* (Vol. 10). Greenwich, CT: JAI Press Inc.

Skuttnabb-Kangas, T. (1981) *Bilingualism or Not: The Education of Minorities*. Multilingual Matters 7, 121–35.

Skutnabb-Kangas, T. (1988) Multilingualism and the education of minority children. In T. Skutnabb-Kangas and J. Cummins (eds) *Minority Education: From Shame to Struggle*. Clevedon: Multilingual Matters.

Skutnabb-Kangas, T. and Cummins, J. (1988) *Minority Education: From Shame to Struggle*. Clevedon: Multilingual Matters.

Skuttnabb-Kangas, T. (ed.) (1995) *Multilingualism for All*. The Netherlands: Swets & Zeitlinger B.V.

Skuttnabb-Kangas, T. and Toukomaa, P. (1976) *Teaching Migrant Children's Mother Tongue and Learning the Language of the Host Country in the Context of the Socio-Cultural Situation of the Migrant Family*. Helsinki: Finnish National Committee for UNESCO.

Slavin, R. E. (1983) *Cooperative Learning*. New York: Longman.

Slavin, R.E. (1995) *Cooperative Learning: Theory, Research and Practice* (2nd edn). Boston: Allyn & Bacon.

Slaughter-DeFoe, D.T. (1991) Parental educational choice: Some African American dilemmas. *Journal of Negro Education* 60, 354–60.

Slaughter, H.B. (1997) Indigenous language immersion in Hawaii. In R.K. Johnson and M. Swain (eds) *Immersion Education: International Perspectives* (pp. 105–29). Cambridge: Cambridge University Press.

Sniffen, M. (1999) FBI: Race motivates hate crimes. November 18. *AP via Newsday.com*.

Snow, C., Barnes, W., Chandler, J., Goodman, I. and Hemphill, L. (1991) *Unfulfilled Expectations: Home and School Influences on Literacy*. Cambridge, MA: Harvard University Press.

Snow, C.E. and Hoefnagel-Höhle, M. (1978) The critical period for language acquisition: Evidence from second language learning. *Child Development* 49, 1114–28.

Snow, M.A. (1986) Innovative second language education: Bilingual immersion programs, Education Report No. 1. Los Angeles, CA: UCLA Center for Language Education and Research.

Snow, M.A. (1990) Language immersion: An overview and comparison. In A.M. Padilla, H.H. Fairchild, and C.M. Valadez (eds) *Foreign Language Education: Issues and Strategies* (pp. 109–26). Newbury Park, CA: Sage Publications.

Snow, M.A,. Padilla, A.M. and Campbell, R. (1988) Patterns of second language retention of graduates of a Spanish Immersion program. *Applied Linguistics* 9, 182–97.

Snow, R.E., Corno, L. and Jackson D. III, (1996) Individual differences in affective and conative functions. In D.C. Berliner and R.C. Calfee (eds) *Handbook of Educational Psychology* (pp. 243–310). New York: Simon and Schuster Macmillan.

Solomon, R.P. (1992) *Black Resistance in High School: Forging a Separatist Culture*. Albany: State University of New York Press.

Spener, D. (1988) Transitional bilingual education and the socialization of immigrants. *Harvard Educational Review* 58, 2.

Spilka, I. (1976) Assessment of second-language performance in immersion programs. *Canadian Modern Language Review* 32 (5), 543–61.

Stedman, L.C. (1987) It's time we changed the effective schools formula. *Phi Delta Kappan* 69 (3), 215–24.

Stern, C. and Keislar, E.R. (1977) Teacher attitudes and attitude change. *Journal of Research and Development in Education* 10, 63–76.

Sternberg, R. and Williams, W. (1995) Parenting toward cognitive competence. In M.H. Bornstein (ed.) *Handbook of Parenting: Vol 4: Applied and Practical Parenting*. Mahwah, NJ: Lawrence Erlbaum Associates.

Stevens, R.J. and Slavin, R.E. (1995) The cooperative elementary school: Effects on students' achievement, attitudes, and social relations. *American Educational Research Journal* 32 (2), 321–51.

Stevenson, H.W., Chen, C. and Uttal, D.H. (1990) Beliefs and achievement: A study of black, white, and Hispanic children. *Child Development* 61, 508–23.

Stipek, D. (1998) *Motivation to Learn: From Theory to Practice* (3rd edn). Boston: Allyn and Bacon.

Sue, S. and Padilla, A.M. (1986) Ethnic minority issues in the United States: Challenges for the educational system. In *Beyond Language: Social and Cultural Factors in Schooling Language Minority Students* (pp. 35–72). Los Angeles, CA: Evaluation, Dissemination and Assessment Center, California State University.

Summary of Hate Crime Statistics (1998). Available : http://infoplease.lycos.com/ipa/A0004885.html

Swain, M. (1983) Bilingualism without tears. In M.A. Clarke and J. Handscombe (eds) *On TESOL 82: Pacific Perspectives on Language, Learning and Teaching* (pp. 35–46). Washington, DC: TESOL.

Swain, M. (1984) A review of immersion education in Canada: Research and evaluation studies. *Studies on Immersion Education: A Collection for United States Educators* (pp. 87–112). Sacramento CA: California State Department of Education.

Swain, M. (1985) Communicative competence: Some roles of comprehensible input and comprehensible output in its development. In S.M. Gass and C.G. Madden (eds) *Input in Second Language Acquisition*. Rowley, MA: Newbury House Publishers, Inc.

Swain, M. (1987) The case for focussed input: Contrived but authentic – Or, how content teaching needs to be manipulated and complemented to maximize second language learning. Plenary paper presented at TESOL 1987 Conference, Vancouver, BC.

Swain, M. (1995) The output hypothesis: Second language learning and immersion education. In J. Arnau and J.M. Artigal (eds) *Els Programes d'immersió: Una Perspectiva Europea [Immersion Programmes: A European Perspective]*. Barcelona, Spain: Universitat de Barcelona.

Swain, M. and Carroll, S. (1987) The immersion observation study. In B. Harley, P. Allen, J. Cummins and M. Swain (eds) *The Development of Bilingual Proficiency: Final Report*. Vol II. Toronto: The Ontario Institute for Studies in Education.

Swain, M. and Lapkin, S. (1982) *Evaluating Bilingual Education: A Canadian Case Study*. Clevedon: Multilingual Matters.

Swain, M. and Lapkin, S. (1986) Immersion French in secondary schools: 'The goods' and 'the bads'. *Contact* 5, 2–9.

Tarone, E. and Swain, M. (1995) A sociolinguistic perspective on second-langauge use in immersion classrooms. *Modern Language Journal* 79(2), 24–46.

Tharp, R.G. and Gallimore, R. (1988) *Rousing Minds to Life: Teaching, Learning and Schooling in Social Context*. New York: Cambridge University Press.

Third International Mathematics and Science Study (1995) Washington, DC: National Center for Educational Statistics.

Thomas, W.P. and Collier, V. (1997) *School Effectiveness for Language Minority Students*. Washington, DC: National Clearinghouse for Bilingual Education.

Thorndike, E.L. (1913) *Educational Psychology: The Psychology of Learning* (Vol. 2). New York: Columbia University.

Tikunoff, W.J. (1983) *Significant Bilingual Instructional Features Study*. San Francisco, CA: Far West Laboratory.

Tikunoff, W.J., Ward, B.A., Lash, A.A. and Dunbar, D.R. (1980) *Review of the Literature for a Descriptive Study of Significant Bilingual Instructional Features.* Far West Laboratory for Educational Research and Development, San Francisco.

Tinajero, J.V. and DeVillar, R.A. (eds) (2000) *The Power of Two Languages 2000: Effective Dual-Language Use Across the Curriculum.* New York: McGraw-Hill.

Tizard, J., Schofield, W.N. and Hewison, J. (1982) Collaboration between teachers and parents in assisting children's reading. *British Journal of Educational Psychology* 52, 1–15.

Torres, M.E. (1988) Attitudes of bilingual education parents toward language learning and curriculum and instruction. *NABE Journal* 12 (2), pp. 171–185.

Toukomaa, P. and Skutnabb-Kangas, T. (1977) *The Intensive Teaching of the Mother Tongue to Migrant Children of Pre-School Age and Children in the Lower Level of Comprehensive School.* Helsinki: The Finnish National Commission for Unesco.

Troike, R.C. (1978) Research evidence for the effectiveness of bilingual education. *NABE Journal* 3, 13–24.

Troike, R.C. (1986) Improving conditions for success in bilingual education programs. Prepared for Committee on Education and Labor, US House of Representatives.

Tyack, D.B. (1974) *The One Best System.* Cambridge, MA: Harvard University Press.

US Census Bureau (1980) *Current Population Survey.* Population Division.

US Census Bureau (1990) *Census of Population.* Population Division, Release Cphl-96.

US Census Bureau (1995) *United States Population Estimates, by Age, Sex, Race, and Hispanic Origin, 1990 to 1995.* Population Division, Release Ppl-41.

US Census Bureau (1996) *Current Population Survey.* Population Division.

US Census Bureau (1999) *Computer Use in the United States: October 1997* (p. 20-522). Washington, DC: US Government Printing Office. [online]. Available: http://www.census.gov/population/www/socdemo/computer.html.

US Census Bureau (2000) *Resident Population Estimates of the United States by Sex, Race, and Hispanic Origin: April 1, 1990 to July 1, 1999, with Short-Term Projection to November 1, 2000.* Washington, DC: U.S. Government Printing Office. [online] Available: http://www.census.gov/population/estimates/nation/intfile3-1.txt.

US Department of Education (2001) *Transforming the Federal Role in Education So That No Child is Left Behind.* Washington DC: US Department of Education. Available: http://www.in.usdoj.gov/graphics/aboutins/statistics/illegalalien/index.htm.

US Department of Justice (1999) *Legal Immigration, Fiscal Year 1998.* Annual Report, Statistics Branch.

US Department of Justice (2000) *Illegal Alien Resident Population.* [online]. Available: http://www.ed.gov/inits/nclb/part2.html.

US General Accounting Office (1987a) Bilingual education: Information on limited English proficient students. GAO/HRD-87–85BR.

US General Accounting Office (1987b) Bilingual education: A new look at the research evidence. GAO/PEMD-87–12BR.

Vallerand, R.J., Blais, M.R., Briere, N.M. and Pelletier, L.G. (1989) Construction and validation of the Academic Motivation Scale. *Canadian Journal of Behavioral Sciences* 21, 323–349.

Veenman, S. (1984) Perceived problems of beginning teachers. *Review of Educational Research* 54 (2), 143–78.

Venezky, R.L. and Winfield, L.F. (1979) *Schools That Succeed Beyond Expectations in Teaching Reading.* Newark: University of Delaware. (ERIC Document Reproduction Service No. ED 177 484)

Verhoeven, L. (1994) Transfer in bilingual development: The linguistic interdependence hypothesis revisited. *Language Learning* 44 (3), 381–415.

Waggoner, D. (1994) Language minority school-age population now totals 9.9 million. *NABE News* 1, 24–25.

Waggoner, D. (1995) Language minority population increased by more than a third between 1980 and 1990. *Numbers and Needs* 5, 1.

Weinstein, R.S., Marshall, H.H., Sharp, L. and Botkin, M. (1987) Pygmalion and the student: Age and classroom differences in children's awareness of teacher expectations. *Child Development* 58, 1079–1093.

Wigfield, A., Eccles, J. S. and Pintrich, P.R. (1996) Development between the ages of 11 and 25. In D.C. Berliner and R.C. Calfee (eds) *Handbook of Educational Psychology* (pp. 148–85). New York: Simon and Schuster Macmillan.

Wigfield, A., Eccles, J.S., MacIver, D., Reuman, D. and Midgley, C. (1991) Transitions at early adolescence: Changes in children's domain-specific self-perceptions and general self-esteem across the transition to junior high school. *Developmental Psychology* 27, 552–565.

Williams, J.D. and Snipper, G.C. (1990) *Literacy and Bilingualism.* New York: Longman.

Willig, A. (1985) A meta-analysis of selected studies on the effectiveness of bilingual education. *Review of Educational Research* 55, 269–317.

Willig, A.C. (1987) Examining bilingual education research through meta-analysis and narrative review: A response to Baker. *Review of Educational Research* 57, 363–76.

Wode, H. (1998) A European perspective on immersion teaching: The German scenario. In J. Arnau and J.M. Artigal (eds) *Els Programes d'immersió: Una Perspectiva Europea [Immersion Programmes: A European Perspective].* Barcelona, Spain: Universitat de Barcelona.

Wong-Fillmore, L. (1985) When does teacher talk work as input? In S.M. Gass and C.G. Madden (eds) *Input in Second Language Acquisition* (pp. 17–50). Rowley, MA: Newbury House.

Wylie, R. (1979) *The Self Concept: Vol 2. Theory and Research on Selected Topics.* Lincoln: University of Nebraska Press.

Yagi, Y. (1991) Motivation and attitudes toward foreign language learning among students in foreign language classes in an American university. Unpublished doctoral dissertation. University of San Francisco.

Youssef, A. and Simpkins, E. (1985) Parent attitudes on Americanization and bilingual education: The Dearborn, Detroit, and Farmington study. *Bilingual Review* 12, 190–97.

Index